Robert E. Rivers

THE PRO QUARTERBACK

THE PRO QUARTERBACK

By MURRAY OLDERMAN

PRENTICE-HALL, INC., ENGLEWOOD CLIFFS, NEW JERSEY

Printed in the United States of America
T   73166
Prentice-Hall International, Inc., London
Prentice-Hall of Australia, Pty. Ltd., Sydney
Prentice-Hall of Canada, Ltd., Toronto
Prentice-Hall of India Private Ltd., New Delhi
Prentice-Hall of Japan, Inc., Tokyo

Acknowledgments

I want to thank all the quarterbacks, past and present, who made this book necessary. I also want to thank them individually for their gracious cooperation in providing the material to justify the product.

On a personal level, the public relations men of both professional leagues opened up their dossiers in a completely helpful spirit: Jim Kensil and Don Weiss for the NFL, Jack Horrigan and Al Ward for the AFL. The pro coaches were also a backstop against gross technical error—particularly Al Sherman of the Giants, Weeb Ewbank of the Jets, Don Shula of the Colts and Al Davis of the Raiders (later graduated to commissioner of his league).

The fine photographic displays merit a special commendation for Malcolm Emmons and Walter Ioss, Jr.

Joyce Eckenfelder deciphered the manuscript so that it was readable. And George Flynn of Prentice-Hall provided the editorial wisdom that carried the book through from the inception of the idea to this fruition.

Finally, a brood in Leonia, New Jersey, provided the patience and inspiration integral to every creative project.

—MURRAY OLDERMAN

Contents

Introduction vii

PART ONE

1. The Pro-T QB 1
2. The Evolution 11
3. The Passing Bit 23
4. The Mental Giant 41
5. The Quarterback's Week 57
6. The Game Plan 69
7. Era of the Blitz 95
8. The Mad Scramble 113
9. The Quarterback Mystique 127

PART TWO

10. The Originals 141
        Sid Luckman
        Sammy Baugh
        Frank Albert, Paul Christman, Tommy Thompson
11. The Stars 187
        Otto Graham
        Bob Waterfield
12. The Old Pros 217
        Bobby Layne
        Norm Van Brocklin
        Charley Conerly
        Eddie LeBaron
        Tobin Rote

13. The Big Guns 281
    John Unitas
    Y. A. Tittle
    Bart Starr
14. The Moderns 325
    Frank Albert
    John Brodie
    Sonny Jurgensen
    Jack Kemp
15. The Young Turks 363
    Francis Tarkenton
    Charley Johnson
16. The New Breed 383
17. The Wrapup 401
18. The Composite 417
    Appendix 427
    Index 433

Introduction

I suppose that to appreciate the quarterback in football you should have at some time knelt in the middle of a bunch of sweaty faces and drawn out a play in the dirt, then turned that design into a real thing—like a virtuoso takes notes and turns them into pure melody.

However, my appreciation also comes from knowing and watching all the quarterbacks who have made professional football the most exciting sport of the midcentury. From Sammy Baugh and Sid Luckman to Francis Tarkenton and Joe Namath—I have seen them all. The apotheosis of the pro quarterback was inevitable with the introduction of the modern T-formation a quarter of a century ago. Johnny Unitas is today what Joe DiMaggio was then.

The purpose of this book has been to define and illustrate the nature of the job and to portray the great quarterbacks of professional football as people within that framework. All but Tommy Thompson were personally researched, and the Philadelphia Eagle alumni association can't even find him. They were stimulating, and they were entertaining. And for me, at least, they opened up a new perspective of the pros and the life they lead. It was like Bobby Layne said after a long, long weekend on the trail in Lubbock, Texas:

"At least, you got to admit, it was different."

—Murray Olderman

1. The Pro T-QB

The quarterback starts his countdown to action. Bart Starr (15) barks the signals—"Hut one! Hut two!"—to set the Green Bay offense in motion.

The Packers' Bart Starr cradles the snap from center firmly in his sure fingers and starts to pivot off his left foot as his linemen charge. . . . Now he's made a quarter turn and holds the ball out for mud-spattered fullback Jimmy Taylor, the most valuable player in the 1965 NFL championship game.

Many years ago, before a professional quarterback was worth $400,000, a member of the old Canton Bulldogs in football's Neanderthal era was called into court as a character witness for a friend on trial. The prosecutor asked him what he did for a living, and he replied that he was a football player.

"What position do you play?" asked the prosecutor.

"I'm a quarterback," replied the Canton player.

"Are you a good quarterback?"

"The best in the business!"

The player had always been a modest type, so when he left the courtroom, the coach of the Canton Bulldogs pulled him aside and asked him why he testified that he was the best in football.

"I had to tell him that, Coach," answered the quarterback. "I was under oath."

In 1960, Dick Lynch, a defensive back for the New York Giants, was consulted over a bowl of minestrone at Mamma Leone's restaurant in Manhattan. It was the week before the Green Bay Packers were to play the Philadelphia Eagles for the championship of the National Football League. All the odds pointed to the Packers who had just started their three-year run of Western Conference titles under Coach Vince Lombardi. They had the better offensive line and the better defensive line. They had a superior running attack, with Paul Hornung and Jimmy Taylor. And their linebackers were the best in football.

"I like the Packers," nodded Lynch. "But if the Dutchman gets hot, it'll be the difference."

That's all he said. The Dutchman. Norm Van Brocklin was thirty-four years old. He was pudgy in the jowls and in the belly, and he couldn't move off a dime. But on the mushy turf of Philadelphia's Franklin Field the day after Christmas, he got hot. And it was the difference, 17–13. Throwing the ball and picking the Packer defenses apart with handoffs to other men, he directed the talent-starved Eagles to a championship. Right after the game Van Brocklin announced the end to a twelve-year career, and the Eagles stopped winning.

The pattern of professional football is like that. One man—the T-quarterback—controls the tableau of violent action. He sets it in motion. He is the most important man in the most explosively popular spectator sport of the midcentury.

In this game of human chess, the quarterback is the general of its destiny. He makes the decisions and sets them into action, moving the bodies around in a master battle plan. He didn't learn his lessons at West Point or the Army War College. His training grounds are the playing field, from high school through college. When he gets into professional football, the process is refined with extensive briefing sessions, intensive study of films, the commitment to memory of an entire system of football and, finally, the dedication of practice sessions which resemble army maneuvers. There is no room for error in the highly technical game that has evolved, and the quarterback triggers the action.

3

Bart Starr, a veteran of ten years, put the Green Bay Packers in motion on a wintry day in Wisconsin. The date was January 2, 1966, and the opposing team was the Cleveland Browns. They were playing for the championship of the National Football League, and in the opening minutes of the third quarter of a tense duel in which the Packers led, 13–12, it was still anybody's ball game.

Starr stood erect behind the center, hand on hips, and surveyed the field quickly, left and right. Was Carroll Dale, in the flanker position, split out wide like he's supposed to be? Did Bill Anderson, the tight end, swing over to the left side of the line next to tackle Bob Skoronski after he came out of the huddle? Bart had called for a left formation. The ball was shaded to the right side of the field. How about the backs—did they have their spacing right? Paul Hornung, at halfback, was lined up directly behind the right tackle. Okay. Out of the corner of his eye, Starr could see that Jimmy Taylor was directly behind, on a straight line from center, in the fullback slot.

Now he came head to head with the real confrontation. He looked first at the three linebackers of the Browns. Galen Fiss to his left on the strong side was up close over Anderson's nose like he was supposed to be. Vince Costello was over the middle, half a step off the line. Jim Houston was over on the weak side, but Bart wasn't worried too much about him. The call was a "68 sweep" with Hornung carrying around end. Since the ball was on the 13-yard line of the Browns, Starr wasn't worried too much about the possibilities of a blitz.

The Packers had been sticking to the ground, moving all the way from their own 10-yard line in 10 plays, with only a couple of third-down passes to keep the drive going. That close to the goal line, the Browns would be expecting another run, so they wouldn't shoot (or blitz) their linebackers at him. Primarily he wanted to see that they were in a normal 4–3–4 defense. They wouldn't zone that deep in their own territory, but he didn't want the front four overshifted into odd spacing with tackle Dick Modzelewski on the head of the center. Otherwise he would have to come off the play and, with an "audible," go to another type of run. The whole trick was to make sure that the Cleveland right end, Bill Glass, wasn't lined up wide where he could get in Hornung's way and jam up the play. Starr had been drawing him in close by sending Taylor up the middle on preceding plays.

All this darted through Bart's mind almost automatically, almost subconsciously, as he scanned the field. He got up behind the center in a semicrouch, his feet set comfortably and hands cupped to receive the short snap of the ball which would set twenty-two men, eleven on each side, into synchronized motion. He barked out, "Set!"

The Packer linemen snapped alertly into a three-point stance ready to drive off on a predesignated signal. In the huddle Starr said they would go on "two."

("Just the way you bark out signals can tell other players if you have confidence in the play you called," says Bobby Layne, who called them for fifteen years as a pro in Chicago, New York, Detroit and Pittsburgh. "Even a quarterback's cadence can throw them off. Linemen must get off the mark the instant the ball is snapped. That's their bread and butter. They have trouble when the quarterback isn't the boss.")

Starr started his cadence countdown.

"68 . . . 34 . . . Hut one! . . . Hut two!"

4

The swift motion of center Ken Bowman's hands thrust the ball into Starr's palms. Starr whirled quickly to his left, faked a handoff to Taylor, who dove into a pile of bodies. Then Starr continued around and smacked the football into Hornung's middle. The moment Hornung swept past him, behind guard Jerry Kramer, who had pulled out of the line, Starr was already thinking ahead to the next play. If they stopped Hornung with a short gain, he'd throw a pass. The ball would be placed on the left hash mark, so he'd make it a wing slant. That's a quick slant-in pass to the flanker on the right side. He remembered from his notes that, three weeks before, the Los Angeles Rams had had some success with that play in scoring position against the Browns.

Hornung swept the left end as Kramer led the way. Skoronski and Anderson teamed to wipe out the defensive end and linebacker. Tackle Forrest Gregg cut across and nudged the safety out of the way. Kramer blocked the cornerback and Hornung zipped into the corner of the end zone all alone.

The touchdown put the Packers safely ahead, 20–12. And they stayed that way to an ultimate 23–12 NFL championship victory behind the whip hand and persuasive guidance of their shrewd quarterback. That day Starr was a brilliant field general, as he should be. One quality separates the quarterback from every other man on the field. He must be the leader. It's the nature of the job.

Johnny Unitas of the Baltimore Colts is generally considered the greatest quarterback of his time. He holds a record of throwing touchdown passes in 47 consecutive games, and the Colts haven't had a losing record since his rookie year of 1956. Some years ago they had a halfback who didn't always put out 100 percent. Sometimes he'd come limping back into the huddle, and the other guys couldn't be sure whether or not he was really hurting. "You okay?" Unitas would ask, coldly. "If not, get your butt out of here and send me someone I can use." The Colt leader explained, "That's the only way I can handle 'em. I've always been that way. I used to send guys out of games when I was in high school. If they gave me any lip, I told them to keep moving. I guess I probably humiliated one kid. He started giving me a lot of horse manure in the huddle. I just told him, 'Get off the field.'

"He came running to the sidelines and the coach asked him, 'What are you doing over here?'

"The kid said, 'John sent me out.'

"If I tell a man I'm going to run this certain play, and he says he can't get me the block, get him the hell out of there. I don't need him. Give me someone in the lineup who can get me the block."

Bobby Layne, the quarterback of the Detroit Lions in three world-championship years, was a tyrant. He got maximum effort out of one Negro fullback by hurling racial obscenities at him whenever he missed a block on pass protection. Bobby got away with it because the fullback realized the epithets weren't inspired by bigotry, but by the quarterback's goading desire to win. He took it as part of Layne's personality. Layne was a competitor, even when his belly bloated and the suppleness went out of his throwing arm and he was peddled during the 1958 season to the Pittsburgh Steelers.

The Steelers hadn't finished above .500 in the league standings in eight years. The '58 season started out like all the rest. They lost the first two games. Then Layne joined

5

Johnny Unitas runs his team, the Baltimore Colts, with a firm hand that leaves no doubt about who's boss. The offensive line sets up to pass block as he whirls to get in position.

Bobby Layne was a tyrannical figure in action. The squint-eyed Texan chewed out any man who didn't do his job and give 100 percent effort in doing it.

them and they split a pair before moving into New York to face the Giants. The field was sloppy from rain and Steeler receivers had trouble hanging on to Layne's passes—when the ball carriers weren't fumbling the ball away. Bobby threw a long pass down the right sideline to Jimmy Orr, then a rookie end with the Steelers, now an all-pro flanker for the Baltimore Colts. Orr let the slick ball slide through his hands with a sure touchdown in sight. As he trotted back to the huddle, Layne was waiting for him.

"Listen, you little Georgia cracker," he fumed. "If you drop another pass on me like that, so help me I'll strangle you with my own hands."

Layne laid down this credo for winning:

"A pro player should take pride in his work. The difference in a champion and an also-ran is very little. A lot of players put out just enough to pick up their paychecks and avoid getting cut from the squad. If they would give that extra 10 percent it would mean victory instead of defeat."

The Layne era right after World War II produced the greatest crop of T-quarterbacks in history. They were a hardy and in most cases hard-bitten breed. Bob Waterfield, Charley Conerly, Y. A. Tittle, Norm Van Brocklin and the peerless winner, Otto Graham.

"To me," says Tittle, "Otto Graham is the most successful quarterback of all time because a quarterback is supposed to win. And Otto always won. He could throw wobbly footballs, not as nice a spiral as some. He didn't throw as hard as some young quarterbacks I've seen. All I know is, Otto was always in the championship game."

Through Graham's four years with the Cleveland Browns in the old All-America Football Conference and six years in the National Football League, they never failed to win a division title.

"A quarterback must assert his right to run the team," says Graham. "Being a good leader gets him respect. You don't have to go out and get drunk with the team. But they must know you're a regular guy, not looking for special favors."

Among the young Turks coming up in the T-quarterback ranks, one of the most spectacular is Francis Tarkenton of the Minnesota Vikings. His father is a Methodist minister. Francis is intelligent, God-fearing and invariably pleasant. But he also adds, "I'm not a nice guy on the field. Winning is the most important thing in the world to me. You've got to build your own personality in football. You have to know which men you can chew out, which you have to pat on the back. I'm charging when I play."

A quarterback named George Shaw came into the league in 1955 with superb credentials. As an all-around athlete he was a major league baseball prospect and led the nation one year in pass interceptions on defense at the University of Oregon. The Baltimore Colts made him the bonus selection in the entire NFL draft of college players, and he justified the choice by becoming that rarity, a starting quarterback in his rookie year. He was intelligent, had a fine passing arm and added the bonus of a running threat. But George was also sensitive and had the mild personality of a banker, which he was between seasons. When he was hurt his sophomore season, Unitas stepped in and won the regular job. Shaw never regained it and never again held a regular job in the pros, though his obvious ability kept him around for half a dozen years with Baltimore, New York and Minnesota. The Giants and Vikings were desperate for quarterback help, but George couldn't pass muster as a leader.

7

"He'd be all right," one coach said in despair, "if he'd just learn to say——." But George was a banker to the last.

The Cleveland Browns once invested a No. 1 draft pick in Bobby Garrett, an All-American quarterback at Stanford. They were searching for a successor to Graham, their perennial field leader. Not until Bobby came to camp the next summer did they discover a fatal flaw. Bobby stuttered. The Browns never got his message, nor did the Packers, to whom he was traded.

Quarterback leadership also manifests itself in subtle ways. A man doesn't have to be a firebrand. Bart Starr came to Green Bay from Alabama as a seventeenth draft choice. He's a sensitive, introverted person and sitting on the bench his entire senior year at college because of an injury, while Alabama lost 10 straight games, didn't help his confidence. "I'm sure," admitted Bart, "I wasn't as mentally tough as I should have been."

But his intelligence and his passing ability earned him a position on the Packer roster, and eventually a starting job at quarterback. He still had to prove his aggressive right to it. In 1959, the Packers showed signs, in their first year under Coach Vince Lombardi, of the power that would produce a championship dynasty. During one early-season game they were trying to pick up offensive momentum for a drive and Bart, breaking the huddle, patted offensive guard Jerry Kramer on the tail and yelled, "C'mon, Jerry, let's go!"

The next day, Bart came up to Jerry and apologized for his effusiveness.

Somewhere along the line in professional football a man's physical mettle is tested. When Ernie Stautner was ravaging pro offenses as a tackle for the Pittsburgh Steelers, he said, "You know where I'm going for on every play? The quarterback's face. I want him to know I'm coming the next time. I want him to be scared. Those quarterbacks can't tell me they don't scare because I've seen it in the corners of their eyes."

One young fellow was burning up the league until the Chicago Bears racked him one afternoon, and he pussyfooted every time a defense put pressure on him. It's tough to question a man's courage because as Coach Lynn (Pappy) Waldorf once said, "The very fact of putting on a uniform denotes courage." But some men stand up better to physical risk than others. They don't let it interfere with their normal pattern of play. John Unitas missed two games with a punctured lung in 1958 but was back playing the third week. Otto Graham had eighteen stitches taken in his face on the field and finished the game. After the Bears mauled him, Pussyfoot was always looking for an escape exit when he went back to pass. His own teammates were first to know and got down on him. The word was whispered around the league, and he was through as an effective pro.

The moment of truth for Bart Starr as a quarterback came in 1960, while the Packers were driving to their first Western Conference championship in sixteen years. The big, bad Bears got into the picture here, too. They had an all-pro middle linebacker, Bill George, whose forte was quickness off the ball. He weighed 245 but could come off the snap like a flyweight and be all over the quarterback before that unlucky guy had a chance to cock his arm. Out of uniform, Bill was a smiling Syrian but on the field punishing people was his job.

The Bears were primarily a blitzing team in his best days, with any or all of the

8

linebackers simulating the Charge of the Light Brigade and only one target in mind—the quarterback. In this case it was Starr. Under such pressure the pass protection cup inevitably broke down. On one play against the Packers, George found a clear alley up the middle. Before Bart could duck away, the linebacker's elbow crashed under his faceguard. Starr reeled back, spitting blood from a cracked lip, and tumbled on his rear. Over him hovered George, glowering.

"And that, pussycat, is what you're gonna get all afternoon," threatened the menacing Bear linebacker.

Starr looked up at him with a cold glint, and his answer was terse. He told George where he could go in language that would cancel second-class mailing privileges. It satisfied the big Bear. He left Starr alone after that.

Nearby, Jerry Kramer of the Packers eavesdropped on the short *tête-à-tête* and slapped his thighs enthusiastically. "Hell, Bart," he said, "until now I never even heard you say, 'Damn!'"

The Packers won the West that year, and world championships the next two years and again in 1965 because they had Starr to put all of the pieces together.

"The thing to remember," said Allie Sherman, the coach of the New York Giants, who tasted a couple of those defeats, "is that some quarterbacks might not win with that Green Bay team. To win in professional football, you need two things—good defense and a top quarterback."

2. The Evolution

Cecil Isbell succeeded Herber as the man on the throwing end to Hutson and once completed a four-inch touchdown pass to the Packer end. Cecil was also a fine running threat.

With the fabulous Don Hutson as his favorite target, Arnie Herber made the forward pass a primary method of attack during the 1930s while playing tailback for the Green Bay Packers.

The T-formation quarterback as a modern species started with the NRA (National Recovery Administration) in 1933. At the time that Franklin D. Roosevelt was declaring bank holidays and shaking up the Depression mood, George Halas and George Preston Marshall, two intrepid pioneers of pro football, uprooted the tight structure of their sport. They did it by pushing through a pair of important rules changes that 1) restored the goalpost to the goal line and made the field goal a key offensive weapon, and 2) allowed a forward pass to be thrown from anywhere behind the line of scrimmage.

The second change led directly to the birth of the T-quarterback as we know him today. The T-formation was almost as old as the Poe brothers at Princeton. When Amos Alonzo Stagg went West from Yale all the way to Chicago in 1892, he brought the T-formation with him. There was as much resemblance between Stagg's T and the slotted, flankered, flared T that's in operation today as there is between Henry Ford's Model T and a synchro-meshed, chrome-styled Continental. The horsepower ratio's about the same, too.

The concept of football in the embryo days of the T was linemen, including the ends, squatting shoulder to shoulder, and everybody pushing as one. The defense massed against this phalanx and the result looked like a battle scene from David W. Griffith's "Birth of a Nation." The theory today is to spread the defense by spotting attackers almost from sideline to sideline in a wide-open version of grabbag.

"The T Formation was the first formation generally used," wrote Glenn (Pop) Warner. "It was called regular formation because it was the original. The positions were descriptive of where the players played—the ends were on the end of the line, the guards were guarding the center, the quarterback was approximately a quarter as far back as the fullback, and the halfbacks were half as far back as the fullback."

Warner, who produced fabled halfback Jim Thorpe at Carlisle Institute and had a noteworthy career in college coaching from 1895 to 1939, was the first to open up the game with his invention of the single-wing and double-wing formations. The football rules had been changed in 1910 to prevent mass play. There was no shoving or helping a runner. Seven men had to be up on the front line. Guards and tackles could no longer line up behind the backs and push. The Warner-coached Carlisle Indians sprang the single-wing on Army in 1912 and routed the Cadets, 27–6. The wing was a halfback who lined up outside the tackle. Later Warner devised the double-wing, with both halfbacks lined up outside the tackles.

Most teams abandoned the practice of a man directly behind the center. A tailback stood 5 yards back and took a direct snap from the center, who kept his head down over the ball to insure accuracy. The teams that still lined up in a T quickly shifted to the single-wing or other formations.

For more than a quarter of a century, carrying through the 1930's, in college as well as professional football, the wing formations and the Notre Dame box (developed by

Knute Rockne as a shift from the T) were in vogue. The left halfback, or tailback, was the hub of the offense and the glamour man of the game. It was primarily power football, featuring off-tackle plays with two and three blockers preceding the runner through the hole. An occasional reverse to the wingback or a buck into the line by the fullback broke the monotony. The so-called quarterback was used primarily as a blocker.

The glamour men of football were those halfbacks whose forte was running—Red Grange, Chris Cagle, Jay Berwanger, Clint Frank, Marshall Goldberg, Whizzer White, Tom Harmon. Beattie Feathers of Tennessee astounded the pros by joining the Chicago Bears in 1934 and becoming the first man ever to gain more than 1,000 yards rushing in a season. He averaged 9.9 yards in 101 carries as a rookie that year, and the figure still stands in the NFL Record Manual as the best in history.

But the pros recognized quickly that they couldn't move mountains of men consistently and developed the forward pass as a complementary weapon. They didn't discover it, of course. The forward pass was legalized in the college rules in 1906 as an antidote to the charge that football was brutal mayhem. The first recorded completion was on October 3 of that year when Sammy Moore of Wesleyan astounded Yale by spiralling the pumpkin (the bloated football of that day almost looked like one) to Irvin Van Tassell for an 18-yard gain. In 1913, Gus Dorais and Knute Rockne, a couple of student athletes at Notre Dame, a small Catholic school in northern Indiana, spent a summer on the beach at Lake Erie. Rockne, a 160-pound end, would run down the beach and Dorais would throw the ball toward him from all angles. Dorais weighed 145 pounds. The year before the rules had been liberalized to allow the ball to be thrown more than 20 yards beyond the line of scrimmage, and a pass caught over the goal line was also declared legal. In the fall of 1913, Notre Dame came East to play Army on the plains of West Point. The Dorais-to-Rockne passing combination devastated Army by a 35–13 score and revolutionized offensive football.

When the National Football League was formally organized in 1920, on the running board of a touring car at Canton, Ohio, the forward pass was a recognized weapon. And good passers were in demand. Benny Friedman to Benny Oosterbaan was the famous Michigan passing tandem of the 1920's. Friedman went into professional football with the Detroit Wolverines, organizing the club himself. In 1929, Tim Mara, the founder of the New York Giants, tried to lure Benny to New York with an offer of a $10,000 contract. When Bennie wouldn't budge, old Tim bought the whole franchise, with Coach LeRoy Andrews included, so he could get Bennie to New York.

"Friedman was the first pro I was conscious of strictly as a passer," recalls Wellington Mara, son of the Giant founder and now president of the club. "The pass in those days was a third-down play. Friedman, who was probably ahead of his time, would throw on first down and was criticized for it."

After Friedman, the Giants signed Harry Newman, another passing ace from Michigan. Ironically, Newman is one of the few old-timers whose name remains in the record book—for a running exploit. In a game against the Green Bay Packers in 1934, he carried the ball 38 times, which is still a league record. Newman was followed on the New York scene by Ed Danowski, a local product of Fordham University.

14

Concurrently the Green Bay Packers under Curly Lambeau, their founder, built a winning tradition. In 1930, they signed a Green Bay native named Arnie Herber, who had played his college football in Colorado. Herber had an elastic arm that could hurl the ball in the air accurately up to distances of 60 yards. In 1935, he acquired the perfect target for his pitches—Don Hutson, a Rose Bowl hero for the Alabama Crimson Tide. For the first time, the pass became a primary part of the attack rather than an auxiliary to the running game. Hutson led the league in receptions eight times. In eleven seasons he caught a total of 100 touchdown passes. When Herber started to wear down, the Packers signed Cecil Isbell of Purdue, more versatile than Arnie as a passer and runner. For a couple of years Isbell and Herber played in the same backfield, passing to Hutson, a double-edged throwing blade that lasted through 1942. In a game against the Cleveland Rams that final year, the nose of the ball rested 4 inches away from the goal line. Isbell faked a plunge into the line, stepped back and threw into the flat to Hutson for those final 4 inches and a touchdown.

In 1937, a lanky Texan with a buggywhip arm named Sammy Baugh, stepped off a plane in Washington, D.C., dressed in a 10-gallon hat, chaps and cowboy boots. His feet hurt because he wasn't used to the footwear. The pointed boots with high heels were on order of George Preston Marshall, the flamboyant owner of the Redskins, to advertise the fact that he had signed the most publicized passer ever to come out of the Southwest. Baugh was already a legend for his exploits at Texas Christian University. When the Redskins put regular cleated football shoes on slim Sam, the era of the forward pass in the pros officially began. He played sixteen years and in the NFL Record Manual under the subheading, Efficiency in Passing Statistics, there are three categories: Passing Efficiency, Lifetime; Passing Efficiency, Season; Passing Efficiency, Game. The last two still list Sammy Baugh first. He remains in the top three for the career department.

Two years after Baugh, another flinger from TCU made the trek North to the land of the pros. The Philadelphia Eagles unfurled Davey O'Brien. Davey stuck around only two seasons before he went off to fight organized crime for J. Edgar Hoover and the Federal Bureau of Investigation. He wasn't geared for the long haul like Sammy. Davey was only 5 feet 8 inches. But in his short stay he left his mark. The last game Davey played for the Eagles was on December 1, 1940, against the Washington Redskins. O'Brien vs. Baugh. Davey threw 60 passes, an all-time record for one game, and completed 33. None was intercepted. None went for a touchdown, either, as the Eagles lost, 13–7.

Another arrival with O'Brien was Parker Hall, an All-American from Mississippi. He joined the old Cleveland Rams in 1939 and immediately exceeded the league record for pass completions by 25 as he hit his target 106 times in 208 attempts (for a new accuracy mark of 51.9 percent) and led the NFL in passing as a rookie. He was voted the league's most valuable player.

The next year, 1940, marked the epoch of the T-formation as the dominant force in professional football. The Chicago Bears had always lined up in the T-formation, going back to 1920. They were called the Decatur Staleys and one of the quarterbacks on the

Before he left the Philadelphia Eagles to become a G-man, Davey O'Brien proved a little man (5 feet 8) could throw over the heads of the big pros, and accurately. His 60 passes in one game still constitute an NFL record. Davey played only two seasons.

The modern T-formation took shape when the Chicago Bears put a man in motion in 1931. The quarterback then and for eight seasons was Carl Brumbaugh. Carl, a fine runner himself, races around left end against the New York Giants in the 1933 title game, won by the Bears, 23–21.

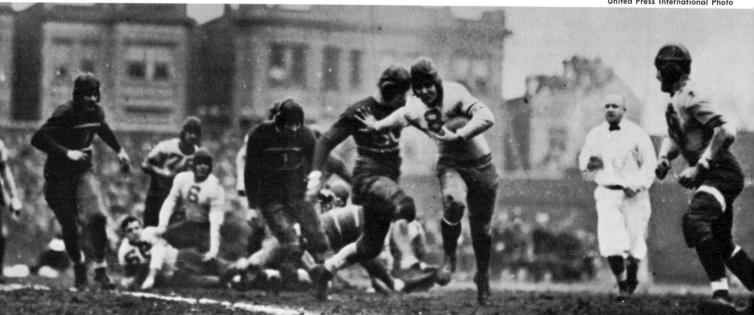

team was a little fellow named Charley Dressen, who eventually concentrated on baseball to become manager of the Brooklyn Dodgers and other major league teams and bring greater renown to the letter "I"—meaning Charley Dressen.

"In 1920," recalled George Halas, the founder of the team, which moved to Chicago two years later, "we used a variety of offensive formations including the loose T. By splitting the ends and moving the halfbacks another two steps away from the fullback, we achieved greater mobility, particularly on end runs. What the Bears did was to put the T and the man in motion together and then gradually add refinements, such as the signal system and counterplays and spreads. This was a period of evolution spanning almost twenty years and was the product of the Bears' organization rather than of one individual."

In 1930, owner Halas fired himself as head coach for a three-year interlude and hired Ralph Jones, a tiny, bald-headed mentor from Lake Forest Academy, just north of Chicago, to run the Bears. Jones stayed three years, then gave the job back to Halas but continued to work with the team. In 1931 he made Red Grange the first man-in-motion. Before the snap of the ball, Grange at left halfback would turn to his right and run parallel to the line of scrimmage while quarterback Carl Brumbaugh called out the signals. It was timed so that the center would snap the ball just as Grange turned again and cut toward the line of scrimmage. This tended to spread the defense which had to overshift to Grange's side.

Legalizing a forward pass anywhere behind the line of scrimmage in 1933, as noted earlier, added another wrinkle. The Bears' fullback was Bronko Nagurski, the scourge of all tacklers. Bronko had some passing ability. Now, if the defenses massed too tightly against him, he ran up to the line of scrimmage, stopped short, jumped and flipped a pass over the line. In the championship game played in the first year of the new rule, the Bears trailed the New York Giants, 21–16, in the fading moments of the fourth quarter. With a minute to play, they were on the New York 36, powered by Bronko's rushes. He headed into the line again. The Giants braced. Nagurski leaped and passed the ball to left end Bill Hewitt, cutting over the middle of the line. Hewitt lateraled to Bill Karr, the other end, who went the distance for the winning score.

The quarterbacks could get into the passing act, too, so Brumbaugh and Keith Molesworth and later Bernie Masterson gradually took over the passing responsibilities. The T-quarterback was starting to take shape.

In the meantime an ascetic technician named Clark Shaughnessy was coaching the University of Chicago team on the South Side of the city. With President Robert Hutchins exorcising the "evils" of big-time football from that school, Shaughnessy found himself with plenty of time on his hands and started hanging around the Bear practice sessions. The possibilities of refurbishing the T intrigued him. A sliding 5–4–2 defense had been devised by Detroit and Green Bay to negate the man-in-motion by rotating the four-man secondary in his direction.

By 1939, Halas, Shaughnessy and Jones concocted an antidote to the new defense. It was called a counter play. With the man-in-motion, the flow of movement was to the right and the defense was sucked in that direction. So the quarterback handed the ball off to one of the other backs against the flow, to the left. It was a variation of the old reverse from the single-wing, except that with the trickery involved in the T, the quarterback hiding the ball from the opposition, the runner didn't need the protective facade of blockers who would tip off the ruse.

The T-revolution started on two fronts in 1940. Shaughnessy went to Stanford University as head coach and picked out a scrawny, lefthanded, tailback named Frank Albert to learn the art of quarterbacking. He backed him up with a pair of swift halfbacks, Hugh Gallarneau and Pete Kmetovic, and a bull of a fullback, Norm Standlee (Gallarneau and Standlee later played with the Bears).

"I thought he was crazy," said Gallarneau. "Like everyone else in college football, we had always played the single-wing or double-wing. When Shaughnessy diagrammed a play which sent me, a halfback, into the line without a blocker ahead of him, I laughed."

Meanwhile in Chicago, the Bears got much the same kind of reaction from the man they had picked out to launch the modern-T assault. Sidney Luckman, an All-American single-wing tailback for Lou Little at Columbia, joined the team in 1939. It was his first exposure to the T. Halas wanted to convert him to quarterback. An assistant coach, Luke Johnsos, outlined the plays on a blackboard in training camp the first day.

"Gosh, Luke," Luckman said, "those halfbacks go through the line all alone. They'll get killed."

"Don't worry, Sid," answered Johnsos. "As fast as they get killed, we'll send in new ones."

The next season, with Luckman directing the attack exclusively in the T-formation, the Bears won the Western Conference championship, though they lost to the Washington Redskins, 7–3, in the last regular-season game. The rematch with the Redskins, on December 8, 1940, was for the National Football League championship. The Bears won, 73–0, in one of the most significant games of football history.

On the first play from scrimmage, Luckman sent his left halfback, Ray Nolting, in motion to the right, then handed off to George McAfee, the right halfback, on a quick-opener between guard and tackle. McAfee gained 8 yards. But the important thing Luckman noticed was that the Washington defense reacted as expected, the linebackers going in the direction of the motion.

On the second play, he faked a handoff to Nolting, going to the right. Bill Osmanski, the fullback, turned in the same direction as if to lead the play, then spun and took the ball in his belly from Luckman. He started to drive over his left tackle, but the hole didn't open up fast enough so he bellied wide around his left end and found daylight along the sidelines. The Washington linebacker on that side, overshifted, was easily blocked by the Bears' left guard, Danny Fortmann, who had penetrated beyond the line of scrimmage.

As Osmanski raced along the stripe, two men in the Redskin secondary—safety Ed Justice and Jim Johnston, backing up the middle—recovered and threatened to pin Osmanski along the sidelines. But George Wilson, the Bears' right end, had raced across the field ahead of them. He turned and wiped them both out with a spectacular block.

18

Sid Luckman, holding the ball out for George McAfee, brought finesse to the quarterback's role in the T. With his clever faking, the Bears could brush block the Brooklyn defenders here and still open big holes.

That set the pattern of the day. The Redskins couldn't handle anything the Bears tried. At halftime the score was 28–0 and Luckman didn't bother to get off the bench after the start of the third quarter.

On the train ride home to Chicago, one of the player's wives couldn't forget the image of the two Redskin defenders being blocked in one swoop. Everybody in the stadium saw the collision and the Redskins stretched out.

"Who was the big monster," she asked, "who knocked those two poor fellows up in the air?"

The Bears in the parlor car roared. The wife who asked the question was Mrs. George Wilson. (George Wilson went on to coach the Detroit Lions to the NFL championship and now is the head man of the Miami Dolphins in the American Football League.)

Some three weeks later, on January 1, 1941, the Stanford Indians, undefeated in their regular-season 9-game schedule and using the revolutionary T-formation, met a strong Nebraska team in the Rose Bowl at Pasadena, California, and won a convincing 21–13 triumph.

The next fall the T-formation flourished on both the collegiate and pro levels as smart coaches hopped on the bandwagon. Some single-wing operators like Baugh held out against it. From his tailback vantage point, five yards behind the center, he felt he had a neutral zone between himself and the hard-charging defensive linemen and a better passing field of vision. The dimension Baugh didn't appreciate at first was the flexibility of the formation. True, the quarterback had to retreat from his post behind center to get into passing position. But all the while he faked handoffs to other backs which kept the defensive linemen guessing. And the linebackers were unable to commit themselves because the quarterback masked the ball with his body. In the single-wing it was always visible. The T-formation also provided better balance to the attack because a team could strike at either side of the line with equal effect and prevent defensive overshifts, which were common practice against the unbalanced lines of the single-wing. Finally, the deception of the T provided the necessary blocking angles to move the large and fast breed of linemen that took over pro ball.

"In the Bears' football alphabet," said innovator Halas, "*T* stands for Total. T-formation football is Total Offense Football because, from the T, the attacking team can shift into combinations which make up the sum total of virtually every known method of scoring touchdowns."

In the colleges, when Frank Leahy abandoned the sacrosanct Notre Dame box, the conversion to the T became a stampede. In the NFL, the Philadelphia Eagles wasted no time emulating the Bears. "I stole the whole Bear system," admitted Coach Earle (Greasy) Neale. "I figured any offense that could score that much was good enough for me." The Eagles became the power of the NFL right after World War II when the pros returned to normalcy.

In 1943, when the Redskins met the Bears again for the NFL title, Sammy Baugh still operated from the single-wing, but in practice sessions Sammy asked Dutch Bergman, the Redskin coach, to install half a dozen plays from the T as a surprise gimmick. Dutch did, but the Skins never got around to using them (and lost again, 41–21).

20

Two years later, however, Sammy was operating full-time out of the T. Coach Steve Owen of the New York Giants succumbed grudgingly after the 1948 season, when he brought in a little lefthanded quarterback from the Philadelphia Eagles, Allie Sherman, to teach the intricacies of the T to Charley Conerly, whose only previous experience was in the single-wing at Mississippi. Steve still clung part-time to his A-formation, with Conerly as the tailback, until he left the Giants in 1952.

The last complete holdout was Pittsburgh, which had persuaded Dr. Jock Sutherland, the collegiate apostle of single-wing power football, to become head coach in 1946. Dr. Jock stayed two years and in 1947 produced a Steeler powerhouse which won eight games and lost four, the best record in club history. The Steelers tied Philadelphia for the Eastern Conference title but lost the playoff, 21–0. Sutherland's health broke before the next season, but his understudy, Johnny Michelosen, a blocking-quarterback disciple at the University of Pittsburgh, succeeded Jock and maintained the old system for four more seasons. The decreasing number of single-wing teams in college football made it difficult for the Steelers to stock their formation with the right kind of players. The old triple-threat tailback and the slashing, pulling guard were in short supply. So were Steeler victories, and in 1952 Michelosen was replaced by Joe Bach, who installed the T-formation and made the roster of NFL converts complete. Except for a brief revolt in 1961 by the San Francisco 49ers, who used a shotgun formation with three alternating tailbacks for half a season, all professional football teams in the National and American leagues have conformed to the same offensive style of play.

In this historical context, the T-formation quarterback has emerged as the single most important man in the game.

3. The Passing Bit

John Unitas of the Baltimore Colts shows off his classic passing form, with perfect overhand motion and the weight coming forward on the left foot as he throws.

A closeup of Unitas shows the intense concentration of the Colt passer and the perfect cradle of the ball as he brings his passing hand forward.

"The most essential element of a pro quarterback," says Sid Luckman, the prototype of them all, "is to be, number one, a great passer. Because no matter how smart you are, how great a leader, no matter what you know about football, if you can't throw under pressure, you're never going to be a great quarterback."

An assistant coach at Baylor University wrote a thesis for his master's degree at the University of Illinois on the analysis of football passers. His name is Charles Gordon (Chuck) Purvis, and he played halfback at Illinois. He broke the components down like this.

"In determining the forces involved while executing the short and long pass the equation $F = MA$ was applied where F = force, M = mass ($\frac{W \text{ lbs.}}{g \text{ feet per second}}$) and A = acceleration. Since the acceleration is equal to the increase in velocity in a given time increment, it was necessary to calculate this velocity increase ($A = \frac{dv}{dt}$). Since it was desired to determine the maximum force applied to the ball, the velocity and time increments were taken at the instant the ball was released. In order to determine the force the velocity had to be measured."

Sammy Baugh wasn't aware it was possible to refine his form like that when he first reported to the Washington Redskins from TCU. Coach Ray Flaherty diagrammed a pass play for him the first day of practice. "The end," outlined Flaherty, "goes down 10 yards and flares to the right. When he reaches this point," and Flaherty drew a big X on the board, "you hit him in the eye with the ball."

"Which eye?" drawled Sam.

For one of his guinea pigs, Purvis used Tommy O'Connell, who played quarterback for Illinois and had one season of glory with the Cleveland Browns when they won an Eastern Conference title in 1957. From his dissection of Tommy's form, Purvis concluded:

"Speed (in throwing a ball) depends upon reaction time; the speed at which the nerve tissue conducts a stimulus has been estimated at 300 feet per second. . . . (Note here that the stimulus is probably conducted a lot faster when fellows like Willie Davis of the Green Bay Packers or Deacon Jones of the Los Angeles Rams, premier defensive ends, are bearing down on the passer.)

"The primary muscles used in throwing a football are the pectoralis major, which contracts, and the latissimus dorsi, which acts as an antagonistic muscle when the arm is being thrown forward. Passers need continuous practice throwing to condition the reflexes, so that the antagonistic muscle acts at the proper time to give accuracy by braking the motion at the proper instant."

Paul Christman, an All-American passer at Missouri in 1939, a championship quarterback for the Chicago Cardinals in 1947 and an astute pro football television commentator in recent years, had a more succinct appraisal of what makes a passer tick.

"A hundred kids today," he said, "can throw the ball as good as Sammy Baugh did. In practice. They've got the arm and the strength. And they can fire it on a line, overarm, sidearm, any way you name it. But what makes a passer is this: there's a fraction of a second after a receiver makes his break when he's going to be open by half a step. That's when you've got to hit him."

Christman drew a straight line indicating the pass route of the receiver. Then he made the line veer left to indicate the receiver cutting. He drew a circle at the point the line veered and another circle where that change of direction ended.

He pointed to both circles and said, "If you hit him with the pass here . . . or here . . . no good. The pass defender is with him in the first case and he's had time to catch up with him again in the second. The point where you've got to him is right between those two circles. That's what makes a passer."

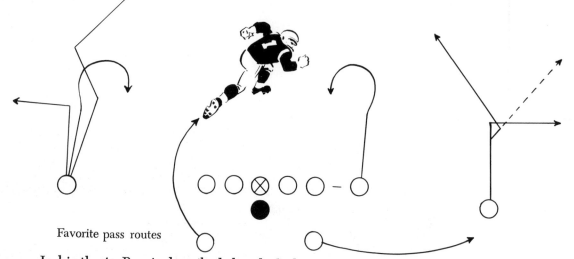

Favorite pass routes

In his thesis, Purvis described the ideal physiology of a passer:

"Armspread to the individual is very important in that the length of the throwing lever, as determined by the position of the axis of rotation in the forearm, functions as a factor in the control of the accuracy of the throw. The longer lever, as represented by the distance from the axis of rotation to the fingers, allows a greater range of rotation. . . . The ideal passer should have a longer armspread to overall height, six feet tall, large hands and long fingers. The ideal passer should be of mesomorphic classification, with stress being on smooth and lengthy muscles, rather than being of the short, stocky, muscular type."

Sammy Baugh was mesomorphic, all right. So is Johnny Unitas.

Allie Sherman threw a football like a lame duck trying to maintain altitude. "He couldn't throw a pass longer than 10 yards," said Emlen Tunnell, who played defensive back in the NFL for fifteen years. Emlen works for Sherman as an aide on the New York Giants, and his disrespect hasn't got him fired yet. The first time Greasy Neale saw Sherman in a training camp of the Philadelphia Eagles, during the war year of 1943, Allie could have been the office boy waiting to grow big enough for selective service.

But little Allie Sherman, out of Brooklyn College, who learned the T-formation from a book, lasted five years in professional football as a backup quarterback for the

26

Although he wasn't the fastest man in the world, Norm Van Brocklin had the superb timing to get the ball launched before tacklers, like George Strugar of the Rams, caught up with him.

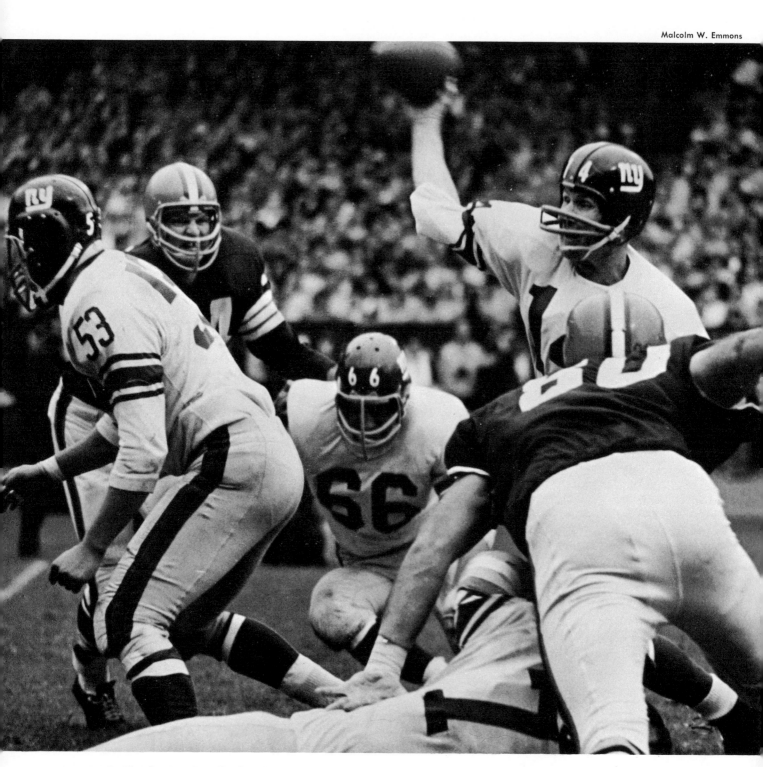

With Cleveland ends Bill Glass (80) and Paul Wiggin (left) converging from both sides, Y. A. Tittle of the Giants hung tough to get his pass off.

Eagles in the days when they won championships. When he saw that his physical limitations would keep him from ever being a regular performer on the football field, he turned to coaching. Like every coach, Sherman looks for the man who can get the ball to the receiver. He delivered the following set of requirements:

"If a man is 6 feet tall or more, he has the ideal passing plane. He's got good vision from that height, and he can get up above those men rushing in on him. That's basic equipment. He's got to be sturdy enough, too. He's going to be hit by a lot of big people. He needs at least rawhide toughness. He could wear down over a number of weeks if he doesn't get the kind of blocking he's been used to in other years.

"The man's arm has to be accurate. That's almost an innate quality, eye and hand coordination. You can help sometimes if a passer has a slight mechanical defect. Don Heinrich, who played for the Giants, had a defect in his form. I think we helped him a little in changing his game. He came up during Charley Conerly's regime and was trying to throw the same kind of passes that Conerly would throw—the 'bomb,' trying to lay it out there down the sidelines on fly patterns. (A "fly pattern" is a maneuver in which the receiver sprints straight down the field as fast as he can, trying to outrun the defender.) Heinrich didn't have that kind of arm or wrist. What we tried to do was get him to put the ball out there 18 to 25 yards. He used to throw off his back foot a lot and when he'd throw to his left, he'd fall away. That's a habit a lot of quarterbacks have and can be fixed. A man throwing left or right should lead out in that particular direction with his left foot. That's basic to passing.

"But the great passers you never have to mess with, because their timing and rhythm compensate for any little defects in form. You take a great passer like Y. A. Tittle. If you asked a young quarterback to work with him, and he didn't have Y. A.'s arm and reflexes, it would be a waste. He couldn't make the same techniques work. Tittle would stride out too far. He'd throw with different motions—sidearm, overhand, three-quarters—using a lot of wrist. He was a natural. You can find an analogy in baseball, with Stan Musial. Young batters weren't taught to copy his form because they're usually not gaited physically to use the same corkscrew stance which was okay for Stan.

"Now Unitas has more or less classic form. He has a perfect overhand motion and followthrough, and he still has the ability to throw sidearm when he has to. Baugh threw from every position. Off his ear, off his hip. He was all wrist. Charley Conerly had the perfect cradle of the ball with his hand. That's why he was so good with a wet ball. His footwork was excellent, too. If you ever gave him enough time, he'd step forward just like a baseball pitcher. He very rarely missed.

"Otto Graham wasn't a classical passer. He was a big man with a strong arm and had excellent timing. That's a thing I want to stress in passing. The arm isn't worth a damn—you're just a heaver—unless you have timing. You must possess the faculty of either releasing quickly or holding on to the ball until the last split second even though somebody is coming into your eyeballs. And then you have to snap the ball off. It takes instinct to recognize the situation and react to it. This is what differentiates between the ordinary passer and the extra-good one. He has to know the time when a man is wide open and is coming off a break, right now, and the ball has to be there.

"Norm Van Brocklin had superb timing. When they talk about quick release, nobody could match him. Nobody had quicker hands. He was great on the slant-in pass, those types where you have to get rid of the ball immediately or the pass is no good.

"In his early years the Dutchman was very bomb-conscious because he grew up with a ballclub that was like that. The Los Angeles Rams had the fastest group of receivers in the league. Elroy Hirsch, Bobby Boyd, Tom Fears, 'Vitamin' Smith, Tommy Kalmanir, and others. The quarterback very rarely threw the ball under 35 yards to any of them. Those Ram teams didn't win many championships (*note: they won an NFL title in 1951 and Western Conference championships in 1950 & 1955*). They won big, high-scoring games. They depended primarily on the bomb. The day their execution was off a little, by either the receivers or the passer, or the pass rush was extra tough, they were done.

"But in the last couple of years, when Van Brocklin came to the Eagles, he impressed me. Here was what I thought was great: he geared to his personnel. He had to throw a lot. The Eagles were often overmatched in talent. But the types of passes he threw—quick look-ins and square-outs—and the selection of them were superb. Those last couple of years, 1959–60, were as good as I've seen a passer have. I changed my opinion of him.

"I consider timing the cap to all of it. You can have everything, the equipment and the arm. If you don't have that sense of anticipation in pro ball, you're finished. On a pass play where the blocking is 85 percent effective, the passer should get the ball off in fairly good rhythm. Even if there's a man rolling off the block and getting to the passer, the good one can throw with color (i.e., the other team's jersey) looking him in his eyes.

"I'll add one other element, a feel to the ball. When most young quarterbacks have to throw into that vital 8-to-12-yard zone where most passes are completed, they snap the thing off. It zips right in there, hard. There are times when it's a perfect pass, the receiver is wide open but the ball is dropped. The good passer can control the revolutions of the ball, putting a little more spin on it when he has a pure situation.

"There's a feel to throwing short. Sometimes that thing should come right now, wham, just as hard as it can. Sometimes he takes a little spin off the ball, and yet doesn't hang it up too soft so the defender can pick it off. When a man is going out on an angle, it's tough to handle a hard ball.

"Now when you get to the next area of throwing, from a 12-yard depth to 20 or 30 or 40 yards, you begin to put a little trajectory on your pass. Craig Morton came out of California to the Dallas Cowboys with a tremendous arm. He could throw the ball 50 yards on a string no higher than 10 feet in the air. But like others, he has to learn to get a little lift to the ball. When a man throws the ball 40 or 50 yards on a line, and very few are capable of doing it, he's got to wait longer behind the line of scrimmage to get rid of it. He's hitting that receiver, bang, when he's 40 yards down the field. That means the man must have time to get there. It increases the pressure on the pass protection. It's a better deal all around to release the ball a little earlier, when the receiver is 25 yards downfield, lofting the ball so he runs under it 40 yards from the line of scrimmage. Plus, the percentage of catching a ball with a low trajectory is smaller. It's harder to hold on to.

30

United Press International Photo

Heavy pressure exerted by the New York Giants in the 1963 title game didn't divert quarterback Billy Wade (9) of the Chicago Bears from sighting his primary target.

DRAWING A

By far the most popular grip with pro passers is the one that has the ring and little finger on the laces. It's also called the overhand grip. Generally, the index finger is spread wider than the others so that it's almost touching the tip of the ball and offers direction at the moment of release. To get the ball into position to pass, most pros favor holding it with both hands, then raising it on a level with the right ear, cocking it and bringing the arm forward on a straight plane with plenty of wrist snap at the moment of release. The index finger, as noted, controls the flight and should be the last finger to feel the ball. It's not necessary to grasp the ball tightly with all four fingers. The thumb is on the underside of the ball, at almost a right angle to the index finger.

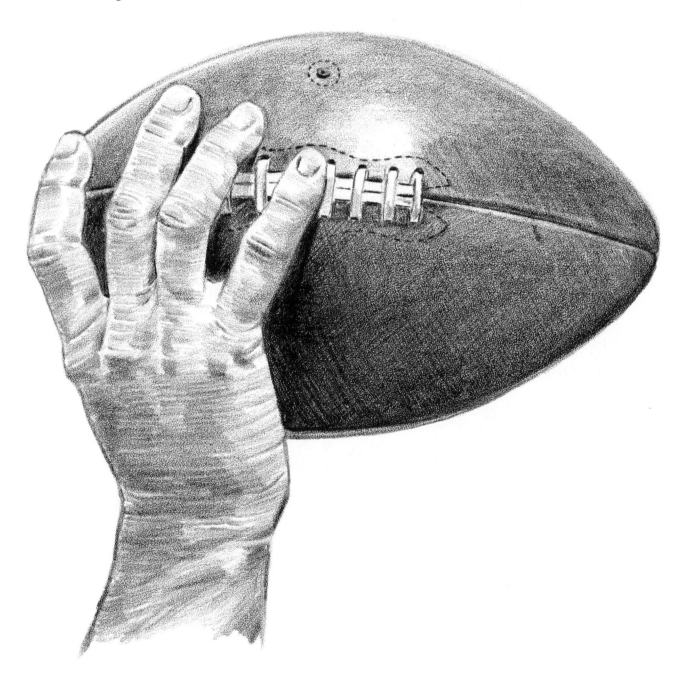

DRAWING B

Some passers—notably Bob Waterfield and Bobby Thomason—have successfully used the thumb grip. This ignores the leverage provided by the laces. The thumb is either on the laces or just slightly above it. Generally, to use this grip, the passer must have big hands and long fingers to control the rotation of the ball and compensate for the lack of "feel" that the overhand grip passers get from using the laces. In either case, the fingers do most of the work, since the ball shouldn't even touch the heel of the palm. Passers have varied both grips to fit their individual styles, much as Willie Mays doesn't swing a bat exactly the same way as Henry Aaron.

With Giants' defenders Jim Katcavage (75) and Andy Robustelli (81) dragging him to the ground, Norman Snead, then a rookie quarterback with the Washington Redskins, still managed to maintain passing balance.

"I don't mean you should put the pass up there, hanging, where the defense has a chance to gather under it for an interception. The thing that made Sid Luckman was his ability to get the ball out ahead of the receiver. Greasy Neale thought he was the greatest and made us study it.

"Of course, Sid was gifted with receivers like Ray Nolting, Harry Clark, Ken Kavanaugh and Bob Swisher. They were a lot of fast people. The passes would travel 35 yards, but Sid would have the ball in the air when the receivers were only 18 yards down the field. He had a perfect feel for trajectory where the ball was not too high and didn't hang, yet the receiver could run under it. I couldn't do it, though I practiced for weeks. I couldn't train myself to throw into space. I was trained to hit the guy on the break, or a step and a half ahead of the defender, leading him with the ball. Tommy Thompson, an excellent passer for the Eagles, couldn't do it either. We spent a month and Greasy finally gave up.

"The great ones have a feel. Unitas can put the ball up there softly and there are times when, wham, he has to rifle the ball inside. Say there are two defenders around the receiver. The ball isn't a foot to the right or the left. It comes in where it should with the nose up, on a wonderfully sharp plane. This is an instinct, feel and accuracy that the truly great ones have. Unitas is superb. So was Y. A. Tittle at the high point of his career.

"Strangely enough, there's a mentality to passing, too. There's a difference between a quarterback coming away from the center and saying to himself, 'I hope I find him.' And a quarterback coming away and saying, 'You better stop this one, pal. I'm putting it right there in your gut.'

"Say there are thirty passers in our league. I bet there aren't more than five passers that come away from the center saying, 'I'm putting it in there, baby.'

"You got to have mental toughness. That was Tittle's greatest strength. He believed he could throw the ball better than any guy could run three yards."

It bugged the bald quarterback to hear the fans or critics, or even players and coaches, say, "That Tittle was sure off today. The bum was throwing bloopers."

"I would venture to say," argued Tittle, "that 99 percent of the poor throws are not caused by the poor arm or the poor fakes by the receivers, but only because of the poor play selection in the huddle and the failure to adjust. I read so many times that Unitas is off today or John Brodie is off today.

"Well, they don't throw curve balls or knucklers or balls that are supposed to hop and dance and suddenly aren't hopping that day. I can't recall any day I threw differently."

"I look back," claimed Otto Graham, "and I don't think I threw more than half a dozen bad passes in my whole career. I had some passes intercepted because of deflections—lots of times short passes are thrown between arms and heads—or a linebacker was hidden."

Otto was voted in a national poll of sportswriters and sportscasters the greatest quarterback in pro history. His explanation for his success was simple: "I was born with a God-given gift of coordination and I could throw a football—that's basically what a quarterback does."

But Otto also appreciated that a passer must have a feel for his job.

"I handled the College All-Star team for nine years," he said, "and all those years I had to teach kids to throw softer balls. They tend to fire those rollout passes on the run, like they've been trained in college. Even those who used a straight dropback before throwing—like George Mira of Miami—had to be taught to pull the string. The idea is to loft the ball over the linebacker's head under ideal conditions, not to try to throw through his hands. Throw it just hard enough to complete the pass."

Francis Tarkenton, the quarterback of the Minnesota Vikings, remembered his first exposure to Graham.

"He probably threw as soft a ball as anyone ever threw," recalled Tarkenton. "I watched him playing catch with Adrian Burk, who once played quarterback for the Philadelphia Eagles. (Burk is a co-holder with Luckman and Tittle of the record of seven touchdown passes in one game.) Burk threw real hard. Otto couldn't hold the ball. Otto turned to me and said, 'See how hard Adrian throws the ball? That's why my passing percentage is better than his.'"

Tarkenton came into professional football with some question about the caliber of his passing.

"My throwing improved 100 percent in three years," he said realistically, "because I disciplined my arm to know what kind of ball to throw in different situations. I can whip it out there toward the out marker; I can whip something in the middle, and if I need to lob the ball I can do this, too. When I came up I had questions about my ability to do these things because I had never done them before. In college it's mostly short stuff. I needed to strengthen my arm somewhat. It's taxed more in pro ball. But now I have no more questions about my ability."

The proof, however, is in the doing. The issue came up sharply in the first game of the 1965 season. The Baltimore Colts played the Minnesota Vikings. The official temperature registered 94 degrees, hottest ever recorded for September 19 in the crabcake country of Maryland. The offenses of both teams sizzled, too.

With Unitas at the controls, the Colts stepped out to a 14–10 lead at halftime. The young Vikings, with definite championship aspirations in their fifth year of operation, came storming back with the third-quarter kickoff. They marched deep into Baltimore territory.

From the 30-yard line on second down, quarterback Tarkenton faked a handoff to fullback Bill Brown and faded straight back to throw. Paul Flatley, the Vikings' split left end, ran a post pattern. He broke straight down the field, feinted defender Lenny Lyles to the sideline and then veered in on a path to the goal posts. Flatley was all alone crossing into the end zone as Tarkenton arched the pass. But Francis, who had been harassed by Colt defenders most of the afternoon, put too much on the ball and it sailed past Flatley's groping left arm.

Third-down play coming up. Flatley faked a slant-in over the middle as Tarkenton again set up in his protective cup. Lyles lost his balance chasing the receiver and fell down as Flatley cut back toward the left sideline. Again he was alone, like one of those go-go dancers in an elevated cage. Tarkenton's pass wobbled over his head. The Vikings had to settle for a field goal and still trailed the Colts, 14–13.

36

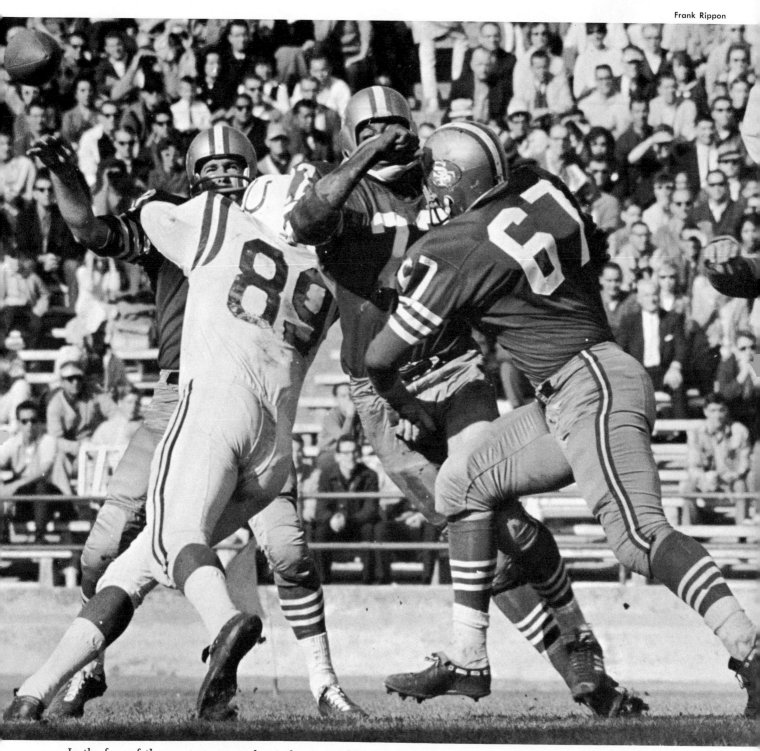

In the face of the greatest pass rusher in history, Baltimore's Gino Marchetti (89), John Brodie of the San Francisco 49ers stands his ground to release the ball.

Passers must be able to flip the ball under, around and over assorted arms, as Frank Ryan of Cleveland did here, with tackle Joe Rutgen of Washington coming at him.

Now it was Unitas' turn. He hit Raymond Berry, split left, with a sideline pass for a first down. Jimmy Orr, the right flanker, worked on George Rose, the Vikings' defensive halfback. Rose was overplaying him to the inside of the field. Orr started to break in, saw Rose pick up the move and broke his pass pattern by running straight down the field. Unitas, tuned to Orr's tricks, pumped once and then lofted the ball softly into the little flanker's hands for a 52-yard gain.

One play later, Orr again faked Rose inside and ran a zig-out pattern into the end zone to grab Unitas' perfect pitch for a touchdown. The way it turned out, that was the ball game, eventually won by the Colts, 21–16.

And that was the difference. When Tarkenton had his man open, twice, he missed. Unitas didn't. Tarkenton is a potentially great young quarterback. Unitas is a great seasoned quarterback who has had the benefit of working with his deep receivers, Berry and Orr, a total of fifteen years.

"We knew we could throw to the outside," Unitas said later. "The Vikings were covering us inside, not giving us too much there. So we just took what they gave us. Passing, you know, is a sort of hit-and-miss kind of thing, backed by solid, basic thinking."

And throwing.

4. The Mental Giant

The Cleveland Browns pulled one of the great upsets in championship game history, defeated Baltimore 27–0 in 1964, because Frank Ryan outdueled John Unitas. He's ignoring the dark figure of big Gino Marchetti (89).

Coach Sid Gillman of the San Diego Chargers places his entire stress in football on results. "Statistics," he says, "are for losers."

There's a curious argument in favor of Sid's statement:

• On December 1, 1940, Davey O'Brien of the Philadelphia Eagles threw 60 passes against the Washington Redskins, an NFL record, and completed 33.

• On September 23, 1962, Sonny Jurgensen of the Eagles threw 57 passes against the New York Giants and completed 33.

• On October 25, 1964, Billy Wade of the Chicago Bears threw 57 passes against the Redskins and completed 33.

• On November 21, 1948, Jim Hardy of the Los Angeles Rams threw 53 passes against the Chicago Cardinals and completed 28.

• On December 5, 1948, Charley Conerly of the Giants threw 53 passes against the Pittsburgh Steelers and completed 36, an NFL record.

• On November 10, 1963, Don Meredith of the Dallas Cowboys threw 48 passes against the San Francisco 49ers and completed 30.

No passer in National Football League history has ever thrown more passes in a single game than any of the above, or completed more. In every case, the passer's team LOST!

The American Football League record for passes thrown and completed in a single game is held by George Blanda of the Houston Oilers. He went 37 for 68 and 393 yards gained against the Buffalo Bills on November 1, 1964. Buffalo won the game, 24–10.

"I like to throw the ball as much as anybody," said Y. A. Tittle, who threw and completed more passes, for more touchdowns, than any quarterback in professional football history, "but unless it's put up there at the proper time with proper thought behind it, the passing game will not win for you.

"A quarterback has to know when he comes out of the huddle, the pass-defense habits of the other team and the pass-defense habits of its coaches. Whether it's a strong man-to-man club, whether a zone or full-roll team, whether they have a tendency to double-team the weak-side split end."

Certain types of pass patterns are not good at all if certain defenses are applied against them. Throw a turn-in pass to the weak-side end who is double-covered inside-outside by the weak-side safety and the cornerback, and there's no way in the world he can do anything about it. That's the way Del Shofner was covered most of the time in the 1963 championship game against the Bears."

Shofner was Tittle's favorite receiver with the Giants. He failed to catch a single pass in the title game. When Tittle didn't go to him, the Bears knew his other favorite play was a screen pass. They intercepted two of the screens to set up both their scores in a 14–10 upset.

"It's absolutely necessary for a quarterback to anticipate and recognize defenses," continued Tittle. "In the past, a decade ago, it didn't make a lot of difference. Individual effort was the big thing. The defensive team could make a mistake and not get hurt because it had a good back who could recover and run like a deer. Now they play team defense and they don't make mistakes. Therefore, you don't make mistakes. Or can't afford to.

"You throw a down-and-in pass pattern to a receiver into the hole (the short area over the middle of the line) and their guy backs up in the hole, you might just as well line up your defensive unit because he's got an interception. How does the quarterback know the defender's going into hole? If he watches and doesn't feel what he ought to see—the weak-side safety doesn't look right, he's a little too relaxed—he should come off that play (i.e., change it on the line of scrimmage) and maybe go to a running play.

"This is the part of football that makes it mentally tougher than ever and likewise more satisfying for a quarterback. I don't want to mesmerize people with the idea that football is a game for brains to play. Basic simplicity is still the keynote. You don't outsmart anybody anymore. All you want to do is be right, percentage-wise.

"Where do these percentages come from? Not from the quarterback. They come from the staff before the game, from the receivers, maybe from some linemen, from the coaches on the sidelines and in the spotter's box."

On a street corner in Columbus, Ohio, one Saturday night in 1958, Allie Sherman said that Lee Grosscup of the University of Utah was the best passer he'd seen come out of college ball in a decade. Sherman was doing some personnel scouting for the Giants. That year the Giants drafted Grosscup No. 1, probably on Sherman's recommendation, and Allie got back his old job as assistant coach in charge of the Giant offense a year later when Vince Lombardi moved on to Green Bay. It's part of the toughness of Sherman that Grosscup was destined never to play a full game for him in regular league competition because he didn't measure up to Allie's mental concepts of a pro quarterback.

Sherman's success as a coach has been in the area of quarterbacking. Weeb Ewbank gets credit for developing Johnny Unitas at Baltimore, but chances are Johnny would have been great eventually for any coach. Sherman's credits are tangible. He started Conerly on the right track in the T and then nursed several great seasons out of Charley when the Mississippi flinger wore white sideburns and played on creaking legs. His greatest job was with Tittle. Yat had never been a winner and the 49ers were ready to dump him in 1961 when Coach Red Hickey installed the shotgun offense as a basic attack. Tittle was too old to run from tailback. He came to the Giants almost on the eve of the season because Sherman decided Grosscup would never make it as Conerly's successor. For one thing, Lee wouldn't cut his hair short like Sherman wanted.

Sherman read Tittle's limitations as a quarterback immediately. Around the league there were derisive nicknames for Tittle's mental capacities as a quarterback. With the 49ers, too much stuff was thrown at him. Yat had a great arm as standard equipment and great confidence in his ability to throw. He didn't need to master 400 plays and twice as many variations thereof to lead a pro team. Sherman grasped this. He simplified his offense to suit Tittle's personality as a quarterback, and Yat produced three divisional

United Press International Photo

Coach Allie Sherman of the Giants (right) simplified the pro offense for Y. A. Tittle and spurred the veteran quarterback to the best three years of his career when he came to New York in 1961.

Besides his obvious passing gifts, Norm Van Brocklin was like a coach on the field for the Philadelphia Eagles, looking over the defense to find porous spots.

Jules Schick Photography

championships in three years. When the string ran out on Tittle's elasticity—he was injury-prone in 1964, his last season, and painfully slow in setting up against the blitzes other teams threw at him—Sherman didn't waste any time in making it clear to Tittle he should retire. There is that hardness in the little General.

"A quarterback must have a very positive approach in what he's trying to make the other team do. A lot of quarterbacks go out there thinking, 'Well, it looks like they'll probably have the linebackers close, so I'm going to pump the ball up in the secondary. If they drop off, I'll run some draw plays.'

"But the real good quarterback says, 'They're going to red dog a lot and I'm going to open this ballgame up. I'm going to throw the quick slants and the circle pass as the red-dog man is coming. I got a halfback who can beat the linebacker because they're up tight and dogging a lot. When they fall off to the outside to help on the flanker or the spread end, I'm going to use the halfback.'

"Confidence. That's what the quarterback needs. He knows right now what counteracts the other team. He doesn't float around."

The quarterback's life has become very complicated. He has to consider the basic frequency or tendency of the other team, how it reacts to the particular down, field position and game situation. He has to know the opposing personnel. Who's the weaker tackle or linebacker or deep back? What kind of coverage do they favor, zone or man-to-man?

In the early days of the T-formation, the quarterback's life was relatively simple. The defenses were fairly static, with five- or six-man lines. The quarterback could influence the defense by sending a man in motion or handing off to one of the backs on a quick dive up the middle. Those were the basic plays. If a quarterback just wiggled his elbow, it would send a couple of linebackers flying in that direction. They reacted to all the fakes. In those first years of the T, everybody on defense watched the quarterback.

It's not so anymore. A defensive genius named Tom Landry, who now coaches the Dallas Cowboys, figured out tendencies. He developed his system as the defensive player-coach of the New York Giants. When the Cleveland Browns, for instance, lined up in a particular formation, they ran only certain plays in their repertoire. Landry refined it to frequencies. When it was second down and 5, at midfield, you could expect this. On third and 3 within the 20-yard line, they favored a different play. Landry would stand on the sidelines when the Giants played the Browns and call the plays before Coach Paul Brown of Cleveland would send his messenger in from the sidelines. He was right 90 percent of the time.

Now the defense keyed on formations and personnel other than the quarterback—halfbacks, fullbacks, guards, tackles. It became a game of cat and mouse.

"When Vince Lombardi came to Green Bay (in 1959)," says quarterback Bart Starr, "he gave us offensive men keys to look at a defense. If we throw a certain pass pattern, a definite key's going to tell us if the pattern'll work. For example, take the free safety on a pattern where the guy breaks inside. All you got to do is look at one guy—the safety. He'll tell you right now if he's going to break the pass up, if it's going to be dangerous. If he's there, then you've got an alternate man to throw to. This stuff is basic and simple and you should know it the first time you go on a practice field. On pass patterns, if the defense changes the last minute and goes from man-to-man to zone coverage, right now that tells me our men are going to change their routes. Maybe the route I called in the huddle isn't as good against a zone as it is against man-to-man."

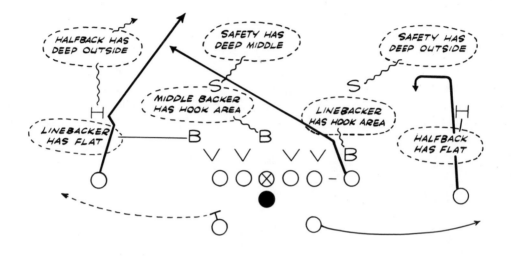

In a zone defense, the field is split into segments (see diagram), with each man responsible for his area. It's particularly effective against the bombs, so most passers try to flood a zone with an extra receiver or hit the receiver in the twilight area, or cracks between two zones, where the responsibility of coverage is not quite fixed. The passer doesn't have to keep his backs in for pass protection because blitzes are unlikely by the linebackers, who have their own zones of responsibility. The man-to-man is just what it implies. Every pass defender picks up a receiver according to his position (i.e., the right cornerback on the split left end) and stays with him all over the field. It's best to throw to the strong side of the field against the man-to-man because the strong-side safety and cornerback are in single coverage. Most teams combine these two types of pass defenses—zoning one side of the field, using man-to-man on the other.

Starr has taken a favorite pass pattern and carried it through against the different defenses he might encounter. It's called a Flare Wide L and R Wing Trail, and Bart used it at a couple of crucial points in the 1966 (played at the end of the 1965 season) championship game against Cleveland. Here he diagrams it against possible defenses he might see as he comes out of the huddle, and adds his own explanatory notes to describe his thinking:

47

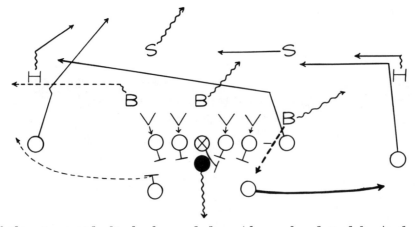

"If the strong-side linebacker red dogs (shown by dotted line), the quarterback merely dumps the ball to the fullback in the flat. He would have good running room because the secondary defenders are going in an opposite direction.

"Note the wide area the tight end has after he passes the middle linebacker. The halfback, after checking for a red dog, flares wide, taking his weak-side linebacker with him. The right end or the flanker is usually the first-choice receiver against this defense.

"Note also that if the strong-side safety covers the tight end as he's supposed to, the wing (or flanker) has a huge inside area in which to operate. He has only the linebackers to concern himself with."

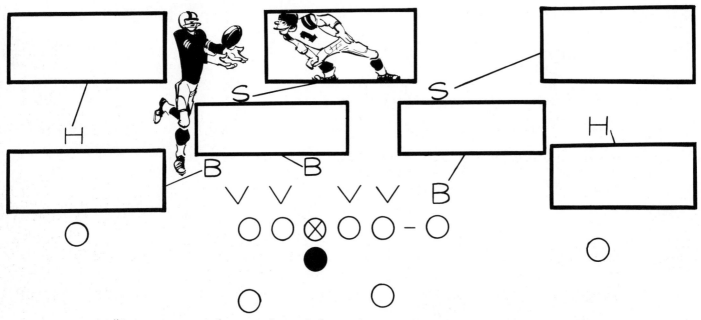

"Against a zone the most logical choice for a primary receiver is the wing, since he can turn in just inside the cornerback on his side and pull up short of the strong-side linebacker, who has dropped straight back into the hook area.

"This is an excellent pass against a zone defense, and many times we have hit the tight end between linebacker zones.

"On this defense the coverage is by areas or zones rather than man-to-man, the exception being that the right cornerback will have the split end all to himself for a while."

48

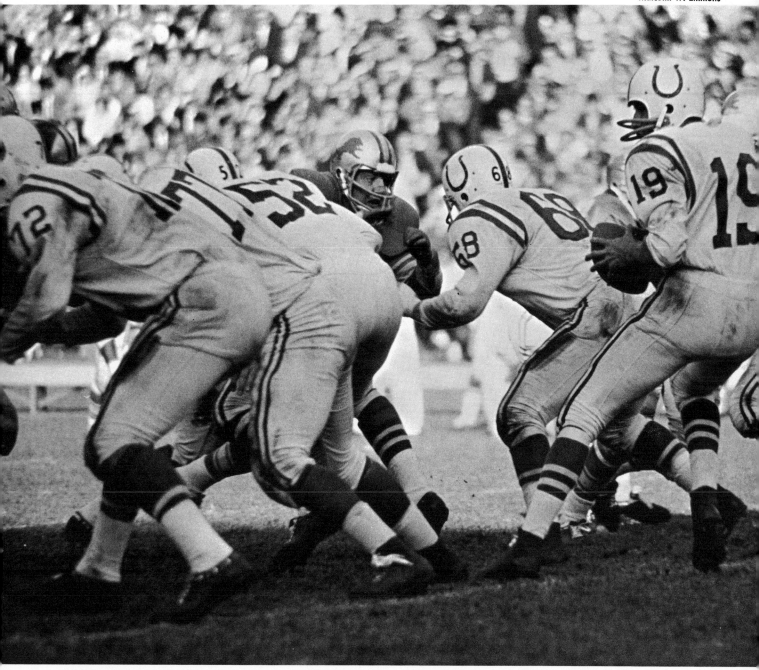

As John Unitas of the Colts (19) starts to set up, he's looking for the linebackers to pick up a blitz and the strong side safety to tip him off on the defensive alignment.

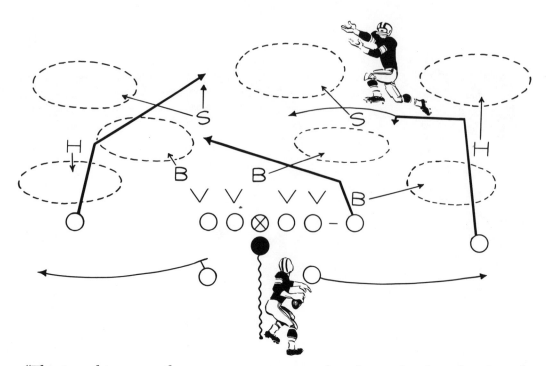

"This is nothing more than zone coverage rotated to the weak side rather than the strong side as in normal zone.

"The defense may play the split end inside-outside, rather than short or long. The strong-side defensive halfback and safety are man-to-man on the wing and tight end but will play rather loose.

"The wing is an excellent choice again. See the big hole he can veer into either in front of or behind the middle linebacker."

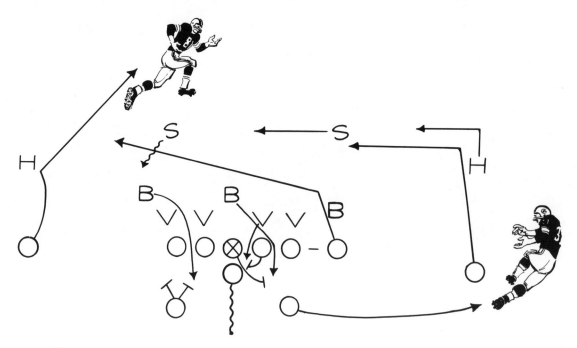

"If the linebackers blitz, this pass becomes even more effective since there is no dropping or rotating by the linebackers, forcing the pass to be spaced between them. The secondary defenders must also be especially careful in their coverage because there is no linebacker support. The receivers 'show' immediately and are easily picked up by the quarterback.

"If the weak-side linebacker red dogs, the safety on his side normally has the remaining halfback man-for-man, thus allowing the split end running room on a post pattern with only the right cornerback to pick him up.

"Against this coverage, all three receivers may be open.

"If all three linebackers blitz, the quarterback merely dumps the ball to the fullback flaring right.

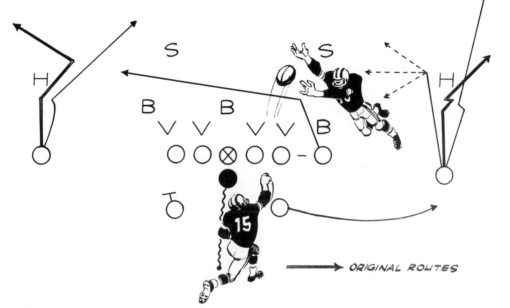

ORIGINAL ROUTES

"The defenseman covering the wingback is coached to expect an 'in' break by the wing when the fullback flares wide; with this in mind, note how easily a quick move inside by the wing, followed by a 'corner' or flag route is a simple takeoff of the original pass route, which was a square-in. The wide route by the fullback doesn't interfere or draw the linebacker into a dangerous position at all.

"With the same thinking in mind, it's also easy to see how the wing can run a 'fly' pattern on the cornerback with a slight dip to the inside as an initial fake. One or two of these suffice to make the cornerback deep-conscious, and you can throw short all day.

"The wingback can run several angles on his breakaway from the defender, thus giving the latter no indication where his path to the inside will take him.

"The split end can have companion routes that operate the same as the wing."

This all sounds very complicated to the layman, but it's the basic bread-and-butter thinking a quarterback must master before he can hope to lead an offense into action.

Francis Tarkenton came right out of the University of Georgia into a job as a starting quarterback with the Minnesota Vikings in 1961. "It scares me to think back," he says, "of the things I didn't know. I didn't know pro defenses and offenses. Why they go to a zone, why they go to a weak-side zone, why they go to double coverage on some re-ceivers. On third and long, I didn't have any idea what kind of coverage they were going to, or on second and short. I didn't know how to evaluate these things, how to reason them out. No quarterback knows until he has studied them and learned them and watched people react to situations. I think it's impossible for any rookie ever to come up and be a polished quarterback."

The recognition and "reading" of defense has become the most important mental function of a quarterback. Tarkenton outlines the possibilities: "They may have single (man-to-man) or they might have a strong-side zone coverage and therefore take the long ball away from us on the strong side. (*Note:* the "strong side" is always that on which the tight end lines up, with a flanker outside him.) They may go to a weak-side zone and revolve their defensive backs around to the weak side. They might go to a double coverage and have two men on each side of our three ends. They may go to a combination coverage, which is a strong defense against our slot end and our flanker back."

Since he's gone into pro coaching and progressed to head man of the Washington Redskins, Otto Graham has tried to simplify this problem of recognition.

"I've always felt the key to quarterback is reading linebackers," says Otto. "The first thing I teach my boys is to look for them. They're going to red dog or they aren't. They don't stand there for a couple of seconds after the snap and start coming. They come right now. If they come right now, you've got to unload the ball to a tight end or swing back. If they don't come, then you look back at your strong-side safetyman. If he turns and starts running diagonally backwards, at 45 degrees to the outside, you know damn well they're going to revolve their defenses on you. The left cornerback has moved up to the line of scrimmage and is waiting for you. So if you throw a pass to your swing man (one of the backs flaring wide), that cornerback is going to pick it off or else tackle the guy for no gain. But you also know that from over on the side of the field, the free safety has to come across and protect against the tight end as a possible receiver. Now your spread end over on the left is one-on-one with the right cornerback. You know that. So you look for him. Or if you have a swing man going to the weak side (left in this case), you're in business."

After the recognition, comes execution. On a gray December day late in 1964, the Cleveland Browns met the Baltimore Colts for the National Football League champion-ship. The Browns were 10-point underdogs. In the 19-mile-an-hour wind blowing off Lake Erie, neither team scored in the first half, and the 80,000 people in Cleveland's Municipal Stadium sat hushed, slightly frozen and pleasantly surprised. The Colts were, after all, the highest-scoring team in football, with the incomparable Johnny Unitas at quarterback.

Early in the third quarter a quick Cleveland penetration put the Browns on the Baltimore 36-yard line in a fourth-down situation. The wind was at their backs. Lou Groza came on the field and kicked a 43-yard field goal to start the scoring. The Browns held after the kickoff and gained possession of the ball again on their own 34-yard line. Quarterback Frank Ryan brought them out in a double-wing formation practiced spe-cifically for this game. The Baltimore weak-side linebacker, Don Shinnick, didn't adjust.

52

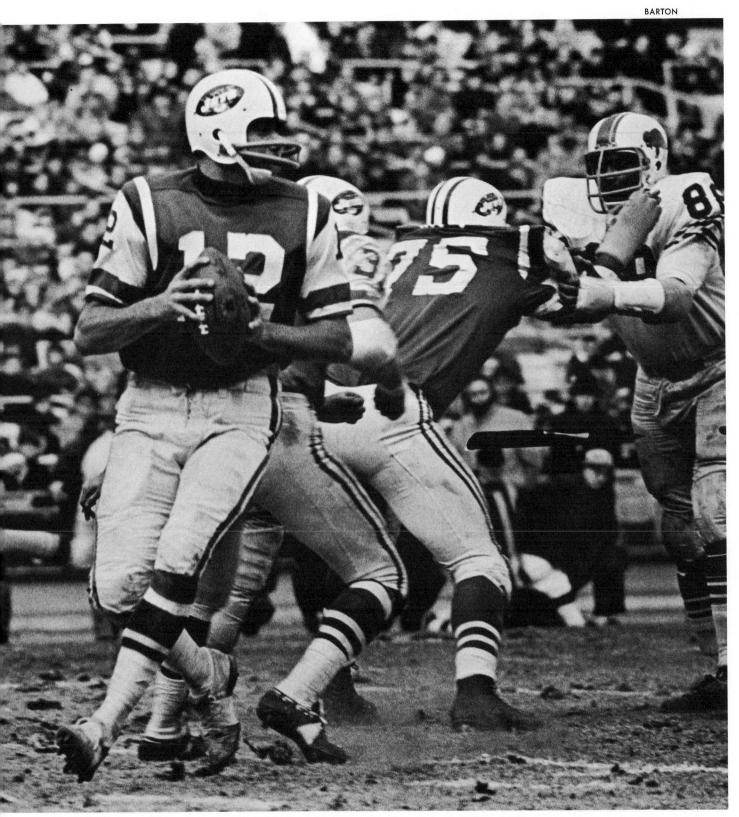

The toughest part about a rookie quarterback breaking in, like Joe Namath did in 1965, is to look over the field and recognize the type of pass coverage being used by the defense.

He stayed in close, on the inside shoulder of his defensive end. Halfback Ernie Green of the Browns flanked left, outside his end, and had a good blocking angle on Shinnick. Ryan pitched quickly to fullback Jim Brown. As Green sliced down Shinnick, guard Gene Hickerson pulled out of the line and raced around to nudge the cornerback out of the play. Behind him, Brown swept his left end and glided swiftly down the sideline.

"I'm trailing the play thinking maybe he's going to break all the way for a touchdown," Ryan reviewed the situation. "Then I see him tackled on their 18-yard line. The first real threat of the day. I have a feeling I have to do something to take advantage of this tremendous break. Now this was my reasoning. I didn't want to run the ball again on the next play. If we run outside, they might have a blitz on, like they do in such situations lots of times, and we could lose big yardage. If we run inside, they might stack it up. And second down and 8 is a defensive play in my book. If we pass and it doesn't work, it's still second and 10. So why not pass?"

In the huddle, Ryan called the same formation as on the previous play. A close double-wing, with Paul Warfield, normally the split left end, lined up tight, close to tackle Dick Schafrath. The backfield action simulated a run, with Brown the obvious ball carrier, since he lined up alone behind the quarterback. Ryan didn't say much in the huddle.

He barked briefly, "Two double-wing 70, slot-inside release. Check the Blitz. Cross. Rip deep, shake. On two. Break."

"The 'two' means Jim Brown is directly behind me and the slot end is on my right," explained Ryan. "That brings Warfield in tight and Green flanking him. The 'slot-inside release' tells him whether to go inside or outside of the linebacker. He checks the blitz. If it's on, he heads over the middle. The 'rip deep, shake' means that the slot end, or Gary Collins, goes down, fakes to the inside and then veers deep into the corner of the field.

"On the 70's series of plays, the fullback is always blocking or flaring to the weak side. The halfback is always in a pattern to the weak side. Normally, I like to throw a hook pass on a 70. On this play, I wanted to hit Gary because I figured they'd be looking for Warfield as a receiver. Even double-teaming on Paul, they can slough off. Hopefully, I completely isolated Gary with Bobby Boyd, their left cornerback."

At the word "break" in the huddle, the Browns clapped hands simultaneously and turned toward the line of scrimmage. When they got up there, the quarterback yelled, "Set."

"I was checking the spacing of the defensive line," continued Ryan. "I have a picture in my mind of where everybody's supposed to be. If something's out of place, it'll register. Like, for instance, normally, the strong-side linebacker is on top of the slot end. Sometimes, though, they have a little game going. They slide the defensive end to the inside shoulder of the slot end and drop the linebacker off a little.

"On this play against the Colts, I was also conscious of Jim Welch, the weak safety, and Boyd. They were slow breaking the huddle, and they were talking to one another, like they weren't sure. It was part of my awareness. At the snap of the ball, I went right to their coverage, looking to pass there. It's not a conscious effort. In this case, I just felt the defense was a little hesitant. The noise was so bad I couldn't hear what they were saying to each other."

54

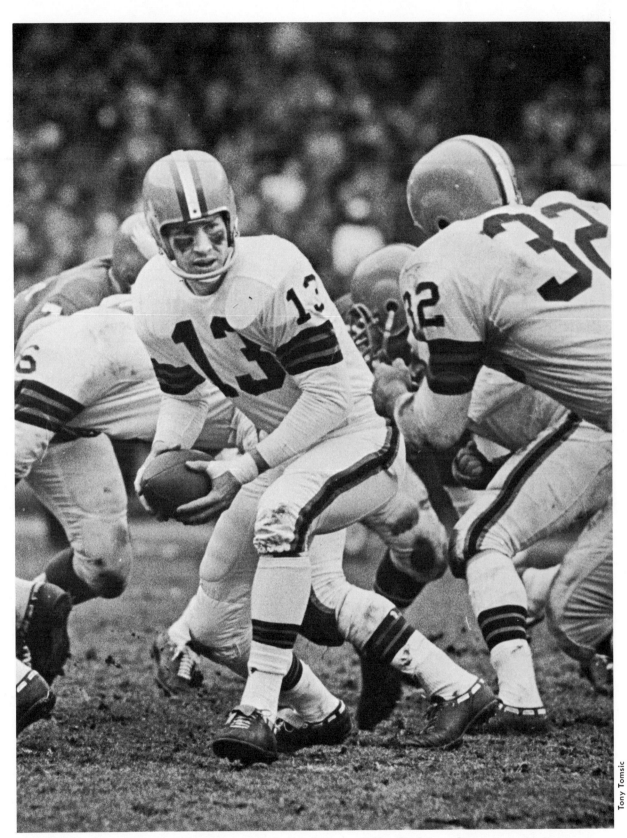

You don't have to be a mental giant, though Frank Ryan of Cleveland is, to know your smartest move as a Brown quarterback is to slip the ball to fullback Jimmy Brown (32), coming from the right.

His signals before the snap were brief: "Set . . . Red 84 . . . Hike . . . Hike."

As he backed up with the ball, he checked the middle linebacker and the strong-side linebacker quickly. If they were coming (i.e., blitzing) he was prepared to dump the ball quickly to his tight end, John Brewer. If only the middle linebacker, in this case Bill Pellington, blitzed, Ryan was going to stick with the play because he was sure center John Morrow would pick up the blitz. As it turned out, the linebackers held their places. Ryan, fading, tried to pick up Collins. ("There was a whole bunch of junk out there where he was supposed to be," Ryan said. "He was obviously cut off deep to the outside.")

The Cleveland offensive lineman had formed their protective cup around Ryan and forced the Colt rushers around him as he stepped up. The middle linebacker, Pellington, was chasing Brown on the left side of the field. An alley opened up the middle, and for a moment Ryan was tempted to run. Just then he saw Gary shake loose from his coverage. Boyd and Welch weren't quite sure who was to pick him up. Neither did. Collins simply broke his pass pattern and cut toward the middle, under the goalposts in the end zone. He was all alone.

As Ryan threw the ball, he worried about it hitting the crossbar, not about the accuracy of the pass. "I can complete that kind blindfolded," he said. The ball caught Collins perfectly in the stomach for a touchdown.

"Damn," yelled Ryan, "we did it!"

With a 10–0 lead, the Browns had control of the game and went on to rack up a spectacular 27–0 upset for the NFL championship. After seven erratic years in professional football, six of them as a substitute, Ryan proved he had the recipe for signal-calling.

Loser Unitas sent word to the Cleveland dressing room: "Tell Frank Ryan I said congratulations!"

56

5. The Quarterback's Week

BART STARR *of the Green Bay Packers:*
YOU MEET A GUY ON THE STREET ON
MONDAY MORNING, AFTER A GAME, AND
HE'LL SAY, "BOY, YOU GUYS REALLY
HAVE A SNAP. GREATEST LIFE IN THE
WORLD." IT'S A GREAT LIFE, THE HOURS
YOU PUT IN ARE FINE, AND IT'S VERY RE-
WARDING AND YOU'RE PAID WELL. BUT
I DON'T THINK THAT THE FAN EITHER
STOPS TO REALIZE OR KNOWS WHAT
GOES INTO IT. COACH LOMBARDI SAYS
YOU PUT IN TWENTY-SEVEN TO THIRTY-
THREE HOURS OF PRACTICE FOR EVERY
HOUR OF TIME YOU PUT IN ON THE
FIELD DURING A BALLGAME. THAT'S A
LOT OF WORK. I DON'T THINK A FELLOW
SITTING BEHIND A DESK PUTS IN THIRTY
HOURS OF PRACTICE AT HOME FOR
EVERY DUTY HE HAS TO PERFORM IN
THE OFFICE. MAYBE A DOCTOR DOES. I
DON'T THINK THEY REALIZE THE TIME
WE SPEND AT A BLACKBOARD, LOOK-
ING AT MOVIES AND EVERYTHING ELSE
THAT GOES WITH BEING A QUARTER-
BACK.

Bart Starr, in practice togs, surrounded by Green Bay kids, is a familiar sight in the parking lot outside the Packer dressing room. He holds son Bret, 2.

In mid-week practice sessions, Bart Starr, passing, breathes life into the plays diagrammed on the blackboard by the Green Bay Packer coaching staff.

Cherry Starr waited outside the link-wire enclosure that marks off the dressing-room entrance of the Green Bay Packers. It's just north of Lambeau Stadium and surrounds the low, yellow-brick building that serves as the home and lifeblood of the Packers.

Sometimes, if the crowd presses too close, especially after a Packer win, the attendant lets the wives inside the enclosure. This was after a loss. By the time Bart Starr sweated out the reporters and a slow, grim shower, the crowd had thinned out. He was dressed in a neat gray sportscoat with dark slacks and a mackintosh. A couple of kids stopped him for his autograph.

He spotted Cherry, smiled feebly and escorted her to the Ford stationwagon on the other side of the building. Bart, Jr., and his friend, Steve Cristigna, were inside it, waiting. Bart slid behind the driver's wheel.

The house on Chateau Drive is only five blocks away, walking distance, so it didn't take them long to drive it. "Why did you let (Jim) Marshall get in on you?" asked young Bart. His dad shrugged. "I noticed you overthrew (Carroll) Dale on that sideline pass," the youngster continued. "Were they rushing you?"

"They sure were," nodded Starr.

Starr parked the car and walked through the front door into the living room. He slammed his coat into a chair, in a motion of disgust. He heard a thump and turned around, startled. Young Bart had also whipped off his coat and slammed his coat down.

> STARR: That's what you got to watch out for. These kids imitate everything you do, on and off the football field.

In a couple of minutes, Zeke and M.E. (for Mary Elizabeth) Bratkowski drove up. It was late afternoon on a Sunday in Green Bay, Wisconsin. Bart broke open a couple bottles of beer. The girls had Cokes. They tried to unwind. The radio was on to see if they could pick up the other pro football scores of the day. By six o'clock, Bart realized he hadn't eaten a thing since breakfast. The Starrs and Bratkowskis got into the stationwagon and drove downtown to Washington Street, the main drag. He stopped in front of the Downtowner, a big restaurant. They walked into a private dining room where they wouldn't be bothered. Bart ordered the usual: shrimp cocktail, filet mignon medium rare, salad and hashed-brown potatoes. He had a beer with it and it relaxed him.

"How about those Vikings," mused Bratkowski, who was on the sideline telephones all afternoon as the second-string quarterback of the Packers. "In that odd defense, they blitzed on second down. That's something we didn't figure on." An "odd" defense finds one of the defensive tackles playing right over the center's nose.

"No," agreed Bart, "I wasn't expecting it. Or the way (Rip) Hawkins plugged." Hawkins is the middle linebacker for Minnesota and did a lot of moving around along the line, jumping in and out.

Except for the technical football talk over dinner, it was just like two couples of the junior-league set out for a quiet Sunday night dinner. They weren't too late. By ten o'clock, after lingering to make chit-chat with some friends in the restaurant, they wrapped it up. Bart dropped the Bratkowskis off. He paid the babysitter $10 for being there all day, then drove her home.

Later he pulled off his coat and tie, loosened his collar and joined Cherry in the kitchen. Bart's a worrier, but he didn't cry too much over the game. After ten years you're still not used to losing, but you try not to let it stay with you, either. Cherry said it wasn't one of his better games.

> STARR: Cherry's a fine little student of football. She didn't know beans about it when I first met her. When we're on the road, she won't go to hen parties. Because she wants to watch the game, not talk. But she's emotional. She throws the tranquillizers down like a—oh, golly. Before one title game, she was downing these things. I just put my hands on her shoulders and said, "Sweetie, don't worry about it. I've got to play, not you." She broke up.

That night, Bart slept fitfully. He always has trouble after a game, win or lose. On Monday morning he was up early to help Cherry with the kids. Besides Bart, Jr., there's little Bret, just learning to walk. Monday's a big-breakfast day. Hotcakes (which he won't eat later in the week), bacon, scrambled eggs, orange juice, milk and hot chocolate. Bart won't drink coffee. Cherry keeps some instant coffee around the house in case friends drop in.

The weather looked bad, so Bart offered to drive the older boy to school in the family's second car, an Oldsmobile sports coupé. He continued on to the Model Cleaners to drop off some clothes and laundry. He also deposited a couple of rolls of film at the Camera Corner in the Beacon shopping plaza. Then he drove downtown to pick up a shotgun he'd ordered earlier. He wanted a recoil pad put on. "Go get 'em next week," said the man behind the counter. Bart swung the car out toward Highland Avenue, which goes past the Stadium. A couple of Packers were already there. Bart joined them in the slick new sauna bath for 10 minutes of baking tired muscles. On the way out he stopped at the table in the middle of the dressing room and rifled through a stack of mail for the stuff addressed to him.

> STARR: My wife answers most of my fan letters. I hate to write letters. I do it once a week, on Mondays. And then I have a lady down the street type them up.

He wrote letters most of Monday afternoon, horsed around with young Bret and, when the other kids on the block came home from school, stepped outside to throw passes to them. After a leisurely dinner, he watched television briefly. Bart's trying to kick the TV habit. Around ten o'clock, he sneaked downstairs to the finished basement. There's a filing cabinet stacked in a corner. He pulled the middle drawer and took out a folder marked "San Francisco 49ers." It was the first sign of attention to the week's work ahead. He checked over the reports he had written on them last year.

60

STARR: I like to read my notes on 'em. "This guy can be beat on an outside pattern. . . . To throw inside on him, favor the left hash mark. . . . The screen pass is good under certain conditions." And I write what those conditions are. The next morning, when I get the scouting report and see films, I already have a little idea of what I want to keep in mind about the 49ers. I file all my game plans and reports on each team in this cabinet. That way I've got a permanent record on them.

On Tuesday morning, the butterflies in his belly started to quiver. Time to go to work. Coach Vince Lombardi wants his team there sharply at nine-thirty for the first meeting. He starts it at nine-twenty-five. Bart was there at nine. He drove to practice alone in the Olds, then put on grey sweat togs. Those are his workclothes except in the early season, when it's warm enough for shorts. Lombardi's opening remarks were terse and to the point. He wasn't happy.

STARR: He's fair. He gives a great deal of thought to what he says to us on Tuesday. It's always very apropos. It sets the pace for the coming week.

The room was darkened and Lombardi flicked on a screen projector. Movie time. Sunday's game was the feature. It was already broken into offensive and defensive segments. The defensive unit watched its segment in the visiting team's dressing quarters. Starr and his offensive pals stayed behind and listened to Lombardi and three of his assistant coaches deliver terse comment as their film was run and rerun. Starr saw himself getting clobbered as the Viking ends penetrated past the Packer tackles and swarmed him. The memory made him wince.

"You should have stepped up there," cautioned Lombardi at one point.

"Yes, sir," agreed Starr.

The moment the reel was run, Lombardi snapped, "All right. Out there, men." They jogged or walked across the parking lot that surrounds the stadium and across Oneida Avenue, which separates the stadium grounds from a big indoor arena, to the Packer practice area. When they assembled, out front stood Fuzzy Thurston. The offensive guard and whoop leader started them off on their exercises. "Let's get Herb out there," came a yell from the back row.

"Way to go, Herb," the defensive unit chorused. Adderley, an all-pro cornerback, had made a couple of interceptions in the last game. This privileged him to lead the exercises. Lombardi called the offensive unit together. He wanted to run a play which bugged him on execution. The Packers moved through it at three-quarter speed, Starr handing off to Jimmy Taylor on a 34X, the fullback hitting the hole between left guard and left tackle on the weak side. Then all the linemen got together for a touch-football game. Starr and Bratkowski took the backs and ends to an adjoining field and alternated throwing passes. They were on the field for only 45 minutes but worked up a good sweat.

When they came in, Wally Cruice was waiting for them. Wally is the Packer scout who prepares the advance reports on the upcoming opponent. On an upright screen in the dressing room using an opaque projector, he flashed the defensive patterns the

Packers might expect. Starr studied them closely. When Wally was through, the Packers hustled to the showers.

> STARR: As far as most of the fellows are concerned, that day is over right there, about noon.

But for the quarterbacks, the work was only beginning. Lombardi and his staff started running films again in the Packer quarters. Bart asked assistant coach Red Cochran to get him a can of film on the 49er-Chicago Bear game. Starr and Bratkowski hustled down to the visiting dressing room where the spare projector was still set up.

> STARR: That's so, when we go out to practice the first time Wednesday against the 49er defenses, we'll have in our mind, having looked at a film, a little bit of an idea of what we're trying to accomplish. If you haven't seen 'em on film, you can't appreciate it, even though the coaches have given you a plan of attack.

As Zeke reversed the film and repeated a running play, Bart noted, "That sweep into the short side of the field looks good. . . . But don't run a sweep on their left end. He's tough." Mostly, however, he noted how they reacted to passing situations.

> STARR: I think the running game tends to take care of itself. If you see a tackle chase real hard, you might look for a 'give' play, or you can see if we can run our sweeps well against them or our screens. But the coaches set that up. I try to concentrate on the passing stuff that should go against them.

At twelve-thirty, they had the film back in the can and were headed downtown. Bart took Zeke along as a passenger. The first stop was Chili John's just up the street from the Northland Hotel. "Great chili," said Starr. "I feel like a bowl. Let's get it out of our system early in the week."

They stopped at the bank before Bart went on to get a haircut. Window walking along Washington, he saw a pair of pants he liked and went in and bought them. He left Zeke downtown and went home. With him were individual report forms passed out in the morning session. Bart spent 40 minutes filling out his game report of the Vikings encounter. He jotted down the plays he thought had worked best. He also noted the Viking personnel who had impressed him. "That Carl Eller," he mused, "got to me real good." Eller's a huge (6–6), 260-pound defensive end who stepped into a regular job in 1964 as a rookie. "That Marshall on the other side," Starr said, shaking his head, "he's a good rusher, too. He makes you step up in the pocket."

Now Bart was caught up in the fever of thinking football. He headed back down to the cabinet in the basement and pulled out his most recent file on the 49ers, the one from their second game of the previous year, played on the West Coast.

> STARR: I checked them again to see if any of the things in the reports were noticeable on the film of their game against the Bears just a week before. In a nutshell, I was trying to get myself in shape thinking 49er thoughts.

After dinner, he put on a conservative dark suit. Bart had made a date to speak to a bunch of high school kids at the First Methodist Church. Normally he turns down all engagements during the season, but this was his church, and he'd committed himself a long time ago. He spoke informally to the boys about the benefits of being a pro football player. As he spoke he thought to himself, "I'd rather be home right now looking at films." But on Tuesday night the Packer coaches are using them. So Bart was stuck with this gaggle of youthful, scrubbed faces looking up at him. He muddled through, telling them how he located a pair of extra tickets for Bart, Jr., and his buddy Steve to attend a game against the Colts earlier in the season. He wasn't sure of the seat locations. Early in the first quarter, Cherry Starr trained her binoculars on a special section of Colt rooters who'd come all the way from Baltimore and were whooping it up. Smack in the middle sat young Bart and Steve. She rescued them at halftime.

He was home early for a good night's rest. Wednesday and Thursday are the key preparatory days in pro football, when the heavy work is done. The Wednesday assembly time was ten o'clock, but Bart checked in an hour early. He wanted to examine his playing shoes and other gear. He also wanted to be handy in case Coach Lombardi had anything on his mind. He did. The Packer coach huddled briefly with Starr and forewarned him of a couple of changes the 49ers had made in their pass coverage. When the whole squad arrived, they broke into platoons again. Coach Lombardi had the Packer offense for the week neatly drawn out on cards and flashed the plays on the opaque projector. Starr, along with the other men on the offensive unit, jotted down the plays in his notebook. When he was through, he had a set of offensive alignments to use against every defense the opposition had shown up to that time.

> STARR: That's our ready list. It might contain 25 running plays and 10 or 11 pass plays. But we may only use 8 or 10 plays altogether during the game. Many of the plays we carry every week because we feel we can run these plays against any team, and we like to. For instance, everybody in the league knows we're going to run the power sweep.

The bread-and-butter play of the Packer offense is called the 49-Sweep. Both guards pull to form a blocking convoy for the left halfback, who comes hard, then bellies out slightly (see diagram) and makes his cut according to the way the openings develop. The center and left tackle both have to make tough, onside blocks (blocks in the direction of the play, which means extra quickness on the part of the blockers to get an angle on the defensive tackles). The play can also go the other way with the fullback carrying.

> STARR: We add and subtract plays because we think a certain play can be run against a certain defense. We also get a defensive report—how they charge, how they like to play in various field positions, their characteristics, their secondary coverage.

The Packers broke up into little groups within their units. Starr was with the backs and ends. On a blackboard, backfield coach Red Cochran took each pass on the ready list and threw it up against every defense the opposition had shown to prove its soundness.

63

"This fellow played an 'in' break real tough a year ago," noted Starr as he saw a diagram which called for Carroll Dale to run an inside route against the right corner-back, cutting toward the middle of the field.

"Well, this year," said Cochran, "he's not doing it. He's much more outside-conscious."

The group meetings lasted half an hour. Then the team went out on the field and started polishing the plays they'd been given. The offense had 45 minutes, with the defense simulating the opposition. Lombardi was at Starr's elbow as he ran the offensive unit through its repertoire. Then it was the defense's turn. Paul Hornung, who still likes to make believe he's a quarterback, simulated the other team's passer. Meanwhile, Starr took his receivers over to another part of the practice field and threw to them. Dale and Dowler were rusty on zig-out routes, which weren't used for a couple of games, and polished their moves, while Starr hit them consistently as they made their breaks. The Packers finished their workout with wind sprints. They ran a series of 20-yard bursts, then lengthened out to a couple of 50-yard sprints. Starr ran with the rest of the backs. He was in good shape. The bumps of last Sunday were three days old and forgotten.

Back they went to the Packer headquarters building, and a catering service sent a man around to take lunch orders. Bart settled for a cheeseburger and a coke. (Sometimes he packs his own lunch, a ham or chicken-salad sandwich that Cherry prepares.)

Immediately after lunch, the movie projectors whirred again. The defense was back in the visiting dressing room. The offense was in the normal Packer surroundings. "See," said Lombardi, "this is why I laid out that pass pattern to Dale. Watch that halfback laying off him. . . .

"You can see why we're going to run this play against them because when the guard pulls, he influences their middle linebacker over to the strong side."

After the movies, Starr borrowed a couple of reels to take home and added pictures of the previous year's game against the 49ers. He had time for a quick romp with the kids while Cherry got supper ready. At eight o'clock, the other quarterbacks—Bratkowski and young Dennis Claridge—dropped by. They went downstairs to look at films.

> STARR: We feel the more we can look at somebody and the more we can see of what they're doing, the quicker recognition we'll have when we see it on the field in front of us.

After an hour and a half, the eyes started watering and Bart shut the projector off. Wednesday was just about shot. Zeke and Dennis took off, and Bart pulled out his play book and extracted the ready list for the week. He tried to couple the plays with the images the screen imprinted on his mind and felt he could pretty well visualize what he wanted to do on Sunday. He checked his watch. Eleven o'clock. He was ready for the sack.

On Thursday, it was a repeat. Report in sharply at ten o'clock. The team and group meetings were shorter in the morning. They changed a couple of pass plays, though, after reviewing the stuff ran the previous day. Lombardi decided they didn't look so good in execution. "We're running a strong-side turn-in to the wing man," he said to Bart. "Maybe the 'out' would be better." So the wing on the strong side, Dowler, was to go down 10 yards, then cut to the sideline instead of veering over the middle. "On that post route to the wing," advised Lombardi, "use it only from a double-wing formation." With those two brief changes, the game plan for Sunday was finalized.

During the field work, Bart hustled toward a goalpost with center Ken Bowman and kickers Babe Chandler and Hornung. It was time for kicking drill. Bart is the holder for the Packers. He's held the job since his second year with them in 1957.

> STARR: Tobin Rote started to make a holder out of me in my rookie year so he could have more time to concentrate on his quarterbacking. I didn't hold that season, but I have ever since. I can't really break down the job because it's almost reflex now. I like to take the snap around knee level. I have to get the ball down quickly and on the same spot, and also spin it to get the laces in front before the kicker hits it. It happens so quick you don't have time to think.

Starr spent the other part of the Thursday field drills working with the offense, integrating the running and passing plays. He also went through a two-minute drill. It's an exercise to get as many plays as possible into a two-minute period. The routine is valuable in the frantic moments just before halftime or at the end of a game. Starr is convinced he could squeeze fifteen plays in under pressure if he had to. The field work wound up with the usual pass polishing to the different receivers.

Lunch was followed by another movie session. But this time the Packers looked at themselves in action against the 49ers in the past. Lombardi wanted the players to see how the opposition reacted to them. Every team has certain characteristics and tendencies and must be careful not to get into a rut where the enemy can anticipate their moves.

Before he got home, Bart had time to get the car washed, pick up the cleaning he'd left on Monday and drop by the camera shop for the finished film. After dinner with the family, Zeke and Dennis dropped by again. It was a lot more relaxed. Cherry fixed some popcorn and brought it downstairs while they watched film. "You can't look at movies too much," said Bart. They had a beer to liven things. The mood was one of anticipation. Bart was eager for the real thing.

> STARR: By Thursday night, I want to have a real good picture in my mind, without having to refer to the game plan, of what we want to do. I want it to start to come into focus.

So he and Zeke took turns at a blackboard he rigged up. They outlined the plays they'd use in most situations. They boiled it down to three or four passes.

> STARR: I believe in a simplified offense. Cutting down is a real problem because you know everything is designed to work. But we're both thinking as one by the time the session is over. In case anything happens to me in a game, the other quarterbacks should be ready to go in with the same ideas.

On Friday, the tapering-off process started. The meeting was short. Lombardi gave Starr his goal-line offense, what he should call when he got inside the other team's 10-yard line. He also outlined the best plays for short-yardage situations at midfield. He

65

reviewed the defenses favored by the 49ers so Bart would recognize any switch and be prepared to check off. A lot of it was old stuff because like every team the Packers have a few basic short-yardage plays. The workout on the field was brief. Starr sharpened up on his short passing, throwing flares to Hornung and quick slant-ins to the tight end, plus hooks to Dowler and Dale, the wide receivers. Lombardi put the offensive unit together for a quick drill on a couple of plays that he felt needed more polish: a pass to the halfback off the double-wing, and a new goal-line pass installed just for that game. Bart concluded the drill by throwing overtime to all his receivers to get his timing sharp.

He got home in time for a late lunch, then sat down and finalized his notes to keep up with the coach's last minute look at the new plays. He wanted to lounge around the house all afternoon, not actually working at football, but circles and checks crept into his thoughts. Outwardly he was relaxed. He even crept upstairs for a nap, a Friday ritual.

Friday night was a treat for the kids. Bart and Cherry took them out to dinner. They met Zeke and M. E.—the Bratkowskis—at Proski's, a restaurant that specializes in sea food. Bart revelled in the boneless perch. It was an early dinner, starting at five-thirty, because Bart promised to take the boys to the movies. Bret fell asleep before the show was over.

Bart woke up Saturday morning and checked the weather for the weekend. It could affect his passing. No rain in sight. The workout was extremely brief. From the time he left home at nine-thirty to his return, he was only gone an hour. The Packers stayed just long enough to break a sweat. He ran the offensive unit through a couple of plays to get the feel of the ball. They all scattered to their television sets around town. Bart switched on the college game of the week, a Big Ten tussle between Purdue and Michigan. He didn't try to dissect the action. He just sat back and enjoyed it, chewing on some peanuts. That way he shot most of the afternoon.

After dinner, it was more television. Bart, Jr., wanted to watch "Flipper" so his dad drifted to the set in the basement for more adult fare. He would end the night with "Gunsmoke." That night he slept like a log. He never has trouble the night before a game, secure in the knowledge that he's as prepared as he's ever going to be.

On Sunday morning he was up at seven o'clock. He had orange juice, two eggs over medium, extra-crisp bacon and a slice of toast.

> STARR: I get real hungry later on because that's my pregame meal. On the road I'm luckier because I can wait until ten o'clock to eat for a two o'clock game.

At home, he had to bundle off the family to church, which was a four-mile drive downtown. Out of a habit he took a notebook along, but he never referred to it during the drive to or from church. At ten-thirty he picked up Bratkowski, who lived eight blocks away, and drove to the stadium. The girls would double up later, and that way they'd each have their cars.

Bart took his time hanging up his clothes neatly in his stall, which is in the middle of the dressing room, on the left side as you walk in. He walked across the room to the

66

trainer's quarters to get his ankle taped—a "must" for all pros. He kibitzed with Hornung, who had the next-door stall. Bart studied the game program, observing the uniform numbers of the other team's defensive personnel to keep them in mind. The wait was becoming oppressive, and he was glad when Coach Lombardi wagged him to come over to the coach's private office at the far end of the big room.

Lombardi had a play scrawled on the blackboard. "I want you to open up with a trap on the defensive end," he said, pointing to the right flank. "He plays wide and looks for the sweep. Get him to realize he's going to be trapped if he keeps on playing that way. That'll open up our sweep later."

It was Lombardi's only instruction for the game. Too late now to learn anything. At noon sharply the dressing room was cleared of all outsiders. Fifteen minutes later Bart led a parade out onto the field, through the open gate at the north end of the stadium.

A week's work was imprinted on the quarterback's mind. For the next two and a half hours it was a game again.

6. The Game Plan

Under the pressure of game conditions, a young quarterback like Charley Johnson of St. Louis, framed here between Cleveland tackle Frank Parker (78) and guard Ed Cook (75), must discipline himself to stay with the game plan.

In a watering spot called the Pink Poodle, hidden in the maze of old Wrigley Field, George Halas of the Chicago Bears brandished a piece of paper in his right hand and shouted triumphantly, "This did it—our war plan!"

The Bears had just demolished the Green Bay Packers, 26–7, the key game in a processional to the championship of the National Football League in 1963. They did it by controlling the ball for 55 plays on the ground, guided by a quarterback, Billy Wade, who used to think that throwing a long pass was the only way to advance the football.

The "war plan" flaunted by the exultant Papa Bear Halas contained a mass of figures, phrases and hieroglyphics that would be mystifying to the average reader but actually spelled out for the Bears the strategy used to destroy the Packers.

It's commonly known as the *game plan*, which has become the "in" phrase of modern pro football. Coaches mention it with mystical reverence. If a team wins, the game plan did it. If a team loses, the quarterback strayed. In that same Year of the Bear, the St. Louis Cardinals were in Yankee Stadium to do battle with the New York Giants and emerged with a 24–17 victory.

Normally this should have made Charley Johnson, the Cardinals' quarterback, an elated young man. But he stood in his stall in the dressing room, a bruise on his nose and a fever blister on his lower lip, and reproached himself. "I got disillusioned," he said, "about the way the Giants were covering us. Our game plan called for running plays between the tackles and short passes to the outside. They were giving us the outside pass patterns and I wasn't recognizing it. It looked to me like the linebackers were dropping off and they weren't."

So Charley threw bombs down the middle in the first half and completed a miserable 3 passes in 15 attempts while the Cardinals dropped behind, 10–3. At halftime, assistant coaches Fran Polsfoot and Chuck Drulis, descending from their aerie on high in the pressbox, convinced quarterback Johnson he'd better get back to the original game plan, pronto.

"They ordered me to do it," admitted Charley simply.

On the first play of the third quarter he hit Sonny Randle, the split end, on a quick sideline pattern for 15 yards. When the Giants blitzed, he sent fullback Joe Childress 28 yards up the middle on a draw play. From the 11-yard line, he connected with Randle for a touchdown to tie the score. Following the same pattern, he pulled out the victory. Another triumph for the game plan.

Here's how it evolves. On Monday the coaches preparing for a game study films of the opposition's defense. Perhaps 60 to 70 defensive plays are contained in each of the game films. The defensive formations and calls are charted. They reveal definite tendencies on first down, on third down and long yardage, etc.; maybe they like to red dog most of the time on second-down-and-long situations. By Tuesday morning the quarterback gets a list that contains, say, 9 running plays and 6 pass plays, plus a couple of draw plays and screens. These are the plays that the coaches, after studying the films, think have the best chance to work against the opposition defenses.

In quarterback meetings, the signal callers are briefed on their usage: here's your best running play when it's first and 10, your best pass on first and 10 at midfield. Here are your best second-and-5 running plays, your best short-yardage calls.

Through refinement in practice sessions the rest of the week, the 9 running plays are boiled down to 4. And if they're stopped early in the game, they use the others on the list. The 6 pass plays are narrowed down to the best 3. Of the 2 draws, this is the one you go to first. When you see how the middle linebacker or the defensive tackle takes the influence block, try this next.

Finally, the coaches prepare their quarterbacks with a list of automatics, the changing of plays through audible signals on the line of scrimmage. Let's say, for example, 48 sweep is okay against a 4–3 or a 4–4 defense, but not against an odd defense (the line shifted over so that a defensive tackle plays right over the center). Then if the quarterback calls 48 sweep, and the defense lines up odd, the quarterback instantly switches to an automatic. To keep the operation simple, a team like the New York Giants will have no more than 2 running plays on their list of automatics. They'll have many more passing automatics because pass defenses are easier to read—they're based on recognizing red dogs or the positions of the secondary man.

When Y. A. Tittle was with the New York Giants, he thrived on the simple game plan. He came to them in the twilight of his career as a master of two tactics—the screen pass and the play-action pass. A play action simulates a running play and does what a toupee might have done for Tittle—hide the real thing. The way old Yat pulled it off, he could make Little Egypt look like Dame Margot Fonteyn.

Yat teased the ball into the runner's belly as deftly as a blackjack dealer cuts a deck and then retracted it, like a guy dealing off the bottom. The linemen blocked aggressively to carry through the masquerade. Then Tittle whirled and threw to his favorite deep receiver, Del Shofner, behind the sucked-in defense.

"It immobilizes the linebackers," explained Tittle. "They destroy the passing game with drops (a drop is a retreat to cover potential receivers in the short zone behind the line of scrimmage). Without linebackers, I could have completed 80 percent of my passes."

The danger in the play-action pass is that if the defender isn't fooled, he can step around the blocker and catch the quarterback as exposed as Tittle's bald head. So a play-action pass isn't called on third down with 12 yards to go when even Grandma Moses could have painted a throwing situation. Third down and 2 yards to go is a more logical situation when the defense has to be wary of a running play.

"The play-action pass is best," continued Tittle, "when your running is going good. If slant 34 off tackle has gained consistently, they're going to respect it when the play starts that way. Then you can fake the run and throw."

The Giants made a living off the play-action pass with Tittle. They operated on a cardinal principle—work what's going well. Work just a couple of plays to death. Because when the defense stops them, they've had to make some visible change. When an offense is spraying different plays all over the lot, it's not aware of defensive reactions.

Y. A. Tittle was a master of the play-action pass. Tittle, right, has tucked the ball on his hip after simulating a handoff to the fullback, who carries out the running fake.

After he retired, Tittle became an offensive coach for the 49ers. To illustrate the form a game plan takes, he assumed a team was preparing to play the Green Bay Packers and he put together a hypothetical game plan:

GREEN BAY DEFENSE

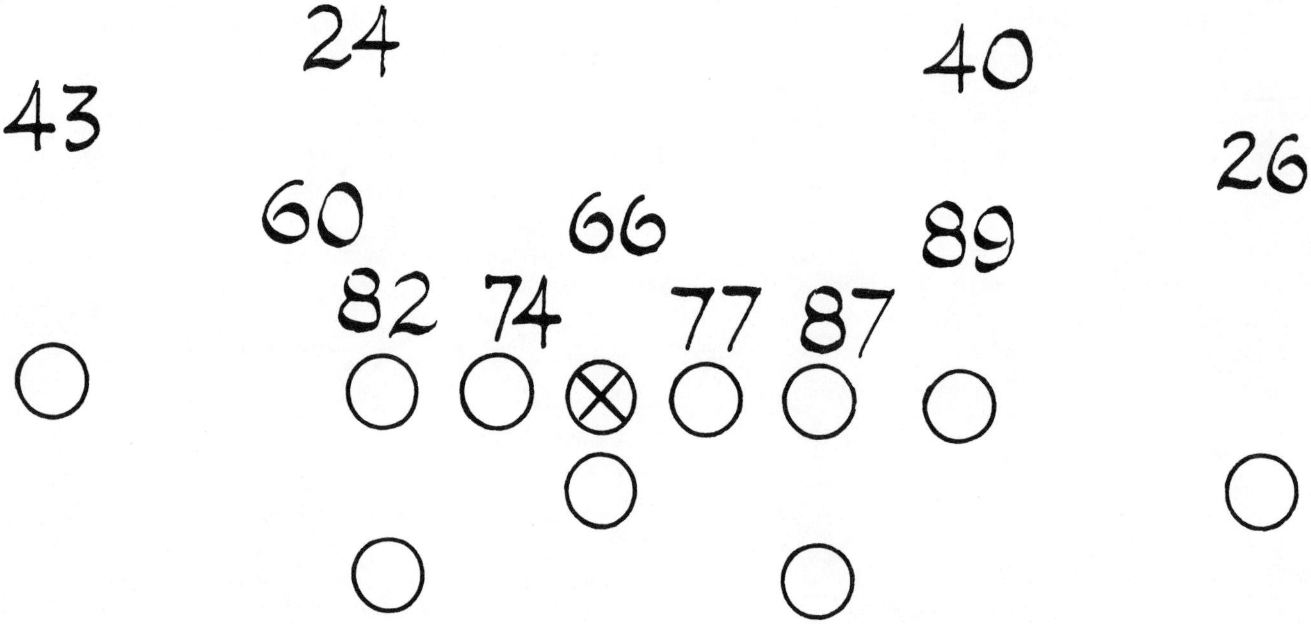

43   24   40

        60   66   89   26
     82   74   77   87

LB–Robinson #89
LE–Davis #87
LT–Kostelnik #77
MB–Nitschke #66
RT–Jordan #74
RE–Aldridge #82
RB–Caffey #60
RH–Hart #43
RS–Wood #24
LS–Brown #40
LH–Adderley #26

Defenses Used: 3 games
        170 plays–33 dogs

74

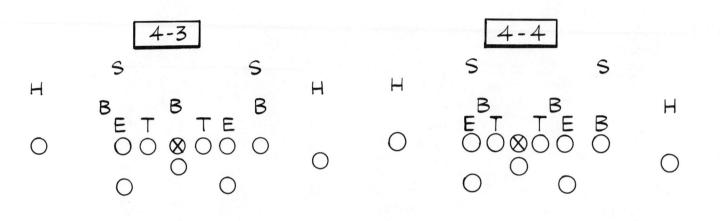

4-3

4-4

112 times
18 dogs

20 times
3 dogs

Odd to End

Odd to Flanker

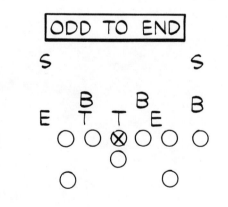

ODD TO END

ODD TO FLANKER

12 times
9 dogs

26 times
3 dogs

On the sidelines, while the offense took a breather, Coach Vincent Lombardi of Green Bay refreshed his quarterback, Bart Starr, on the game strategy.

Sid Gillman, the coach of the San Diego Chargers, made a point to his veteran quarterback, Tobin Rote, before he rushed back on the field to take command.

Open Left
48 Sweep
46 H
44 Trap
40 Quick Trap
25 Trap
29 Sweep
Draw 4 (HB)

Cross-Over Left
36 H
24 Quick
30 Quick Trap
25 F
27 Full
Draw 5 (HB)

Open Right
29 Sweep
27 H
25 Trap
21 Quick Trap
44 Trap
48 Sweep
Draw 5 (FB)

Cross-Over Right
37 H
45 Quick
31 Quick Trap
44 F
46 Full
Draw 4 (HB)

Notes:
1. Play-action pass off 21 and 40 Quick Trap
2. Man-to-man coverage
   a. 80% key
   b. 20% combo
3. Most automatic Draws, Play Passes, Screens, End Runs vs. Odd to End
4. Hold FB on passes to help on Davis
5. Flanker left when going on top
   (must occupy Wood)

READY LIST: PASSES

Patterns:
#1–(do not throw on Adderley)
#2–(right side only)
#3–(left side only)
#4–(do not use except on first down)
#5
#6–(hold FB)
#7
#8
#9

The actual patterns are not listed because football people are notoriously cautious about giving away their secrets. The Giants have a slightly different method of putting together their game plan. A master card has the defense laid out across the card, with the offensive alignment under it, and then nine big squares across the card designating the possible holes through which a play might be run. In each of those squares are listed the various plays designed for those holes. Coach Allie Sherman is perfectly aware of the fact that Giants traded to other teams take along his secrets, but he feels to expose his operational procedure would reveal his approach to the game.

What follows now, however, is an authentic ready list of plays prepared by Coach Al Davis of the Oakland Raiders for a game against the Houston Oilers on November 14, 1964. The game was won by the Raiders, 20–10. The notes with certain plays that went well are Davis' comments after the game.

OFFENSIVE READY LIST–HOUSTON OILERS NOV. 14, 1964

I. Normal Formations

RUNS	FORMATION

1. 40–41 Ice Round — Far
2. 48–49 Y Even–Cloud — Far
   (note: "Best long-gainer")
3. Fake Delay, Trap 14–15 Ace — Far
4. 64–65 Bluff Odd — Far
5. 18–19 Bob Odd — Full
6. 18–19 Bill Round–Crack — Half
7. Aud 52–53 Man (Weak vs Orange–Tackle pull) — Full
8. Aud 32–33 Double (Strong vs Orange)
   (note: "Consistent gains for audible runs") — Full-Half
9. Aud 16–17 (Weak)–18–19 Boom Man O Sky — Full-Half
10. Fake Trap, FB Delay 8–9 — Far

PASSES

1. 89 Turn-In Flare (8–9 In) (8–9 Swing) (18–19 In)
2. 89 Turn-In and Up Flare 8–9 In
   (note: "Bomb to Art Powell")
3. 91 Out Flare 12–13 Hook
4. 93 Swing Check 4–5
5. Waggle *Left* 89 Cross, 83 Cross (1st or 2d Back Weak)
   (note: "Have shown weakness against")
6. 94 Corner Flare 6 Flat

SPECIAL COVERAGE (FAR RIGHT)

1. P.P. 65 Y Hook In–Z Out at 10
2. Fake 65 Waggle Right, 89 Cross
3. Aud 24 P–5 (Roll strong; circle weak) (*Far*)

4. Aud 26 Flare 6 Flat (Far)
5. Aud 92 Roll Strong (92 Corner–Z Out–Y Hook-In) Vs. 6 or 3
6. Aud 93 Roll Strong (93 Flat–Z Out–Y In Slot) Vs. 6 or 3

II. East Formation

1. 18–19 Bob Odd
2. 16–17 Bob Queen–O
3. Aud Away 8–9 (Vs Stack Weak side)
4. Aud H 4 or 5 Strong
5. Ice 4 or 5
6. Aud 52–53 Man (Tackle Pull vs. Orange)
7. Aud 32–33 Double (Vs. Orange)
   (note: "Consistent gains")
8. QB Draw–Flare 7
   (note: "Cotton Davidson broke game open with")

PASSES

1. Aud 24 Flare 7 (8–9) (20)
2. Aud 25 Flare 8–9 *Weak* (7) (14–15 Curl)
3. Aud 26 Flare 2–3 Flat (8–9 Flat)
4. Aud 27 Flare 20 (Vs. 3 Sky)
5. Aud 28–29 Flare 7 (U In)
6. Aud 99 Flare 7 (Vs. 3 Red)
7. Aud 78–79 (Weak)
8. 94 Short Out and Up–Z Turn-In–Flare 7
   (note: "Best pass this formation")
9. Aud 22 K 30–31 (Fake Trap–U Corner, HB Fan)
   (note: "Play passes worked well")
10. Aud 24 K 30–31 (Fake Trap–U Hook, HB Swing)
    (note: "Play passes worked well")

III. Gadgets

1. (Far) Screen Left–Right to Full
2. (Full) Screen Weak to Half (4 Counts vs. Orange)
3. Aud 86 K 54 Screen Right to Full
4. Aud K 10–11 vs. *Dog #1 Man*
   (note: "Went great vs. Dog")

IV. Spread Formation

1. 94 Corner Flare 7 Post
   (note: "Billy Cannon open in spread. Covered by linebacker")
2. 94 Corner Flare 7 Hook
3. 94 Hook Flare "R" 4–5 Corner
4. Aud 99 Flare 7
5. QB Draw Flare 7
6. B–C Motion Trap 4–5 Ace
7. B–C Motion Aud 52–53 Man

V. Tight U

1. Aud 24 B–C Motion Flare 2–3 Flat
2. Aud 23 B–C Motion Flare 4–5 Wheel
3. Aud 22 B–C Motion Flare 2–3 Flat
4. Aud 86 Flare 8–9 *Weak*
5. Roll, 94 Sneak Flare 4–5 Corner

VI. Goal Line—Short Yardage

REGULAR FORMATIONS	FORMATION
1. Trap 14–15 Bluff Ace	Full
2. QB 18–19 Boom Man O Sky	Far
(note: "Davidson for score")	
3. 68–69 Boom Man O Sky (64–65 Man)	Far
4. Aud 16–17 (Weak) 18–19 Boom Man O Sky	Half
5. C Motion 31 Man, B Motion 30 Man	Half-Full
6. Near Right QB 48 Bob Even—Cloud	Near

PASSES

1. QB 18–19 Pass—82 Flat
2. Aud 89 B–C Motion Flare 4–5 (Look Quick)
3. Roll 94 Sneak Flare 4–5 Corner
4. Aud K 64–65 (X Slant–83 Flat)
5. 91 Quick Slant—Fire Zone

80

EAST

RUNS

1. *East Far* QB 18–19 U Man O
2. *East Far* 69–68 U Man
3. 18–19 Bob Odd (Weak)

PASSES

1. Aud 25 or 27 Flare 8–9 Wheel or Flat
   (note: "First back open every time")

VII. Weak Safety Cover 1 End (Yellow Dog)

1. 28–29 Flare 70 or 71
2. Aud 28–29 B–C Motion
3. Aud 89 B–C Motion Flare 4–5 (Look Quick)

For the cognoscenti, an explanation of some of the terms, with diagrams where appropriate, will help decipher some of the Raider strategy and show it's not as complicated as it sounds.

The numerology of the Oakland system designates the holes by number, as follows:

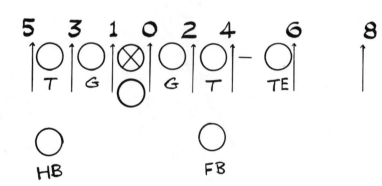

So the number 48, for example, means a play from the "4" series of their repertoire through the "8" hole.

East Formation means both of the deep receivers, split end Art Powell and flanker Bo Roberson, line up on the same side, with the tight end opposite. East Far positions the two set backs away from the flanked receivers, one behind the left tackle, the other behind the center.

81

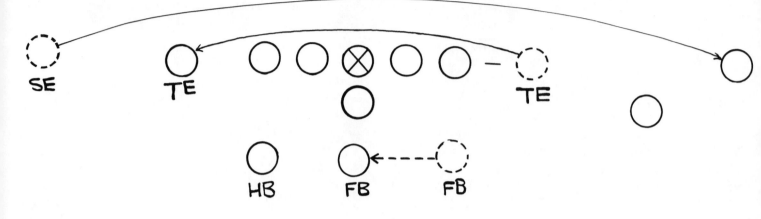

Other terms:

1. Ice Round—Ice is a term where a back isolates a lineman at the point of attack. Round is a blocking combination for the linemen. (diagram 1.)

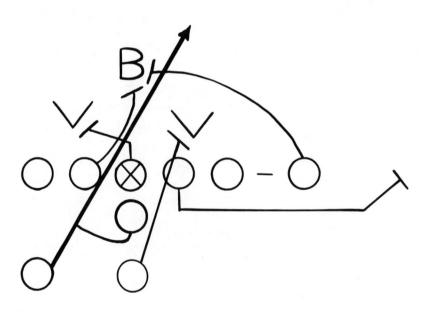

2. Y Even–Cloud.—"Y" stands for the tight end. He takes the end man (in his case, the outside linebacker) in or out depending on the hole. Cloud means that the flanker blocks the defensive halfback (or corner).
3. Trap 14–15 Ace–Ace means a double team between the tackle and guard on one man. (diagram 2.)

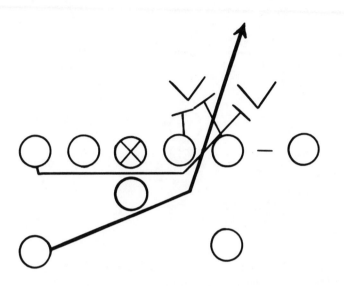

4. Bluff Odd–Bluff influences defensive linemen to be odd or trapped at point of attack.
5. Bill Round—the back blocks to the inside. (diagram 3.)

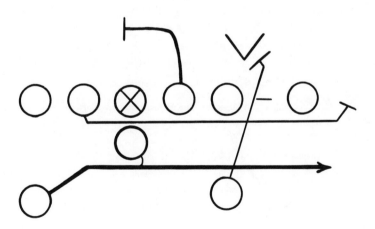

83

6. Bob Odd—the back blocks the end man in or out.
7. Crack—the weakside end (split end) takes the first man to his inside (the weakside linebacker).
8. Orange—name of a basic 5–4 Oklahoma defense.
9. Boom Man O Sky. Boom means the weakside near back blocks the end man. Man designates man-for-man blocking on the line. O is the off-guard pulling. Sky means the spread end takes the weakside safety. (diagram 4.)

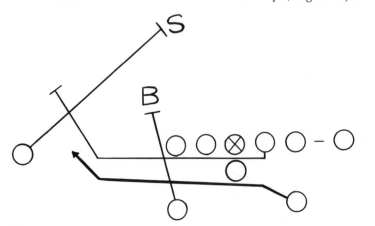

10. Y Hook In—the tight end hooks in on his pattern.
11. Wheel—a type of pass pattern run by the strongback
12. Stack Weakside—Overshift by the linebackers on the weak side. (diagram 5.)
13. Far, Full, Half-Full—designates where both of the running backs are to line up.

Oakland, held scoreless in the first half, set up a field goal in the third quarter when halfback Clem Daniels broke for a 41-yard sprint on 48 Y Even-Cloud. The Raiders took a 10–3 lead on Davidson's 26-yard pitch to Powell and scored their last touchdown the same way.

By Friday night of each week, the Raiders expect their quarterbacks to memorize a ready list (or game plan) such as the above word-for-word.

While all this offensive plotting is going on, the defenses aren't sitting by idly. Here, for instance, is a sampling of notes prepared by the defensive strategists of the Minnesota Vikings for a game against the Los Angeles Rams:

1. Goal line and very short yardage—strong safety play tight on slot for outside pick.
2. Same at goal line when slot spreads 3–4 yards. Look for bootleg and blitz the gap. Stop Q.B.
3. Tight weak side in and out play the end hooking tough.
4. Linebackers be sure to stay with the weak back always. They will always do something with him (check flare, screen, pause), especially to wide side of field.
5. Flanker into short side of the field, force slot outside. Do not let him inside.
6. Slot slow. Stay with him.
7. 6–1. Free safety be sure to go with flow and pick up slot.
8. Flex weakside. Inside out on weak end and halfback. Remember TD pass to Baker vs. Bears.

84

With a chalk board as his guidepost, Coach Blanton Collier of the Cleveland Browns outlined the plays which carried the Browns to the championship in 1964.

"The average person who hears just a little bit of this says, 'Oh my gosh, there's more to this than I realize,'" said Bart Starr of Green Bay. "He might think the job of being a quarterback is like that of an IBM operator. In a way it is. Once you get the hang of it, it's not that tough at all. I never did real well in math. I don't think I enjoyed it. I enjoy being a quarterback.

"We have a very simple system. In fact, when our coach gets teed off at us, he'll say, 'This is a system for simple-minded people.'

"We used to have a system when I first came into pro ball where the quarterback called the entire play—the formation, the play number, the blocking, the whole works. Under Coach Lombardi, I call the play, period. The line calls the blocking. I might say, 'Brown right 69 on 2. Break.'

"'Brown' denotes the formation, strong right for an end run by the halfback.

"Before Coach Lombardi, we might call that play '69 Bill O Grace Ed. 'Bill' meant a back on a certain blocker. 'Grace' was a guard. The 'O' was the other guard. 'Ed' was a block on a linebacker. That's a lot to remember. If you said 'Bill O George' you were in trouble. You had to learn a lot of names associated with blocking—George, Grace, Bill, Ed, and so on. Coach Lombardi took all that out. It makes it easier for a quarterback.

"I doubt we use as many as 20 different plays a game. We use 6 or 8 running plays and not that many pass plays. You don't need them."

In 1964, when Cleveland clinched the Eastern Conference title on the last day of the season by beating the Giants, 52–20, quarterback Frank Ryan revealed the Browns used only 5 different running plays and 3 different passing plays. Mixing those 3 passing plays smartly, Ryan threw for five touchdowns.

And in the ensuing 27–0 defeat of the Baltimore Colts for the NFL championship, Ryan restricted his running and passing plays to 8 of each. "Only 3 or 4 have to work per game," said Frank.

The 1964 championship game is an interesting study in game plans—how one succeeded and one failed.

First, Coach Don Shula explained the Baltimore strategy:

"Number one, we knew the Browns had a potent offense and would be hard to stop. We wanted to control the ball ourselves, both running and throwing, to keep it away from them. That's where we started with the game plan.

"We had seen six or seven films and thought we could run straight at them. They had given up the most yards per try in the league. We felt the two tackles were stepping up the majority of the time and Vince Costello (the middle linebacker) was stepping up, and we could block out their tackles with (center Dick) Szymanski and (guard Jim) Parker. Then we'd also have Sizzy pulling on Costello and our backs would be able to follow on his block on straight-ahead plays.

"Their ends play pretty wide. They don't come shooting across. They'd be difficult to block in on sweeps so we didn't think we'd be able to sweep them too effectively. We felt our 4-hole trap to the right with Parker pulling on (end Paul) Wiggin was going to be a good play for us. Other clubs had hurt them with it. We execute this basic play real well. It broke real well for us on the second play of the game. Lenny Moore shot through for a 15-yard gain to midfield.

"We felt you couldn't sucker block them because their linemen weren't charging that hard across the line of scrimmage. They didn't key and go with the guards.

"On a passing situation, (tackle Dick) Modzelewski would take a tough inside rush and a lot of times we thought we could draw between him and Wiggin. (Jim) Kanicki, the other tackle, came real hard sometimes on passing situations and their linebackers drop deep in their coverage, particularly Costello. We thought our trap draw with Parker pulling on Modzelewski and Szymanski blocking back on the other guy had a chance to break.

"And with their linebackers dropping deep, we felt that we could screen. If their linebackers drop deep, they're zoning and the cornermen don't press it. The screens on the strong side, we felt, were very good."

Altogether, the Colts had 34 different running plays in their repertoire, from four different formations, and 27 passing plays, from four formations. But in the game, Baltimore only had the ball for 45 plays and Cleveland had it for 70. Cleveland played the Colts with more single coverage of receivers than Shula had anticipated, and more odd spacing in the defensive line. The screens, like he said, should have been good plays for the Colts. But fullback Jerry Hill dropped one with long yardage in sight, and Lenny Moore had an open route on another until corner linebacker Galen Fiss came up and made a tremendous tackle behind the line of scrimmage. When Cleveland broke the game open with a 17-point scoring burst in the third quarter, the Colts discarded their game plan and were dealt their first shutout in 32 games.

Coach Blanton Collier described how he prepared for the game:

"We decided to run Ernie Green at the start to see what they were going to do about covering Jim Brown. It didn't take long for me to see they weren't going to stop Jim. You could see this was going to be another of his good days. In the first half we found he could run up the middle but we hadn't scored, so in the third quarter we made a revision in our plan and went to the double-wing. We put Green outside and Paul Warfield in tight on the left. John Brewer was in tight on the right and Gary Collins was the flanker.

"If the linebacker tries to hold Collins at the line of scrimmage, he can't get out to stop Brown going wide. If the linebacker moves outside to stop Brown, that leaves Collins with a one-on-one situation against their safety."

When it works, it's all so simple. Brown ran the ends, including a 46-yard sweep that set up the first touchdown. Ryan connected with Collins for 3 scoring passes.

And maybe Shula miscalculated. Colt owner Carroll Rosenbloom, who headquarters part of the time in New York, likes to get to Baltimore on Thursday before an important game to catch the last two workouts of the Colts. But business commitments kept the Baltimore owner in New York. He called Shula to say he was sorry ". . . but I won't be down for a couple of days."

"That's all right, boss," answered Shula glibly. "We'll have plenty of time to put your stuff in on Saturday."

The Cleveland Browns, dealing from strength, use Jim Brown (32) as their bread-and-butter man, taking the ball from Frank Ryan (13), while Gene Hickerson (66) pulls out from his guard position to block.

It was called at the time it took place "the greatest game ever played." And that judgment has stood up. The New York Giants met the Baltimore Colts on the last Sunday of 1958 for the championship of the National Football League.

The game ended in regulation time with the score tied, 17–17, after Steve Myrha kicked a 20-yard field goal with seven seconds left to play. In the sudden-death overtime, first in the history of professional football, the Colts forced the Giants to punt. Starting from their own 20-yard line, they moved inexorably down the field under the superb direction of Johnny Unitas.

After ten plays, they had a first down on the Giant 8-yard line. A slant up the middle by fullback Alan Ameche gained two. A daring pass to Jim Mutscheller put the ball on the 1-yard line. Ameche burst through a big hole over the right side to make the Colts champions of the football world for the first time in their history.

On the sidelines, Coach Weeb Ewbank carefully folded over two sheets of paper, twice, and put them in his pocket. Later, after the tumult of victory had subsided, he unfolded the paper and made a notation in the upper right hand corner of the first sheet: "Won 23–17."

He underlined it for emphasis.

The sheets were filed in a big binder to preserve a document that's a legitimate part of pro football history, for it spelled out the preparations for football's most exciting game. Ewbank, the coach of the Baltimore Colts, had compressed his basic game strategy against the Giants on the two sheets. Unitas, the quarterback, had studied them to recognize the defenses that might be thrown against the most potent offense in the game, to memorize the list of plays he would use against the basic 4–3 alignment. There were also special instructions directed to all members of the offensive team.

Ewbank had carried the two sheets onto the field at Yankee Stadium for quick reference as the game unfolded. He had written quick notes to himself on the back of the first sheet, which contained the basic game plan.

This was the first sheet:

Weeb had laid out the various defenses Unitas might expect to see from the Giants. In the two boxes at the top, he had written in most of the plays from the Baltimore repertoire which were to be used against the normal New York defenses, both running and passing, and had drawn in the pass routes of his deep receivers—split left end Raymond Berry and flanking halfback Lenny Moore.

Ewbank credits this type of visual preparation for teaching Unitas quick recognition of defenses. Where he wrote numbers in defensive positions, he wanted to alert the Colts to the individual personnel there. Sam Huff was 70, the middle linebacker. Dick Modzelewski, 77, and Roosevelt Grier, 76, were the defensive tackles. Cliff Livingston, 89, was the strong side corner linebacker. Emlen Tunnell was the strong side safety, 45.

On the reverse side of the sheet, Weeb added some plays and special alignments as they occurred to him before the game, and during the action. These notations were made in pencil.

Finally, from his analysis of the Giants, Ewbank had prepared a set of written instructions keyed to the abilities of weaknesses of the opposition and related to the habits of the Giant players. And at the last minute, he had written at the bottom of the page some notes directed to the game officials to cue them on certain thoughts he had about Giant techniques, both offense and defense.

The fifth Ewbank note at the bottom in script—"LT–holding"—is obviously trying to alert the referee that Roosevelt Brown, the Giant offensive left tackle, sometimes holds. And next he points out that their offensive linemen penetrate downfield, on passes. After which he added magnanimously, "We may do same—just call them as you see them."

Ewbank also wanted to warn the officials that the Colts would use a quick lineup on their first play of the game, and to be prepared for it. Weeb diagrammed the lineup for his quarterback (see back of first page).

Unlike almost everything else in this document, it never came off. The Giants won the toss for the game and received the kickoff.

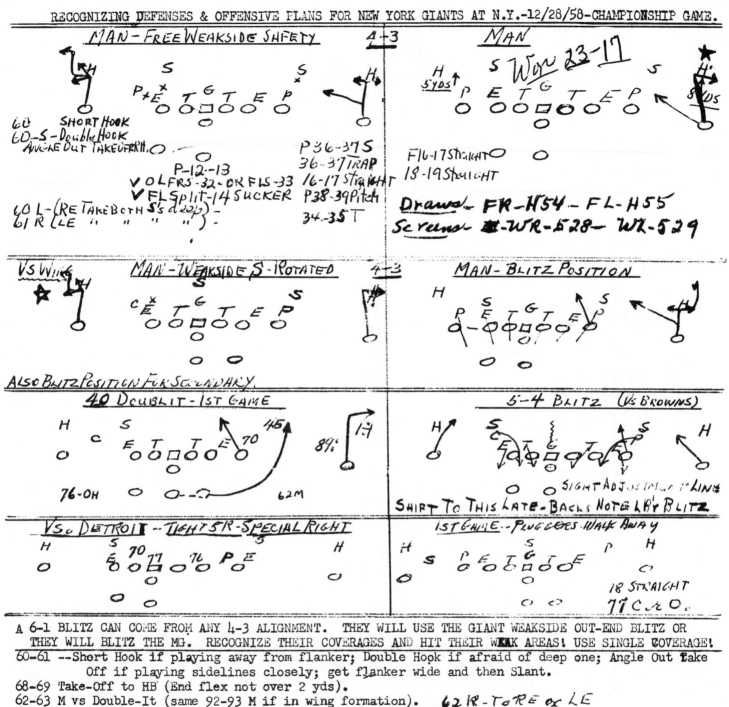

A 6-1 BLITZ CAN COME FROM ANY 4-3 ALIGNMENT. THEY WILL USE THE GIANT WEAKSIDE OUT-END BLITZ OR
   THEY WILL BLITZ THE MG. RECOGNIZE THEIR COVERAGES AND HIT THEIR WEAK AREAS! USE SINGLE COVERAGE!
60-61 --Short Hook if playing away from flanker; Double Hook if afraid of deep one; Angle Out Take
      Off if playing sidelines closely; get flanker wide and then Slant.
68-69 Take-Off to HB (End flex not over 2 yds).
62-63 M vs Double-It (same 92-93 M if in wing formation).   62 R - TO RE or LE
70-71: 70 C-71 C--hit man open, do not force any pass-key off linebacker.
***70-71 Angle Out Take Off to HB--FB Block.
76-77 (flanker hold and watch for 270-271 Screen); 76-77 C; 76-77 Oh vs Man in Walk-Away (same for
78-79 (beyond 50)--(good to score).   86-87 if Wing)
90-91 (same as 60-61)--Individuals & Combinations that might present themselves.
92 Slant to RH--RE pick LB'r then occupy safety. Hit HB late down field.
FR-28 Pass: FL 29 Pass; ****WR 28 Pass.
WR 428 WL 429. FR Split 438
      Reverse Left Pass; Double QB R 438 Flea Flicker.
      To Score: D.W. Delay to RE (RH slant in deep)(QB look to the left then hit RE late).
Always look for 22 & 23--FB continue on with same rule-MG go away from play, no MG, go with play.
R-114 : R-115 (Angle In to HB at about 20 Yds.)
   128 - TO RE to E - hit HB.
   62 -R - TO T.E. OR L.E.

QB Run Into Short Side.
Short Yardage   (P.P. ☐ Side Teams)
                      (O Side Our Teams)   Goal Line

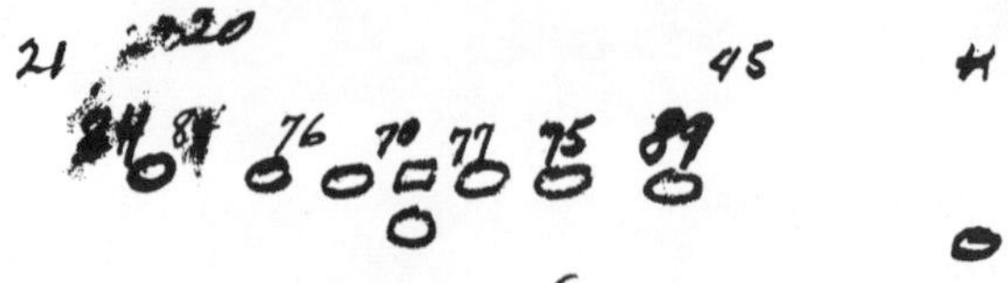

21 →20   H   20   45   41
○4○4 ○6 ○○○○ ○○   ○   81 76 72 70 77 78 75 87
                                              ○ ○ ○ ☐ ○ ○ ○ ○   ○
                                    ○
                                              ○   ○   ○
OL   ○   ○   (Emergency)
FRP 36 S   OL FR R 14   FR 17 P   OL-FR Split - 428   6 0 (Individual)
FRP QB Sneak - Backs fake 17 P (At boks best) FR 17 Fowrn   WR-   6 Q Slant,
FR 17 R   6 Q Slant fr
FR 114 (LE Block) (RH Slant In) FR-R115 (RE B1)   (Keep 78-79 in mind.)   + out.
OL-FR-119 Straight (RE B2   (LH Slant In)
    Gamble
  2-1 - 3-1 - FR 116 Giant
  21   ↑20   ↑   ↑45
  ○   ○ ○○○○○   ○   ○
      ○   ↑
      ○   ○

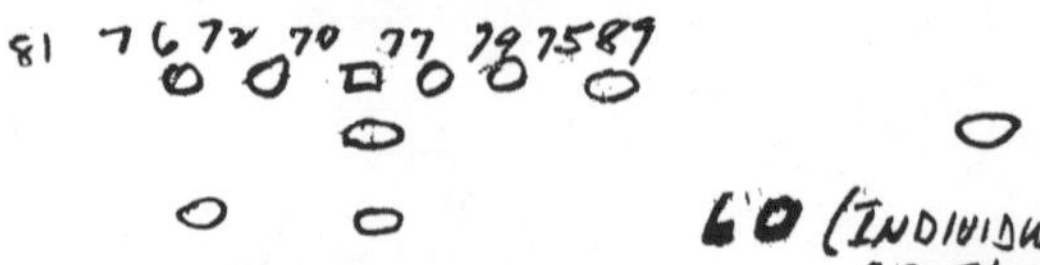

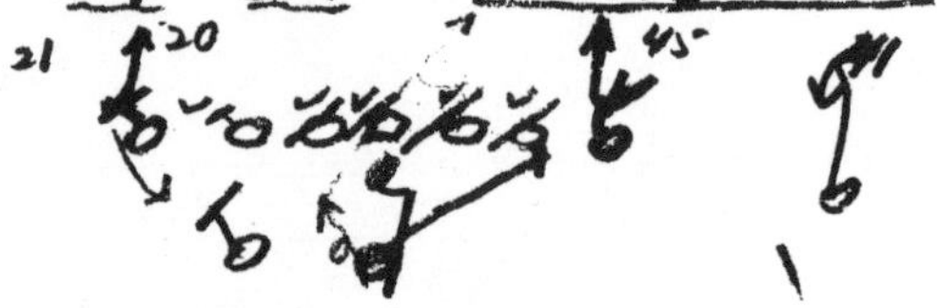

1st Play Quick Line up 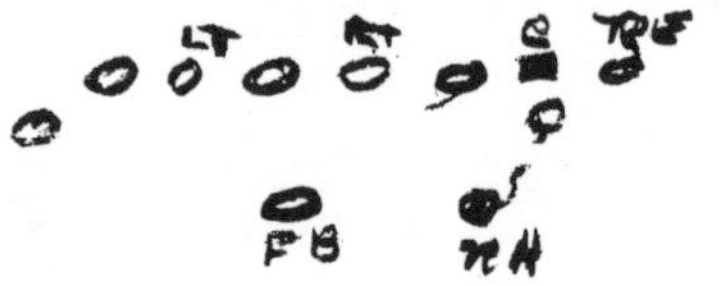
        LT   RE
○ ○ ○ ○ ○ ○ ☐ ○
             Q
      FB   RH

WR - F 17 S - OR FR - P 37 S - F 39 Reg   35 T   H 50
FLE To Hit Berry.   37 Trap   36 T
OR - FL - 61 Bow Out - Fake Draw Left   17 St   16 St

60 - 41 Slant   R 15 G   36
60 - 61 55 E BLP   F 39 Reg   F 38 Reg
70 C - LE Hook at 6   55   P 12
60 X Deep
FRE 60 Bow Out To
92 C RH a out

Line keep good splits-will aid both running plays and pass protection.
Out Ends and flanking backs be sure to keep as wide as possible in order to open up passing lanes.
FB-flare away from 22 or 23 if a MG; if no MG, then flare with the play. Should be easier to
   throw 22 than 23 because Little Mo (77) is shorter than Grier (76).
   n away from 70 if he does not stay in the middle of their 4-3--make him wrong.
Go on early counts to discourage defensive moving and to help pass protection.
Do not run plays into the out end side if the LB'r is in Giant Blitzing area.
FB's-keep varying your 60-90 series passes with split backfields.
HB's-when passing, if you do not have a Blitzing LB'r or are not needed to help a lineman, then
   you can roll off like a screen.
~~Run 68-69 with end flexed about 2 yds this week.~~
One of the keys to our winning this week will be predicated on how well we pass protect, pass the
   ball, and how well we catch it. Run good patterns--study your opponent--make him wrong.
Run 32 & 33 traps from split and hit it fast HB's--FB fake 28 & 29.
Traps should be good-particularly vs. 77 (LT).
34 & 35 traps should be outstanding also. ~~If MG comes up into line or defense becomes a 5-4 at~~
   ~~the last possible moment, the SSG should call~~ Solo ~~then block the MG-T will then solo. The~~
   ~~faking back should set up the man to be trapped and then turn-out on the 1st man to his outside.~~
36 & 37 Traps -C be ready to pick up MG if he shoots.
~~P~~-14 & 15 Sucker, particularly 14--run from split ~~and~~ HB fake an end run--it is a counter play.
Start 38 & 39 regular blocking.
P-38 & 39 Pitch will go with P-12 & 13 which should be good.
P-36 & 37 Solid look very good-the best bet looks to go up thru the 4 & 5 holes-guard lead play.
Run 18 & 19 straight into wing side in order to eliminate the Giant Blitz on the Out-End side.
Remember the 5-4 Blitz comes about late-line and backs must be alert-backs get shooters no matter
   where they come--it could be inside as well from the outside. *(Start Pass Protection)*
On traps-guard use the influence that will bring tackle in fastest.
On 38 & 39 the flanking backs fake a slant in and get the Safety. *(Pop Pass - Use 44 Fire For Chuck Off)*
Trapping guards-keep inside angle and block the area-if MG reads keys well, it might be him to
     block.
QB's-use FLE to get a single coverage for Berry on 21. FR got one for Moore last game--Dupre
   always had it from FL.   WL should get a single coverage for Moore on 21. RH.
Whenever throwing long to Moore-the LE must angle in deep to hold weakside safety or be open self.
FL-Bow Out to LE was good for a TD last time (61 Bow Out to LE). *For Re Draw*
QB-affect the weakside Safety by looking his way before throwing deep on the opposite side from him.
Can't say it is a Zone when there is a Safety in the middle-can be a Blitz; may get it from wing.
On Screens: Back flaring away from the way of screen--check blitzer before flaring--protect the
   QB's blind side--the man flaring may have to screen off of a blitzer.(28-29 Pass best screen)
On goal line 79 will replace 84.
On draws-HB looks best--# 70 will follow the FB quite a bit. On draws and inside plays the out-
   end tackle should take the inside of a game between his E and LB'r blitzing.

F.B. - same rule on slants as on 22-23

OFFICIALS 1st Play- Quick Lineup
   "IN" End pushing with hands
   CRACKBACK Blocking By OUTSIDE Men
   QB-LT-LG- Downfield On Screens.
   LT- Holding -
   men down field on passes - linemen go straight thru.
  We may do same - JUST call Them as you see Them.

7. Era of the Blitz

A quarterback is exposed to physical danger when a 250-pound defensive end like Sam Williams (88) gets past the blocker, tackle Bob Vogel, on ground, and clambers over Johnny Unitas of the Colts.

From his bed in Room 511 of Union Memorial Hospital in Baltimore, John Unitas of the Baltimore Colts relayed the message that he was resting comfortably. And feeling unlucky. His right knee reposed in a cast after a quick operation that Sunday afternoon in December, 1965, to remove a cartilage and mend the torn medial ligament.

John didn't remember a thing. In the second quarter of a game in which the Colts trailed, 7–0, Unitas was hit, as he prepared to throw the ball, by tackles Earl Leggett and Stan Jones of the Chicago Bears. All around him were enemy bodies, with corner linebackers Joe Fortunato and Larry Morris prominent in the crowd.

"I didn't see anybody coming at me," he said. "You're not supposed to. But I felt the knee snap as I was going down."

It also snapped the Western Conference championship chances of the Colts, who held a comfortable game-and-a-half lead at the start of the afternoon. The injury emphasized the risk quarterbacks are running.

"It has to be a matter of luck," shrugged Unitas. "For most of ten years I was lucky. You get hit the wrong way, something's got to give."

In the same season, quarterback Bill Munson of the Los Angeles Rams was hors de combat in the tenth game of the campaign when end Clark Miller of the San Francisco 49ers jolted him on the knee. He needed an operation. Norm Snead of the Philadelphia Eagles missed three full games with a bad hinge. Bill Nelsen of the Pittsburgh Steelers played on virtually one leg most of the year, then submitted to surgery. A slight shoulder separation kept John Brodie of the San Francisco 49ers out of one game. Bad shoulders rendered Charley Johnson of St. Louis and Bart Starr of Green Bay useless at various times. A bad arch caused Frank Ryan of Cleveland to spend one Sunday in street clothes.

Unitas called it a throw of the dice, figuratively, but the popular theory is that the actuarial tables have gone up on quarterbacks in recent years because of the increasing use of the defensive tactic called the blitz.

It has been variously called the red dog, storming, shooting the gap, gaming and dealing.

Charley Conerly stood in the jaws of danger for fourteen years with the New York Giants and lived to become a male model. He's the rugged western character with a tattoo who sometimes adorned cigarette ads. Charley commented, "I suppose the increased use of the blitz since 1961 has something to do with the injuries. Sometimes there are not enough blockers to pick them all up. And these guys are coming full blast. They hit when you don't expect it, and that's how you get hurt. There's no way you can protect yourself as a passer. You're not watching the tacklers. You wouldn't be doing your job."

The blitz increases overall pressure on the quarterback fading to pass. One little breakdown in the protective cup and he's up for grabs like a bridal bouquet. For the un-initiated, it's a nerve-wracking experience, anticipating the rush. As a rookie with the

Dallas Cowboys in 1960, Don Meredith was put into an exhibition game against the New York Giants. As he broke from the huddle and stepped up to the line of scrimmage, the Giant defense looked inert. The front-four linemen sagged in position waiting for the Cowboys to line up over the ball. The corner linebackers stood with their hands on their hips, and in the middle Sam Huff was in his usual crouch, hands on his knees.

Meredith started to bark the signals. Right end Andy Robustelli of the Giants moved a step to the outside and corner linebacker Harland Svare jumped into the gap between Andy and Dick Modzelewski, coiled to rush the passer. Meredith quickly sang out a color, orange, to tell his teammates he was changing the play. Svare jumped back to his initial position outside the end and Robustelli squeezed close again.

There was a flurry of motion on the other side of the Giant line. Corner linebacker Cliff Livingston moved up even with the ball and Huff poured into the space between Rosey Grier and Modzelewski. Jimmy Patton, the safety on the Giant right side, edged closer, too. Now Meredith was in a frenzy. The clock was running. He tried to call another color change. Svare took a couple of catlike steps in his direction. Meredith's 30 seconds to get the play off were almost used up. His mind went blank. He just threw his hands up against the stunting Giant defenders and exploded, "Aw, s——."

Meredith was caught in the trap of not knowing for sure which way the Giants were coming at him, or with whom, and what to do about it. Their stunting tactics—moving around before the snap of the ball—masked their intentions. Would one or two or even all the linebackers rush him with the snap of the ball? Or would they play their normal positions and leave the rush up to the front-four linemen?

Bobby Layne once boiled the essentials of quarterbacking in pro football down to a 7–4 guessing game: "There are either seven men coming at you (the front four and the linebackers) and four laying back (the deep secondary) or four coming at you (the line) and seven laying back. You've got to recognize, by instinct and the game situation which it's going to be."

But the blitz isn't quite that simple any more. In 1961, Frank (Pop) Ivy, coaching the Chicago Cardinals, introduced the safety blitz. Larry Wilson, playing the weak-side safety, moved up to the line of scrimmage with the start of the play and joined the linebackers in their little game of mayhem on the quarterback. He ruined the debut of Allie Sherman as head coach of the New York Giants. The Chicago Bears, who gambled extensively on defense when Clark Shaughnessy was their strategist, frequently sent eight men in on the passer.

So the blitz introduced the unknown factor into the life of a quarterback. The unknown factor is the number of bodies trying to pile in on him. In the early days of the T-formation, the quarterback looked across the line of scrimmage and knew pretty well what to expect. A linebacker was just that. He covered his own area. The 5–3 alignment became the favorite. Five men on the line of scrimmage were anchored by a 300-pound middle guard like Les Bingaman of the Detroit Lions, who played right over the center and didn't budge.

When teams started to put one of the three backs out on a flank, the 5–3 started to get hurt because a linebacker couldn't cover that back in a single (man-to-man) situa-

The huddle is more than a ritual. It's the nerve center of the battle. The field general briefs his troops. On his knees, Sonny Jurgensen, the quarterback of the Washington Redskins, issues the command. . . .

In a moment the battle will be joined as Bart Starr, the signal caller of the Green Bay Packers, starts his cadence countdown which will lead to the snap of the ball. . . .

"Hut 2!" Bart's fingers grasp the football. He turns in the face of the enemy, a lunging Dallas tackle. But already a Green Bay helmet is moving over to fill the gap as the quarterback wheels into action. . . .

It takes courage to concentrate on the job, follow through with fluid motion while 250 pounds of hostility jerk you off your feet and pound you to the ground in counterattack. But the pass is already under way, and that's all that really matters. . . .

Barking his orders, John Unitas of the Baltimore Colts is a drill master leading a disciplined command. From his perch above them, he checks the opposition. His forward unit is tensed, taut and symmetrical before the thrust. . . .

Now the logical design of the play has dissolved into a melée of hard-hitting bodies as teammates Dick Szymanski (52) and Bob Vogel (72) struggle to protect Unitas. The quarterback peers through small openings for his target. . . .

Malcolm Emmons

When the protection has held up according to game plan, the quarterback, Frank Ryan (13) of Cleveland, can set himself deliberately and look over the periphery of his passing area while his sensitive fingers stretch to get a firm grip on the football. That's fullback Jimmy Brown (32) offering him a final measure of security. . . .

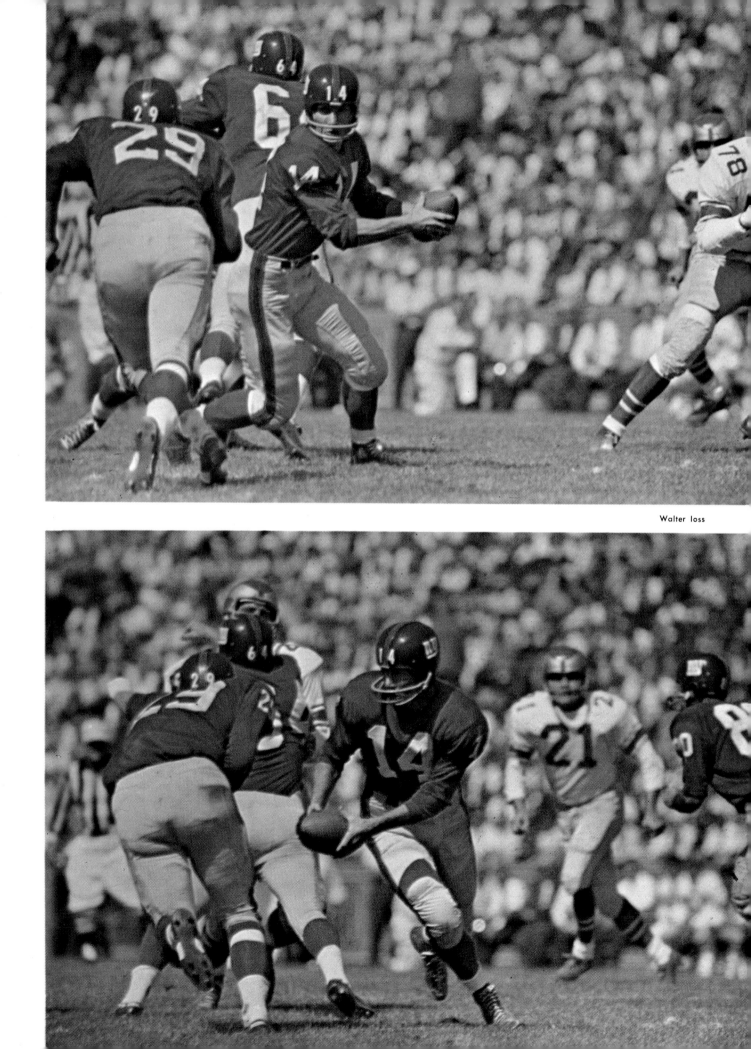

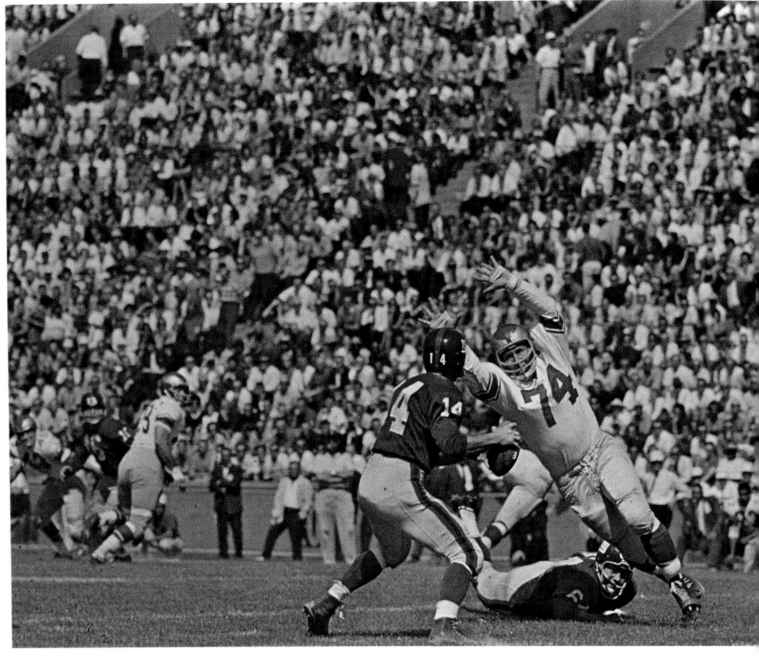

The quarterback uses many ruses—fake checkoffs, slick ball handling feints—to throw the enemy off. In actual execution, one of his best maneuvers is the play action pass, brought into focus here by Y. A. Tittle with the New York Giants. As he pivots with the ball, upper left, Alex Webster (29) plunges straight ahead in a simulation of a running play. While an Eagle defender moves over, Webster tucks his hands to his stomach lower left, but Tittle has withdrawn the football and is fading to pass. He cocks his arm, above. Too late, an Eagle tackle leaps at him. Frank Gifford (16), on the left side of picture, is already cutting between two Eagles to catch the pass. . . .

The unerring hand of the quarterback is also used to pitch the ball short to one of his backs, and Johnny Unitas has completed a full turn from the line of scrimmage to give the Colts a running start against Cleveland. . . .

Passing has become a pressure-packed existence in recent years because of increased use of the blitz, or red dog. In this case, Frank Ryan was able to get the ball off in good style against the charge of Detroit's all-pro middle linebacker, Joe Schmidt. . . .

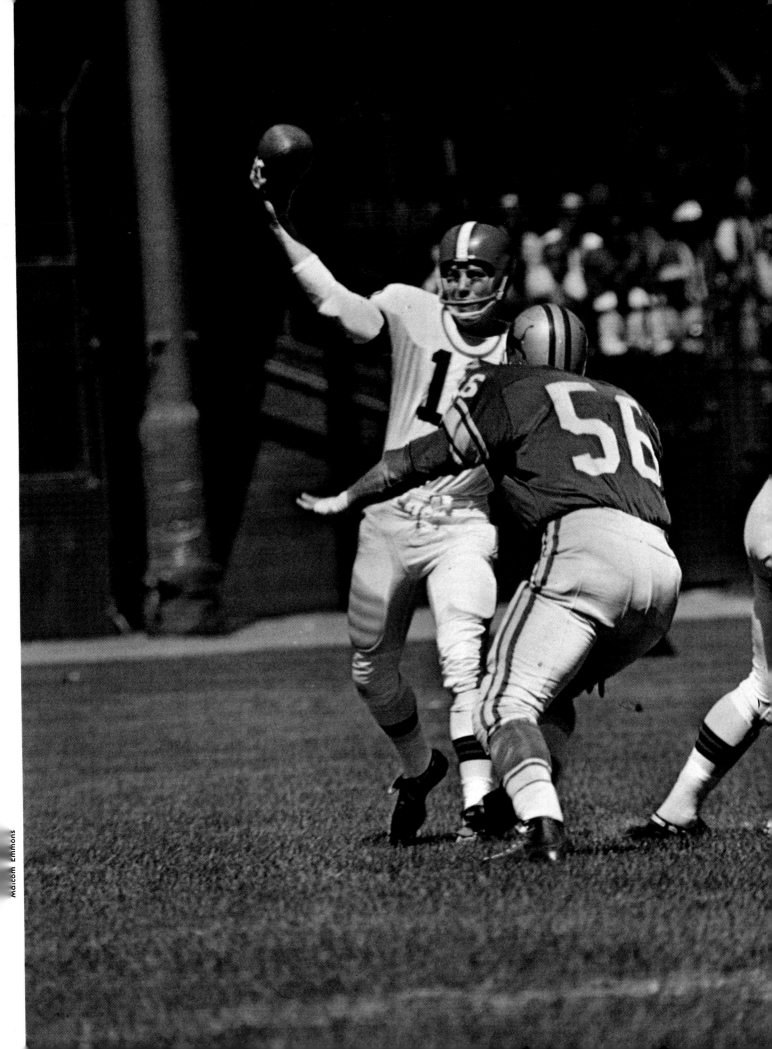

The red dog doesn't faze the experienced general who recognizes it as a gamble that actually weakens the secondary defense if it doesn't succeed. To get at him, the linebacker must leave his area of pass responsibility. If the passer is smart enough to muster extra blocking support, he can head off the blitz. Bobby Layne (22) stands firm in the midst of a swirl of fallen bodies and brings his arm back to throw. He disregards the tardy rush of middle linebacker Sam Huff (70). . . .

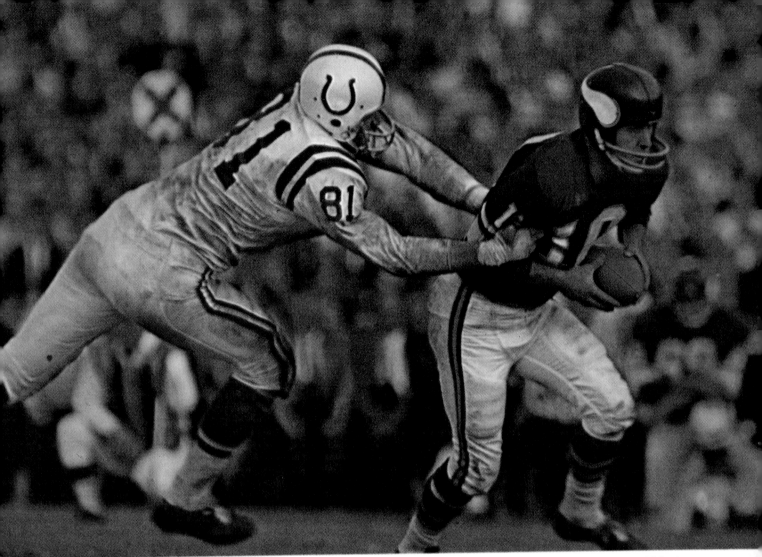

The scramble is the passer's physical resort to escape trouble, and its foremost practitioner is Francis Tarkenton, the elusive eel of the Minnesota Vikings. Upper left, Francis is grabbed by Ordell Braase, the defensive end of the Baltimore Colts, but the grip is tenuous and Tarkenton's already looking for other fields to roam. Even when running, however, the Viking scrambler has an eye peeled for passing possibilities and the ball balanced in his right hand for a quick flip. Tarkenton is at his best threading through a maze of bodies, with an instinctive feel for daylight. . . .

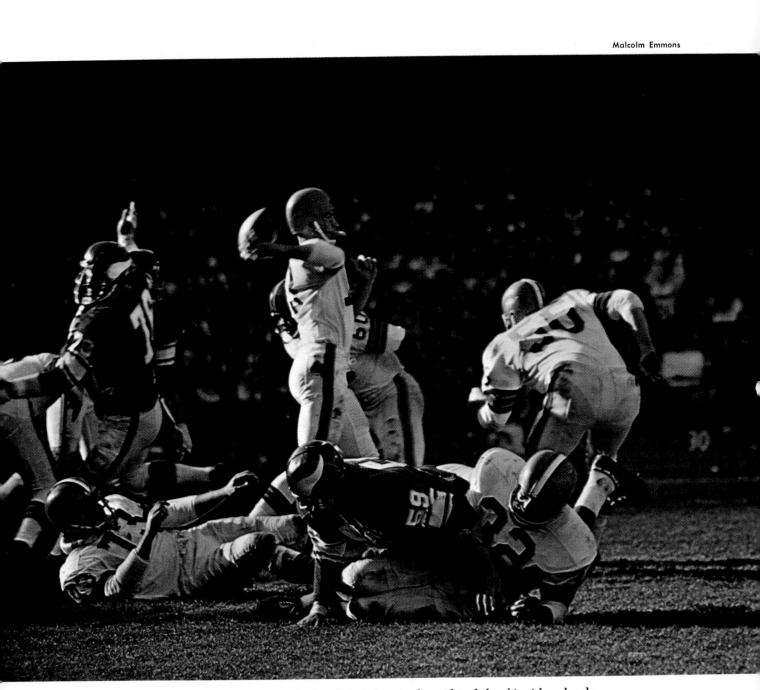

The classic pose of the quarterback still finds him in the midst of the skirmish, a lonely figure of command, surveying the scene, arm drawn back to pass. Frank Ryan has stepped forward with confident stride to launch the football.

The safety blitz finds Jim Bradshaw of the Pittsburgh Steelers enveloping Y. A. Tittle (14) of the New York Giants, though Tittle got his pass off.

One of the great middle linebackers in football history, Joe Schmidt (56) of the Detroit Lions zeroes in on Bart Starr of the Green Bay Packers as he retreats with the ball, gets a secure grip on his midriff and wrestles him to the ground to complete a successful blitz, or red dog.

tion. So the 4–3–4 was evolved in the mid-1950's and became the standard defense. It still is. Four men were found sufficient to provide a basic forward wall against the running play. The three linebackers had to be in the range of 230 pounds each to augment the defense against the run but with the mobility to drop back on pass defense. The back four were swifties whose primary job was pass defense.

As quarterbacks started to attack the 4–3–4, the defenses went out of their simple coverage and into the maneuver originally called red-dogging. The origin of the term is rather vague. Bob Kelly, a broadcaster who went with the Cleveland Rams to Los Angeles in a transplant back in 1946, first popularized it on the air, but Sid Luckman, the original T-master in the pros, said he first saw a blitz by the New York Giants in 1941. The Bear coaches quickly had him counter it by throwing short pitches over the middle of the line. "They worked beautifully," he recalled, "and I didn't see a blitz again for a dozen years."

The T-formation was still something of a mystery in those days, and some teams took peculiar measures to defend against it. The old Cleveland Rams were puzzled, so they actually put a linebacker up on the shoulders of the middle guard.

"He looked like a guy coming at me out of a tree," said Luckman, "so I called time. In the huddle, Bulldog Turner, our center, said he'd drop back and hit him where it did the most good." After a couple of swipes by huge Bulldog, the Rams abandoned that device in the interest of health preservation.

For the initiates, it's important to remember that a lineman does not red dog. He's only doing his job when he attacks with the snap of the ball. When, however, one of the linebackers or backs tries to penetrate the offense at the start of a play and tackle the quarterback before he can get rid of the ball, you have a red-dog situation.

From 1960 on, pro football became the biggest gambling game in America, which is not to make commissioner Pete Rozelle queasy about the threat of a betting coup. The red dog, or blitz, simply worked a complete change in the philosophy of quarterbacking and made the field general's job more hazardous. It used to be called a rocking-chair job, and the guy who got his shirt soiled was a ninny. Sammy Baugh scoffed, "I could play quarterback in white tie and tails."

The blitz put him in the line of fire, as if he'd just been offered at discount. A man who stands up to such pressure without cowering or ducking like a cat assailed by a pack of dogs qualifies for marshal of Dodge City. It has also changed the language of football.

On the New York Giants, for instance, Meg, Wanda and Sara became important members of the cast in a man's world. They were the identifying tags for the blitzing linebackers. Note the initials. Meg was the middle linebacker. Sara was the strong-side linebacker. Wanda was the weak-side linebacker. (The strong side, explained earlier, is determined by where the tight end lines up, with a flanker to his outside.)

So before a game Coach Allie Sherman was outlining to his offensive unit a type of blitz they might encounter. As he raced his chalk across the board in circles and checks, Phil King interrupted him. "Hold it, Coach," said the fullback they called "Chief." "I just thought of something."

BARTON

The multiple blitz possibilities the defense can spring on him are part of Joe Namath's awareness as the young New York Jet signal caller prepares to get the snap from center.

"Let's hear it, Chief," answered Sherman benignly.

"Well, if I'm called on a route, say a shoot—"

King was outlining a pass pattern in which he went at the corner linebacker and then flared out straight to the sideline.

"—and Wanda comes with a tango move. . ." (A "tango move" is a loop to the inside by the weak-side linebacker.)

"Yeah?" nodded Sherman, picking up the pattern on the blackboard.

"Then I don't have to pick him up, right?"

"That's right," agreed the coach. "The center, Greg Larson, will pick up your side."

"Okay," said the Chief, "but what if Meg comes, too?"

Meg normally would have been picked up by the center. Sherman creased his forehead, studied the situation on the board and frowned as King waited anxiously for the answer.

"If Wanda comes in a tango and Meg comes, too," Sherman finally replied, with a sigh, "we sent in a new quarterback."

The blitz has proliferated for a number of reasons. Mark Duncan, the head of the National Football League officials, used to be the defensive coach of the San Francisco 49ers. He keeps up on the defenses by watching 100 league games on films every year. He noticed the change.

"In the old blitz," he said, "you had two outside guys going. There are more combinations possible now because the linemen are getting more agile, with tackles like Billy Ray Smith (Baltimore) and Henry Jordan (Green Bay) who can do more things. They're using a lot more slants and cross charging in the defensive line. It's not unusual to see a team shift into odd spacing (one of the tackles moves over the center) and put two linebackers on the weak side, thereby coming from that direction. Teams have had to bring the weak-side split end inside to help with the blocking."

All teams use the blitz in varying degrees, depending on the mobility of their linemen, the solidity of their personnel and the degree of their success in the won-and-lost column. The New York Giants, who started the glamourization process for the defense, used to disdain the blitz. They were smug in their ability to analyze offensive patterns and confident in the ability of their personnel to handle anything. But in 1964, after three straight Eastern Conference championships, they suddenly woke up losers. At midseason they showed one victory in seven games as they prepared to play the St. Louis Cardinals, who were just one game behind the leading Cleveland Browns. Sherman and Andy Robustelli, the veteran defensive end who doubled as an assistant coach, made a drastic revision in strategy. By the intermission the Giants had smothered quarterback Charley Johnson five times for losses of 55 yards, moved into a 24–10 lead and went on to a 34–17 upset. It was one of two Giant victories for the year.

"They blitzed more against us," moaned Cardinal Coach Wally Lemm, "than they did altogether the whole first half of the season."

"When a team isn't winning," shrugged Robustelli, "you have to do something. Blitzing gives you incentive. It gives you a reckless type of play. When linemen are 'reading' (reacting to the flow of the play), they're stationary. When a team is firing, it gets momentum."

The blitz has become in recent years a many-pronged weapon. Besides the three linebackers shooting at the quarterback from any of the spacings along the line, the safeties have started to come from the outside as well as up the middle, from the strong side as well as the weak side. And occasionally the halfbacks will change off to fire in on the quarterback while the safety covers for them. The possibilities are endless.

The American Football League has generally been more blitz-conscious than the National Football League, and the New York Jets had a special problem because they had a rookie quarterback in 1965, Joe Namath, who had never been exposed to a pro blitz. Cleve Rush, the offensive aide to Coach Weeb Ewbank, listed the many different combinations to which they had to expose Namath (the terminology is that of the Jets— it varies with all teams):

> 6–1—both of the outside linebackers coming
> WP—weak plugger (or linebacker) only
> SP—strong plugger only
> MG—middle guard (actually middle linebacker) only
> Wham—combination of weak plugger and MG
> Slam—combination of strong plugger and MG
> A.O.—All-out, all three linebackers coming
> WSSB—Weak-side safety blitz, in combination with any of the seven listed above
> SSSB—Strong-side safety blitz, in combination with any of the seven listed above

Furthermore, Namath had to look for any and all of these blitzes from the three basic defensive alignments the Jets expected to encounter: the standard 4–3, the 5–1 with the tackles moved over to the strong side so that one of them is head-on with the center, 5–1 undershift with the tackles moved to the weak side. The middle linebacker in both those cases compensates for the shift by plugging to the opposite side.

Complicated?

Get out the slide rule. It reveals that Namath had to learn to look for 21 different types of blitzes from each of the three basic defenses, which multiplies out to 63. The possibilities multiply further if the other team springs a "bastard" defense as well. Finally, on all the variations, the blitzers take many different routes. A corner man can attack either inside or outside the end. He can slide over and shoot the gap between tackle and guard, or guard and center. The middle man can go either side of the center or between guard and tackle. The safety can come shoot inside or outside anywhere along the line.

(See diagrams)

The denouement of Y. A. Tittle as a professional quarterback began in the first game of the 1964 season when Don Burroughs, a veteran safety man of the Philadelphia Eagles, looked like a ten-armed octopus as he swarmed the Giant quarterback from every angle of the field. Poor Yat sat down so much he began to look like a Buddha.

The next week, with the Pittsburgh Steelers continuing the harassment, Tittle was blind-sided by defensive end John Baker and sidelined with a bruised rib cage that robbed him of his mobility the rest of the year and sent him into retirement. Even if it isn't the blitzer who actually accomplishes the damage (for example, Baker), he puts so

What happens when a blitz succeeds is shown here as corner linebacker Matt Hazeltine (55) of the San Francisco 49ers parts Detroit's Milt Plum (dark jersey) from the ball, while linebacker Mike Dowdle pressures him from the front.

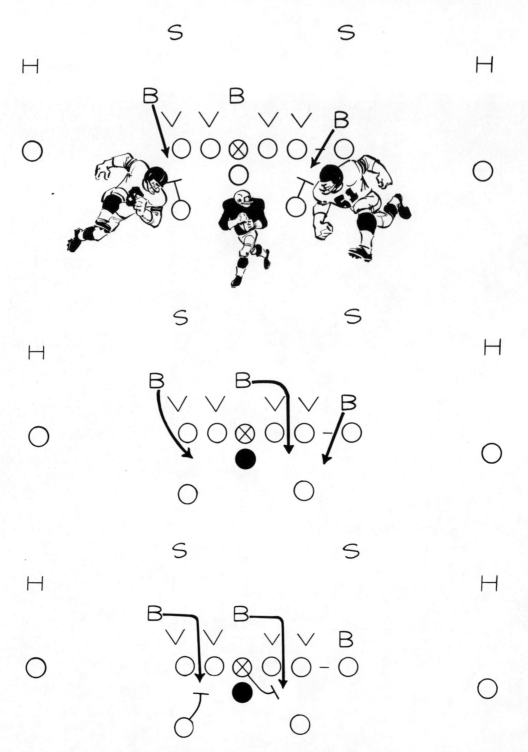

much pressure on the protective cup built around the passer that any leak leaves the quarterback prey to a strong shot in the ribs or the legs. In 1964, besides the crippling blows to Tittle, young quarterback George Mira of the San Francisco 49ers suffered a shoulder separation. So did Frank Ryan of the Cleveland Browns. Milt Plum of the Detroit Lions was encumbered by a wrenched and bruised elbow on his passing arm. Earl Morrall was decked with a broken collarbone. "If those guys keep getting much

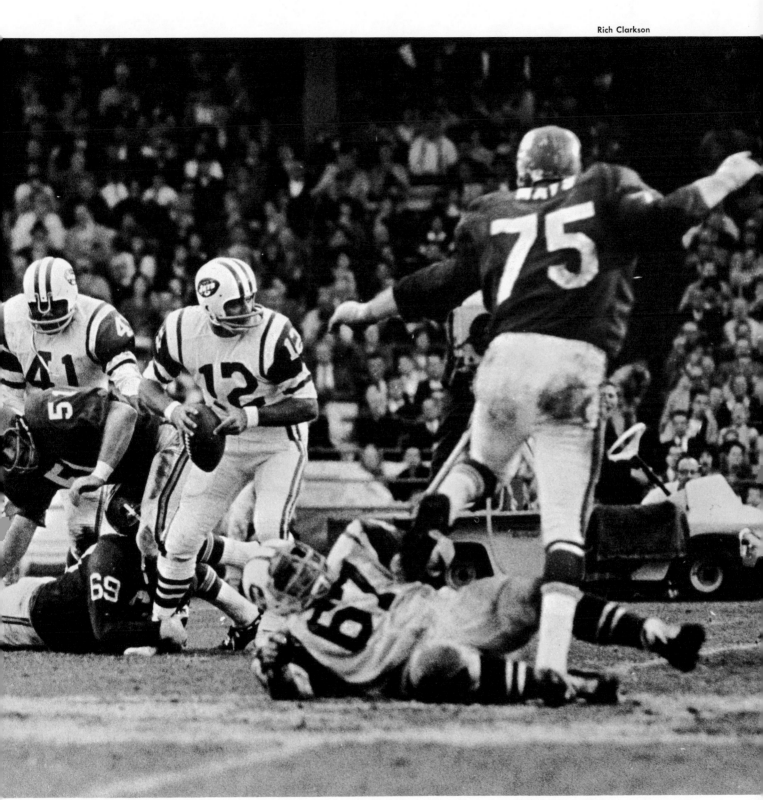

Joe Namath maintained his cool while Sherrill Headrick (69) grabbed him around the ankles and Jerry Mays (75) leaped over Dave Herman. That didn't leave the New York Jet quarterback much time to throw against Kansas City.

Sometimes it's not the blitzing linebacker but a defensive lineman, Alex Karras (71), who hits the quarterback, John Brodie (12) before he can get his arm up to pass.

bigger, stronger and faster," he complained, "I'm going to take up salesmanship." The havoc increased in 1965, culminating with the decimation of the quarterback corps at Baltimore.

Yet the blitz doesn't scare the good ones. "I'd just as soon see a team blitz," said Unitas, "because then it puts them in one-on-one coverage on every receiver. Unless they get to that quarterback within a period of two and a half seconds, he's going to eat them up."

Two things can kill the blitz. Recognizing it and then getting the pass off in good form by holding back enough blockers to pick up the blitzers. The maneuver is an inherent gamble. The good defensive teams, like Green Bay, Detroit and Cleveland in the National Football League, and San Diego and Buffalo in the American Football League, use the blitz sparingly. They regard it more as a change of pace than a way of life, to keep the quarterback wary of the threat and thinking about it.

"Usually," said Francis Tarkenton of the Minnesota Vikings, "you can detect a linebacker sneaking up to the line of scrimmage. He's got to get close to the line at the time of the snap of the ball in order to get the maximum effect of the blitz. If he's off the line at the snap, the blitz is delayed and we should be quick enough to get the ball off. When we recognize the blitz, we may call an audible—it may be a run audible as well as a pass audible."

The blitz has been responsible for the growth of the big back. Teams like to have two big men in the backfield for the necessary blocking. "For every blitzer," explained Unitas, "there's supposed to be a man to pick him up. Now don't get the idea I'm overjoyed about being blitzed, but such tactics do make the defense more vulnerable to draws, flares and screen passes."

Tittle, who went back to San Francisco to coach the 49er quarterbacks, added a qualification: "In your normal alignment, there is one type of blitz where you don't have men back there. That's the safety blitz."

He drew it out.

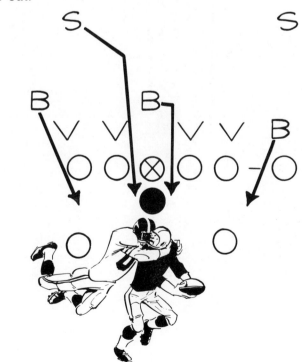

"Now here's one way to handle it," he continued. "Bring this weakside end in."

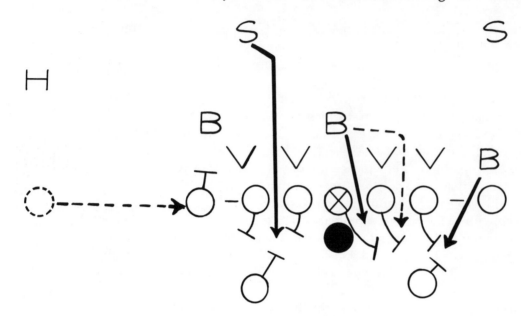

"And here's another way. 'Shout 70.' "

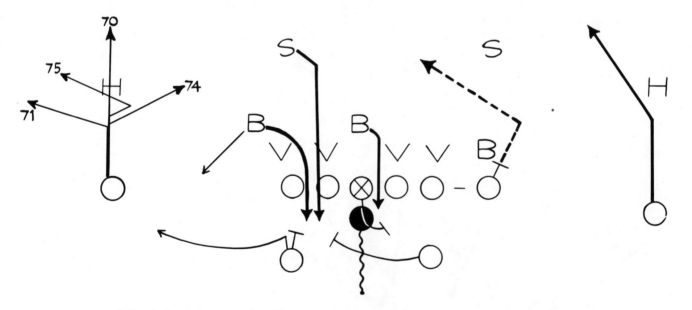

"That's how we completed a lot of passes to Dave Parks, our split end. On an audible to Dave on one of our 70 series of passes, he has several possible routes—a square-out, which is 71; a slant-in, 74; a zig-out, 75, or a straight 'fly' pattern. The halfback's out there covering him all alone. Meanwhile, the halfback takes a step up, then flares left,

When the defensive tackle, Ernie Ladd (77), stands 6–9 and weighs 320 pounds, Lenny Dawson (16) of Kansas City doesn't have much of a passing alley.

drawing the linebacker with him. If the linebacker's shooting, he'll stay in and block. The fullback comes over and picks up the safety. The tight end checks the linebacker on his side and then slants across the middle."

The Green Bay Packers have always invited the blitz against them because Coach Vince Lombardi is confident in the ability of his backs to pick up the extra man and in the poise of quarterback Bart Starr to withstand the rush and get the pass off.

The Packers invaded Baltimore the second Sunday in December of 1965 absolutely needing a victory to keep the race alive. It would put them in first place. A loss meant the title clincher for the Colts. The Packers held a slim 7–3 lead late in the first quarter and had the ball at midfield. Quarterback Bart Starr sensed a blitz and called for a simple option pass. The weak-side linebacker, Don Shinnick of the Colts, came strong and was picked up by fullback Jim Taylor. Starr had a choice of throwing to Boyd Dowler, the split left end who ran a quick post pattern to the center of the field, or half-back Paul Hornung, who swung to his left and then ran a fly pattern on the outside along the sideline. Dowler pulled cornerback Lenny Lyles in with him. No one was even near Hornung as he caught a long pass and waltzed into the end zone.

Late in the fourth quarter when the Colts rallied to cut the Packer lead to 35–27, with five and a half minutes remaining, the Packers took the kickoff out to their 35-yard line. Hornung lined up in the slot on the right, outside his tackle. The Colts came at Starr with an all-out blitz, the three backers rushing. Hornung made a quick break to the inside. Starr quickly flipped the ball to him over the middle on the dead run, and there was no one between Hornung and the goal line. The ball game was over right there.

And the Packers were on their way to the NFL championship, by beating two blitzes for touchdowns.

8. The Mad Scramble

In his young days with the Green Bay Packers, Tobin Rote was the most effective running quarterback in football.

Big Roosevelt Grier slowly lifted his 300 pounds off the pile of bodies. At the bottom he located a white uniform with red piping on the sleeves. He lifted George Mira of the San Francisco 49ers by the scruff of the neck and got him on his feet again. George shook his head to get his bearings.

"In this league," said the huge tackle of the Los Angeles Rams, "you don't run, little man."

The word hasn't gotten out to all precincts, particularly in the upper Midwest where the Minnesota Vikings play. Francis Tarkenton, a minister's son, is the leader of *la nouvelle vague* in quarterbacks. He runs.

Wilt Chamberlain passes off. Jayne Mansfield blushes. Perry Mason loses a case. Y. A. Tittle grows hair. Ned Sparks smiles. Ted Williams tips his hat. General Motors shows a year-end loss. Bill Veeck wears a necktie. Miami freezes over. Leo Durocher shuts up. You get the idea?

A quarterback who runs isn't supposed to happen. He's the most valuable piece of *bric a brac* in professional football, and coaches like to keep him away from the mainstream of contact. Norm Van Brocklin, Tarkenton's coach at Minnesota, was a great passer for the Los Angeles Rams and Philadelphia Eagles because he believed in staying in his pocket.

"I run," said the Dutchman in a phrase that was to become memorable as the credo of all quarterbacks, "only from sheer fright."

From the start there have been exceptions. Frankie Albert was a great bootlegger for the 49ers. Faking a handoff and tucking the ball alongside his hip for a run around end was an integral part of the San Francisco offense. Sid Luckman ran from scrimmage only once in the 1946 season. That 19-yard dash to the end zone led the Chicago Bears to a championship-game victory over the New York Giants. In 1952, Bobby Layne carried the ball from scrimmage 94 times in 12 games as the Detroit Lions introduced elements of the split-T offense in which the quarterback ran along the line of scrimmage and had the option of pitching out or keeping the ball and slanting off tackle. He gained 411 yards rushing, only 46 fewer than the team's leading rusher, Bob Hoernschemeyer. The Lions won the NFL title that season, their first since 1935, and Layne scored the first touchdown himself in a 17–7 playoff win over the Cleveland Browns.

Oddly enough, Bobby went into pro ball with the idea that the quarterback led a sheltered life. He was drafted by the Pittsburgh Steelers, who were still playing the single-wing, because they wanted him for the vital tailback job. Bobby wanted no part of them, having tasted the joys of a protected existence when the University of Texas switched to the T-formation his senior year and put him at quarterback. When the Chicago Bears secured the rights to Layne from Pittsburgh, he quickly signed and eventually wended his way to Detroit. But Layne was a competitor who didn't hesitate to stick his neck out if the situation called for it.

Gino Marchetti, recognized as the greatest defensive end in the history of the game, recalled one encounter with Layne's brashness. As the left end for the Baltimore Colts, Gino had cruised along the line and smeared a couple of Detroit plays on the opposite side of the field. To keep him honest, Layne faked a play the other way, kept the ball and bootlegged around Marchetti's end for 27 yards and a touchdown. Later in the game, when Layne faked a bootleg, Gino crashed into him full tilt and knocked the quarterback to the ground. As they got up he taunted Bobby, "I'm waiting for you to bootleg."

Layne didn't wait long to pick up the challenge. On the next play he kept the ball himself and skirted around Marchetti for a 30-yard gain.

When Tobin Rote joined the Lions in 1957, they probably had the best two running quarterbacks in the business. Rote had been the leading ball carrier on the Green Bay Packers. He was their No. 1 groundgainer in '56. Tobin was 6–3 and weighed 215 pounds, built to take the punishment. He continued to lug the ball when he moved to the Lions and was their second leading groundgainer as he led them to a title in his inaugural season. For his ten years in the NFL, Rote gained more than 3,000 yards on the ground and averaged five yards a carry, figures which would do justice to almost any running back.

As recognition of the quarterback's vital role in the offense as a passer increased, so did his timidity as a runner, and by the time Rote played out his string as a pro with the San Diego Chargers of the AFL in 1964, he said, "Nowadays I don't run because they don't want me to, and it's a lot healthier."

The colleges, however, have kept supplying the pros with quarterbacks who can run the ball. The average college passer throws on the run in the rollout offenses that are prevalent on the campus. He generally has to be something of a running threat to warrant a spot in the lineup. The All-American quarterbacks of recent seasons have been fellows like Roger Staubach of Navy who made a career out of running for his life. When Otto Graham coached the College All-Stars against the NFL champions each August, he said, "I was hesitant to take Roger for the All-Star game, great as he is, because he ran too quickly. His main thought as quarterback at Navy was to go back and scramble. He was taught this."

In 1961, Francis Tarkenton joined the Minnesota Vikings in training camp at Bemidji, Minnesota, and the battle over scrambling quarterbacks was joined.

"There are those times when, by the nature of its rush, the defense overextends and leaves itself open to a run," wrote Green Bay coach Vince Lombardi in his classic book, *Run to Daylight*, "so the quarterback who can also run has a great advantage."

When Tarkenton fades back to pass, all hell breaks loose if he cannot find his primary receiver or the pass rush is too severe. The first thing he does is head for the nearest open space, right or left, by ducking under arms and squirming out of tackles. This takes a great deal of agility in the face of the quick defensive giants who populate pro ball. Francis weighs 193 pounds, and the average defensive lineman goes at least 250, so that gives the Viking quarterback a shade on quickness. As he takes off in full flight with the posse of tacklers on his heels, Tarkenton becomes alert to the possibilities of finding an open receiver. There's no way a defensive back can keep a receiver bottled

116

Super scrambler Tarkenton wheels to get away from Willie Davis (87), Green Bay.

Malcolm W. Emmons

Malcolm W. Emmons

Francis Tarkenton of the Minnesota Vikings slips the clutch of Paul Wiggins (84), Cleveland. He's off and running.

Defensive end Lionel Aldridge of the Packers grabs a handful of Tarkenton's shirt, as the quarterback struggles to keep his balance.

up indefinitely. The more time the latter has to maneuver, the greater his chances of getting open. Tarkenton in a scramble gives the receiver all the time in the world.

The problem now is for the two of them—passer and receiver—to make contact because Tarkenton's got the enemy breathing down his neck and can't afford the luxury of stopping to look around downfield. He'll zig left, twist and go back the other way, all the time retreating, slipping out of tackles. . . . Before defenses got wise to his abilities, Tarkenton ranged all over the field. Against the New York Giants one afternoon, he ran at least 90 yards crisscrossing the field, wound up 30 yards behind the line of scrimmage, turned and threw a pass all the way across the gridiron to tight end Hal Bedsole that was good for a 30-yard gain. Minnesota fans didn't even blink.

Now defensive ends try to contain him by keeping their pass rush to the outside, forcing Francis to look for an inside alley where the traffic's generally heavier. The average drop (retreat from center) for a pro quarterback is 7 yards and he has from 3 to 3½ seconds to get rid of the ball before he's snowed under. The protective cup around the passer is so designed that the offensive linemen force their rushers outside and around an imaginary arc. The quarterback's supposed to step up into the middle of the cup and throw.

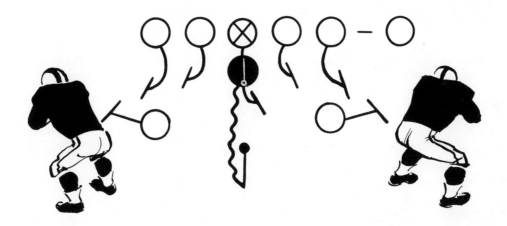

Tarkenton and his fellow scramblers, who leave the cup, offend the purists. The critics maintain he breaks down the blocking coordination between line and backfield. Since they don't know in which direction he's going to scramble, the linemen don't know how to direct their blocks.

Francis argues, "I don't think a quarterback can say, 'I'm going to drop back 7 yards and not run.'"

119

It was pointed out that his own coach, Norm Van Brocklin was a gluefooted quarterback who never sashayed out of his pocket.

"But he hasn't played since 1960," shrugged Tarkenton. "Dutch compensated for the fact he couldn't run. He released the ball so quickly. My way is to get out of trouble.

"When the pass pattern doesn't develop the way you anticipate it, then what do you do? Do you say, 'Okay, I'm going to sit there and take a 10-yard loss and maybe we'll get it back next down.'? Or are you going to adjust and say, 'I'll try something else off the same play because I don't want to lose the down.'?

"The down is precious. So I'm going to come out of there and compensate so we can get the pass off and maybe get some ground gained on it. This is my philosophy. I don't think a quarterback's job is done when he goes back 8 or 9 yards to pass, gets pressured from the inside and he steps up and there's no pocket and he says, 'I better not step outside because the pattern will be broken. I'm going to take my loss and forget it.'

"That's not my personality. That's not my type of play. The scramble comes out of a situation that is not ideal, not a perfect blocking situation where the ends are open."

The Viking scrambler made an important distinction. When fellows like Layne and Rote ran the ball, it was usually by design. There were set plays for them. When Tarkenton runs, it's strictly make-it-up-as-you-go. The scramble is born from desperation. Today there are virtually no set running plays for the quarterback except for the sneaks when the ball is inching up toward the goal line and the man who gets the snap from center has the best chance to wedge the ball across.

"I used to think Otto Graham ran around a lot," continued Tarkenton. "They didn't call it 'scramble' back in those days. But he moved around a lot in the backfield. In the lines today we've got an unusual animal. He has tremendous speed, tremendous strength. And I don't care how good your offensive linemen are, your defensive linemen are going to beat them occasionally. Offensive linemen generally scale smaller. The tackles are from 240 to 255, the guards from 230 to 250. The defensive linemen are all 260, 270, 280, rangy, with great speed. They're going to get in sometimes and if they close down the pocket, I think the quarterback has got to be able to skip to the outside.

"When a team gives you the outside, it's in trouble. The offensive tackle, you must remember, takes the inside and runs his man to the outside. Some time during a game, a defensive end becomes frustrated because he knows the guy is playing him to go to the outside. He says, 'Maybe I can beat him inside one time.' Then he'll fake outside and try to come inside.

"When you're dropping back and looking down, you can kind of see the arc. You've got two big men rushing over there. If one of them is shut off inside, you can sense this. When I do, well golly, I know I've got yards. I can step out there and nobody else is around to bother me. It gives me more time for my pass pattern to develop. When the frustrated end gets pinched off, he's dead."

Many coaches argue, however, that Tarkenton's progress as a quarterback is in inverse ratio to his scrambling. The more he cuts down on it, the better he'll be. The Vikings haven't won a championship with him. The winning quarterbacks who didn't scramble—like Van Brocklin, Charley Conerly, John Unitas—had an inside move that

Not even the shirt dragged off his back discourages the Viking scrambler.

Quarterback John Hadl of the San Diego Chargers rolls out like a halfback. He can either run or pass.

threw tacklers off. They needed only a 4- to 6-inch lateral step to elude defenders. Unitas does most of his running to the inside holes.

"I get a kick out of carrying the ball once in a while," admitted Unitas, "but I know that I'll never run like a halfback. I think we quarterbacks have been blessed with a sixth sense that warns us of impending doom. We've got to counter by sidestepping, juking or just plain taking off. I'll run up the middle. Quarterbacks get an awful lot of legwork as it is just pulling the ball away from the center and racing back 7 or 8 yards to set up on every pass play."

Tarkenton, the apostle of the scramble, has become sensitive on the subject.

"What's the definition of 'scramble'?" he asked. "Is it every time you run? Against the Giants in New York a couple of years ago I ran twice, and then I ran around and passed to Bedsole. That amounted to 3 out of 29 times I handled the ball. People are looking for something different, which calls attention to it.

"If it's third and 15 and the other team's giving me a strong rush, what have I got to lose? I'd be willing to give up 10 or 12 yards. The situations determine whether or not you scramble.

"It's been argued that I don't function well on a bad field. Against Detroit, on a rainy, muddy field, we scored 20 points and got beat, 23–20. Then we played the Rams in three-degrees-above zero, on a frozen field. That day I threw for over 200 yards and three touchdowns. I didn't run a lick.

"I don't think a bad field bothers me because generally I'm still a drop-back passer. I'm a passer; I'm a quarterback. On a day you're not going to be able to move around quite as well, you don't. You have to take that 7- or 8-yard loss when they rush you.

"I think I do stay in the pocket more now."

Former Coach Buddy Parker of the Steelers declared that the quarterback who can run with the ball is becoming a necessity because of the increase in rushing linebackers. The added pressure of the blitz has forced the pros to use occasional rollout patterns to get the quarterback free of the pack. It has placed a stress on mobility.

"There is a trend in the direction of better scrambling quarterbacks," agreed Coach Tom Landry of the Dallas Cowboys, "but not in the direction of a planned running attack for them."

There are plenty of good scramblers besides Tarkenton in both pro leagues. John Brodie of the 49ers has been evading tacklers with success since 1957. When the 49ers tinkered briefly with their shotgun offense in 1961, Brodie was adaptable enough to take his turn at tailback (in an alternating rotation with Bill Kilmer and Bobby Waters). He didn't like it, but he got out alive. Brodie's stand-in, Mira, came up to the pros with a reputation as a superb scrambler. He has strong, thick legs and likes to run. The 49er quarterbacks were trapped fewer times behind the line than any others in 1965. Mira has a bit of a height problem. He's under six feet. With that type, coaches frequently put in rollout patterns in which the quarterback takes the ball from center and instead of dropping straight back, fades to his right or left where he can get an angle of vision to spot his receivers. Otherwise he's staring into the upraised arms of linemen who tower as much as 6–8. When Eddie LeBaron, 5–7, came into professional football, the

Washington Redskins and later the Dallas Cowboys had to take that tack with him. A quarterback rolling out is already on the run, so it becomes tempting in a broken pattern to tuck the ball under his arm and take off for the wide-open spaces. Charley Johnson of the St. Louis Cardinals is probably Tarkenton's chief rival at zig-zagging away from a rush. Charley's a compact six-footer with good running ability. Frank Ryan of the Cleveland Browns is a nifty runner when he has to be, though he lacks the speed of Mira, Tarkenton or Johnson. He has a long, deceptive stride. Don Meredith of the Dallas Cowboys is built like Ryan and doesn't hesitate to take off under duress. Bill Munson of the Los Angeles Rams comes from the same mold.

In the American Football League, Jack Kemp of the Buffalo Bills and John Hadl of the San Diego Chargers actually prefer to take to their heels under a strong rush. The've both been criticized periodically for not staying in the pocket long enough, but since the Bills and the Chargers both manage to win with them, the arguments are academic. In fact, Kemp's alternate on the Bills, Daryle Lamonica, is a replica of the early Tobin Rote in both size and running style and makes a fetish of keeping the ball. Oakland coach Al Davis felt he lost a good shot at ousting the Chargers for the Western Conference title of the AFL in 1965 because a preseason injury cost him the services of Cotton Davidson and left him with a pair of quarterbacks, Tom Flores and Dick Wood, who were immobile in the face of a severe pass rush. Cotton's a rabbity type of passer who fires his passes on the run and would have been effective against certain teams that put the pressure on. Or so Davis felt.

The prototype of the breed, though, is still Tarkenton, who shaded to the conservative side after five years of scrambling but stayed ahead of his contemporaries in sticking out his neck, and that of the Vikings. One scrimmage play against the Detroit Lions started out at the Lions' 45-yard line, and twenty seconds and half a dozen grabbing arms later, Tarkenton was running laterally at the 10-yard line of the Vikings with tackle Alex Karras and end Darris McCord in thundering pursuit. One of the Viking linemen had already thrown three blocks on the play, took a pause that refreshes at midfield, and yelled out to a teammate, "Look out, he's coming back the other way."

"Where?" screamed the other Viking. "I don't see him."

"Not here," answered the lineman. "Down there by our goal line. Where the hell else did you expect him to be?"

Whereupon Tarkenton started upfield again, weaving in and out like Red Grange, then stopped and threw the ball. Fullback Bill Brown caught it along the sideline and quickly stepped out of bounds to ease the suspense. The Vikings lost 13 yards on the play.

The Los Angeles Rams, backed up to their 35-yard line one day, with the Vikings driving to break a tie, chased Tarkenton back, back, back with an all-out blitz—their huge front four plus all the linebackers. He tried to run to the left. They cut him off. He reversed to the right, and they were there to meet him, too. He was still scrambling wildly when all the Rams hit him at once on his own 25-yard line. He coughed up the football, and Los Angeles recovered. Total loss: forty yards plus the football.

But the Vikings estimate he has also completed 35 touchdown passes off broken plays, none of them rehearsed. Though when Coach Don Shula of the Baltimore Colts

124

On his ground forays, John Unitas of the Colts prefers to take an inside route up the middle.

handled Francis in the Pro Bowl game a couple of years ago, he took him aside during one practice session and said, "It's getting kind of late. Why don't you take part of the afternoon off to work on your scrambles." Shula, they say, was serious.

"A man has to be cunning to play end for the Vikings," said one of the Minnesota receivers. "The thing you learn first is never to stop running. Francis never gives up on a play."

It's a hazardous way of making a living, the cat-and-mouse game he plays with the defense. He weaves and turns in designs that would do justice to a Jackson Pollock painting, depending on a sixth sense to alert him to danger from the blind side. "The kid's going to get killed!" said Gino Marchetti of the Colts the first time he saw Tarkenton skip around.

The irony is that Tarkenton, who should be the most vulnerable to injury because he challenges tacklers more than any other quarterback in football, was virtually alone among the frontline signal callers who escaped serious injury over his first five years in pro football. He was shaken up in a Baltimore game of 1962 and against the Detroit Lions in 1964. He had to be spelled for just a few minutes in each case. The Chicago Bears clotheslined him early in a 1963 game. Dave Whitsell, a defensive back, impaled Tarkenton on his forearm as he tried to scoot out of bounds on a scramble. But before the game was over, Tarkenton was back calling signals and running around.

A final twist is that when Shula of the Colts answered a questionnaire before the '65 season on the trend toward scrambling, he wrote, "The running quarterback is not for Baltimore. We only have two (John Unitas and Gary Guozzo) and want to keep them both healthy."

Both Unitas and Cuozzo were cut down by crippling injuries late in the year, and Shula discovered the glory of the running quarterback—in Tom Matte, a hastily converted halfback.

126

9. The Quarterback Mystique

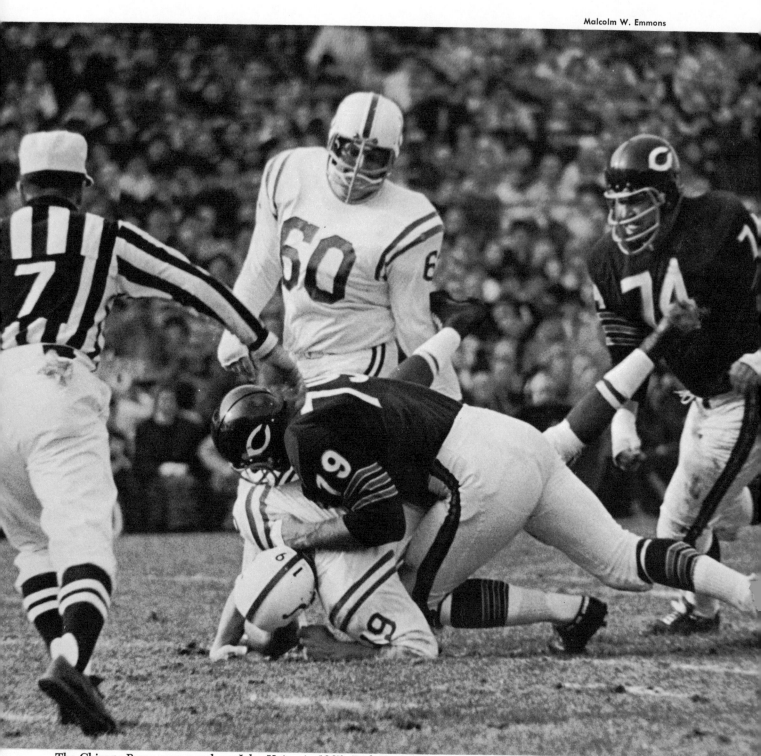

The Chicago Bears were rough on John Unitas in 1965. Dick Evey (79) upended the Colt quarterback, while George Preas (60) stood by helpless.

The mystique of the quarterback, that allegory for omnipotence in professional football, was severely bruised in the final weeks of 1965.

The Baltimore Colts were sailing serenely along at the top of the Western Conference of the National Football League, secure under the generalship of John Unitas. "With Unitas," said one rival coach, "they're great. Without him, they're nothing."

A couple of seasons earlier, Coach Vince Lombardi of the Green Bay Packers was more specific in his appraisal: "Take him away, and they're a fourth-place team."

The Chicago Bears delivered a shot to Unitas' ribs in the eighth game of the '65 campaign, but Gary Cuozzo, his substitute, took over and threw a touchdown pass to Raymond Berry, which was eventually decisive, 26–21. The following week against Minnesota, Unitas' ribs were still tender. He suited up and was available in case of an emergency, but the Colts never needed him. Coach Don Shula entrusted his offense to Cuozzo. Gary was shaky in the first half, but Unitas encouraged him each time he came back to the bench: "Keep up what you're doing, Gary. You'll get to them."

Gary needed the pat on the back. The Colts were down, 7–3, with 23 seconds left in the first half and barely across midfield. Jimmy Orr, the flanker, faked a turn-in and took off on a fly down the right sideline. He turned just in time to find a long pass thrown by Cuozzo nestle in his hands and trotted into the end zone for a 43-yard touchdown play. In the second half the young quarterback threw 4 more touchdown passes to complete a 41–21 rout against the strong Vikings and keep the Colts in first place.

In fact, he even sent Coach Norm Van Brocklin of the losers into retirement for a day. The Dutchman, despairing after a second-stringer cannoned his team and destroyed their chance to become a factor in the Western Conference race, went into conference with himself at midnight and the next morning announced he was quitting the Vikings. A day later he reconsidered. An ex-quarterback is allowed one change of signals.

Cuozzo's Cinderella story ended abruptly with the return of Unitas, and the next two games, John was again the spearhead of the Baltimore offense in a high-scoring 34–24 victory over the Philadelphia Eagles and a 24–24 Thanksgiving Day deadlock with Detroit. With a record of 9 victories, 1 loss and 1 tie, the Colts were a game and a half ahead of the slumping Green Bay Packers.

Then those big, bad Bears confronted them again, and late in the first half with the Colts trailing, 7–0, Unitas went back to pass from his own 32-yard line. As his arm completed the throwing arc, tackle Earl Leggett hit him from one side and tackle Stan Jones from the other. Unitas hobbled off the field on his own power, but by seven-thirty that night he was in surgery for a knee operation. The time left on the clock when Unitas walked off was 4:42. The pass he threw was way over the head of tight end John Mackey, though the Bears were called for defensive holding on the play to give the Colts a first down.

Cuozzo came into the ball game and quickly moved the Colts to another first down and 10 on the Chicago 26-yard line. Then he couldn't get a grip on center Dick Szymanski's snap from center. The ball dropped at his feet, and while Gary looked around vainly to locate it, Leggett of the Bears dropped on the football to end the threat.

Nevertheless it was still the cue for Cuozzo to come on with another set of heroics and prove that Unitas wasn't the indispensable man. Gary wasn't quite up to it against a tough Bear defense that day. In the third quarter he couldn't move his team past the Bear 36-yard line. On the first series of the fourth quarter he threw a 48-yard pass to Orr that carried into the end zone, but one of the Colt linemen was holding, which nullified the touchdown. Later in the fourth quarter, Baltimore moved to the Chicago 29 and lost the ball on downs. On the next-to-last play of the game they made their deepest penetration when Gary fired to Orr, who ran to the Bear 17, was hit and fumbled the ball away. The Colts were shut out, 13–0.

Now the Colts were faced with Green Bay next and no Unitas and their grip on first place imperiled. A tough spot for young Gary in his third season as a pro. He blew it all on one play just before the half.

The Packers led, 14–13, but Jimmy Taylor fumbled as he tried to sweep right end. Alert Bobby Boyd, the left defensive halfback, scooped up the bouncing ball and tight-roped down to the 3-yard line before he was knocked out of bounds. The clock showed 1:13 until intermission. Plenty of time to push across a touchdown. Fullback Jerry Hill bucked over his right guard for 2 yards. Just 1 more yard to go for a score and a Baltimore lead. The Colts were all hopped up. The eerie fog which rolled over the stadium and closed off the airport couldn't muffle the roar of the 60,000-plus crammed in the stands as the Colts broke the huddle.

They expected to see Hill hit the middle again, or maybe Lenny Moore over tackle. Cuozzo might even try a keeper.

On the line of scrimmage, defensive end Willie Davis of the Packers sensed something else was up. It was in the way George Preas, right tackle opposite him, lined up. Soft. His hands barely brushing the grass, as if he were prepared to rear up and get in a pass-protection stance instead of firing out as he normally would on a running play. Willie decided it was going to be a pass. So did Dave Robinson, the linebacker behind him.

Instead of charging on the snap, they drifted. Cuozzo in the huddle had called a simple little flare-out pass to his fullback swinging to the open side of the field on his right. He hoped to catch the Packers by surprise. Instead, Davis abandoned his normal inside charge against the obvious running play. He hit against Preas' outside shoulder and drifted wide to cover the flank. Robinson, the linebacker, moved laterally with Hill.

As Cuozzo faked a handoff to halfback Moore and turned to his right to throw, Davis was in his line of vision. Gary floated the ball softly over Willie's outstretched fingers. A more experienced quarterback, sensing the Packers were tipped off, might have thrown the ball clear out of bounds to avoid danger, knowing he could hit them with two more plays.

Before the pass reached Hill, Robinson stepped in. He had 4 inches in height on the Colt fullback and simply snatched the ball away from him on the dead run. The Packer linebacker had clear sailing ahead and a convoy of blockers. But 245-pound defenders aren't geared to run the length of the field. Robinson pooped out and faltered after trudging 87 yards. Lenny Moore, angling across the field, pushed Robinson out of bounds on the Baltimore 10-yard line. On the next play, however, with seconds remaining in the half, quarterback Bart Starr of the Packers threw to Boyd Dowler in the end zone on a post pattern and Don Chandler converted the extra-point attempt.

So the Colts trailed 21–13 instead of going off buoyed at halftime by a 20–14 lead. The 14-point switch looked insurmountable. On the third play of the third quarter, Cuozzo was under heavy fire of a Packer blitz led by middle linebacker Ray Nitschke. Right defensive end Lionel Aldridge of the Packers was the first man to hit him. The ball was jostled out of Gary's hands, but recovered by Baltimore guard Jim Parker. As the punting team came in for the fourth-down situation, Cuozzo trotted off the field holding his left shoulder. The Packers fielded a short kick on the Colt 39 and moved in to score on a 9-yard run by Paul Hornung. During their march, Cuozzo left the field and hurried into a dugout corridor leading to the Colt dressing room.

On the sideline, Tom Matte, who normally functioned as Moore's stand-in at halfback, started warming up, throwing the ball to reserve end Butch Wilson. The Colts were without any kind of quarterback experience at all.

A year before, the New York Giants were left without a seasoned quarterback when Y. A. Tittle was hurt, and end Andy Robustelli recalled the feeling: "It's like going home and you've eight kids and there are two missing. (Robustelli's a prolific father.) You love the other six, but still you don't feel right without the other two."

In five seasons of professional play, Matte had never handed off a ball in earnest. At Ohio State, under Coach Woody Hayes, Tom was a quarterback. But in the Buckeyes' offense, which consisted of the proverbial 3-yards-and-a-cloud-of-dust, he usually kept the ball himself, looking for holes between tackle and end or scooting around the flank. When he threw the ball, it was always on the run and generally as a last resort. The Colts had given him a little practice at quarterback as a safeguard for just such an emergency. There were a few plays designed for Matte to run. He had a halfback draw, setting up as if to pass, then slipping the ball to Moore. He had a rollout off the halfback draw, faking to Moore and keeping the ball himself with an option of passing or running as he circled the end. Altogether he had a repertoire of half-a-dozen plays.

"Go in there and keep a cool head," advised Shula as the Packers prepared to kick off. Matte is an affable, round-faced young man whose smile hides a history of ulcers. He's a fine all-around athlete but worried because he never held a regular job in the lineup. The Colts considered him an all-purpose man.

"Keep it simple," added Shula. "Start out with that halfback draw."

When the Colts put the ball in play on their 22, Tom took the snap surely from center, retreated with his arm raised, then slipped the football to Moore. Lenny looked for a hole over tackle, found it filled and darted around end for 10 yards and a first down. Matte handed off to Moore over left tackle for 6 yards. A trap over the middle with Hill the runner added 6 more and another first down. Matte took over himself and raced around right end and across midfield for 12 yards to the Green Bay 44. The disconsolate crowd perked up.

But with big, agile defenders, a quarterback who keeps the ball on the ground interminably isn't going to get far or live a long professional life. Matte barely knew the terminology for a pass offense, but he went to the air. He threw to tight-end John Mackey on a square-out pattern. It was incomplete. Too low. He threw again, over the middle, and safety Tom Brown of the Packers intercepted the ball. The Packers quickly moved to another touchdown, lifting the score to 35–13.

Meanwhile, in the dressing room a doctor jabbed a needle into Cuozzo's shoulder, then strapped it tightly in place with a wrapping of tape. The clubhouse boy pulled a jersey over Gary's head and he returned to the field. The young quarterback moved the Colts to 2 touchdowns, but with the score 35–27 the Packers broke Hornung loose again on a pass over the middle that went 65 yards for a touchdown and put the game beyond reach.

In 1½ games without Unitas, the Colts went from a firm Western Conference lead to second place and would be lucky to hold that spot against the challenge of the Bears, hottest team in the league. They had six days left until the season finale with the Los Angeles Rams, a Saturday game on the West Coast, and the news got worse. Cuozzo like Unitas, was out for the season. That left it all up to Matte. On Monday, Tom started a cram course in quarterbacking.

The basic mechanics of taking the ball from center was no problem. Matte was used to it from his college days. It's no big deal. Some quarterbacks take the ball with the right hand on top of the left, some with both hands extended, the little fingers on the bottom, the thumbs on the top. When Otto Graham was switched to a T-quarterback, nobody coached him on the snap. He figured that a baseball player catches the ball with his left hand in the glove and traps it with the right, so that's the way he started. He played his first seven years with the Cleveland Browns using his left hand up and right hand down to take the ball from center. But Paul Brown woke up to the fact one day that the other quarterbacks on the Browns, Cliff Lewis and George Ratterman, did it just the opposite. So in less than one day Otto learned to take the ball with his right hand up and finished his career that way.

"I had no transition problem whatsoever," said Graham. "A lot of coaches overcoach. In the split-T they say you should have both thumbs up because the ball comes up with a point. Their reasoning is that when you get the ball, you can turn your hand equally as fast either way. I don't think it makes a bit of difference. I liked to get my hands on the center of the ball, the meat of the ball."

And how about the positioning of the quarterback's feet?

"We played a game against the Philadelphia Eagles," recalled Graham, "when Tommy Thompson was their quarterback. I studied him and noticed that whenever he was going to throw a pass, his left foot was forward under the center. When it was a run, his feet were parallel. Tommy played that way 99 percent of the time. So we taught Alex Agase, our middle linebacker, to look for it, then signal the rest of the defense. We killed them."

The smart players pick up little cues, so the trick for quarterbacks is to be consistent in their habits. Most of them keep their feet evenly placed in a comfortable stance. Foot-

132

Tom Matte's success as a rollout quarterback, at the dramatic close of the 1965 season, has inspired the Baltimore Colts to put in a "Matte offense" for emergencies.

work and faking are a matter of practice. Graham was not a slick artist on handoffs because he didn't work at it. After he planted the ball in the runner's midsection, belt-buckle high, he generally turned around to see how the other guy was doing. Bobby Layne played the spectator when the Detroit Lions met the Chicago Bears in 1956 for the championship of the Western Conference in the last game of the season. Early in the second quarter, Layne spun and pitched the ball to Gene Gedman, a halfback, then turned around to follow the action, when the lights went out. Ed Meadows, a defensive end for the Bears, jumped him from the blind side and Layne woke up in the hospital with a brain concussion to find out the Bears had won the title.

Artisans like George Ratterman and Eddie LeBaron were virtual Houdinis. Ratterman would retire to his room in sneakers, before a mirror, and practice his footwork and sleight-of-hand.

Quarterbacks vary on how they drop back to pass. Frank Ryan of the Cleveland Browns retreats facing the line of scrimmage, keeping his receivers in view. Y. A. Tittle of the Giants favored a cross-over step, hustling back to his predesignated spot, 7 yards behind the line, as fast as he could get there. That's how most of them do it.

To prepare Matte for his unveiling as a quarterback was nevertheless primarily a mental exercise. He had to be drilled in recognizing defenses, and then he had to be trained in running the club. This can get fairly complicated because teams frequently must switch their plays at the line of scrimmage (called an "audible," or "automatic") to meet a changing defense. The Packers use a number system. In the huddle, quarterback Bart Starr says the ball will be snapped "on two" and that becomes the live number. If he hollers "Set . . . two . . ." the Packers are immediately alerted to the fact the next number he calls will be the new play. Running plays are numbered simply by the back and the hole he will hit. Fullbacks and halfbacks are generally "3" and "4" while the holes from end to end are also numbered—thus "34" means the fullback through the "4" hole. The Colts use a color system.

"For the Ram game," said Coach Shula, "we completely changed our cadence of calling signals. Normally the quarterback calls a live color, followed by a check-off (the new play). Or a fake check, if the color isn't live. (*Example:* orange might be the live color, so anytime the quarterback yelled it, the other Colts knew the play was being changed. Any other color didn't count.) We forgot about the colors. Instead we just set our linemen, and Tom went into his 'Hut one, Hut two, Hut three,' depending on what count he wanted the ball snapped. That gave him enough variety to keep the other team from anticipating the snap."

Later in the week, on Thursday, the Colts got a break. They picked up Ed Brown from the Pittsburgh Steelers on waivers. He was a thirty-six-year-old quarterback riding the bench on a last-place team, but back in 1956 he had led the Chicago Bears to a division title, and he was experienced.

"With him," said Shula, "we could throw more passes. With Tom in the game we used two tight ends, Mackey and Wilson, with Alex Hawkins as the flanker. All are good blockers. The problem we had with Brown was that our numbering system was just the opposite of Pittsburgh's. Baltimore numbers its holes even to the right, odd to the left.

134

The Steeler system was odd to the right, even to the left. It would have been too confusing for Brown to adjust so quickly, so he just called plays by formation and name: split right, sweep right; split right, short-trap right; split right, long-trap right; dive right; special right, and so on."

Matte went into the Ram game with the plays taped to his left wrist. Facing the biggest defensive line in the National League, he wasn't supposed to run the ball. The Rams averaged 275 pounds per man on their front four and had the best record against rushing in the NFL. The team had won three straight games, including victories over both division leaders, the Packers and the Browns. They were without their No. 1 quarterback, too, Bill Munson hobbling in a cast after a knee operation, but the late-season drive was led by Roman Gabriel, an on-and-off regular for four seasons.

Yet the Colts zipped into a 10–0 lead at halftime. Matte slipped through the Rams for 99 yards in 16 carries in the course of the afternoon. Altogether the Colts gained 214 yards rushing, a season high against Los Angeles. At the start of the second half, however, Gabriel spurred the Rams to two quick touchdowns and command of the game. A field goal in the second minute of the fourth quarter stretched the lead to 17–10, and the Colts looked dead as they lined up to receive the kickoff. Alvin Haymond ran the ball out to the 28-yard line. Shula sent Brown into the game. He flipped a quick pass to Hill for 4 yards. Matte replaced him. A running play failed to gain. Shula sent in Brown with the important third-down play.

"The Rams were zoning to the strong side of the field all day and were open for a slant-in," he explained. Mackey caught the ball, perfectly thrown over the middle, ran right by safety Ed Meador and had clear sailing all the way. The revived Colts moved the ball next time they gained possession and Lou Michaels kicked a 23-yard field goal to win the game, 20–17.

The race hinged on the Packers-49ers game the next day in San Francisco. If the Packers lost, the Colts were champs. If they tied, there'd be a playoff. In the closing minutes, quarterback John Brodie threw a touchdown pass to Vern Burke, an unknown end, to tie the Packers, 24–24, and create a conference playoff in Green Bay on December 26.

The whole country, or that part of it impassioned by pro football, was gripped by the drama of the Colts, who were trying to win with a quarterback whose sole experience as a pro now consisted of four quarters of play. For the playoff game with the Packers, the whole load was on Matte. Under league rules, Ed Brown was ineligible to play because he had joined the club too late. For depth the Colts had all-pro defensive back Bob Boyd, another ex-college quarterback, at Oklahoma. Like Matte, he'd never handled a handoff previously as a pro and in college was a split-T rollout runner. Unlike Matte, he didn't even know the plays.

Shula barely considered Boyd. His cram course for Matte continued. Again Tom taped a plastic band around his wrist listing formations and plays. In practice, he got a chance to work more with the receivers and improve his timing on pass plays, but basically Shula planned to continue his system of two tight ends with a stress on the running game. The only man who wasn't nervous was Matte, who had ulcers.

Shula played the percentages. Next to the lowly Steelers, the Packers were the most vulnerable team in the NFL to running, yielding an average of 141.5 yards per game. On the other hand, they were the most effective team in the league on pass defense. Their two all-pro linemen up front, Willie Davis and tackle Henry Jordan, were among the most agile in football, featuring great lateral mobility, yet not especially big and therefore vulnerable to running plays massed right at them.

The first play from scrimmage after the kickoff produced a tremendous break for the Colts. Green Bay's Starr threw a pass in the left flat to tight end Anderson. Anderson was hit hard by Lenny Lyles and fumbled the ball. Linebacker Don Shinnick picked it up and ran along the sideline as Starr angled across to cut him off near the goal line. The other Colt linebacker, Steve Stonebreaker, picked up the action and ran escort for Shinnick. He met Starr with a solid shoulder block and crumpled the Packer quarterback. While Shinnick ran into the end zone for a quick score, Starr grimaced in pain on the ground. He was led off the field with severe rib contusions. When he tried to throw the ball, he couldn't lift his arm above the waist.

Zeke Bratkowski, who never held a regular job in ten seasons with the Bears, Rams and Packers, came on to replace Starr. The odds were evening out a little for the Colts. Inspired by the quick break, they moved into field-goal range in the second quarter and Lou Michaels toed a 15-yarder to establish a 10–0 halftime lead. But the Colts never crossed midfield again under their own power in the third and fourth quarters. With one minute and fifty-eight seconds left to play in regulation time, Don Chandler kicked a 22-yard field goal to send the game into sudden-death overtime. The Colts claimed later in the winter that pictures revealed the ball was wide of the goalpost, but that's not what the record book says.

In the overtime the Colts got good field position at their own 40. On the first play, Matte ran a "statue" left and almost broke for a long gain. It's a variation of the old Statue-of-Liberty play. The quarterback stands up and turns like he's going to throw the ball to a halfback flaring wide, then pivots and runs the other way. A great tackle by linebacker LeeRoy Caffey saved the Packers. The Colts hammered into Green Bay territory. When they had third down and 4 on the Green Bay 37, Shula himself called a quarterback draw to the left. But the Packers jammed the middle against Matte, forced him back to the right and a loss of three yards. A low pass from center complicated a field-goal try from the 47 by Michaels, who kicked wide. The Packers charged back up the field, with Bratkowski throwing effectively to put Chandler in position for a 25-yard field goal in 13:39 of the overtime, and a Green Bay championship.

The result boiled down to a matter of the Packers having a quarterback, although an ancient and rusty one, who could come off the bench and given them a balanced attack with his passing, while the Colts in a pinch tried to run the ball down the Packers' throats. Matte carried the ball himself the last three times Baltimore had it. The Colts reached Green Bay territory twice the entire afternoon. Yet if Michaels had kicked that 47-yarder . . .

On such slender threads, the mystique of the quarterback was saved. The Colts, everybody agreed, failed to win primarily because they missed the gifts of John Unitas in the final crucial weeks. But there's a sequel.

136

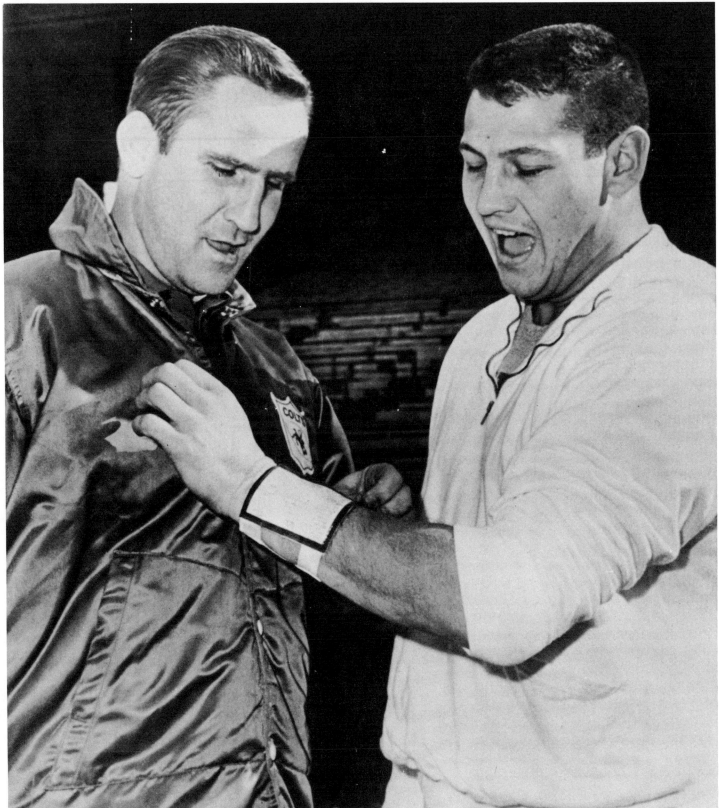

To help him with his signal calling, Coach Don Shula of Baltimore, left, taped a play card to the wrist of reserve quarterback Tom Matte before the start of the 1965 Western Conference playoff with Green Bay.

The Colts qualified for the Playoff Bowl in Miami, with Matte again the quarterback. He was strangely relaxed and catching on to the role. Dropping straight back to pass, rolling out occasionally, he completed 7 of 17 passes against the Dallas Cowboys for 165 yards and 2 touchdowns, both to flanker Jimmy Orr. He also connected on a 38-yard pitch to Mackey and a 52-yarder to Hill. Tom was voted the game's most valuable player and rushed off to show U.S. servicemen abroad how he'd done it—in game films.

Shula awaited the return of Unitas and Cuozzo in 1966, fully recovered, but had the additional delightful dilemma of Matte.

"We learned a lot," he said. "Like the value of a quarterback getting to the outside, putting pressure on the corner man. We can play Tom as a quarterback, but treat him as a halfback. We probably will keep our Matte offense as part of our system."

For emergencies only, of course.

138

Part II

10. The Originals

Sid Luckman

HAVING SID LUCKMAN AT QUARTERBACK WAS LIKE HAVING ANOTHER COACH PLAYING ON THE FIELD. HE WAS THE GREATEST PLAY-DIRECTOR I HAVE EVER SEEN.

—George Halas, owner-coach,
Chicago Bears, 1920—.

When Sid Luckman leaves the office in the Randolph Tower there's a black limousine waiting for him at the curb as he comes down from the seventh floor. It looks slightly out of place in the concrete maze of dingy gray skyscrapers and elevated railways which circle the area they call The Loop in the heart of the Chicago business district. A black-capped chauffeur is at the wheel of a long Cadillac limousine and the interior is air-conditioned, keeping the heat of summer out. If Sid is going to stay in town, he'll pull the telephone out of its crib along the rear seat and dial his wife Estelle.

The Luckmans live in the fashionable northern suburb of Highland Park. Sid built the big home two years ago, but his boy Robert is married and living in another house in town and Ellen is away at Syracuse University, while Gail's down at the University of Miami in Florida. So they ramble in it alone.

After the call, he'll direct the chauffeur to head to the exclusive North Side nearby for a dinner rendezvous at the Drake. There's a big round table reserved for him in the International Room overlooking Michigan Boulevard. His companions are the chairman of the board of a vending company, the founder and president of a national bakery chain and an oil magnate who made $20 million in the last three years. The talk is of Palm Springs and Honolulu and New York.

Sid's impeccably dressed in a conservative dark suit. Approaching fifty, he is still trim—almost slight for a former pro star—black-haired and tan. He's a solicitous host, very much at home with people, genuinely friendly, although like most high-level businessmen he never seems to sit still. Allie Sherman, his good friend, says that when Sid has a little pregame gathering at his home, twenty couples show up and there are favors for all the women.

This is how all former T-quarterbacks should wind up. If Sid Luckman isn't a millionaire, as he's reputed to be, he's close enough to keep the income-tax boys aware of his financial standing.

He is also listed with the Chicago Bears as a coach (George Halas doesn't believe in assistants). It isn't fulltime with Sid, since he's vice-president of a packaging corporation. On Thursdays he generally picks up the practice sessions of the Bears to see what's going on, and when the team travels on the road, he accompanies it as companion and confidant to Coach-President-Owner Halas. There's a father-son relationship there that's difficult to define. Papa Bear, as Halas is often called, developed (with Shaughnessy) the T-formation as the most formidable offensive weapon in football and Sid was the Baby Bear who wielded it. Together, coach and quarterback, they revolutionized the game and became rich men in their own spheres. Sid's niche is secure as a member of the Pro Football Hall of Fame.

The beginnings were humble enough. It was an Indian summer day in 1924, and Meyer Luckman came home to the flat in Flatbush, a section of Brooklyn which encompasses Prospect Park, with a package under his arm. Sidney Luckman was a curly-headed

143

kid of eight, crazy about sports. When they lived in Williamsburgh, a ghetto area under the Brooklyn Bridge, he threw a tin can in the streets. Meyer wanted him outside like the other boys in the neighborhood, not to dodge traffic, but over in the park a couple of blocks away. He unwrapped the box and tossed a brand new football to little Sid.

Red Grange was the big hero of American football in this era of the Golden Twenties in sports; in the summers all kids wanted to carry ice like Red had back home in Wheaton, Illinois, to build up his muscles. Facing Michigan in that fall of 1924 the Galloping Ghost of Illinois ran for five touchdowns, four of them in the first 12 minutes against a team that had not been beaten in three years. But for a little Jewish kid from Brooklyn, there was a basic division in the cult of the hero. Why be like Red Grange, dodging people on the sidewalk like they were imaginary tacklers, when you could be like Benny Friedman of the University of Michigan, throwing the football to Benny Oosterbaan? Sid preferred Friedman as his beau-ideal, and since it was his football and none of the other kids in the gang were affluent enough to own one, he got to be the passer in the pickup games in the park.

The knack which he developed for passing sustained the boy from Brooklyn for a quarter of a century. He became a schoolboy star at Erasmus Hall High School in Flatbush, where, for the big game with Manual, Sid was put on display before 30,000 at Ebbets Field, the "haimische" home of the zany Brooklyn Dodgers. The depression had hit by the time Sid was ready to go to college, but his football abilities attracted the attention of Coach Lou Little at Columbia University, which still glowed with the glory of having beaten Stanford on a sloppy Rose Bowl field on January 1, 1934, as Al Barabas ran the naked reverse called KF79 for the only touchdown of the rain-slogged game.

Sid enrolled at Columbia College on Morningside Heights in upper Manhattan, making the trip over by subway, in the fall of 1935. There were no athletic scholarships then, but he had an NYA (National Youth Administration) job for everyday expenses, and he washed dishes at the Zeta Beta Tau fraternity for his meals. "The first time I saw him," recalled Little, "he had class written all over him." A marginal student at first, Sid skipped the freshman football schedule to concentrate on his books. As a sophomore, he started the opening varsity game against Maine and ran 40 yards for a touchdown, then passed for two more scores. He ran the ball, punted, passed, called signals and played an alert brand of safety on defense. Grown to a solid 195 pounds, he was built for endurance, but he sometimes wondered if it was worth the physical punishment. The light Blue of Columbia lost more than it won during his three varsity seasons because Little found no replacements for his graduated Rose Bowl gang. Luckman never made a recognized All-American team in college.

There was an occasional bright spot. In his senior year, Army was upset, 20–18, as Luckman completed 18 passes for two touchdowns and ran a kickoff back 85 yards for a touchdown himself and also kicked an extra point. The Cadets lost only one other game that season, to Notre Dame, and Gar Davidson, the Army coach and eventual superintendent of the Academy, raved, "He's the perfect football player." In the next-to-last game of his college career, Columbia lost to Syracuse, 13–12, and Luckman was almost indistinguishable in the miserable mire and rain of Baker Bowl, but George Halas of the Bears had made a special trip to scout the chunky prodigy.

144

Halas didn't tell anybody, but he was looking for the perfect passer to become his quarterback and unveil the modern T-formation as the Total offense. The Bears had peddled end Eggs Manske to the Pittsburgh Steelers in exchange for the rights to the Steelers' first draft choice. Since the Steelers finished last, Halas had the choice pick of anyone in the country. He could select Davey O'Brien, who was breaking all of Sammy Baugh's passing records at Texas Christian while leading the Horned Frogs to an undefeated, untied season and an ensuing Sugar Bowl victory over Carnegie Tech. Everybody expected him to. Or he could gamble on Luckman. Halas liked the way the kid from Columbia got up after he was knocked down.

"It was a hunch more than anything else," Papa Bear said. "Maybe it was a question of size. Sid was at least 3 inches taller than Davey, and that advantage in height means an awful lot when you're under the center."

In the pro draft of college players on December 10, 1938, Halas directed the Steelers to pick Luckman as payment for Manske. Halas wasn't even sure he had a player. Sid was discouraged from the pounding he had received at Columbia. His nose had been broken three times—the carnage eventually reached eight breaks before he called it a professional career, and ridges and slants still remain on his nose as the residue of those beatings. It was big news around New York, headlines, when Luckman announced he was quitting football. In those days not every All-American rushed eagerly into the pro ranks. That year, Eric Tipton and Dan Hill of Duke's great Rose Bowl team and Brud Holland, Cornell's inspiring end—all now enshrined, as is Sid, in the college football Hall of Fame at Rutgers—passed up the pros. Clint Frank of Yale hadn't been interested the previous year, though Byron (Whizzer) White of Colorado, now a Supreme Court Justice, postponed his Rhodes scholar studies to accept a contract from the Detroit Lions. Luckman forgot the bruising memories when Halas offered him a deal worth $10,000 for his rookie year. For one thing, Sid planned to get married, and he joined the Bears after the College All-Star game in 1939.

"I was completely shocked by what I saw," Sid now recalls. "It was the first time I'd seen the T-formation, and I didn't realize it could conceivably work, where you had no blocking in front of the ball carrier. Then when I saw it in operation, I knew right there it was the most wonderful thing that could happen to me because I wasn't fast enough to be a good ball carrier.

"You also had to use your imagination. It was simple for me at first because George Halas told me to learn the left-halfback position. The Bears used the man in motion in 1939, and I was the halfback going in motion."

Records show that Luckman, with nine-year-veteran Carl Brumbaugh at quarterback, threw only 51 passes that first season. O'Brien, who went with the Philadelphia Eagles and played tailback, threw more than that in a single game. But every day, when the regular Bear practice sessions were finished, Luckman stayed at Wrigley Field and worked with Brumbaugh, just ball-handling and spinning and maneuvering. At Columbia, the tailback did a lot of spinning—Luckman cites Barabas' KF79 play as an example—so he found the adjustment easy. Playing halfback that rookie year gave him a knowledge and appreciation of the T from an angle other than the quarterback, who sat in a rocking chair and handed off while the other men gathered most of the bumps.

Sid Luckman was intense about his passing even warming up before a game.

In his first year with the Bears the former Columbia star played halfback and was the man in motion.

The debut of Sid Luckman, T-quarterback, took place in 1940, a historic year in professional football. In Sid, Halas found a sponge for his new theories. The serious, intense kid from New York—the patois of Brooklyn conspicuous in his talk despite the soft tone of his voice—absorbed the system completely. Halas had given the Bears 400 plays on his offense. Luckman knew not only his assignments, but those of every other man down to the last block.

"Sid," said Halas, "had to be familiar with over a thousand different assignments and formations."

The job wasn't quite as complicated as the myth built up around it. The Bear offense could be broken down to 60 or 70 plays, with 6 or 7 variations of each. But Luckman was so adroit in handling them that when he finally retired after a dozen seasons and the Bears skidded as a power because they lacked real direction, Halas admitted, "Sid was so smart he spoiled us."

Until Luckman took over at quarterback, the Bears had failed to win an NFL championship since 1933. It was an inspiring first year. Brumbaugh had retired, but Luckman had help at quarterback from Bernie Masterson and rookie Bob Snyder.

"In those days," says Sid, "everybody played defense—through 1942. There was no conversing between the bench and the field. If you talked, it was a 15-yard penalty. I think it put a tremendous load on any signal caller."

The Bears won the Western Conference title with an 8–3 record, unseating the Green Bay Packers. One of the losses was to Washington, 7–3, in the ninth game of the season, and the Bears weren't happy about it. With 40 seconds left in the contest, and the Bears in possession at midfield, a pass to George McAfee carried the ball to the 1-yard line. McAfee tried to feign an injury, but the Bears were penalized back to the 6. Two passes thrown by Bob Snyder, in the game for Luckman, fell incomplete, the second of them bouncing off fullback Bill Osmanski's chest in the end zone. The Bears felt Frank Filchock of the 'Skins had interfered with Osmanski on the play, costing them the game, and complained bitterly to the officials.

"Cry babies!" taunted the Redskins, led by owner George Marshall, the sharp-tongued Redskin boss who sneered: "They're strictly a first-half club. They give up."

Luckman remembers it vividly.

"We thought we'd gotten a pretty rough deal in that game," says Sid. "Some of the calls against the Bears were very unusual. We vowed we'd win the other 2 games on our schedule. We hoped the Redskins would win the Eastern Conference. That's exactly what happened, and we met on a cold day."

The date was December 8, 1940, and the site was Griffith Stadium in the nation's capital for the world championship (there was no other pro football league in those days to dispute the claim). From the Bear standpoint, the buildup to the game was a fantastic emotional experience.

"When we took the train from Chicago, like we did in those days," relates Luckman, "strange thing, there wasn't anybody talking or joking or fooling around or playing cards. Everybody had their playbooks out. Everybody was studying, and you could see there was tremendous determination and desire.

"It will probably go down in history as the greatest football exhibition of all time. It was the kind of game you dream about." That is if you happened to be a Chicago Bear. On the second play from scrimmage, fullback Osmanski took the ball from Luckman and raced 68 yards down the left sideline for a touchdown. This was the famous counterplay to the weak side that, according to Luckman, was the start of the modern T.

Max Krause of the Redskins received the kickoff on his 4-yard line and, finding an alley up the middle of the field, sprinted to the Chicago 32-yard line. Tailback Sammy Baugh worked the ball to the 26, then faded back and located end Charley Malone in the clear at the goal line. His pass was rifled on target, but Malone lost the ball in the sun and it slithered through his fingers. A Redskin field-goal try was wide. That was their last chance to score. The Bears started from their 20, and Luckman ignored the pass. Alternating his backs—Osmanski, McAfee and Ray Nolting—on straight dives through the Redskins' line, Luckman generaled the Bears to the Washington 6-inch line on 16 straight running plays. He sneaked the ball across himself. Minutes later, halfback Joe Maniaci raced 42 yards for a touchdown and the rout was on. A Luckman pass to end Ken Kavanaugh made it 28–0 at halftime. Back in the dressing room, Halas reminded them, "They say you guys are quitters, that you give up." When the Bears stormed back, he didn't even bother to put Sid in the game. The quarterback watched the action from the bench the rest of the afternoon. The Bears had one failing that day. They missed four extra-point attempts in the second half. Otherwise, they ran up a score of 73–0.

That led to Sammy Baugh's laconic reply when asked if the game would have turned out differently had Malone held the ball in the end zone for a tieing touchdown in the first quarter. "Yup," drawled Sammy. "The score might have been 73–7." Or 73–3 if the field-goal try had succeeded.

Luckman didn't make the official all-league team that year. Ace Parker, a versatile triple-threat for Brooklyn, did. But Sid made it in 1941 and again in 1942 and a year later he was voted the Most Valuable Player in the NFL.

On November 14, 1943, the Bears played the New York Giants in the Polo Grounds. It was Luckman Day; among the gifts were a $1,000 War Bond from Chicago and New York fans and another for $1,000 from the Bears. Sid was due to report shortly as an ensign in the Merchant Marine (later he served in Atlantic waters on tankers and on an army transport). A guy could fall flat on his face under such circumstances. The Giants weren't exactly patsies. They tied for the Eastern Conference title, and Steve Owen was known as the best defensive coach in football, inventor of the umbrella defense which put four deep men in a perimeter that was the best weapon yet against the passing game.

Early in the first quarter Luckman hit Jim Benton with a touchdown pass; before they changed sides he connected with Connie Berry on a 44-yarder to the end zone. The Giants got one of those scores back, but in quick order, Sid fired a goal-line pass to Hamp Pool, varied the routine by letting Harry Clark run 4 yards for the score after a long pass set it up, then flipped to Clark for 33 yards and a touchdown, located Benton again for 6 points and finally flipped a slant-in pass to George Wilson over the middle for still another. Total: 6 touchdown passes in one game, tying Baugh's record.

The Bear coaches (Halas was already in service) thought he might need a rest. They started to send Snyder in as his relief. The players waved the substitute off the field,

Luckman prepares to throw one of seven touchdown passes he completed against the New York Giants on Nov. 14, 1943.

crowing, "This is Sid's day. Let him go for it." And late in the game he threw to Hamp Pool, who made an acrobatic catch and dragged a couple of Giants over the goal line to climax a 56–7 show. The total of 7 touchdown passes in one afternoon—he threw for 433 yards altogether—still is the record, shared now with Adrian Burk of Philadelphia and Y. A. Tittle of the Giants.

But Sid doesn't consider it the big moment of his career. "My personal thrill," he said, "was throwing for 5 touchdowns in the championship game against the Redskins that year."

Those Redskins again!

As usual, the passing duel was between Luckman and Baugh. Early in the game, Luckman fielded a punt by Sammy near the sideline and, coming up the field, was hemmed in by two Redskins cutting across to cover. Sid abandoned all finesse and tucked the ball in tight while he ducked his head to drive straight ahead and try to bust through the traffic. He looked up to see Baugh bearing down on him full speed after trailing his own punt downfield. Luckman braced himself and pumped his knees a little harder. They collided like a couple of engines accidentally switched to the same siding. Baugh dove for Luckman's legs. Luckman's knee, churning like a piston, hit Sammy in the head and knocked him cold. Baugh wasn't much good the rest of the afternoon while Luckman pitched the Bears to a 41–21 victory.

A myth started to spread around Chicago that the Bears never sent Sid's football pants to the cleaners. He never got the chance to get them mussed. Maybe not his pants, but Sid's nose was broken five times while he was with the Bears, so somebody got to him. He was knocked around enough to cater to a superstition. Every Sunday, when he trotted on the field, he was careful to step across the chalked sideline with his right foot first. Once in college he turned around to acknowledge a friend's hello, forgot about the line and stepped over it with his left leg. That afternoon Brud Holland of Cornell broke two of Sid's ribs with a ground-shaking tackle. Sid was a six-footer all through his playing career. The pounding of many tackles hammered his vertebrae down to a present height of 5 feet 10½ inches.

But Sid was also smart on self-preservation. When Fred Davis, a mammoth tackle, joined the Bears, Luckman grabbed him for a roommate. While Davis had been with the Redskins, he had broken Luckman's nose. "I figured he'd be wonderful to have around for protection," Luckman said.

By 1946, the aging field general had reduced his exposure to danger to one carry from scrimmage for the whole year. He made it a memorable one. The Bears were locked in a 14–14 duel with the Giants in the fourth quarter of the championship game. The tension was heightened by the revelation that Alvin Paris, a gambler, had tried to get two Giant players to dump the game. Fullback Merle Hapes of the Giants was suspended because the offer had been made directly to him, and he hadn't reported it. Frank Filchock, the passing ace of the Giants, knew about the offer, too, but only through Hapes, so he was allowed to play, although he drifted out of the NFL to Canada the following winter.

Filchock passed brilliantly for the two Giant touchdowns, but the Bears kept pace with a Luckman pitch and an interception, and late in the game they carried a threat deep into Giant territory. On 2 straight plays, Luckman swept halfback McAfee to the left and reached the Giant 19-yard line. As he huddled the Bears, Sid reached deep into his repertoire of plays. The quarterback snapped, "Okay, boys, let's cross them up. My turn. Spread left, 97 bingo keeper . . . on four!"

The play simulated another McAfee sweep to the left, with exactly the same blocking patterns as on the previous two plays. The difference was that Sid didn't bother to feed the halfback the ball. He tucked it behind him and drifted to his right as the Giants, influenced by the blocking, went chasing after McAfee. When Sid was far enough away from the pack, he tucked the ball in the cradle of his right elbow and set sail for the goal line. By the time the Giants got wise and turned in strong pursuit, Sid had too big a lead and sprinted across for the decisive touchdown of the game. It was the one and only time he carried the ball in 1946.

It was also, really, his last hurrah. Sid had two more very active seasons as the field general of the Bears, but they never won another title. When the All-America Conference was organized in 1946, the Chicago Rockets offered him a job as player-coach at $25,000 a year—the highest salary ever paid a player until that time—and they deposited $125,000 in the bank to cement a five-year deal. But Sid turned them down because of loyalty to the Bears and because his own business interests outside football were starting to thrive. As his career waned, he also refused a couple of head-coaching jobs elsewhere in the NFL. As a player, he gave way slowly to the influx of postwar quarterbacks on the Bear roster—Johnny Lujack of Notre Dame, George Blanda of .Kentucky, Bobby Layne of Texas, Nick Sacrinty of Wake Forest (there are those who say he would have been the best but he quit after one season to become a doctor), Steve Romanik of Villanova. In 1949, working closely with Luckman, Midwest hero Lujack took over the Bears' first-string job and might have had a long and successful career but for a shoulder injury (suffered on defense) which crimped his passing style and forced him into early retirement after 1951.

Luckman quit after the 1950 campaign, making it an even dozen seasons on the pro rolls. With him, the Bears won five division titles and four world championships. He was as self-effacing at the end of his career as he'd been the day he came in, a rookie bewildered by the mechanics of a new offense and a new position. Early in his career he convinced himself there was no such thing as the indispensable man. The Bears had the ball on their opponents' 20-yard line, leading handily, so Sid promised each of the long-suffering seven linemen up front they could call the signals in rotation. Within 5 plays the Bears had scored a touchdown. "The right tackle and end were mad at me," grinned Sid. "They got gypped out of their calls."

Although Halas, and many others, rate him the smartest quarterback in history, he wasn't infallible. In 1948, the Chicago Cardinals played in the Western Conference of the NFL and challenged their North Side neighbors for the title. They came down to the last game of the season tied for first place. With two minutes left on the clock, the Bears trailed, 24–21, but were in excellent field position with a first down on the Cardinal 10-yard line. Their running game was going good, but Luckman abruptly switched tactics and called for a down-and-out pass. It was intercepted by Red Cochran of the Cards and

Luckman, an infrequent runner as a quarterback, surprised the Washington Redskins by bursting through this gaping hole in the 1943 title game.

As an elder statesman in 1948, Sid Luckman found himself surrounded on the Bears' quarterback corps by Johnny Lujack, left, and Bobby Layne.

cost the Bears the title. "It was a nightmare for me," said Sid. "I should have called for an off-tackle play. I'm sure we could have rushed the ball across in 4 plays."

His career passing statistics, 904 completions in 1,744 attempts, are respectable but modest alongside the career totals of such later flingers as Tittle, Layne and Unitas. He never officially led the league in passing, and some critics said he threw rainbows. But for the decade in which he flourished, Sid was Sammy Baugh's only serious challenger as the greatest passer in football. Sammy threw short. Sid threw long. And they made a pact at the peak of the debate about their merits. They respected each other. Sammy would always say Sid was the greatest and Sid would always say Sammy was the greatest.

And neither was too far wrong.

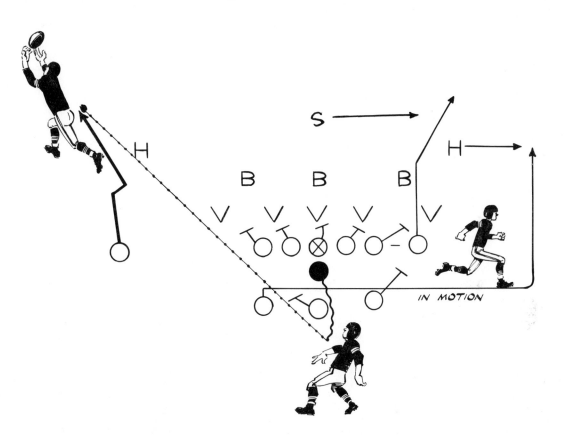

Sid Luckman describes his favorite play:

"The Chicago Bears had a lot of success in my early days of the T formation with a pass to Kenny Kavanaugh.

"Ken was our left end and isolated man-to-man with the defensive halfback by splitting left.

"Our halfback on the same side went in motion ·to the right, making the defense conscious of that side. Our right end went down several yards and also broke right.

"Because he was an experienced and excellent receiver, Kavanaugh called for the maneuver he preferred. In the diagram shown, it was a zig-out.

"My job was simply to get the ball to him."

SID LUCKMAN

BORN: Nov. 21, 1916   HEIGHT: 6'0"   WEIGHT: 195

Chicago Bears, 1939–50

PASSING RECORD:

Year	Att.	Comp.	Yards Gained	T.D.	Pct.	Longest	Int.
1939	51	23	636	5	45.1	62	4
1940	105	48	941	6	45.7	57	9
1941	119	68	1181	9	57.1	65	6
1942	105	57	1023	10	54.2	57	12
1943	202	110	2194	28	54.5	66	12
1944	143	71	1018	11	49.7	86	11
1945	217	117	1725	14	53.9	65	10
1946	229	110	1826	17	48.0	48	16
1947	323	176	2712	24	54.5	81	31
1948	163	89	1047	13	54.6	53	14
1949	50	22	200	1	44.0	34	3
1950	37	13	180	1	35.1	44	2
TOTALS	1744	904	14,683	139	51.8	86	130

RUSHING RECORD:

Year	Att.	Yards Gained	Longest	Ave.
1939	24	42	11	1.7
1940	23	−65	14	−2.7
1941	19	21	20	1.1
1942	13	24	9	1.9
1943	22	−40	8	−1.8
1944	20	−96	7	−4.8
1945	36	−118	22	−3.2
1946	25	−76	25	−3.0
1947	10	86	40	8.6
1948	8	11	18	1.4
1949	3	4	14	1.3
1950	2	1	1	.5
TOTALS	205	−206	40	−1.0

PUNTING RECORD:

Year	No.	Ave.	Longest
1939	27	44.4	67
1940	27	42.0	70
1941	13	41.0	52
1942	24	40.6	60
1943	34	35.9	78
1944	20	34.2	63
1945	36	36.0	61
1946	33	37.4	69
1947	5	35.4	42
1948	10	38.4	49
1949	1	16.0	16
1950	—	—	—
TOTALS	230	36.7	78

Sammy Baugh

IN FOOTBALL, YOU HAVE THROWERS,
AND YOU HAVE PASSERS . . . AND THEN
YOU HAVE SAMMY BAUGH.

—Hugh (Bones) Taylor, end,
Washington Redskins,
1947–54.

Professional football first felt the influence of Samuel Adrian Baugh in 1937. He was a stringbean from the west of Texas, too skinny even to be called a lanky Texan. Still is.

It was his first season in the National Football League. The Washington Redskins played the Chicago Bears for the championship, and they were backed up against their own goal line. Baugh was a rookie tailback for the Redskins. The philosophy of those days was that in such a situation you were supposed to punt out of danger.

As the 'Skins huddled in their end zone, Baugh drawled, "We're a-goin' into punt formation but we're really gonna pass." The ball was on the 9-yard line. The goalpost shaded Sammy as he took the snap from center, fingers extended. The Bears edged closer to try to block the kick. Sammy straightened up and fired the ball like a slingshot downfield to Cliff Battles, his halfback, for a 42-yard gain. And the Redskins drove in for a touchdown.

Sammy threw 3 touchdown passes that afternoon—on tosses of 55 and 78 yards to end Wayne Millner and 35 yards to halfback Ed Justice. The last produced the decisive score in a 28–21 thriller for the title. He gained 335 yards on 18 completions. For that era they were extraordinary figures. For that matter, and especially in a championship game, they'd be great any time. The career of Sammy Baugh, the greatest passer in history, was under way.

The city of Washington has been notably devoid of champions, except for some self-proclaimed entries in the Congressional Record, but it has been blessed with two unsurpassed virtuosos in throwing. Walter Johnson pitched for the Washington Senators over a 21-year span and won 416 games. In a more rugged area, Sammy Baugh slung passes for the Washington Redskins from 1937 through 1952, sixteen seasons, and was responsible for five division and two NFL titles—although, like Johnson, he was generally surrounded by mediocrity, especially in the last half of his career.

There are still a couple of testimonials to his finesse in the record book. In 1945, he completed 70.3 percent of his passes, and in a game against the Pittsburgh Steelers that season he set a standard by hitting 18 of 21. Both are NFL records. From an historical standpoint, they're noteworthy because Sammy was playing his second season as a T-quarterback. He successfully bridged the transition from the single-wing to the T, though he was reluctant at first. "Why that's the easiest position in football," he scoffed, "quarterback in the T-formation. All you do is hand the ball off and pass."

But then he mused, "If they'd had the T when I started playing pro, I could have lasted until I was forty years old."

Sammy Baugh was bred in the era of the whole football player. He passed, ran, blocked, called signals, punted and played a nifty brand of safety on defense. Some of it shows in the figures. He led the NFL in punting more times (five) than any other kicker in history; he holds the highest punting average for a season (51.3 yards) and for a game (59.4 yards on 5 boots against the Detroit Lions in 1940). And here's one that'll surprise a lot of people: he shares the record for most interceptions in a game, picking off 4 against the Detroit Lions in 1943.

What doesn't show is the unique personality and toughness of Baugh, an authentic rawhide character out of Texas. Right today, he wears a 10-gallon hat and faded jeans, with scuffed, pointed boots and a big chaw of tobacco bulging in his cheeks. He speaks the pokey ranch language, maybe faster than most Texans because it fits his taut, muscular frame. The wit is quick and dry.

When Sammy was inducted into the Texas Hall of Fame (he's already in both football halls of fame), his old college coach, L. R. (Dutch) Meyer made the introductory remarks. "I want you to know the greatest gambler I ever saw in a football suit," Dutch pointed to his former passing ace.

And Sammy got up and grinned, "You heard what he said. So I want you all to know the guy who was telling me what plays to call out there."

Sammy came a long way from the country boy who in 1938 sat through a long eulogy at the National Press Club of Washington and was called upon to get up and say hello. Sam stood up, tersely said, "Hello," and sat down.

But although he first arrived in Washington in cowboy regalia, Sam wasn't a product of the wide-open spaces. The pointed boots worn on orders of owner George Preston Marshall pinched and hurt his feet, and he felt just plain silly. Sammy was originally a town boy from Sweetwater, a switching stop for the Atchison, Topeka and Santa Fe, at the bottom of the Texas panhandle. His father worked for the railroad as a checker. They had a backyard, and Sammy suspended an old tire from a tree. He'd set the tire to swing like a pendulum, then he'd step back 10 or 15 paces and try to throw a football through it. That's how he developed his skill as a passer, and right until the day he quit, at the age of thirty-eight, Sam was still throwing footballs tirelessly (no pun intended) to sharpen his accuracy.

Because he was skinny and tall, his first position was end at Sweetwater High. At a practice session, he picked up a poorly thrown ball 40 yards down the field, turned and fired it back on a line to the scrimmage line. The coach whistled and said, "From now on, boy, you're a passer."

Actually, he was a baseball player, the best third baseman in Nolan County, and went over to Abilene to play on weekends. Dutch Meyer saw him there. Dutch then coached baseball at Texas Christian while handling the freshman football team. He told head grid coach Francis Schmidt, "I found me a real baseball player. Incidentally, I think he plays a little football, too." Schmidt frowned after his first look: "Too fragile. He won't last."

By Sammy's sophomore season, Dutch was the head football coach and young Baugh was his boy. He recognized the brilliant talent for passing and went overboard, even in that air-crazy Southwest Conference. Sam led the Horned Frogs to the Sugar Bowl his junior year, and his great punting (14 times, averaging 50 yards) on a wet field set up the winning field goal in a 3–2 triumph over Louisiana State. As his reputation spread so did his sensitivity about his role as a passer and the way his teammates kidded "the great Baugh."

158

Meyer finally called a squad meeting and said, "We believe the best way for us to win is for Sammy to pass, so quit kidding him about it."

Against Texas, during his senior year of 1936, All-American center Ki Aldrich broke from the huddle and before squatting over the ball, addressed the opposition Longhorns: "Gentlemen, Mr. Baugh is about to launch a pass again. I can't tell you where it'll go, but it'll be good. So be ready." Sammy kept Ki's word and drilled a 25-yard completion. As they lined up again, Ki shook his head at the Longhorns, "Now I hate to be an old I-told-you-so, but—."

During his three years for Texas Christian, Sammy completed 274 passes in 599 attempts for 3,439 yards and 39 touchdowns.

Sammy was an All-American the last two years, but the baseball fires still blazed in his ambition. After graduation he signed a contract with the St. Louis Cardinals and in the summer of 1937 made the tour of their farm system—Sacramento, Columbus, Rochester. He whipped the ball so hard from third base they switched him to short for the longer throw, and for the preservation of first basemen. That's where he really got his nickname, Slingin' Sam. There were two things wrong. First, he couldn't hit the curve ball. Second, the Cardinals were bringing along another young shortstop named Marty Marion, who eventually made it all the way to St. Louis.

Meanwhile, the football Redskins had just moved their franchise from Boston to Washington. George Preston Marshall, a flamboyant promoter, was looking for something to jack up the attraction, and Baugh was just the ticket. He went real "big"—$5,000—in his offer to the TCU star. It was the best investment Marshall ever made. His first year, Baugh straightened out the Skin finances so that the team showed a profit of $20,000 compared to an $85,000 deficit in '36.

With Marshall shrewdly promoting the Baugh image, the Redskins at one point had forty consecutive sellouts. "He took the Redskins out of the red," gloated the owner, "and put them in the black."

Sammy did more than that. He won games. He fulfilled a commitment to play with the College All-Stars and threw a touchdown pass to Gaynell Tinsley of LSU which beat the champion Green Bay Packers, 6–0. In his season debut with the Redskins, he faced the sturdy, defense-minded New York Giants. Sammy passed 16 times, completed 11, for a 13–3 win. He took the Skins to an Eastern Conference crown, applying the clincher in a showdown against the Giants in the Polo Grounds. Sammy went 11-for-15 in a 49–14 rout, then had to run for his life as the fans broke through the cops' lines to demonstrate their adulation. Sammy was the league's leading passer and voted, as a rookie, to the official all-league team.

Of course, he had good company on the Redskins. With him in the backfield were Cliff Battles, one of the greatest runners in history, hard-hitting Ernie Pinckert and Riley Smith, a demon blocker. The line was anchored by all-pro tackle Turk Edwards, with ends Charley Malone and Wayne Millner to catch passes.

For the next ten seasons, the Redskins never had a losing record, winning five division titles. Sammy prospered, too. As long as people thought he was a cowboy, Sam decided to oblige and invested in a ranch at Rotan, Texas, due north of his old home

He was called Slinging Sammy Baugh because he could fire it like a shot from any angle.

town of Sweetwater. Eventually he increased his holdings to 6,500 acres and bred pure Hereford cattle.

Over the years his football income was estimated at $300,000, and Sam said pithily, "Half went into taxes, and half went into Texas."

His spread is in the red-brush country at the Double Mountain fork of the Brazos River. He began to dress the part of a rancher and learned to use a lariat, competing in local rodeos. He went Hollywood, too, making a serial called "King of the Texas Rangers." He had one big line. He mounted his steed and said to the heroine, "C'mon, gal, we gotta git goin'." No one was quite sure if the command was addressed to the girl or the horse.

In reality, Sam became a master of the bon mot. He was invited to address a gathering of FBI men, at a time when the Redskin line was weak and he was getting plastered every Sunday. He squinted at the G-men sharply and said, "This is the most protection I've had all year."

A big rookie reported to the Redskins and was introduced to Baugh. "Gee whiz," the young giant gushed, "I've always dreamed of playing with the great Sammy Baugh."

"What position do you play, son?" asked Sam.

"Tackle."

"Tell you what," said Sam. "You knock hell out of some of those opposing linemen, and I'll dream of you."

As football, with its complex defenses, got more complicated, he observed, "The algebra teacher used to be the football coach; now the football coach is the algebra teacher."

The most famous Baugh retort came after the 73–0 lacing by the Chicago Bears in the 1940 title game. Sam was asked if the game would have been different had an end not dropped a touchdown pass in the first quarter.

"Yeah, 73–7."

Hidden in the history books is the fact that Baugh and the Redskins avenged the 1940 73–0 debacle a couple of years later when they met the Bears again in the 1942 championship game. With their famed T attack carrying them through the regular 11-game schedule undefeated, the Bears were heavily favored. During the regular season they had outscored Washington, which still used the archaic single-wing, 376 points to 227.

Tackle Lee Artoe of the Bears scooped up a Redskin fumble in the second quarter and lumbered 50 yards to a touchdown. The extra-point attempt was missed. Stuck deep in his own territory on the 12 after the kickoff, Sam faked a pass and drove his foot into the ball for a surprise 83-yard punt that rocked the Bears. A pass by Sid Luckman was intercepted, and Baugh retaliated quickly with a 32-yard touchdown pitch to Wilbur Moore. The conversion by Bob Masterson made it 7–6 at halftime.

In the third quarter, Baugh changed his strategy. The Bears spread to stop his passes, so he ran the ball at them twice and on third down, when they were sure he'd throw, he ran it once more himself for a first down. He kept the ball on the ground for 12 straight plays as the Redskins drove to a touchdown. That's how it ended, 14–6. Sammy played the full 60 minutes.

161

The Redskins have never won another NFL title. The Bears clobbered them in 1943 as Baugh missed most of the action with a brain concussion. The merits of the T were now obvious, so the Redskins converted in 1944, putting Baugh up behind the center. "It's like playing with top hat and tails," he cracked. But the adjustment wasn't easy. He never became a slick ball-handler, yet by 1945 he had the Skins on top of the Eastern Conference again. The championship game was played in raw, cold Cleveland Stadium, the winds blowing off Lake Erie so cold they froze the valves in the band's trumpets and so strong they made Baugh look like a scarecrow in a wintry breeze. The Cleveland Rams (fated to move West to Los Angeles the next year) were their opponents, featuring their own brilliant passer, a rookie quarterback named Bob Waterfield whose greatest fame till then was that he was married to Jane Russell. Each team scored two touchdowns, all on passes, though the Rams missed one conversion. There was a whisper of the future, however, in the fact that both Redskin scores were flipped by Frank Filchock, a young passer from Indiana who filled in for Baugh. The decisive action came early in the first quarter when Sammy was in the game. Daring as ever, he backed into his own end zone to throw a pass.

"Everyone expected Sam to punt," recalled Wayne Millner, the intended receiver, "because we were backed up to the goal line. There was no one within a mile of me when I broke into the clear. But as Baugh threw the ball, the wind shifted and blew the ball into the goalpost. Instead of being ahead, 7–0, on a 105-yard play, we were behind, 2–0."

The play later caused a change in the rules, so that a pass hitting the goalpost was simply grounded, but at that time it meant a safety. And that safety was costly, as the Redskins lost, 15–14. The final irony was that on the Ram conversion, which meant the ball game, Waterfield's kick hit the crossbar, and then crawled over the bar for the point.

The Redskins began to produce possible successors to their aging passer. Filchock was followed by Harry Gilmer of Alabama. Each year as Sammy reported to camp he was asked if it would be his last, and he replied laconically, "Got to see how I do here. Maybe last year was my last year."

In 1947, his eleventh season, they finally arranged a Baugh Day in Washington. The fans' contributions produced a new stationwagon on the field, and a few people suspected it might be needed to cart Baugh's body away. The Redskins were in miserable shape. Marshall, with a phone to the bench, was running his coaches in and out of Washington on a shuttle, ten in ten years. Ray Flaherty, the prewar coach, never came back, skipping to the rival All-America Conference. When Baugh Day came up, it was against the Chicago Cardinals, destined to win the Western Conference title, and the Skins were in the throes of a five-game losing streak.

The field was muddy as Baugh took charge at midfield in the first quarter. He threw twice, and the ball was on the 4-yard line. Once more, and Dick Poillon clutched the bullet throw in the end zone. From his 42, he started again and wound up with a pass to Paul McKee for a touchdown as the second quarter started. His first-half statistics showed 11 for 13, and the Redskins, adding a field goal, led, 17–7.

He was just warming up. A 36-yard pass to Doug Turley, followed by a 34-yarder to Bones Taylor produced a quick touchdown at the start of the third quarter. This was a tough Cardinal team, with its dream backfield of Paul Christman, Charley Trippi, Elmer Angsman and Pat Harder, plus Marshall Goldberg to spark the defense. Baugh stunned them with two more touchdown passes in that period, then added a final one late in the game to wrap up a 45–21 victory. The totals for the day added up to 25 completions for 355 yards and 6 touchdowns.

Baugh considered it his greatest performance—"I guess because it was my day and I did pretty good."

Bones Taylor, by then his favorite receiver and later a coaching cohort, remembered precisely when the zing went out of Baugh's passing.

"Sam was born with a sense of timing," said Taylor. "I asked him once how he decided whether he was going to give the ball to you in a hurry or loft it for you to run under. He said, 'I don't know. I never did stop to think about it. I just do it, and it either works or it doesn't.'

"We were playing the Giants in the Polo Grounds back in 1950. Sam called a 'quick' where I break out of the line of scrimmage and look back at him. He pumps the ball at me. A quick and go. The defensive man would come up on me at the fake. He'd be coming at me in one direction, and I would go by him. Well, I went by Emlen Tunnell and Sam didn't give me the ball as he normally had all these years.

"He'd flip and I'd run under the ball. This time he held on to the ball. I had to turn around and catch it 25 yards down the field facing back toward Sam. He had lofted the ball and waited too long to throw it. So I thought to myself, right then, 'Sam's reflexes are gone. He's through.' The next year he didn't play much."

And 1952 was his last, mainly as a counselor to Eddie LeBaron, the little man from College of the Pacific who had returned from the Korean War. Sam went out with a bang. The Cardinals opened the season. Sam had alternated with LeBaron in the exhibition games and hurt his throwing hand. But with the real shooting, he trotted out to start his sixteenth active season. For a moment the clock was turned back.

He flicked a quick completion. A second. A third. The Cards couldn't stop him. He had 9 straight, and they were beginning to bruise the old man—thirty-eight years old now—before and after he released the ball. On his tenth straight, Don Joyce, a defensive tackle, climbed all over him and then, using 255 pounds as a lever, rode Baugh to the ground. Sharp, stinging pain traveled from Sam's bad right hand up to his shoulder. He couldn't touch it as he dragged himself up and back to the huddle.

He threw just once more, completing a short toss—11 straight—and Joyce was on him again. As the tackle charged, Sam's fist shot out and rocked the Cardinal back. Joyce came up swinging. The fight was short, indecisive, but vicious, and the officials threw them both out of the game. That was it for Sammy Baugh as a passer. He came in once more late in the season, on a token appearance to hold the ball for an extra-point attempt, allowing Washington one last look.

At 6–2 and 180 pounds, Sammy had managed to protect himself for a long time. Early in his career he returned a punt against the Giants when the lights went out—his own—and Sammy hit the ground with such force the seismograph needle at Fordham wavered. Out of the haze, he was aware of someone helping him to his feet and saying,

In this remarkable sequence, taken early in Sammy Baugh's career, the fabled Redskin played tailback. He took the direct snap from center, straightened up to throw as blocking back Riley Smith (11) came across to head off a rusher (99) and give him precious extra time to set for the throw. That's Baugh (33) getting the ball off in good style, though hit around the waist. And it heads straight for the receiver.

"Ain't this a helluva way to make a living, Sammy?" It was Mel Hein, the all-pro Giant center who had hit him.

After his playing days, Sam coached at Hardin-Simmons in Abilene, Texas, which fitted in fine with his ranching at nearby Rotan. He later moved into pro ball, serving two stormy years with the New York Titans (now the Jets) in the American Football League and another with the Houston Oilers as head coach. The results were mild, the work demanding. "If I could coach during the season and spend the rest of the time on my ranch, I'm happy," said Sammy. His old Washington teammate, Harry Gilmer, signed him as a backfield assistant for Detroit in 1966.

Over the years he wore out 100 jerseys and 60 pairs of shoes, but he managed to stick with the same shoulderpads, tattered remnants which eventually were called Blue Jays because they shrank to no bigger than a corn plaster.

Once a lineman on the other team was digging him with elbows and knees on every play, and Wee Willie Wilkins, a hulking tackle for the Redskins, offered to exact reprisal.

"Never you mind," snapped Sam.

On the next day the lineman came piling in on him as usual, and in those days face guards weren't worn. Sam waited till the last instant—as per directions to the Revolutionary soldiers at Yorktown—and then drilled the football right into the face of the enemy. It hit him square between the eyes.

One thing Sammy Baugh could always do was hit the target.

SAMMY BAUGH

BORN: March 17, 1914   HEIGHT: 6'2"   WEIGHT: 180

Washington Redskins, 1937–52

PASSING RECORD:

Year	Att.	Comp.	Yards Gained	T.D.	Pct.	Longest	Int.
1937*	171	81	1127	7	47.3	59	14
1938	128	63	853	5	49.2	60	11
1939	96	53	518	6	55.2	44	9
1940*	177	111	1367	12	63.7	81	10
1941	193	106	1236	10	54.9	55	19
1942	225	132	1524	16	58.7	53	11
1943*	239	133	1754	23	55.7	72	19
1944	146	82	849	4	56.2	71	8
1945*	182	128	1669	11	70.3	70	4
1946	161	87	1163	8	54.0	51	17
1947*	354	210	2938	25	59.3	74	15

Old No. 33 trotted off a Washington gridiron for the last time, after 16 seasons, on Dec. 15, 1952.

Year	Att.	Comp.	Yards Gained	T.D.	Pct.	Longest	Int.
1948	315	185	2599	22	58.7	86	23
1949*	255	145	1903	18	56.9	76	14
1950	166	90	1130	10	54.2	56	11
1951	154	67	1104	7	43.5	53	17
1952	33	20	152	2	60.6	20	1
TOTALS	2995	1693	21,886	186	56.5	86	203

* led NFL

RUSHING RECORD:

Year	Att.	Yards Gained	Longest	Ave.
1937	86	240	41	2.7
1938	15	35	9	2.3
1939	14	46	13	3.2
1940	20	16	5	.8
1941	27	12	16	.4
1942	20	61	28	3.1
1943	19	−42	4	−2.3
1944	19	−38	17	−2.0
1945	19	−71	34	−3.6
1946	18	−76	13	−4.2
1947	25	47	19	1.9
1948	4	4	7	1.0
1949	13	67	17	5.2
1950	7	27	11	3.9
1951	11	−5	7	−.5
1952	1	1	1	1.0
TOTALS	318	324	41	1.0

PUNTING RECORD:

Year	No.	Ave.	Longest
1937	—	—	—
1938	—	—	—
1939	26	38.0	69
1940	35	57.4	85
1941	30	48.7	75
1942	37	46.6	74
1943	50	45.9	81
1944	44	40.6	76
1945	33	43.3	57
1946	33	45.1	60
1947	35	43.7	67
1948	—	—	—
1949	1	53.0	53
1950	9	39.1	58
1951	4	55.3	58
1952	1	48.0	48
TOTALS	338	44.9	85

Frank Albert, Paul Christman, Tommy Thompson

WHEN FRANKIE ALBERT IS QUARTER-
BACKING, IT'S LIKE HAVING A COACH ON
THE FIELD, AND THAT'S GIVING THE BEN-
EFIT OF THE DOUBT TO THE COACHES.

—Dud DeGroot, coach,
Washington Redskins,
Los Angeles Dons

Frankie Albert was too small and too slow, and his Stanford University team of 1939 won only 1 game. Paul Christman could pass like a guy on a hot streak in Las Vegas, but he wasn't fast enough to cross the street on a green light. Tommy Thompson could see out of only one eye, and couldn't run much either.

In a nutshell, there's the proof. The profession of T-quarterback brought out the best in three men who made notable contributions to football in the 1940's, when the pros were just beginning to win acceptance.

Clark Shaughnessy, one of the original architects of the T-formation, argues to this day that "Frankie Albert was the greatest quarterback of all time."

Pretty bold statement coming from a man whose coaching included the handling of such men as Sid Luckman, Sammy Baugh, Tobin Rote, Bob Waterfield and Norm Van Brocklin!

It also indicated that maybe some sentiment had penetrated the crust of "Old Soup," as they used to call Shaughnessy when he went to coach Stanford in 1940 and took over a disreputable squad with a 1–8–1 record. In his briefcase Shaughnessy had the outlines of a new system he was going to introduce into college ball, the same one the Bears were already unfurling on the pros—the modern T. And he looked around for an engineer.

He settled on a cocky kid named Albert. The physical dimensions certainly didn't impress Shaughnessy. The kid was 5–10 and weighed 160 pounds, and he didn't look as if he'd grow any more (he didn't all the time he played football). Down south in Glendale, a suburb of Los Angeles, the high school coach wouldn't give him a uniform when he turned out for football as a sophomore.

But he had a certain brashness and leadership. Shaughnessy had brought along Bernie Masterson, the quarterback of the Chicago Bears, to help him install the new system. Masterson looked at Albert and indicated to young Frank he was puny for a rugged contact sport like football.

"Yeah," flipped Frankie, "but I'm strong as a bull and six times as smart."

Later, Shaughnessy was to observe, "He took hold of something entirely new, untried and untested in college ranks and made it a championship operation as well as setting a pattern which 90 percent of all football teams still use today."

The first time Shaughnessy met with the Stanford squad, he diagrammed a play on the board and said, "You boys will make 8 touchdowns with this play this season." Albert led the laughers. A week before their opener they scrimmaged the freshman team and were beaten.

The first game was with the University of San Francisco, picked in a preseason forecast to finish seventh in the nation. The Dons were 7-point favorites. "We knew we had something good," recalled Albert, "but we never figured it would leave USF completely mystified. They never had the faintest idea of what was coming. On our man-in-motion stuff, they never covered Pete Kmetovic. They didn't know what to do. I've never had as much fun in a football game."

Stanford upset the 7-point favorites, 27–0, and the Albert era began. Just what qualified the unsuccessful tailback of '39 to be the All-American quarterback of '40?

"A superb ball-handler," noted Shaughnessy, "a magician with the ball, wonderfully observing and a gifted field general. He was neither strong nor fast. His talents were primarily those of a faker; he could fool people and by temperament he ate up that sort of assignment."

Legerdemain kept Albert in business for seven years as a pro with the San Francisco 49ers. He was a lefthanded passer, and the purists frown on that because the ball rotates opposite to the way most receivers are used to catching it. He couldn't throw the long ball, and he had a limited field of vision because of his height, but he almost patented the bootleg play as a compensating device.

Over the years the favorite San Francisco image of Albert was the little southpaw faking a handoff to Norm Standlee, his fullback mate at Stanford, too, then tucking the ball alongside his hip as he drifted to his left, either stopping to throw a pass to end Allyn Beals or continuing around end with deceptively long, splay-footed strides.

Albert was a natural for the 49ers. It meant coming only 30 miles up the Peninsula from the site of his heroics as an All-American. As a varsity junior he took Stanford to the Rose Bowl and a 21–13 verdict over Nebraska. Standlee was graduated to the Chicago Bears, but Albert repeated as an All-American in 1941. He wrote Standlee, "Tell the Bears to save me that quarterback spot. . . . We'll have fun." So what if a guy named Luckman was running the Bear offense. After graduation, Frankie even picked up $6,000 for a quick Hollywood epic called "The Spirit of Stanford."

However, Pearl Harbor came along. Albert spent most of the next four years as a damage-control officer aboard a naval vessel in the Pacific, cruising the waters of Sitko Bay. Meanwhile, the All-America Conference came into being, with San Francisco blueprinted as a member. One of owner Tony Morabito's first acts was to track down Albert while he was still in the Navy and sign him for the embryonic team, which would need a lot of local color. Together they went to Standlee in early 1946 and enticed the fullback away from the Bears. The 49ers had the makings. With Buck Shaw, another northern California favorite from Santa Clara, as the coach, they had successful seasons as long as the AAC lasted, four years. Their cumulative record was surpassed only by the fabulous Cleveland Browns—the Browns lost 4 games over that span, 2 of them to San Francisco, including an astounding 56–28 pounding at Kezar Stadium in which Albert threw five touchdown passes. However, the 49ers were unfortunate to be in the same division as the Browns. And Albert was unfortunate to come along at the same time as Otto Graham, the super passer of the Browns. The all-league quarterback spot was automatically allocated to Automatic Otto, who had Paul Brown to call his plays for him.

Albert had a flair that captivated strategists. He was unorthodox. Once he threw 4 passes in a row to Beals, all using the same pattern. He ran halfback Johnny Strzykalski into the line to change the pace, then came right back with exactly the same pass pattern 3 more times.

He was unpredictable. No other southpaw has ever made it as a pro quarterback. Sometimes he passed on fourth down. Early in a game against Buffalo, he tried a pass that went for a long gain. He never tried it again the whole day. Why?

172

Frankie Albert of the San Francisco 49ers was the only successful lefthanded quarterback in pro ball.

With teammate Norm Standlee (72) on the ground, Frankie Albert is still a threat against the Bears as he rolls out on a run-pass option.

"I liked the defense they were in," he explained. "I was afraid if I used the play again and it worked, they might change their defense."

There's a tendency to downgrade Albert because his passing was sometimes erratic and he didn't have the arm to put the ball out there 50 or 60 yards with accuracy. One San Francisco critic wrote that he was a "cutie with a million-dollar head and a 10-cent arm." Still, he completed better than 50 percent of his throws (53.8, to be exact, for his career), and in 1948 threw 29 touchdown passes, an AAC and team mark that stood until John Brodie broke it in 1965, seventeen seasons later. Albert shared the Most Valuable Player award with Graham in '48. The next year, the last for the AAC, he was also voted to the all-league team, as a halfback, a token recognition of his versatility.

Not generally known was the fact that Albert had impaired vision in his left eye and wore contact lenses on the field.

When the 49ers were absorbed into the NFL in 1950, Albert was starting to slide as a player. A touch of the quickness—the kind that enabled him to retreat hastily from his spot behind the center and quick-kick on third down in strategic spots—had faded. The competition in the NFL was slightly stiffer. The gambles were a little riskier.

"In 1952, we were leading the boys of Halas U. (Chicago Bears) by a score of 17–10," said Albert, recalling one blooper. "It was fourth down (seems as though I always have my troubles on fourth down), about 4 yards to go with the ball on our 34-yard line. I called for a punt in the huddle but as I stood the normal 10 yards from center, hands outstretched, awaiting the snap of the ball, I noticed old No. 7, Ed Sprinkle, was coiled directly in front of our left end, planning to jam him and thus prevent his covering my punt.

"Knowing that he did not plan to rush the kicker, and realizing there was a very stiff wind blowing in my face, I elected to take several quick steps to my left and watch the development of the play before punting a 'rugby' kick—on the run and, in this case, a low spiral that would travel better into the wind.

"Well, at this point I made what turned out to be the *wrong* decision. I thought Sprinkle was too far to the inside and I could run around him for the first down. The so-called 'meanest man in football' saw my move and recovered in time to tackle me 1 yard short of a first down."

From that point, the Bears shortly kicked a field goal by George Blanda, later added a touchdown in the final minutes for a 20–17 victory.

"I should have punted, of course," mused Albert.

In 1951, when the Baltimore franchise folded and the players were split up among the various teams, the 49ers tapped a bald-headed passer named Y. A. Tittle as their choice. Buck Shaw kept him on the bench most of the first season, letting him absorb the 49er system. He turned Tittle loose in the last three games, all won by San Francisco to produce a second-place finish, only half a game away from a title. And in '52, the younger Yat gradually took over the quarterbacking job from Albert. Frankie's pride was piqued. He was too far along in his career to start warming the bench, so he abruptly retired. The following June the itch got him and he accepted an offer from Calgary to play in the Canadian league. It was an abortive experience and Frankie quit for good after the 1953 season.

174

"If I had it to do over again," he said, "I think I would have stayed in football a little longer as a player. I quit when I was only thirty-two years old and such men as Tittle went on and on."

He became an assistant coach with the 49ers, and in 1956 was elevated to the head job. Frankie hung on almost three years. In 1957, the 49ers got as far as a divisional playoff with the Detroit Lions, blew a 27–7 lead in the third quarter and have yet to win in their division. The odd part about Albert as a head coach was that he delegated almost all the strategy to his assistants. The brainiest quarterback of them all was only a figurehead as a strategist. He resigned late in the 1958 season. "I was too emotional a guy to coach," he said. But Albert was businesslike enough to retain a 5 percent interest in the 49ers. He moved to beautiful Pebble Beach, south of San Francisco. His daughter Jane is a nationally ranked tennis player, and Frank occasionally dabbles with football as a television color commentator.

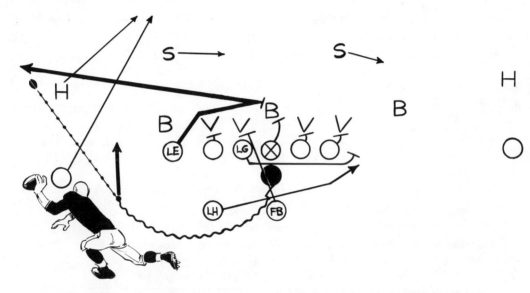

Frankie Albert describes his favorite play:

"My pet play, called 27 Cross Buck Bootleg, is best executed in a short yardage situation, when the opposition is looking for a running play.

"In the diagram, notice the swing of the play is to the right with off guard (*left guard*) pulling and then all the interior linemen putting pressure from right to left, thus indicating the power of the play is to the offensive team's right.

"It's imperative the quarterback make excellent fakes to the fullback and left halfback. For the next four steps he should look as though he has completed his duties and is merely observing the success or failure of the ball-carrying left halfback.

"From this point the quarterback is on his own and whether he runs around the weak side of the defense or elects to pass is dictated by the situation. The left end, you'll note, has actually placed a block on the middle linebacker, then recovered, and hopefully is open in the left corner of the field.

"If the play is effective, the result will be an excellent gain by the quarterback running or a touchdown pass to the left end. In other words, it's designed for a long gain or real catastrophe.

"For years, both John Brodie and Y. A. Tittle (and, I suppose, Albert) have used the play effectively inside the opponents' 20-yard line."

175

Which leads us to another glib ex-quarterback, Paul Christman.

The man you see on television delivering piquant comments during American Football League games and not afraid to second-guess looks more like a football player now than he did a quarter century ago. Then Paul Christman had a bit of a paunch, a sharp right arm and a sharp tongue.

The Chicago Cardinals, with fabled storyteller Jimmy Conzelman as their coach, signed Paul to his first professional contract in 1941. The Cards had finished in last place the season before.

"Get a smile on your face, Paul," advised Conzelman as the photographers flashed their powder. "You haven't been asked to commit suicide. We're a much better team than the sportswriters say we are."

"You'd almost have to be," said Christman.

Christman reported to his first training camp, and the big man was Marshall (Biggie) Goldberg, the All-American halfback from the University of Pittsburgh who was already a seasoned pro. Goldberg briefly acknowledged Christman's arrival. "Hello," he nodded to the All-American back from Missouri. "And exactly what do you play?"

"Poker, pitch and pinochle," answered Christman. "And what do you play, Mr. Goldberg?"

In its proper context, the veteran's question was a legitimate one. Christman was a slow-footed tailback with a protruding belly, a good head and a good arm—which sounds exactly like a description of some latter-day quarterbacks (Bobby Layne, for instance)—but Christman wasn't tailored to the football of 1941 when a man had to be a triple-threat to play tailback and double on defense as well. What do you do with Christman?

Perhaps fortunately, the answer was delayed. Christman had a prior commitment with the United States Navy which kept him busy for the next four football seasons, and by the time he got out in 1945, football had been redesigned to fit his singular abilities.

Nevertheless, as a football player, Paul Christman was a victim of poor timing. He should have come along a decade later and there's no telling what he might have accomplished as a T-formation quarterback, or how long he would have lasted.

As it was, he flashed briefly, with fewer than half a dozen seasons to show off his passing, and bowed out at the age of thirty-two, when that age was considered antique for a football player.

They called him "Pitchin' Paul" when he flared into national prominence as an All-American halfback at the University of Missouri in 1939. He came from an athletic family. His older brother Mark was a major league infielder, a journeyman who lasted nine years in the American League. Mark could also fling a football 65 yards in the air and hit the target. He did it once in a high school game in Maplewood, the St. Louis suburb where they were raised. Paul followed him in both sports and decided football was his business. He tried to go to Notre Dame and was turned down. He enrolled at Purdue but lost his scholarship when the freshman team got down to hard work. Weight was a bit of a problem then. He'd balloon if he didn't watch his diet. When he turned to his state University as a last resort, Coach Don Faurot saw a blond blimp who had puffed out momentarily to 240 pounds.

176

Eventually he trimmed down to a fighting 205 (the Christman of today is 190). The year 1938 was a big one for the Christmans. Mark reached the majors as a third baseman with the Detroit Tigers. Paul played in his first varsity game for Missouri against Colorado and threw 2 touchdown passes.

Faurot retooled the single-wing and put Christman a couple of steps farther back, in a modified short punt formation where he could look the field over and get more time to zero in on his target. Occasionally, for diversity, he had to run. He wasn't a complete bust-out carrying the ball. A 22-yard touchdown scamper against NYU in Yankee Stadium in 1939 helped propel him to All-American honors as a junior. Paul passed the Tigers to the Orange Bowl, with a pair of twin ends named Bud and Babe Orff as his primary targets. Ironically, Faurot converted Missouri to the T-formation in 1941, the year after Christman's departure. Paul was the indirect inspiration for Faurot's invention of the split-T offense, which initially featured the quarterback as a blocker pitching out to the halfbacks. Because he had no passer like Christman, Faurot felt the split-T was his only hope for a strong running game.

When Christman came out of the service in 1945, he was a rusty twenty-seven years old. He had played some with the famed Fleet City football team. "They had me running the fifth team," shrugged Paul. "I was no more sensational there than I was at Purdue." The Cards of '45 were no better than they had been when Christman last had contact with them. They won exactly 1 game. Preparing for the 1946 season, the Cardinals sent out questionnaires to all men who had been in the service, including this question: What was your most hazardous experience?

Christman filled it in blithely: "Playing behind the Cardinals' 1945 line."

But, with Conzelman returning as coach in 1946, they started to climb. The "Dream Backfield" of Christman, Charley Trippi, Elmer Angsman and Pat Harder was assembled. Paul became adjusted to taking the snap from center, and he was smart in the use of his personnel. The passing was integrated with the great running talents at his command.

The Cardinals were locked with the Bears in a rouser in 1946. With 4 minutes to go on the scoreboard clock, they led by 14 points; 3 minutes later the score was tied. Christman threw a long pass from midfield to Mal Kutner, who was knocked out of bounds on the 3-yard line. With time out, Christman asked the referee if the scoreboard clock, which showed 17 seconds left, was right. The referee nodded. Paul wanted to go for a field goal, but there was a crosswind and the angle was bad, so he figured he'd try a pass first. It clicked for a touchdown.

"I was congratulating myself," he reminisced, "when the Bears took the kickoff and used up more than 2 minutes before we finally stopped them at midfield, as the game ended. The clock was more than 2 minutes off. In the excitement neither the referee nor I had taken the time to check it with the umpire.

"In retrospect, with 2 minutes to get 3 yards, I would never under any circumstances have called a pass. Anybody who did, with a backfield of Angsman, Trippi and Harder, should have his head examined."

The Cardinals were the emergent power of the West in the postwar era. They beat their arch-rivals, the North Side Bears, in the season finales of both 1947 and 1948 to win the division titles. Their counterparts in the East were the Philadelphia Eagles, led by Tommy Thompson, a subdued quarterback like Christman, who wisely used the thunderous running of Steve Van Buren.

Paul showed his disciplined quarterbacking at its best in the 1947 championship game, played on a frozen field in Comiskey Park. He threw just enough, 14 times, to keep the Eagles wary. But he sent Charley Trippi through the line on a quick-opener for 44 yards and the first touchdown. Then it was Elmer Angsman's turn to bust for 70 yards. When the Eagles bounced back on a long touchdown pass, Trippi returned a punt 75 yards for a touchdown. And in the fourth quarter, Angsman again sprang off tackle on a trap play to run 70 yards for the deciding touchdown of the 28–21 seesaw battle.

As pro football increased in complexity, Paul was the thinking man's quarterback.

"Signal-calling is much more involved than ever before," he said back in 1950. "No longer does the quarterback chant, 'No. 2 to the right on three, hip!' It resembles a chess game with moves and countermoves."

He offered a case in point:

"On first down, at midfield, a play gains 9 yards. In the old days, the logical play would have been a line plunge for first down. Now pro teams think of this as a 'free' down. Try for a long-gainer—usually a pass—and if it fails, you still have third down and 1 to go.

"Consequently, instead of the seven-man line he saw in the past, the quarterback usually is greeted with a loose five-man line all set for that pass to come off. So the offensive team must go them one better, as the Cardinals did against the Boston Yanks in 1947.

"With second down and 1 yard to go, we faked a plunge to our left half, Trippi. This brought the linebacker up to meet him. While this was going on, our left end, Billy Dewell, slipped behind the linebacker. After faking my handoff to Charley, I straightened up and threw a quick pass to Dewell, who sidestepped the safetyman and went 40 yards to score.

"In this way, we double-checked them. They expected a pass so we faked the plunge to cross them up and passed anyway."

The Cardinals unloaded Christman on Green Bay in 1950, and he just stuck around briefly before he retired after the season to become a successful manufacturer's representative, and later emerged as a vibrant television personality.

Christman was accompanied in his exit by Tommy Thompson, his old Eagle adversary. Their careers paralleled, but Tommy had eight full seasons to show his stuff. Possibly his greatest asset was poise.

"He was the most nonchalant guy I've ever seen," said Allie Sherman, who was his backup quarterback for three years on the Eagles. "He never got ruffled at all. I spent all that time with him, and I never really got to know him."

Tommy was a taciturn Texas who drifted up to Tulsa to play his college football and joined the Eagles with a fair reputation as a tailback. He was even better with golf sticks, as Coach Greasy Neale found out. Greasy was an avid linksman. As a kid, Tommy had been a caddie at Ben Hogan's old golf club in Fort Worth and was close to a scratch golfer. Greasy became his pigeon. It was a fair trade. Tommy became his T-quarterback

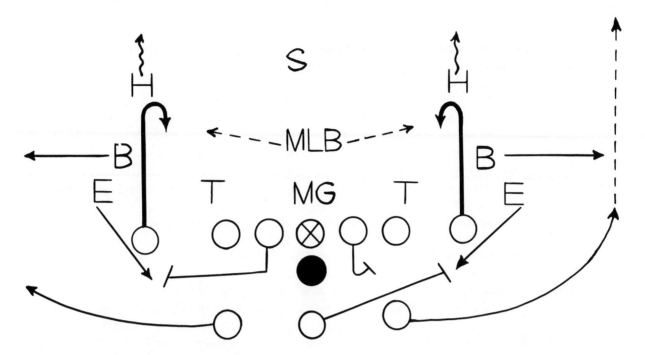

Paul Christman describes his favorite play:

"Here was our bread and butter pass against the 5–3–3 defense we so often ran into in my day. It wasn't the home run, but it sure pecked people to death for at least 10 yards a try and was almost impossible to stop.

"We called it Green Right, Double Hook, Double Divide. Green immediately informed everyone in the huddle a pass was to be called. Green Right indicated the blocking assignments to the guards and fullback. The fullback blocked right on this call, so the pulling guard blocks left and the other guard retreats to pick up strays, or 'dogs' against an odd defensive line.

"We were working on the middle linebacker. When both of our halfbacks divided, the outside linebackers went with them. The defensive halfbacks gave ground until our ends both hooked, making them too late to recover. The safety spent his time trying to decide who to take. This play hit fast.

"The only defensive man free and bothersome was the middle linebacker. This is where 'eye-faking' came in. The MLB had no time to do anything else than look where the passer was looking and run in that direction. Knowing this, I would back-pedal instead of turning my back to the line as I retreated. As I faded, I would deliberately follow the path of my right end with my eyes. When the MLB ran to cover him, I would turn slightly and hit the left end (and vice versa). There was really no difficulty following the patterns of both receivers because they were only 8–10 yards apart on their routes.

"On fiendish afternoons, when we had a comfortable lead, I would look at neither end as I retreated, but directly at the MLB, and then at the last moment throw to one of the ends. The only way I can describe the retreat of the MLB is to compare it with a chicken with his head cut off. The poor guy tried to run two ways at once and frequently ended up back where he started.

"Against the Bears in 1947, for the Western Division title, we used a variation of this play to open the game with an 80-yard touchdown pass. We had Babe Dimancheff at right halfback just for this one play. We flanked Charley Trippi, the left halfback, because we knew they'd pull the safety and corner back over to that side to double cover him. Thus, we isolated Babe with their left linebacker. Babe was once the Big Ten sprint champ, so it was no trouble to hit him on a deep swing pattern for the score."

as the Eagles won three-straight division titles from 1947 through 1949, and won the NFL championship game the last two years.

Thompson got his big break when he reported to the Eagles in 1941. Neale had just taken over the team from Bert Bell, who eventually became commissioner of the league. Greasy was impressed by the Bears' 73–0 massacre of the Redskins and decided to install the T-formation. He bootlegged films of the Bear game over the winter, broke them down and copied the offense. Now he needed a quarterback who could pass. He settled on the rookie from Tulsa.

"Tommy was my guinea pig," admitted Greasy. "We made a lot of mistakes learning the T and every mistake seemed to boomerang on Tommy.

"When our blockers missed assignments protecting the passer, Tommy was tackled for the loss. And the fans blamed him. But he learned quickly and was close to being the best quarterback in the league in two years."

But in 1942 Tommy went into the Army. The draft board ascertained he could breathe. He couldn't see out of his left eye. As a boy of eight, he was struck by a stone, and a blood clot blurred his vision. His success as a passer was remarkable since monocular vision restricts judgment of depth and field of vision. When he went back to throw, Tommy couldn't sweep both sides to look for openings. He had to cock his head in the direction he was throwing, and frequently he was swiped from his "blind" side. He was on limited service with the Army, but he somehow went ashore with an infantry division at Normandy.

When he returned to the Eagles in 1945, ex-sergeant Thompson was catcalled everytime Neale put him in a game. The Eagle fans had a new pet, Roy Zimmerman. Rusty Tommy fumbled, overshot his receivers, but Greasy decided only one quarterback could be boss, and Tommy was his man. He dumped Zimmerman.

"If Tommy hadn't come through," Neale admitted, "the fans would have run me right out of Philadelphia. That's one reason I didn't mind making an occasional contribution to the Thompson Welfare Fund on the golf course."

Against the Washington Redskins in 1946, the Eagles trailed 24–0 at halftime. Steve Van Buren, at that time the greatest runner in the NFL, the man who kept the pressure off Tommy's passing, was on the bench with an injury. Tommy rallied the Eagles to 2 quick touchdowns in the third quarter, but with 5 minutes left to play, they still trailed, 24–14. Tommy got them another touchdown with his passing. Time was fading as the Redskins took the kickoff and tried to keep the ball on the ground. On fourth down and 1 at their own 40, the Redskins gambled on a plunge into the line and were stopped. Tommy coolly took charge and threw two short passes to move the ball up 10 yards, trying to draw the Redskins in. Then he retreated and located end Jack Ferrante for the big bomb in the end zone and a 28–24 upset.

A year later, the Eagles had their first division title in history.

In 1948, Tommy led the National League in passing, with 141 completions in 246 attempts for 1,965 yards and 25 touchdown passes. Parenthetically, Luckman and Baugh were still playing regularly at the time. Sometimes luck rode on his throws. In a game against the Giants, Tommy looked for end Jack Ferrante on a pass over the middle, then nonchalantly flung the ball deep into the left corner of the end zone, his "blind" side.

180

Halfback Ernie Steele sprinted under the ball, jumped and snared it for a touchdown. But on the sidelines, Coach Neale was puzzled.

"You were supposed to hit Ferrante," he said to Thompson as the teams lined up for the ensuing kickoff. "What happened?"

"He was covered," shrugged Tommy. "A couple of Giants were coming at me, so I decided to get rid of the ball, quick. I guess I didn't throw it quite hard enough to get it out of bounds."

"You mean," said Greasy, laughing, "you didn't even see Steele."

"Shucks," said Tommy, "you can't expect an old one-eyed guy like me to keep track of every pass-chaser you put in a ball game."

Sometimes guts rode on his throws, too. When the Eagles played the Bears in mid-season, Tommy sustained a painful shoulder separation in the first half. During the intermission, a doctor jabbed a shot of novocaine into him to ease the agony.

When the Bears rallied to tie the score, 7–7, Tommy hustled back into the game and directed the Eagles within field-goal range, then held the ball and spun it for Cliff Patton to kick the winning field goal.

The championship game against the Cards in December was played in a blizzard at Shibe Park, Philadelphia. One of the heaviest snowstorms in history hit the area that morning and obliterated all the yard-markers. Before a punt, the players trudged around and packed down the area so the kicker would have a free arc for his foot. Passing was hopeless. Tommy became a ball carrier, controlling the ball for 50 yards on the ground. A fumble late in the game gave the Eagles the break they needed to send Van Buren crashing across from the 5 for a 7–0 victory.

In his stoicism, Tommy was a lot like Charley Conerly, who endured years of hard beatings with the Giants before he clicked. Thompson was a good, solid quarterback—not flashy in his execution like Waterfield or Albert. He was great under bad conditions. The '49 championship game against the Rams was played in a monsoon that hit the Los Angeles Coliseum, but Thompson threw a touchdown pass to Pete Pihos and never fumbled the slick ball as the Eagles won their second straight championship.

"This team will hold up as long as Tommy does," said Van Buren. "It can win without me or without key linemen. But it can't win without Tommy."

The words were prophetic. Tommy quit abruptly after the 1950 season, and the Eagles took a decade to get back up on top. Tommy went out without any fuss. He said simply he was going down to Arkansas and go fishing. He built himself a home on Lake Norfolk, near Mountain Home, deep in the Ozarks, and he fished.

Thompson left just one mystery. His age. He was one of those guys who was always twenty-nine going on thirty-five. It was the only thing prima donna about him.

FRANK ALBERT

BORN: Jan. 27, 1920   HEIGHT: 5'10"   WEIGHT: 160

San Francisco 49ers, 1946—52

PASSING RECORD:

Year	Att.	Comp.	Yards Gained	T.D.	Pct.	Longest	Int.
1946	197	104	1404	14	52.8	54	14
1947	242	128	1692	18	52.9	60	15
1948	264	154	1990	29	58.3	61	10
1949	260	129	1862	27	49.6	48	16
AAC TOTALS	963	515	6948	88	53.5	61	55
1950	306	155	1767	14	50.7	43	23
1951	166	90	1116	5	54.2	47	10
1952	129	71	964	8	55.0	60	10
NFL TOTALS	601	316	3847	27	52.6	60	43
COMBINED TOTALS	1564	831	10,795	115	53.1	61	98

RUSHING RECORD:

Year	Att.	Yards Gained	Longest	Ave.
1946	69	−10		−0.14
1947	46	179	n. a.	3.9
1948	69	349		5.1
1949	35	249		7.1
AAC TOTALS				
1950	53	272	42	5.1
1951	35	146	34	4.2
1952	22	87	29	4.0
NFL TOTALS	110	505	42	4.6

PUNTING RECORD

Year	No.	Ave.	Longest
1946	54	41.0	n. a.
1947	40	44.0	69
1948	35	44.8	n. a.
1949	31	48.2	n. a.
1950	37	38.5	64
1951	34	44.3	66
1952	68	42.6	70

Tommy Thompson, with good vision in only one eye, led the Philadelphia Eagles to world titles in 1948–49.

Pitching Paul Christman directed the Chicago Cardinals Dream Backfield of 1947–48.

PAUL CHRISTMAN

BORN: March 5, 1918   HEIGHT: 6'2"   WEIGHT: 200

Chicago Cardinals, 1945–49

Green Bay Packers, 1950

PASSING RECORD:

Year	Att.	Comp.	Yards Gained	T.D.	Pct.	Longest	Int.
1945	219	89	1147	5	40.6	70	12
1946	229	100	1656	13	43.7	82	18
1947	301	138	2191	17	45.8	80	22
1948	115	51	740	5	44.7	71	14
1949	151	75	1015	11	49.7	50	13
1950	126	51	545	7	40.5	44	7
TOTALS	1140	504	7294	58	44.2	82	86

RUSHING RECORD

Year	Att.	Yards Gained	Longest	Ave.
1945	30	−34	9	−1.1
1946	28	−61	6	−2.2
1947	8	11	3	1.4
1948	8	6	5	.8
1949	4	34	22	8.5
1950	7	18	4	2.6
TOTALS	85	−26	22	−.4

TOMMY THOMPSON

BORN: Aug. 15, 1916   HEIGHT: 6'1"   WEIGHT: 190

Pittsburgh Steelers, 1940

Philadelphia Eagles, 1941–50

PASSING RECORD:

Year	Att.	Comp.	Yards	T.D.	Pct.	Longest	Int.
1940	28	9	145	0	32.1	31	3
1941	162	86	974	8	53.1	50	14
1942	203	95	1410	8	46.8	65	16
(1943–44, U.S. Army)							
1945	28	15	146	0	53.6	27	2
1946	103	57	745	6	55.3	45	9
1947	201	106	1680	16	52.7	69	15
1948*	246	141	1965	25	57.3	70	11

Year	Att.	Comp.	Yards Gained	T.D.	Pct.	Longest	Int.
1949	214	116	1727	16	54.2	75	11
1950	239	107	1608	11	44.8	75	22
TOTALS	1424	732	10,400	90	51.4	75	103

* Led NFL

RUSHING RECORD:

Year	Att.	Gained	Longest	Ave.
1940	40	39	17	.9
1941	54	28	14	.5
1942	93	9	22	.1
(1943–44, U.S. Army)				
1945	8	−13	7	−1.6
1946	34	−116	6	−3.4
1947	23	52	16	2.4
1948	12	46	13	3.8
1949	15	17	5	1.1
1950	15	34	7	2.3
TOTALS	294	96	22	.3

11. The Stars

Otto Graham

THE TEST OF A QUARTERBACK IS WHERE
HIS TEAM FINISHES. SO OTTO GRAHAM,
BY THAT STANDARD, WAS THE BEST OF
ALL TIME.

—Paul Brown, coach,
Cleveland Browns, 1946–62

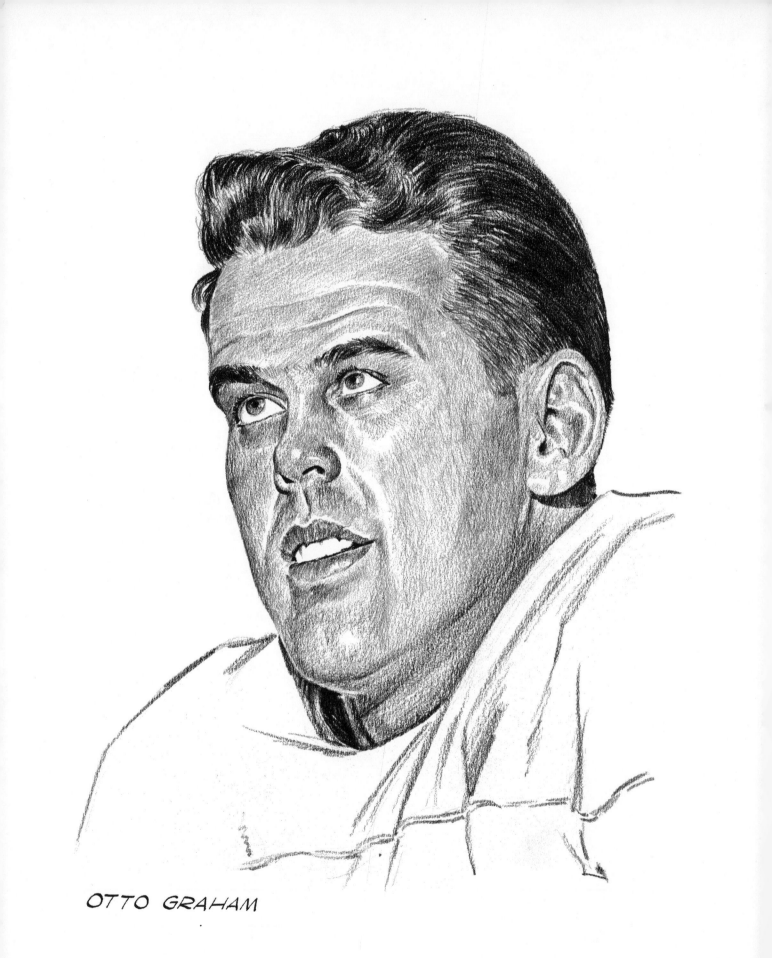

OTTO GRAHAM

If it weren't for the butterflies, Otto Graham would have kept throwing footballs until he was fifty years old. That would have taken him into the year 1971, and probably accounted for 25-straight Eastern Conference titles for the Cleveland Browns.

Automatic Otto was like Rocky Marciano. He went out undefeated. The official tally tells the story: ten seasons of play, ten division titles, four-straight All-American Conference championships, three NFL championships in six playoffs.

In a national poll of sportswriters taken in 1964 Otto was voted the greatest quarterback of all time.

Now the parallel between Graham and Marciano, whose career spanned 49 fights without a loss, is purely metaphysical. Rocky was a Brockton ditchdigger who beat people with raw physical strength and tenacity. Otto was an urbane, smooth operator, with a "God-given" ability to throw a football, who finessed them. When he got nervous about the whole thing—the tensions and the pressures that go with being a big-time athlete—he quit. Rocky retired when the physical grind of training palled.

The mating of Graham and Paul Brown to produce the longest run of success in football history, college or pro, was one of those rare coagulants in sports. Brown was a fanatic, dedicated, stern and tense. Graham was loose, flip, pleasantly cocky and irreverent. One common quality welded them. They were geared to win. Otto wouldn't concede a croquet game to his wife Bev if she were eight-months pregnant.

The Browns had to win their season-opener in 1950 if they were to maintain their esteem as a team. It was the most important game in their young history. The All-America Conference, in which Cleveland was a charter member, had been absorbed into the NFL that season. But a tinge of bitterness lingered from the costly battle to survive. The older NFL teams were openly skeptical of the caliber of football the new entrants would bring in. They regarded the Browns as *papier-mâché* champs. By an "odd" quirk of scheduling their debut would be against the Philadelphia Eagles, who were at the crest of a two-year championship reign.

"This was a game," recalled Otto, "we had been looking forward to for a few years, for obvious reasons. The NFL used to tell us, 'Go get a football before you even think of playing us. Our worst team can beat your best team ten days a week.'

"We would have played them for a barrel of beer or for nothing.

"Paul Brown didn't have to lift a finger or say one word to get us ready."

The issue was further joined for Graham personally by a little contretemps involving him and George Preston Marshall, owner of the Washington Redskins. At a Washington Touchdown Club banquet the previous January, Otto had received a trophy as the most valuable player in the AAC. The presentation was made by O. O. Kessing, the lame-duck commissioner, who remarked, "It is unusual for the head of a defunct league to be invited to such an affair."

Otto accepted and said glibly, "The AAC isn't defunct. We simply absorbed the National league."

Then he looked at Marshall, whose Redskin franchise was so entrenched he had started to dispose of his laundry business.

"Maybe Mr. Marshall better buy back a piece of that laundry business," continued Otto irrepressibly, "if we play the Redskins next year."

Marshall stood up from the floor and hooted, "You probably won't even have a job next year. Maybe you'd like to drive one of those laundry trucks!"

And Otto fired right back, seriously, "Mr. Marshall has caused many men to lose many millions of dollars through his stubbornness during the so-called pro football war."

So Otto's stomach flutters accelerated as he knelt for the pregame ritual of adjusting the laces on his high-topped black shoes. Above him, the concrete bowers of Philadelphia's Municipal Stadium supported 71,327 curious Eagle partisans. Paul Brown leaned over his quarterback and put a hand on his shoulders. "They're going to figure us for long passes," said Brown, "so let's concentrate at first on the square-outs and hooks to Mac (Speedie) and Dante (Lavelli)."

The Philadelphia team quickly moved deep into Brown territory. From the 15-yard line, Cliff Patton kicked a field goal and the Eagles were first on the scoreboard. "You're in the big leagues now," a foghorn yelled down to the Brown bench, and the crowd picked up the refrain.

But the Browns took the kickoff and started grinding out the short yardage according to the game plan, with Graham flipping to Speedie and Lavelli. "We felt they couldn't handle our passing," he said, "and they couldn't. Their defenders just couldn't cover our receivers, didn't realize how fast and effective they were."

As the Eagle secondary started to double on the ends, halfback Dub Jones was isolated with Eagle defender Russ Craft, one-on-one. Dub went down and caught a couple of sideline patterns, a favorite in the Brown repertoire. Craft got tired of playing Jones loose for the bomb and started to edge up.

Dub came back to the huddle and whispered to Otto, "He's ready."

The play sent in from the bench was a hook to Speedie, the left end. The scrimmage line was the Cleveland 41. Jones, on the other side, faked a square-out. Craft came up on him, and Dub broke right past the Eagle back. He caught Graham's pass on the Philly 25 without breaking stride and loped into the end zone. The Browns were out in front.

Their defense, fired up, stopped an Eagle drive on the 2-yard line in the second quarter, and Graham started pecking away again until the Browns reached the Philadelphia 26. Again the play was supposed to be a hook to Speedie, but Otto picked out Lavelli open on a post pattern down the middle and floated the ball into his hands for an easy touchdown. In the third quarter, under a severe rush by Eagle end Norm (Wild Man) Willey, he flipped sidearm to Speedie for another score. When receivers were covered, the Browns varied the attack by sending Marion Motley, the big fullback, up the middle on draw plays that chewed up the Eagle line. The final score was 35–10. The Browns were firmly entrenched as the most powerful team in football, and Otto Graham was the No. 1 quarterback.

In some ways he didn't look the part. In his prime, he was 6–1 and 195 pounds, ideal measurements. But Otto always looked a little slack. There was no hard set to his jaw. His muscles were smooth rather than bulging. And he didn't breathe fire.

190

Automatic Otto Graham was at his best under pressure. With his free hand, he pitched out to fullback Ed Modzelewski as Art Hauser of the Los Angeles Rams grabbed him.

Otto Graham credited his basketball training with making him a good T quarterback.

"T-quarterbacks do the least work," he shrugged, "get the most credit and the most money. The most important thing is to cover up after you hand the ball off to a halfback. After the thud, run over and help him get up, pat him on the back and say, 'Nice try, fella.'

"But when you hand off to a fullback like Marion Motley, forget that other stuff and just get the hell out of the way."

He's so frank it hurts. His wife studied singing when they were going together in college. Otto walked in at the end of a recital. "Your last note was sharp," he commented immediately. She returned the ring and the pin, and it took a little talking to bring them together again. Otto does talk.

He got up at a luncheon in Cleveland and said, "I have always disagreed with the theory of sending in messengers with plays because I think players on the field know the situation better than anybody on the bench." This was the system practiced by Paul Brown, and Otto was still playing for him. Later Brown blackballed him from an announcing job for Cleveland games.

A San Francisco tackle caught him with an elbow in the mouth that opened a gash which required twelve stitches to close, his only real damage as a pro. He was asked if they played dirty in the pros. Otto answered, "Sure they do." But forgot to note that "they" didn't include all players.

He went to a Hall of Fame luncheon in Canton, Ohio, and said, "The Browns won't win anything as long as Jim Brown is there. He won't block." He suggested trading the great fullback for the good of the team. Of course, this was long after Otto had left the Browns.

Graham spent eight years as the coach of the College All-Stars for their annual August game against the NFL champions. He blasted Charley Taylor in 1964 for being lazy in workouts, and the halfback became rookie of the year for the Washington Redskins. He kept Gale Sayers out of the 1965 game, calling him a malingerer, and Sayers electrified the league as a halfback with the Chicago Bears.

But Otto's a man of principle. He turned down big coaching jobs because he didn't want the pressure or lack of security and settled for football coach at the Coast Guard Academy in New London, Connecticut, with a regular commission. "I was the only guy in history to skip from a Navy Air Force cadet to full commander," he cracked. He produced an undefeated season in 1964.

He finally returned to pro ball in 1966 as the head coach on a firm three-year deal with the Washington Redskins and admitted that Buffalo or San Diego of the rival AFL could give any team in the NFL a tough game, and that he'd love to have Joe Namath of the New York Jets playing quarterback for him.

He also laid down a primer for the quarterback: "He must have the complete respect of the players, on and off the field. If I don't think he can command that respect, he will not be my quarterback."

Otto Everett Graham, Jr., brought to football respect and the sensitivity of a musician. Back home in Waukegan, Illinois, his father directed the high school band and orchestra, and his mother taught music. His brother Eugene played the oboe and English horn; brother Victor specialized in the oboe; Richard played the French horn,

192

and Otto spread his talents on the piano, cornet, French horn and violin (like fellow townsman Jack Benny).

At Waukegan High School he was an all-state basketball player, wavered between scholarships to Dartmouth and Northwestern, and chose the school just down the road from home, in Evanston. He was still a music major. Football didn't figure until Lynn (Pappy) Waldorf, then head coach at Northwestern, strolled by an intramural touch game in the early spring and saw this black-haired kid run and throw the ball, a notch in class above all the other scholars in shorts. He invited young Otto to try out for the varsity. Otto made good progress but tore a knee cartilage in a scrimmage. An operation in the fall kept him out of school a year. When he reported again in 1941, Northwestern's big name was Bill DeCorrevont, the schoolboy from Chicago Austin who once attracted more than 100,000 people into Soldier Field for a high school game. DeCorrevont was a senior, Graham a sophomore. They shared the tailback position in the single-wing. Bill played the first and third quarters at tailback; Otto relieved him in the second and fourth quarters. The Minnesota Gophers, riding to their second-straight unbeaten season and another national championship under Bernie Bierman, barely squeaked by the Wildcats, 8–7. A long touchdown by Graham was called back because of an offside penalty.

By coincidence, Graham's three varsity seasons coincided with the college coaching debut of Paul Brown at Ohio State. In his senior year, tailback Otto was an All-American in both football and basketball, then went into service as a naval air cadet. He was sent to North Carolina Pre-Flight school and, of course, turned out for football in 1944.

"We had ten coaches," remembered Otto, "among them Bear Bryant, but none had ever coached the T before. Ray Bray, who played guard for the Chicago Bears, was also an officer there, and he knew the T. So he gave the coaches our plays and really got us started. It was more or less hit-and-miss. Because I could throw the ball, I was a T-quarterback. Our pass protection was poor; sometimes the linemen were back there before I was. So halfway through the season they shifted me to fullback part-time and snapped the ball to me through the quarterback's legs."

That was his introduction to the T. In 1945, Paul Brown, also in the navy, looked up Cadet Graham at the Glenview, Illinois, Naval Air Station. He was signing players for a new Cleveland team in a new pro football league, and Otto was his first target. The salary would be $7,500, with a $1,000 bonus for signing—but meanwhile he'd pay Otto $200 a month for as long as the war lasted. That was persuasive to a young man getting paid $75 a month by the government and about to be married. He and Bev celebrated. They went to the Edgewater Beach Hotel on Chicago's north side and ordered shrimp cocktails and cokes.

Otto got out of service in 1945 before the Browns fielded a team and signed to play pro basketball with the Rochester Royals. Naturally they won the championship, with Otto starring in such basketball company as Bob Davies, Red Holzman and Fuzzy Levane. But a year later football became his business.

"I was lucky," admitted Graham. "I didn't have an established quarterback in the NFL to go up against. We were all rookies. None of the quarterbacks had played pro ball. Paul Brown had never coached it. We all learned together. What helped me more than anything else was the fact I was a good basketball player. The mechanics of quarter-

Graham didn't shy from contact. He scores his second touchdown in the 1955 title game against the Rams.

backing are just the same as in basketball. The footwork and the pivoting are identical. You find a good basketball player, he's a good athlete."

One of the first things they learned together was a pass pattern that revolutionized offensive football. Mac Speedie, the left end, ran a standard zig-in and zig-out pattern but was having trouble with it in practice one day because the defensive halfback was laying back to pick up his cut. So Mac came back to the huddle and said to Otto, "I'm going to break it off sharp this time."

As the halfback, sensing the usual pattern, started to drift back, Speedie broke sharply in front of him and caught Graham's pass just before he hit the sideline. That's how the sideline pass was born.

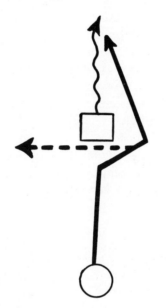

"It's a very tough pass to cover if you have a quarterback who can throw the football," said Graham objectively. "The secret is to have the receiver come back. You tell a guy to make a 90-degree cut, but actually with momentum he's still going downfield. By making the receiver come back, he has the defender beaten by two steps. The defender's even blocked off by the receiver's body. I used to throw the football in relation to where the defensive man was, not where my man was."

Speedie, now the head coach of the Denver Broncos, added, "Otto had a great sense of timing. He could anticipate our breaks." Any time Cleveland needed a few yards, Speedie or Lavelli would cut for the sideline and Graham would hit them perfectly. The maneuver became a delicate mechanism with practice and eventually a standard part of every pro team's passing game.

"Even after a half dozen years," said Graham, "I'd work with Speedie, Lavelli and Dub Jones for hours after practice to keep sharp. It got so if the receiver moved his fanny a certain way, I knew what he was going to do."

The first pro game Graham ever started for the Browns, an exhibition against Brooklyn in Akron, he was so bad he had to be yanked for Cliff Lewis, another rookie from Duke. But he led them to a 12–2 record in their first season and a championship over the New York Yankees, 14–9, on a Graham-to-Lavelli pass in the fourth quarter.

The Brown offense was simple. The staples were the sideline pass and the draw by Motley. Brown stressed execution rather than deception. A genius wasn't needed to direct the offense. Graham's ranking as a great quarterback has been challenged by charges he didn't perform the vital function of calling signals. It's generally forgotten that in the first four years he called 75 to 80 percent of the plays himself.

In their second season, in a game against the original Buffalo Bills, the Browns were backed up to their own goal line. They held and took over with the ball a foot away from the stripe. In the huddle, the players asked Otto what he was going to do (this was before the Browns started the messenger-guard system).

Otto grinned slyly: "It's time, boys, to surprise them with a screen pass."

The play was directly against the book. The other Browns protested.

"Look," the quarterback argued, "if they rush me, I'll throw the ball into the stands. Only thing that can happen is they'll penalize us half the distance to the goal, and what difference does 6 inches make in this spot?"

The Bills bunched into a gap defense as Otto called signals. The linebacker over Speedie slid inside. Mac bumped him slightly on the snap of the ball, then drifted to the left sideline. Graham straightened up and flipped the ball laterally to Speedie, standing on the goal line. There was no one ahead of him except Browns, and he ran 100 yards to a touchdown.

"Everyone, including the coaches, said I was nuts," admitted Graham, "—but it worked."

The schism between Brown and his quarterback started on a point of pride. Brown's first lieutenant, in charge of offense, was Blanton Collier. During the game, Collier sat in the pressbox and kept phone contact with the bench. When the offensive team came to the sidelines, Graham rushed over to the phone hookup with Collier, by-passing the head coach. In a pique, Brown abruptly ended the Graham-Collier hookup and took over all the play-calling, via alternating guards.

"There were times the boys came out with plays we didn't think were too good," said Graham, "so I called my own on occasion. But not too often, because after all I'm not stupid. Paul Brown was not only coach. He was the business manager. You don't go around telling the boss he's wrong all the time.

"Paul Brown said he used to call plays because quarterbacks get stereotyped, which is true. But he failed to realize that he himself was more stereotyped than anyone I've ever seen.

"The only real difference we ever had was on the audible bit. I always felt that with a quarterback who has played a few years, if the play is off tackle to the right and there are five men stacked there, it's ridiculous to run there. Paul just didn't believe in automatics. He felt there was too much chance of a mistake.

"My last few years I know I wasn't as good a quarterback, mentally, as I was my first few years. Somebody makes all the decisions for you, you stop thinking."

196

Otto ran with long, deceptive strides—"I was much better than people realized."

But not executing. Collier, who succeeded Brown as Cleveland's head coach in 1963, said, "I always thought the great passers were the ones who hit with the impromptu pass, the pass that wasn't in the books. And Otto was tremendous at that." Collier remembered one game against the Yankees for the AAC title in which he suggested Mac Speedie run a flag pattern (to the near corner of the end zone, where the flag is).

"As soon as the play started," he recalled, "I knew it wouldn't work. The man covering was laying way back and outside. Speedie saw the trouble and changed the pattern with a cut toward the goal line. Otts (Collier always called him 'Otts') had already started his arm action but somehow managed to change it in midair and threw a perfect touchdown pass."

Once, Motley and Edgar (Special Delivery) Jones, the halfback, were both supposed to go to the right on a pass play. Motley forgot his assignment and went left. They bumped heads and staggered, both groggy. The defensive team, sensing a slipup, forgot about them and barreled in on Graham. At the last moment, Graham noticed Jones coming out of the fog, flipped the ball over, and Special Delivery ran 80 yards to a touchdown.

Graham never could account for his knack of timing and accuracy. In the locker room a Brown receiver took a wire coat hanger, bent it into a diamond shape barely large enough for a football to go through, and stationed Graham 15 feet away.

"Here," said the player, holding the hanger by the hook, "let's see you throw the ball through this." Graham did it 10 times in a row and only touched the sides of the metal hanger once.

In his four AAC seasons, Otto completed 55.8 percent of his passes. In his six NFL seasons, he completed 55.7 percent of his passes. Graham insisted if they didn't count passes he intentionally grounded, he would have had an 80 percent completion average.

He could also run the ball. "I was a much better runner than people realized," the old tailback said with pride. "I deceived the pros because I had a long stride and the sight of a 280-pound lineman bearing down on you gives you added speed." In the Browns' first year in the NFL, the Giants were the only team to contain them successfully, winning both regular-season games to tie Cleveland for the division title. In the playoff, Cleveland took measures to counteract the umbrella defense rigged by Coach Steve Owen of the Giants. The Giants keyed their middle linebacker on Motley, nullifying the Browns' favorite draw play. So Cleveland flared the fullback wide, pulling the linebacker with him. Graham faked the pass to Motley, then ran the draw himself up the middle, through the vacated linebacker's spot. On a frozen field, wearing sneakers, Otto had the biggest running day of his pro career as the Browns won, 8–3.

He showed his clutch ability in the title game that followed against the Los Angeles Rams, led by Bob Waterfield, another great quarterback of the time. The Rams shocked the 60,000 people in drafty Cleveland Stadium on the first play from scrimmage as Waterfield located Glenn Davis along the right sideline and the former Army jackrabbit ran 45 yards to complete an 82-yard touchdown sprint. Six plays later Otto retaliated with a 27-yarder to Dub Jones for a score. They seesawed like that most of the four quarters. There was one tension-inducing factor. After a score in the second period, the Browns had failed to convert because a gust of wind blew the pass from center too high in time to be spotted for the kick by Lou Groza. So when Graham pegged to halfback Rex Bumgardner for a touchdown in the fourth quarter, the Browns still trailed, 28–27.

The Browns weren't perturbed, though. "His teammates felt that no matter how tough the situation, Otts would pull them out somehow, some way," said Collier.

Graham can replay the situation clearly today. He said, "I'll never forget. We were down there with 3½ minutes to go, real close to the goal line. I ran a quarterback draw play and picked up 8 or 10 yards, got hit from the blind side and fumbled the football. I thought then and there I had lost the game. I would have crawled into a hole if I could have found one. I came out on the sideline.

"You know that Paul Brown didn't pat all the guys on the back all the time. It wasn't his way. But as I came up the sideline, he patted me on the shoulder, smiled and said, 'Forget about it. We're going to beat them anyway.'

"I felt I had blown it. The defense went out there and if they'd let the Rams get one first down, it'd be over. But they stopped them. Waterfield punted to the 10. Cliff Lewis caught the thing and ran out of bounds on the 32."

A minute and 50 seconds to go, 68 yards to cover. The Rams went into a prevent defense, dropping everybody back, so Otto ran 14 yards and out of bounds to stop the clock. He threw to Bumgardner, to Speedie, to Jones, to Bumgardner again—all sideline passes, the receiver jumping over the chalk line to preserve time. Now the Browns were on the Ram 11, the spot to play it safe, look for the field goal. Otto wanted to give the ball to Bumgardner on a tackle slant to position the ball for the kick. Bumgardner said his hands were cold and wet from falling into a snowbank the play before. Otto kept the ball himself and burrowed toward the middle of the field. Then Groza came in and calmly kicked a 16-yard field goal to win it, 30–28.

"A lot of people forget," added Graham, "that after we scored there were still 20 seconds left. They ran the kickoff back to the 30 and put Norm Van Brocklin in the ball game for the bomb. Warren Lahr intercepted the ball running toward his own goal around the 20 and was grabbed and half-wrestled all the way into the end zone. It was possible the officials could have called that, incorrectly, a safety."

That championship was followed by two more. In 1954, they met the Detroit Lions in an extra-special game for Otto. He was retiring after the season. The Lions had a perfect 4–0 record in competition with the Browns, including title victories in 1952 and 1953. Otto ran for three touchdowns, threw for three and the Lions were routed 56–10. But there was a loophole in Otto's decision to quit. He told Paul Brown he'd come back for 1955 if the Browns were in a jam for quarterbacks. A court ruling sidelined a rookie hopeful, Bobby Freeman, as the backup man for George Ratterman, already groomed to succeed Otto. So Otto, filled out to a lumpy 208 pounds, reported two weeks before the start of the '55 schedule. The Browns were trampled in the league opener, 27–17, by Washington. And Graham blamed himself for not being mentally ready. They lost only one other game all season. For the title, they met the Rams, led now by Van Brocklin. The Dutchman had six passes intercepted. Graham completed 14 out of 25 for 202 yards and 2 touchdowns. He ran the ball over himself a couple of times. The Browns won in a breeze, 38–14. It was a typical Graham day, the kind he'd had for a decade. And when it was over, there was no reneging. He quit and never played another game of football.

The New York Giants were the only team able to defend against Graham's passes to Dante Lavelli (56). Emlen Tunnell (45) and Tom Landry (49) block the ball off in a 6–0 shutout in 1950.

"The mental pressure, rather than physical wear-and-tear, had most to do with my decision to retire," he said later. "I don't believe the pressure would have been as great with a less successful team."

The next year, 1956, Cleveland had its first losing season in history. Naturally.

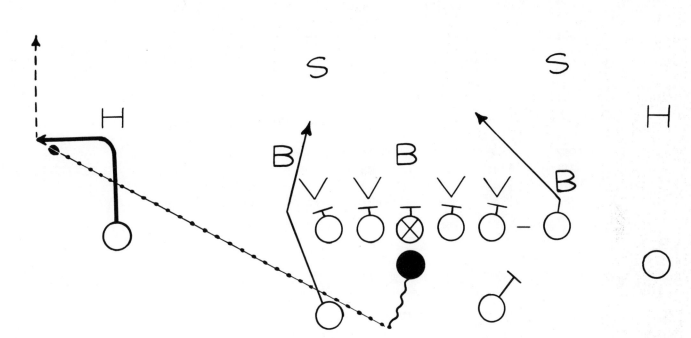

Otto Graham describes his favorite play:

"Ever since my Cleveland Browns days, I've been partial to the short, square-out patterns that are the bread and butter of a passing attack and always good for short yardage. They require delicate timing between the passer and receiver. Once achieved, you're in business.

"For instance, when I coached the College All-Star squad against the Green Bay Packers in 1963, one of my ends was Pat Richter. The quarterback was Ron Vander-Kelen, who had been his battery mate at Wisconsin, so they knew each other well.

"The play is designed actually for a five-yard gain, but when the Packer corner back came across to grab Pat after the ball was thrown, the defender missed the tackle. Pat, playing split left end, had a clear lane down the sidelines for 70 yards and the touchdown that decided the 20–17 upset of the Packers.

"The play can be used to either side. Just flop it over by lining up strong left.

"The quarterback backs out in the direction of the pass only four steps and throws quickly. The receiver breaks out sharply after penetrating across the line of scrimmage and is very tough to cover."

OTTO GRAHAM

BORN: Dec. 6, 1921   HEIGHT 6'1"   WEIGHT: 195
Cleveland Browns, 1946–55
PASSING RECORD:

Year	Att.	Comp.	Yards Gained	T.D.	Pct.	Longest	Int.
1946	174	95	1834	17	54.6		5
1947	269	163	2753	25	60.6	99	11
1948	333	173	2713	25	52.0		15
1949	285	161	2785	19	56.0		10
AAC TOTALS	1061	592	10,085	86	55.8	99	41
1950	253	137	1943	14	54.2	31	20
1951	265	147	2205	17	55.5	81	16
1952	364	181	2816	20	49.7	68	24
1953*	258	167	2722	11	64.7	70	9
1954	240	142	2092	11	59.2	64	17
1955*	185	98	1721	15	53.0	61	8
NFL TOTALS	1565	872	13,499	88	55.7	81	94

* Led NFL

	Att.	Comp.	Yards Gained	T.D.	Pct.	Longest	Int.
COMBINED TOTALS	2616	1464	23,584	174	55.8	81	135

RUSHING RECORD:

Year	Att.	Yards Gained	Longest	Ave.
1946				
1947	19	72		3.8
1948				
1949				
AAC TOTALS				
1950	55	145	20	2.6
1951	35	29	12	.9
1952	42	130	21	3.1
1953	43	143	21	3.3
1954	63	114	14	1.8
1955	68	121	36	1.8
NFL TOTALS	306	682	36	2.2

Bob Waterfield

THE THING I REMEMBER ABOUT BOB
WATERFIELD WAS HIS LEADERSHIP. HE
HAD AN INNER STRENGTH. EVERYBODY
ON THE BALL CLUB RESPECTED THE
GUY.

—Bob Boyd, end,
Los Angeles Rams, 1950–57

Bob Waterfield had everything going for him to be the glamour guy of all the great quarterbacks spawned in that prolific breeding period right after World War II. He looked the part. Brown, wavy hair and a firm set to his jaw; tall and rugged in a John Wayne sort of way; and Jane Russell for a wife.

But the Waterfield personality was wrapped in the skin of a walrus. He was tough. Nobody got inside him. He wasn't aloof. He just didn't project. And Jane, that doll of a movie star, called him affectionately, "Old Stone Face."

Some men lead by the force of their individuality: a Bobby Layne haranguing the Detroit Lions or a Norm Van Brocklin jabbing the Philadelphia Eagles to play over their heads. All winners have a strong competitive urge. And make no mistake—Bob Waterfield was a winner. But the combustible coals were stoked so deep inside him that the average guy never got a chance to see how Waterfield fired up a team.

In 1945 Waterfield took the field against the Detroit Lions with three crushed, separated ribs that had only six days to heal. It was his first year as a pro, and the game was for the Western Conference title of the NFL. In practice he didn't even bother to throw, because he barely was able to lift his right arm, and the shooting pains made him sick, ready to throw up. He told the coach, Adam Walsh, before the game that the ribs no longer bothered him.

"I won't pass," Waterfield assured his coach. "Just let me in to run the team and keep the ball on the ground."

The trainer for the Cleveland Rams shot his right side with novocaine and taped the ribs tightly, the adhesive sticking like a mustard plaster. A sharp wind skimmed across the ice of Cleveland Stadium as Waterfield trotted stiffly out to the opening huddle. He took the ball from center on the first play, spun to hand it to a back but withdrew the football and cocked his arm. He threw it hard and accurately to end Jim Benton. Waterfield didn't feel a thing.

He passed 20 more times that day, totalled a dozen completions and 329 yards gained. The Rams beat the second-place Lions, 28–21, and had their first division title.

Waterfield was a man who led by example. One of the Ram backs whined in a huddle that he didn't feel up to carrying the ball on the particular play Bob called. Waterfield didn't argue with him. He stepped swiftly inside the group of clustered shoulderpads and slugged the back. No more complaints.

In a period when the T-quarterback became the ultra-specialist, Waterfield was the most versatile of all specialists, especially as Sammy Baugh faded out. Bob ran the team; he also ran the ball, with a knack for the deceptive bootleg. He passed and he punted. He has an 88-yard boot in the record books. He was a leading place-kicker in the NFL, and in the early years he played a lot of defense. He justified a salary for any one of those talents. Combined in one man, they made Bob Waterfield a powerful force for the eight years he stayed in pro ball. The Rams won four division and two NFL titles during that time, a ratio exceeded only by Otto Graham among his contemporaries. And Graham had the better supporting cast.

The popularity push of professional football began with the transfer of the Rams to Los Angeles in 1946, the first big-league sport to open up the plush territory of the West. And Waterfield was their best selling point as Los Angeles picked up the ball and showed the rest of the country its potential for supporting sports. Bob was their own boy. He came out of Van Nuys in the bustling San Fernando Valley, which was changing almost overnight from a pastoral outpost to a megalopolis on the north flank of Los Angeles.

Robert Staton Waterfield was born in Elmira, New York, on July 26, 1920. The family moved West when he was four years old to Van Nuys, where his father ran a moving company. In those days, Van Nuys had Bob Burns and his bazooka and little else. For a husky boy, there were lots of hills and ravines to explore, a chance to acquire a taste for the outdoor life—hunting and fishing. His father died when he was nine; his mother became a nurse to support the little family. Bob, reclusive by nature, was alone most of the time. When he got to high school he worked in a concrete pipe yard. "They paid me two bits an hour," he said. "It was pretty good for the back muscles."

He was small, never reached more than 150 pounds in high school, but he played tailback in the single-wing. Football brought him out of his shell a little. He'd stop in the hallway at school between classes to chat with a girl who had long black hair and a dazzling smile, and everything else that was supposed to go with it. Her name was Jane Russell, but Bob never got around to asking her out until after he finished high school. He wanted to play college football, but there was no stampede to get him because of his size. He went to work for two years on the assembly line of an aircraft plant, filled out and enrolled at UCLA in Westwood, just over the San Vicente Mountains from home. He made the varsity in 1941 and a year later led the Bruins to their first Rose Bowl game in school history.

Meanwhile, Howard Hughes had discovered Jane Russell and cast her in a movie called "The Outlaw." It revealed her as a sultry star, but mainly in publicity stills, because release of the picture was delayed for years. Meanwhile, to Bob she was still the girl in the old neighborhood. He married her in 1943. The war was on, and they packed off to Fort Benning, Georgia, where Bob got an infantry commission, while Jane worked in a beauty shop. It was a big deal when they went to downtown Columbus, the football hero and the starlet.

The Cleveland Rams had drafted him for the NFL in 1943. When a knee injury forced him out of the army after fifteen months, Bob skipped the pros to finish out his college eligibility. He played in the Shrine East-West game on January 1, 1945, and gave the pros a sample of what they were getting. Because of the war years, his abilities had been obscured.

The East team, loaded with players like Heisman Trophy winner Les Horvath of Ohio State, carried a 7–0 lead into the last quarter. It would have been bigger if Waterfield hadn't punted for the beleaguered West team. For example, with the ball on his team's 14, Waterfield quick-kicked over Horvath's head to the East 6-yard line. From his own 30, he punted to the East 10. From the West 17, he punted to the East 9. He

206

Bob Waterfield's versatility included rollout runs to surprise the opposition.

Vic Stein

rolled another kick dead on the East 4. Altogether he booted 5 times for an average of 59.4 yards!

Then he swung into action offensively in the fourth period. He threw a 45-yard pass that set up the West's first touchdown of the day. Waterfield had 11 completions for the game. Late in the period, he grabbed a lateral and ran 13 yards for the decisive touchdown, 13–7. Waterfield averaged 6.7 yards a carry.

In today's market that would have made him a half-million dollar prospect for the pros, especially being married to Jane Russell, and the publicity she represented. Waterfield actually signed for $7,500 and the Cleveland critics howled he was being overpaid.

Now a pro quarterback is supposed to take three years to develop. Maybe it was the wartime atmosphere. Japs were still being smoked out of caves on remote Pacific isles where the news of V-J Day hadn't reached. The dispersal of America's millions of fighting men, including the prize football talent, wasn't complete. Whatever the conditions, Waterfield came on immediately as a star. An old Bear T-quarterback, Bob Snyder, took on the coaching job of adapting Waterfield to the pro system. In his first scrimmage, he threw two touchdown passes and won the regular job.

The Rams had been in Cleveland since 1937 without ever experiencing a winning season. They had a new head coach, Adam Walsh, one of Notre Dame's Seven Mules under Knute Rockne; a new T-formation system, and a new quarterback. The other players called him "Waterbuckets"—later it was shortened to plain "Buckets," which is how Waterfield referred to himself throughout his career. Buckets gave them a sample in the exhibition season by outpassing Sammy Baugh in a win over the Redskins, the first in Ram history.

The performance was no fluke. During the regular season the Rams won 9 and lost 1. The key game was that late-season encounter with the Lions. The week before two Chicago Cardinals had busted his ribs with a high-low gang tackle. But Waterfield played, as related earlier, and assistant coach Bob Snyder said, "It was the greatest exhibition of guts I've ever seen."

Waterfield was the last rookie quarterback ever to lead a team to a championship in professional football. The Rams, representing the Western Conference, met the Washington Redskins, with Sammy Baugh still very much active, in the title playoff. Waterfield had his side, where the ribs were tender, tightly taped. Before the game could start in Cleveland Stadium, with the temperature reading 6 degrees above 0, the ground crew had to remove 5,000 bales of hay, and a tarpaulin weighted down by 18 inches of snow.

Baugh, the old master, was the leading passer in the NFL that year with a completion percentage of 70.3 percent for the season, still the all-time record. But that was the game in which Sammy hit the goalpost with an errant throw for an automatic safety. Otherwise, the teams matched touchdowns. Waterfield hit end Jim Benton on a 37-yard scoring play just before the end of the first half. He kicked the conversion, a squibber that hit the crossbar and barely tumbled over. In the third quarter, he connected with halfback Jim Gillette on a 53-yard touchdown play.

The honors for his first season were complete when Buckets was named the winner of the Joe Carr Trophy as the league's Most Valuable Player. Cleveland put him on the same pedestal as Bob Feller of the Indians. The city had the two best pitchers in sports.

208

It quickly narrowed down to one because young Dan Reeves, the grocery heir who bought the Rams in 1941, spirited the Rams out of town to the more hospitable climate of Los Angeles. In winning the championship, the Rams had lost $50,000 on their operation in Cleveland. Reeves found out the Los Angeles Coliseum was available and petitioned the league owners to move his team in January, 1946. When they turned him down, he threatened to disband the championship club. The NFL reluctantly granted permission.

For Waterfield, the shift made sense, too. Jane's career was picking up. They'd be together all the time. Bob had worked at Warner Brothers in the production department, and later got before cameras as an extra in an Errol Flynn adventure, "Burma Road." But he wasn't comfortable making the Hollywood scene. Football was his business.

"There never was anything else," he said curtly to an interviewer, "just football."

For relaxation, he was close to the best hunting and fishing in the high Sierra. "If Bob had his way," said Don Paul, the center on the Rams, "he'd disappear into the woods with a gun for five months of the year and come out when it started to snow."

Playing football in Los Angeles, however, was not quite as serene. His seven years with the Rams on the West Coast were contentious. The club had a phobia for collecting quarterbacks. They already had one of the best in the business. But with the switch to California in 1946, the Rams also acquired Jim Hardy, a local favorite who played at the University of Southern California. When Hardy was peddled to the Chicago Cardinals in 1949, followed by a fog of rumors about a bitter feud between the quarterbacks, the Rams already had signed Norm Van Brocklin, an All-American quarterback at the University of Oregon. And for the next three years, or until Waterfield finally retired, the same disquieting reports of trouble between the quarterbacks popped up periodically. Hardy and Van Brocklin were generally embarrassed by the commotion and publicly denied any feuds. Waterfield, in line with his strong, silent image, generally ignored the brouhaha.

As a spotlighted personality in Hollywood, he needed gossip like Pasadena needed smog. "He's not a gregarious guy," said his wife. "Bob likes honesty in people. It's a passion with him. He'll talk football all night with someone who knows what he's talking about. He hates to yak with people just trying to make an impression."

On the Rams, he acted like any other guy, though Reeves jumped his contract to $20,000 a year on a three-year deal the day the team went West. When rookies like Bob Boyd, a 9.5 sprinter from Loyola with limited football experience, wanted extra work catching the ball after practice, Buckets stayed overtime to throw the ball.

Though Hardy and Van Brocklin cut into his playing time, and the increasing use of the Dutchman probably caused Waterfield to retire prematurely, Waterfield was still the man the Rams leaned on in the clutch.

In 1946 and again in 1951, he led the NFL in passing. As late as 1948, he was still taking a turn on defense and led one of the most memorable rallies in NFL annals. The Philadelphia Eagles, heading for an NFL championship, came out to play the Rams on a Sunday in October of 1948. Steve Van Buren and Company rushed to a 28–0 lead late in the third quarter. There were 4 minutes left in that period, to be exact, and the Eagles confidently held the ball on their own 34. An Eagle back fumbled after a 10-yard gain.

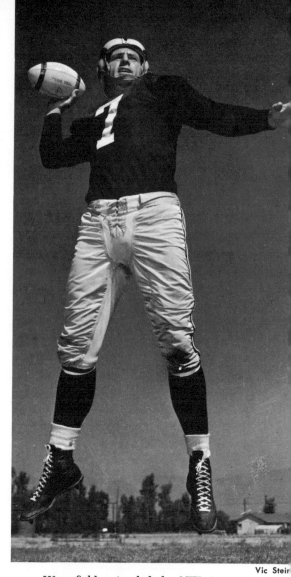

Vic Stein

Old Buckets, as the Rams called Waterfield, was a stylist as a T formation ball handler.

Vic Stein

Waterfield twice led the NFL in passing.

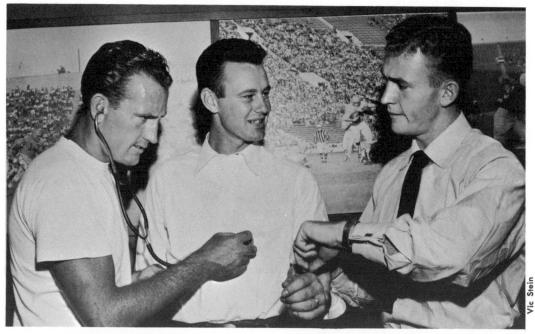

Vic Stein

Norm Van Brocklin, who eventually supplanted Bob Waterfield, joined the Los Angeles Rams in 1949. Bob applies the stethoscope, while Jim Hardy, right, another Ram quarterback, checks the rookie's pulse.

Waterfield swooped in from his defensive position and recovered the ball. He passed twice, to ends Tom Fears and Jack Zilly, for a touchdown. When the teams changed sides to start the fourth quarter, he intercepted a pass on the Eagle 46. In 8 plays, culminated by a 13-yard pass to end Bill Smyth, the Rams were on the scoreboard again. Now it was 28–14 with half the period gone. From the Philadelphia 43, Waterfield fired a 39-yard pass to Fears. Two shots into the line, and the Rams were only 7 points down. After every score, Waterfield kicked the extra point (he still holds the NFL season record of 54 points after touchdown, established in 1950).

With 2½ minutes left the Rams tried to generate a final drive from their own 27-yard line. Waterfield's first 3 passes fell incomplete. With nothing to lose on fourth down, he threw to Red Hickey. The ball and an Eagle arrived at the same time. Red was knocked unconscious but held on for 20 yards and a first down. Two more passes took the ball to the Eagle 29, but the clock was moving. Bob sent Zilly out on a flag pattern to the right corner. The big end was covered. Waterfield, under a rush, lofted it with delicate accuracy, Zilly making the grab as he stepped into the end zone just inside the out-of-bounds line. The stunned Eagles had to settle for a tie.

The next year, 1949, the Rams started a run of three straight division titles with possibly the greatest offensive unit a pro team ever put together. For receivers, Waterfield had Fears and Hirsch as his primary targets. For running backs he had a trio of bulls—"Deacon" Dan Towler, Dick Hoerner and Tank Younger. Outside speed was furnished by Vitamin Smith and Tommy Kalmanir, augmented by Glenn Davis in 1950 after he finished his service commitment.

The 1950 Rams, playing a 12-game schedule (it's 14 now), set existing league records for touchdowns (64) and scoring (466 points). They rolled up a record 70 points in one afternoon against Baltimore. But they still had to meet, and beat, the Chicago Bears in a playoff for the division crown.

On Wednesday before the game, Waterfield contracted intestinal flu. On Friday he ran a high fever. On Sunday he had to be driven to the game. Van Brocklin, playing his second season, started at quarterback and flubbed 8 straight passes. Next time the Rams got possession, Waterfield ran on the field. Jumbo Joe Stydahar, the coach, figured Van Brocklin wanted some relief. Van Brocklin thought Stydahar sent the new quarterback. Waterfield simply took over on his own.

On the first play he slipped the ball to Davis, who scooted 63 yards to a touchdown. It was called back. Waterfield moved the Rams into position and kicked a 43-yard field goal. Then he cranked up and threw 3 touchdown passes to Hirsch, which accounted for a 24–14 triumph.

Hirsch once came back to the huddle and suggested a pass pattern to Waterfield. Buckets nodded and threw the pass. It was intercepted by an alert defender. As they walked to the sideline, Waterfield pulled alongside the end and muttered, "Elroy, if you don't know what you're talking about, keep your damn mouth shut."

In '49 the Rams were thwarted for the league championship by a rainstorm in the Coliseum which made passing impossible but didn't hurt Steve Van Buren's running as the Eagles won, 14–0. The Cleveland Browns spoiled the '50 title game on a last-minute field goal by Lou Groza.

But the 1951 Rams, with Waterfield leading the NFL in passing, gained 5,506 yards, an average of 459 a game, and finally got their championship by beating the Browns, 24–17. Ironically, the decisive touchdown was a 73-yard touchdown pass to Fears, by Van Brocklin, who took over Waterfield's clutch role.

Bob played one more season and saw limited action. He saved most of it for an afternoon in Green Bay, Wisconsin, when the Rams trailed by 28–6 with 12 minutes to play as Waterfield took over for Van Brocklin. The Rams scored 3 touchdowns and Waterfield kicked a field goal to nose out the Packers, 30–28.

When he retired, some of the essential character and stability of the Rams went with him. The next half dozen years were marked by coaching squabbles, player popoffs and a divided ownership which rent the franchise. So in 1960, Bob Waterfield was brought back as head coach, the proverbial calm on the troubled waters. He was in over his head.

Everybody still respected him. With a touch of gray added to his temples, he maintained a pose of dignity. But the players said he was only a figurehead in the coaching

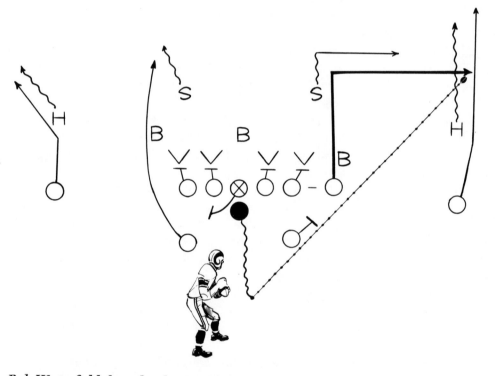

Bob Waterfield describes his favorite play:

"This is not usually a long gainer, but it is fairly safe to throw and a good first down pass. It is usually called a drag pattern.

"The left halfback ties up the weak safety and the strong end drives the strong side safety deep. Meanwhile the flanker on the strong side has taken off on a fly pattern.

"The strong side end then cuts abruptly toward the sidelines and drags in behind the flanker to catch the pass. The action of driving the strong safety deep should generally give him a step on the defender."

212

setup. The owners (Reeves in the early years had taken in Ed Pauley and Fred Levy as partners) couldn't get along. Bad trades had sent away the guts of the club, notably Van Brocklin. Bob stoically endured a couple of losing seasons, and with 4 games left in the 1962 schedule, he quit abruptly.

Silently, too.

BOB WATERFIELD

BORN: July 26, 1920   HEIGHT: 6'1½"   WEIGHT: 191

Los Angeles Rams, 1945–52

PASSING RECORD:

Year	Att.	Comp.	Yards	T.D.	Pct.	Longest	Int.
1945	172	89	1653	15	51.7	84	16
1946*	251	127	1747	18	50.5	57	17
1947	221	96	1210	8	43.4	45	18
1948	180	87	1354	14	48.3	80	18
1949	296	154	2168	17	52.0	71	24
1950	213	122	1540	11	57.3	72	13
1951*	176	88	1566	13	50.0	91	10
1952	109	51	655	3	46.8	63	11
TOTALS	1618	814	11,893	99	50.3	91	127

RUSHING RECORD:

Year	Att.	Gained	Longest	Ave.
1945	18	18	16	1.0
1946	16	−60	6	−3.8
1947	3	6	4	2.0
1948	7	12	10	1.7
1949	5	−4	5	−.8
1950	8	14	13	1.8
1951	9	49	25	5.4
1952	9	−14	19	−1.6
TOTALS	75	21	25	.3

PUNTING RECORD

Year	No.	Ave.	Longest
1945	39	40.7	68
1946	39	44.7	65
1947	59	42.4	86
1948	43	42.6	88
1949	49	44.4	61

Hollywood wasn't Waterfield's beat but he made the scene occasionally with his glamorous wife, Jane Russell.

PUNTING RECORD

1950	52	40.1	61
1951	4	41.5	52
1952	30	42.5	59
TOTALS	315	42.5	88

SCORING RECORD:

Year	T.D.	X.P.	X.P.M.	F.G.	F.G.A.	Total
1945	5	31	3	1	3	64
1946	1	37	0	6	9	61
1947	1	27	3	7	16	54
1948	0	38	6	6	10	56
1949	1	43	3	9	14	76
1950	1	54	4	7	14	81
1951	3	41	2	13*	22	98
1952	1	44	1	11	16	83
TOTALS	13	315	22	60	104	573

* Led NFL

12. The Old Pros

Bobby Layne

I DON'T CARE IF WE'RE JUST PLAYING
SHOWDOWN FOR A NICKEL A HAND. I
WANT TO BEAT YOUR BRAINS IN.

—*Bobby Layne, quarterback,*
1948–62

The football philosophy of Bobby Layne was firmed up on a blustery day in 1953 when he huddled the Detroit Lions on their own 20-yard line. He looked up at the clock on the big scoreboard in Briggs Stadium (since changed to Tiger Stadium) and it showed 3 minutes to play. In electric-bulbed numerals the score read Cleveland 16, Detroit 10. The Lions had been locked up most of the second half in their own territory.

Bobby turned around and looked at Lou Creekmur and Ollie Spencer, Harley Sewell and Dick Stanfel, the hard-bitten members of the Lions' offensive line.

"Awright, fellers," he drawled in that nasal Texas twang with a touch of whiskey in the tonsils. "Y'all block and ol' Bobby'll pass you raht to the champeenship."

"Ol' Bobby'll get you 6 big ones"—that was his credo.

He immediately threw to Jim Doran, the big left end who started out with the Lions playing defense. Doran caught only 6 passes all season, but Coach Buddy Parker knew he had been the nation's leading receiver in his college days at Iowa State. When Leon Hart, the huge end of the Lions, hurt his knee in the first half against the Browns, Doran came in as his sub.

Cleveland, expecting Layne to pass late in the game, concentrated on end Dorne Dibble and halfback Doak Walker, the prime receivers. Layne hit Doran to work the Lions out of danger. After a running play, he fired the ball to him again on a hook pattern to put the Lions across midfield. Two more passes worked the ball to the 33. Coming back to the huddle, Doran nudged Layne, "Hey, the halfback's not picking me up on a slant, Bobby."

Layne nodded. He faded back, and as Doran broke down the middle of the field, Warren Lahr of the Browns let him get a step lead. Layne floated the ball into his hands, and Doran carried the ball into the end zone. Then Walker kicked the point and the Lions had their "champeenship."

The Lions had run 6 plays in less than a minute of play.

"Layne could get in more plays in the last 2 minutes of a game," said Bill Pellington, who played a dozen seasons as linebacker for the Baltimore Colts, "than any other quarterback in history. He was smart. He knew what to do against every defense."

"If I wanted a quarterback to handle my team in the final 2 minutes, I'd have to send for Layne," said George Halas, which was quite an admission for Papa Bear because he had first crack at the blond Texan as a pro and peddled him off.

Robert Lawrence Layne, mean—yes, mean—competitor for fifteen tumultuous seasons in the National Football League, was Gary Cooper in the showdown in "High Noon"; he was Buck Jones heading off the rustlers at the pass; he was Sam Houston leading the charge at San Jacinto, and he was Davy Crockett and Jim Bowie defying Santa Anna as the Alamo crumbled. A slight footnote; he was born in the little "bitty ol' town" of Santa Anna, a dusty whistlestop in the very middle of Texas, on December 19, 1926.

219

If he had been born three generations earlier, Layne would have been the real-life sheriff in the settling of the West; and that would have included the helling on Saturday night. Layne is right out of a western scenario.

He's brash. He's gregarious. He's demanding. He's tough. He's devoted to winning. But he doesn't neglect his funning. All these qualities are reflected in his performance as a football player.

The other thing about Layne is that as a spotlighted pro quarterback, from the 1948 through the 1962 seasons, he always went first class. When he sought libation he went to the nicest joint in town, and he always walked through the front door. This is what he believed in.

"If I feel like a beer or two, I'm not going to sneak around some side-alley joint," he said testily. "It's a little late to be telling me what to do. And no one can ever say I wasn't 100 percent ready the day of a game."

Layne was a legend before his throwing arm lost its zing and he quit—there was a little of the pathos of the graying gunslinger who was no longer the fastest gun in the territory. And the stories of Layne the character were jumbled with his accomplishments as a quarterback and leader, and eventually magnified until his achievements are no longer really appreciated. He came along at the time of Graham, Tittle, Van Brocklin and Conerly, and in his head-to-head duels with all of them he was more often than not the winner.

That's why, perhaps, the most treasured memento of his playing days is a plaque received by him in 1958. It read:

BOBBY LAYNE: the guy Detroit will never forget

With great savvy and skill Bobby Layne did these things for Detroit in eight glorious years as Lion quarterback:

He produced three world championships and four divisional titles.

He completed more than 100 touchdown passes.

He turned a losing proposition into one of the best franchises in professional football. But most of all, Bobby left his mark as a matchless competitor and a great guy. How could Detroit ever forget?

THE DETROIT LIONS FAN CLUB

The Lions let Layne go after the second game of the '58 season, a 13–13 tie with the Green Bay Packers, then the low team on the totem pole in the West. The newspapers in Detroit blamed him for the poor showing and the coaches publicly criticized his execution at quarterback. Bobby got on the telephone Sunday night and called his wife Carol to tell her he was quitting. As usual, she was spending the season with their two school-age boys in their sprawling year-round ranch-style home in Lubbock, Texas.

"If that's the way you feel about it," said Carol, "come on home." But Bobby was dissuaded from packing up during the season and being branded a quitter. Instead, Carol flew up to join him. She arrived on Monday night, and as Bobby escorted her through the airport gate, he heard a page over the public address system, "Telephone call for Bobby Layne."

He turned to Carol and said, "They're probably gonna tell me I been traded. Ha, ha."

That's what it was, to the Pittsburgh Steelers, and his initial reaction was hurt. But Bobby traveled all night so he could make it to Pittsburgh the next morning in time for Tuesday practice. When he walked into the dressing room, all thirty-five Steelers ignored him. Bobby didn't know it at the time, but Harry Gilmer, then an assistant coach with the Steelers and a former teammate of Layne in Detroit, had told the players that Bobby was a salty, no-nonsense guy who was like a marine drill sergeant about practice.

"They acted," said Layne later, "almost like they were scared of me."

The veteran quarterback rallied the winless Steelers to a quick win over Philadelphia, which was nothing sensational since the Eagles won only 2 games that whole season, and then the Steelers relapsed again. The writer walked in on Layne after a loss to the Giants in New York. He was smoking a cigarette furiously, drinking black coffee and fuming, almost incoherent in defeat. Here he was—thirty-one years old, with a pot belly, a fractured ankle that had barely healed, a scarred shoulder and playing out the string with a tailend team. Yet he cared, desperately.

Somebody brought him over to a gray-haired man wearing a hat with a floppy brim, smoking a big cigar, standing next to a jockey. Layne barely acknowledged the hello. He didn't know who the guy was, didn't want to know. Later he found out it was his introduction to Art Rooney, the owner of the Steelers. Rooney was enchanted. He cared, too.

The writer eventually went to Lubbock to spend a weekend with Layne. It's a lonely place to arrive on a Friday night, and Layne wasn't home. A chain of phone calls finally located him. At a party.

"See you at the hotel in the morning," he said. Then he thought a second. "Got a better idea. I'll have somebody bring you by here first. . . . Say, you drink, don't you?"

The writer never reached the hotel. The party was followed by a breakfast of milk punch at the country club, then by a head-to-head gin rummy game in the basement between Bobby and a pipeline contractor which started at $100, then proceeded to $1,000, and when his opponent, down a few grand, clamored for more action, the poker chips came out. Noon wore into afternoon, and one pot reached $10,000. A $25 chip skipped off the table; nobody bothered to pick it up. They left it for the waiter. Everytime Bobby won, he cackled in glee. At seven o'clock, Bobby looked at his watch and said, "Gotta go, fellas. Wife's expectin' me to cook the steaks." IOU's clogged his pockets. "Whooee," he said outside, "Carol's gonna hop on me for bein' late."

Wouldn't the winnings pacify her?

"Just fun money," he shrugged. The pipeline contractor, down $25,000 for the day, dropped by the Laynes later in the evening. He cornered Bobby and said, "I need a man like you. You can keep me out of trouble and come into my business. I'll pay you $75,000 a year. It'll be worth it."

"That's very generous of you," said Layne, "but sorry, I still got to play football for Buddy Parker and Mr. Rooney. I owe it to 'em and I want to."

A blazing desire to compete has characterized Bobby Layne ever since he was a towhead in junior high school and his teammate was Doak Walker. They went on to

Highland Park High School in Dallas together, and the agreement was tacit they'd also play on the same team in college, though Bobby was a year ahead in school. Bobby went on to the University of Texas, and then both Doak and Bobby went into the merchant marine. Bobby hurried back to Texas in November, 1945, and found his buddy Doak had enrolled at Southern Methodist in time to play against the Longhorns (freshmen were eligible then). They matched touchdowns but Bobby missed his extra point. In the fourth quarter, however, he intercepted a Walker pass and fired the Longhorns on a 70-yard march via 3 passes to win, 12–7. In 1947, they both made the All-America teams as SMU went through its schedule unbeaten and Texas lost only once, a 14–13 cliffhanger to Walker & Co. But for Bobby the season had another significance. The Longhorns, with Blair Cherry stepping up as head coach to succeed the retired Dana X. Bible, converted to the T-formation with Layne as their quarterback.

Bobby married Carol Krueger the summer before his senior year. Coach Cherry, eager to indoctrinate him in the new formation, thought it would be a nice wedding present if they went with him to the summer camp of the Chicago Cardinals, where Bobby could watch a smart pro, Paul Christman, perform the mechanics of the T. On the trip north, every time they stopped for gas, Bobby and Carol jumped out of the car and practiced center snaps. It stopped traffic, too.

After graduation, however, the Pittsburgh Steelers, remembering Bobby's earlier tailback experience, drafted Layne for their single-wing attack designed by Dr. Jock Sutherland. He told them flatly he wasn't interested and might have signed with Baltimore of the All-America Conference if Art Rooney hadn't peddled the rights to the Chicago Bears. In 1948 the Bears still had Sid Luckman, and coming in with Bobby was Johnny Lujack of Notre Dame, the most highly publicized quarterback in the country. In that company, Bobby played third-fiddle. His main function was to serve as valet for center Bulldog Turner in the hazing system practiced by the pros. Bobby polished Bulldog's shoes and washed his car and when Bulldog was put on the fat man's table to restrict his eating, Bobby sneaked food to him in his room. The complicated offense of the Bears baffled the young Texan, and the Bear coaches frankly doubted his capacity ever to absorb it. So after one year, Bobby was traded to the New York Bulldogs, a random collection of strays under the haphazard direction of Ted Collins, whose real job was managing singer Kate Smith.

Their following in New York was apathetic, and the morale of the club wasn't much better. They played 18 games the year Bobby reported, including exhibitions, and lost 16 of them. Attendance for one game with Pittsburgh was so low—a smattering of a few hundred dotting the vast decks of Yankee Stadium—that Collins suggested to owner Rooney of the Steelers they clear out all the people, refund the money, and play the game just for the benefit of the two of them to satisfy one of Collins' repressed desires. "We were afraid," mused Bobby, "if Kate ever got a sore throat, we wouldn't get paid."

The experience had a dual benefit. It gave Bobby his first real chance to play quarterback as a pro and absorb valuable experience under fire. He actually set his career high of 156 pass completions in that season, and the fact he lived through that brutal pounding proved to him that he could take anything as a pro.

222

Bobby Layne shunned protection. No face guard or hip pads, special under-sized shoulder pads. The threat of Andy Robustelli (81) of the Giants didn't faze him.

Daniel R. Rubin

Layne in his Lion hey-day. He utilized the whole field. Here Bobby (22) threw a flare pass to fullback Pat Harder (34).

Trouble was, Bobby didn't want to take anything. The Philadelphia Eagles, for instance, had a bonus system in force where they paid 10 bucks for blocking a punt, 5 for an interception, 5 for racking up the quarterback, ad infinitum, and Bobby figured "they made enough money off me to pay their income tax." From his normal 205 pounds he went home to Texas after the season weighing 176 and passed old friend Doak Walker on the street without a sign of recognition from the latter. He was determined to quit football when the Detroit Lions secured him in a trade for a relatively obscure fullback named Camp Wilson (Wilson was smart; he refused to report, and the Lions had to substitute end Bobby Mann in the deal).

Layne and the Lions fitted together like hand and glove. The experience with the Bulldogs toughened him up to take over a club. He was reunited with Walker, who had graduated to the Lions, and Detroit was on a lucky spree with young talent. Among those who reported the next couple of years were such eventual all-pros as defensive back Jack Christiansen, tackles Lou Creekmur and Thurman McGraw, ends Leon Hart, Dorne Dibble and Cloyce Box and guard Dick Stanfel.

With the elevation of Buddy Parker to head coach in 1951, the Lions were on their way. Only a loss on the last day of the season to San Francisco kept them from a Western Conference title that year. They made it to the top the next season and defeated the all-conquering Cleveland Browns, 17–7, for the league championship. Parker ran a loose ship. The Lions were a roistering crew with the ribald spirit of a pirate vessel, and Layne was the first mate. A ritual of training camp was Layne's beer bust for the rookies, to see if any of them could keep up with him.

"You can call it cornball," said Layne, "but it's effective. Football is a team game, and the guys have to belong. This is a feeling you can't get in a day." He wanted the Detroit Lion uniform to mean something and cited the example of the New York Yankees.

Layne, for all his autocratic behavior, was no prima donna. Parker wanted him to run from the split-T in 1952, so he ran, though he wore no hip pads, no thigh pads, disdained a face mask and had special undersized shoulderpads which would not restrict his throwing. The Lions roared to two world championships with their boisterous camaraderie and set serious aim on an unprecedented third-straight, never achieved since the modern phase of the NFL began with the split into Eastern and Western divisions in 1933. They won their third straight division title in '54 and for the third straight time prepared to meet the Cleveland Browns. In regular-season and championship play the Lions had never lost to the Browns and in fact had defeated them, 14–10, in the last game of the campaign. Coach Parker wanted no slipups. He asked all the Lions to be in bed by ten o'clock, and they complied 100 percent, Layne among them.

The Lions got bombed, 56–10, in the greatest rout since the Bears 73–0 mauling of the Redskins in '40.

"I guess," ruminated Parker later, "when a kid's been used to drinking bourbon since he was fourteen, you don't want to change his habits."

Over the years, the sight of Layne making the scene in Detroit or Pittsburgh the night before a game wasn't unusual. Bobby explained it easily: "I'm one of those people who can get along on five to seven hours of sleep. If I go to bed at eleven the night before

224

a game, I'll get up at five. By kickoff time I've already played one game in my head, with the real one still to come. But if I go to bed at two, I'll sleep until eight. Then I won't have so much time to fret before the game."

One night in Detroit he was arrested on a charge of driving while intoxicated. Bobby could have ducked publicity by simply paying the fine but insisted on a jury trial. He was flagged down for driving without his lights on after stopping at a pizza place which was closed. "The officer made a big fuss," said Layne, "because I'd been to Les Bingaman's bar earlier in the evening." Bingaman was the 300-pound middle guard of the Lions. Most of the Lions turned out in court and when the verdict came in—"Not guilty!"—they reacted like after a team victory. Part of the testimony had involved Layne's Texas drawl, which can be a little tough for Detroit cops to understand.

At the post-trial party, a natural consequence of the acquittal, Friday Macklem, the equipment manager of the Lions, fixed up a sign which he carried all evening: "AH-ALL AIN'T DRUNK. AH'M FROM TEXAS."

Late in his career, Bobby became sensitive about his playboy reputation because his two boys were growing up and he complained, "If I had been to all the places and done all the things I'm supposed to have done, I'd have to be Superman."

In the summer of 1955, on a ranch outside Lubbock, Layne was holding the reins for his boy, Bobby, Jr., when a sudden shot made the animal rear and tore the quarterback's right shoulder out of its socket. Bobby played that fall but couldn't throw normally and the Lions dropped to last place. In 1956, facing the Chicago Bears on the last Sunday of the season for the division title, he was blind-sided by end Ed Meadows and suffered a severe brain concussion. In 1957, late in the season, he fractured his ankle in a game against the Cleveland Browns, and although Bobby missed the ensuing championship game rematch with Cleveland, the Lions were in good shape for a replacement.

Tobin Rote, who had starred at Rice, had arrived from Green Bay to share the quarterback job with Layne. They were old rivals from college days in Texas but good buddies. The rugged Rote fitted right into the spirit of the Lions. The quarterback meetings were held in a neighborhood pub, the most convenient and logical place following an afternoon workout. Also with the quarterback corps, though held off the roster, was Jack Kemp, a youngster drafted from little Occidental College in California. Kemp was freckle-faced and wide-eyed and awed by the old pros. He sipped softly on his Coke while they plotted. Layne tapped his glass on the wood after a session, squinted at Kemp and said, "Kid, if you want to make it in this league, you're gonna have to learn to drink."

Despite the personal rapport with Rote, Layne chafed as a 50 percent quarterback. He believed in the one-boss system and didn't enjoy sitting around. "When I'm not playing," he said, "I have a serious weight problem. Part of it goes where I'm sitting and the rest to my stomach." In the long history of the pros, divided field authority has seldom produced winners. The Los Angeles Rams won only one world championship with Bob Waterfield and Norm Van Brocklin on the same squad. The San Francisco 49ers couldn't accommodate Frankie Albert and Y. A. Tittle.

And so after the second game of the 1958 season, Layne was traded to Pittsburgh and stretched his career five more years. He never brought Mr. Rooney and Buddy Parker a championship—the closest he came was his first year with the Steelers.

But Layne left his impact on the times. Coach Paul Brown called him "the best third-down quarterback in football." The third-down play separates the men from the boys, and the quarterback who can produce in the clutch situation is a winner. Layne wasn't a picture-book passer. He never was interested in averages and therefore didn't have the percentage of completions to match the other passers of his time.

"Any game in which we gained 200 yards on the ground was a great day for passing, too," claimed Bobby. Yet playing one season less than Baugh, acknowledged as the greatest passer of all, Layne exceeded slinging Sammy's career marks for passes attempted and completed, total yardage and number of touchdown passes.

"Records?" he smirked. "They're just a reminder that I'm getting old. What's more, they're just made to be busted. Winning is what's important. That's all I'm interested in."

He cited the attitude of old-teammate Bingaman as his ideal. "You couldn't move him with a bulldozer," said Layne, "yet he was a guy who always came to training camp afraid he wouldn't hold his job. From the first moment of practice he gave it everything he had.

"In one preseason scrimmage he was breaking up every play I tried to run over his middle-guard position. He seemed to know exactly what was coming. We had a new boy in our backfield, Don McIlhenny. Bing told me after practice that Don was tipping off the plays.

"I said, 'Look, tell me what he's doing. It might help straighten out the offense.'

"Bing shook his head, 'Oh, no. Not until they make the final squad cut. Then I'll tell you.'

"I want competitors like that playing on my side."

As a pitcher at the University of Texas, Bobby won 26 straight games and had a short fling at minor league ball until he decided he didn't like the travel, the hours or the accommodations. He got Slater Martin, an All-American basketball player, put on the team at Texas so he'd have a poker partner on road trips. "He couldn't throw a fast ball," said Coach Bib Falk, an old major-leaguer, "and his curve wasn't even a wrinkle. But he would have made the majors. All he could do was beat you."

Before he started his fifteenth and last season in 1962, Buddy Parker said, "Bobby's throwing lousy." A blood tumor on his left side restricted his passing and had knocked him out of half the previous season. At the time he had gained more yards than any passer in history. Why not let it rest there?

"It's just like a doctor at thirty-five who's been practicing medicine," explained Bobby. "You don't expect him to quit. It's something I like." When he saw, however, that he couldn't produce a winner, he retired gracefully. A good businessman, he has bowling alleys, oil leases and did some coaching for the Steelers and the St. Louis Cardinals. Puffed out a little and wheezing like a latter-day Wallace Beery, he admitted, "Quarterbacking is a lot tougher now. But—"

Bobby paused for effect.

"There are winners and there are losers, and some of the so-called best never won a league championship. The winners did."

His old friend, Doak Walker, put the real epitaph on the career of Bobby Layne:

"Bobby never lost a game in his life. Time simply ran out on him."

226

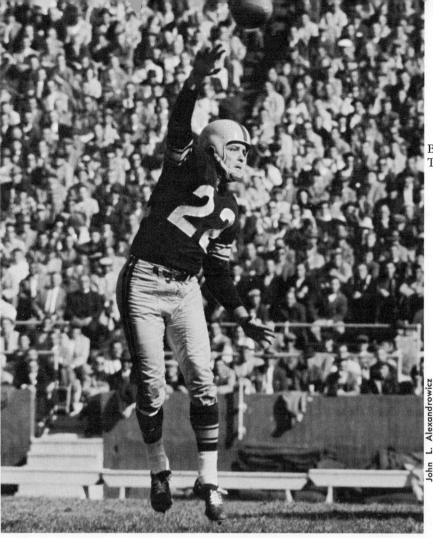

John L. Alexandrowicz

Bobby wasn't a picture book thrower, but only Y. A. Tittle completed more passes in his lifetime.

A fractured ankle against the Cleveland Browns in 1957 hastened Layne's departure from Detroit.

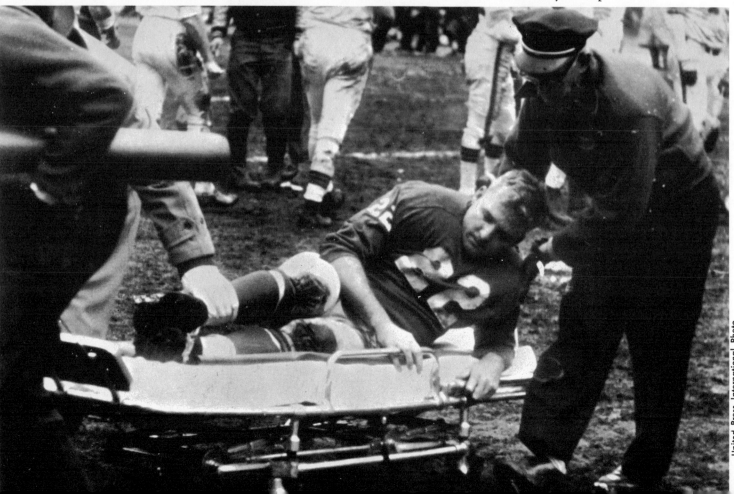

United Press International Photo

Bobby Layne describes his favorite pass play:

"On Thanksgiving Day in 1953, the Detroit Lions were behind Green Bay, 15–7, in the third quarter. The Packers were on our 3-yard line, and it was snowing like hell. Then they fumbled. On the first play, I called a "Green Left X Over Post"—my favorite play at Detroit.

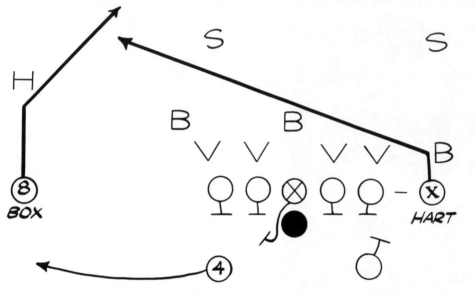

"Green alerts everyone it's a pass. Left tells the 4-back to divide to the left and the center to pull and block to the left. The G-man, Hart, ran an over pattern deep enough to get behind the linebackers. Box ran a 'post,' splitting the cornerback and safety. The pass puts a lot of pressure on the right safety, especially if they doubled up on our flanker—who was Doak Walker—with strong coverage. Viz.:

"Because Box was so fast and usually took both defensive men with him, Hart (quite a bit slower) was usually open. The play timed out perfectly because of Hart's speed. If the safety saw Hart coming across and dropped off, then Box was open. The 4-back dividing to the left flat kept the linebacker from dropping off.

"Against Green Bay that day, the safety man spotted Hart coming across and picked him up. Box beat the cornerback and was wide open for a 97-yard score. This got us back in the game, and we won easily, 34–15."

BOBBY LAYNE

BORN: Dec. 19, 1926   HEIGHT: 6'1"   WEIGHT: 208

Chicago Bears, 1948

New York Bulldogs, 1949

Detroit Lions, 1950–57

Pittsburgh Steelers, 1958–62

PASSING RECORD:

Year	Att.	Comp.	Yards Gained	T.D.	Pct.	Longest	Int.
1948	52	16	232	3	30.7	35	2
1949	299	155	1796	9	51.8	69	18
1950	336	152	2323	16	45.2	82	18
1951	332	152	2403	26	45.8	63	23
1952	287	139	1999	19	48.4	77	20
1953	273	125	2088	16	45.8	97	21
1954	246	135	1818	14	54.9	55	12
1955	270	143	1830	11	53.0	77	17
1956	244	129	1909	9	52.9	70	17
1957	179	87	1169	6	48.6	65	12
1958	294	145	2510	14	49.3	78	12
1959	297	142	1986	20	47.8	48	21
1960	209	103	1814	13	49.3	70	17
1961	149	75	1205	11	50.3	53	16
1962	233	116	1686	9	49.8	62	17
TOTALS	3700	1814	26,768	196	49.0	97	243

RUSHING RECORD:

Year	Att.	Yards Gained	Longest	Ave.
1948	13	80	18	6.1
1949	54	196	27	3.6
1950	56	250	30	4.5
1951	61	290	36	4.8
1952	94	411	29	4.4
1953	87	343	23	3.9
1954	30	119	34	4.0

1955	31	111	19	3.6
1956	46	169	20	3.7
1957	24	99	21	4.1
1958	40	154	18	3.9
1959	33	181	21	5.5
1960	19	12	13	0.6
1961	8	11	9	1.4
1962	15	25	17	1.7
TOTALS	611	2451	36	4.0

SCORING RECORD:

Year	T.D.	X.P.	X.P.M.	F.G.	F.G.A.	Total
1948	1	0	0	0	1	6
1949	3	0	0	0	0	18
1950	4	1	1	0	0	25
1951	1	0	0	0	0	6
1952	1	2	0	0	0	8
1953	0	0	0	0	0	0
1954	2	0	0	0	0	12
1955	0	0	0	0	0	0
1956	5	33	0	12	15	99
1957	0	25	0	6	11	43
1958	3	1	2	0	0	19
1959	2	32	0	11	17	77
1960	2	21	1	5	6	48
1961	0	5	0	0	0	5
1962	1	0	0	0	0	6
TOTALS	25	120	4	34	50	372

Norm Van Brocklin

THE DUTCHMAN WILL BREAK EVERY
PASSING RECORD IN THE BOOK—IF SOME-
ONE DOESN'T BREAK HIS NECK FIRST.

—Hamp Pool, head coach,
Los Angeles Rams, 1952–54

Norm Van Brocklin was pulling off his grimy jersey for the last time. His jowls supported a wide grin. He was giggling. When the Dutchman giggles, it's dangerous. Not malevolent like Dan Duryea playing a deranged killer in the movies, but sticky.

The guy with the mike in the jumbled dressing room stuck it in front of Van Brocklin and asked, "Say, Norm, is this really your last game as a player?"

The Dutchman giggled and snapped, "You're goddam right it is."

The announcer gulped and plunged in with another question: "Now what are your future plans?"

"To get the hell out of L.A. as fast as I can."

That was Norm Van Brocklin's official exit from the active life of a pro quarterback, on January 15, 1961.

Van Brocklin went out in character. He was the quarterback of the East team in the annual Pro Bowl game in Los Angeles. The Dutchman threw a 46-yard touchdown pass to Tommy McDonald, a 43-yard payoff pass to Pete Retzlaff, a scoring 36-yarder to Sonny Randle. He also threw 6 straight passes in a desperate last-minute effort, but the East lost 35–31. And Dutch was a poor loser. He was the kind of guy who would be standing around after the game, looking composed, even affable, then he'd suddenly slam out and hit a metal locker with his fist.

Except for the score, he was on top of the world, figuratively, that January in 1961. It wasn't public, but Van Brocklin had concluded negotiations to step from playing ranks right into the head coaching job with the new Minnesota franchise, at $25,000 a year. Discounting the Pro Bowl, which was just an exhibition game and meaningless, he went out a winner—as the quarterback and coach-on-the-field of the Philadelphia Eagles, recently crowned champions of the National League.

Dutch was awarded the Jim Thorpe Trophy, given by Newspaper Enterprise Association to the most valuable player in the league, with all the NFL players acting as the electorate. At thirty-four, he was ready for a new career.

In the fall of 1965, Van Brocklin was in his fifth year as the head coach of the Minnesota Vikings, and the Pro Bowl scene was replayed to him in a reminiscent conversation. Dutch didn't giggle. He scowled, "Ah, you got it all wrong. I never used any profanity."

The teller reminded him—maybe it was impertinent—that he was right there.

"You're just like those L.A. writers," snorted Van Brocklin.

The Dutchman went through a dozen years as a player with a biting tongue and a sniping passing arm. "Would you want to be a coach?" he was asked as the seasons piled up.

"No," he said, "I want to be a sportswriter, like the rest of you idiots."

He was Ted Williams in shoulderpads—a bit more approachable, not as profane, but just as truculent and equally the artist. What Williams was to hitting, Van Brocklin was to the forward pass.

233

"All he has," once scoffed a San Francisco 49er coach, "is an arm. He runs like a woman trying to get out of her girdle."

George Halas of the Chicago Bears expanded the opinion: "Van Brocklin can throw. Period. In the full sense of the word, he is not a professional football player."

Like they used to say, all Galli-Curci could do was sing. Or to modernize it, Picasso has only his art. Van Brocklin threw a football with the same purity of purpose. He was the absolute derivative of the T-formation in football.

The Dutchman, born in Eagle Butte, South Dakota, grew up in northern California, the only one in a family of nine kids who ever got to college. He came in by way of the back door by spending three years in the Navy during World War II (he enlisted as a seventeen-year-old high school graduate in 1943), which entitled him to an education on the GI Bill of Rights. With a modest sports background he enrolled at Oregon in the company of a couple of buddies from Walnut Creek, California. A baseball scholarship was worth $15 a month extra—Van Brocklin was a pitcher—and football was good for $75. Van Brocklin went for the big dough.

Oregon used the single-wing, and his deficiencies were immediately apparent. He ran slightly faster than a seal on dry land. As the fifth-string tailback, he totalled 11 minutes of playing time in 1946 (freshmen were eligible for varsity play). His record showed 9 passes, no completions, 3 interceptions. Jim Aiken, a gravel-throated character who came out of Ohio high school coaching, took over at Oregon in 1947 and installed the T. He asked for kids who could throw a football. His California buddies pointed to Dutch. Aiken grabbed his stubby fingers, sniffed once and said, "You better give up smoking, kid."

In 1948, Oregon lost only 1 game with Van Brocklin at quarterback and was invited to play against Doak Walker and SMU in the Cotton Bowl. The 21–13 loss was Van Brocklin's farewell to college football after only three seasons. He was enrolled in a biology class, and the lab instructor was a vivacious graduate instructor named Gloria Schiewe. He tried to date the instructress after class. She handed him a test with a flunking grade. When Van Brocklin got his work up to C—, she went out with him. "I fell in love with the big stiff," she said "because he was so helpless."

They were married while Van Brocklin was still in school. With summer studies and Gloria's tutelage, he was able to complete his college credits in three years, a fact that escaped the notice of every pro team, including the Los Angeles Rams. Owner Dan Reeves noticed, however, that on a routine form sent to college players, Van Brocklin had put a question mark after graduation date. He was curious and called Van Brocklin in Eugene, Oregon. Dutch told him he was interested in turning pro right away because he could use the money. So the Rams drafted and signed him for the 1949 season, while Aiken bellowed at the raid of his star.

Clark Shaughnessy was the head coach of the Rams. He could have ignored the curly-headed rookie with the dimple in his chin because incumbent quarterback Bob Waterfield was running one-two with Otto Graham for all-pro honors, and whatever help Bob needed was provided by tested Jim Hardy. But the Ram coach found the right spots to use the kid with the strong right arm and Van Brocklin pulled out 3 games to justify his salary. He completed 32 out of 58 passes and showed enough to let them get rid of Hardy, who was unhappy as a second-stringer.

234

Playing for the East in the Pro Bowl, Van Brocklin (11) teamed with fullback Jimmy Brown (32) on a swing pass.

Norm Van Brocklin (11) sets up quickly behind the blocking of the Los Angeles Ram forward wall. **Vic Stein & Associates**

As a sophomore pro in 1950, Van Brocklin cut into half the great Waterfield's playing time and won the league passing championship. In mid-season, Jumbo Joe Stydahar, who succeeded Shaughnessy as coach, turned the young Dutchman loose against the Detroit Lions. Dutch warmed up by pitching the Rams to a 24–10 lead at halftime. In the third quarter, the Rams erupted with a record-tying barrage of 41 points. These were Van Brocklin's scoring contributions: 31-yard pass to Elroy Hirsch; 43-yard pass to Glenn Davis; 30-yard pass to Tom Fears; 42-yard pass to Bob Boyd. The Dutchman mixed up his receivers pretty well. Stunts like this eventually established him as the greatest long-ball thrower of his time, probably the best ever.

In 1951 he hit Fears with a 73-yarder in the last 5 minutes to beat the Cleveland Browns for the NFL title, and a year later he had definitely unseated Waterfield as the regular, winning league passing honors a second time. He also took over Bob's punting role and was one of the most consistent booters in pro football throughout his career.

Now the real Van Brocklin personality—cocky, hot-tempered—was paraded front and center. A big Ram tackle, Tom Dahms, missed a block that put the quarterback on his rear. On the sidelines, Van Brocklin grabbed a cup of water from the dispenser and flipped it in Dahms' face. The 250-pound tackle blinked, and shrugged. He said tackle Bobby Cross' favorite block was a "look-out" block. "You know," explained Van Brocklin, "he misses his man and he turns around and yells, 'Look out, Dutch!' "

When a tackle on the other team roughed him up, Dutch challenged him to a meeting under the stands later. The tackle might show. Van Brocklin didn't. "I may have a hot head," he explained glibly, "but it's not empty."

In his first year Shaughnessy had given the young quarterback a basic theorem for quarterbacking: "It's just like driving ten mules. You've got ten reins in your hand. You can pull and push and do anything you want with them."

Van Brocklin thrived on the big bomb. He had the arm to put the ball any place on the field, and the Rams had the jackrabbits to complement his firepower. Against the New York Yanks in 1951, he piled up a record yardage of 554 yards through the air.

A teammate questioned Dutch's pinpoint accuracy. He told the quarterback to throw a football downfield. For each time he hit the ball where it landed, Dutch would get a Coke. Van Brocklin flipped the football, which rolled to a stop 35 yards away. Then he proceeded to hit the ball on the ground point-blank 6 times out of 10. Ergo, six Cokes into the chubby stomach. For most of his playing time, the 6–2 Dutchman weighed 208 pounds.

When Stydahar sent in a running play against Green Bay in 1951, Van Brocklin studiously decided that a pass was much more appropriate under the circumstances, so he nonchalantly ignored the instructions. Jumbo Joe pulled him from the lineup and put in Waterfield. Bob got a hot hand and, playing the rest of the game, piled up enough passing statistics to win the league passing title back from Van Brocklin. The Dutchman blew a fuse. That's why he spent most of the title game against the Browns warming the seat of his gold knee-pants—until Stydahar used him to bail the Rams out on that 73-yard bomb to Fears.

It was always merry with Dutch around. The Rams called him "Laughing Boy," and Elroy Hirsch bet him $5 that he could get him to giggle within 5 minutes by telling the corniest jokes. Elroy won the bet.

Van Brocklin's "House of Mirth" began to show cracks, though, after a couple of years. Billy Wade, a tall quarterback from Vanderbilt, was the Rams' bonus pick for 1954, and pretty soon you had the Van Brocklin–Waterfield situation all over again. They were hardly the same types. Van Brocklin was caustic and controversial. Wade was a religious young man who wanted everybody to like him. The Dutchman was the boss man, but there was a Wade claque that felt the young guy deserved more action. In 1955, Van Brocklin led the Rams to the Western Conference title as Sid Gillman, an import from college ranks, took over as head coach. Gillman gave the veteran Rams a loose hand that first season. In the championship game against the Browns, Van Brocklin came up flat. "It was the worst game I ever played," he said. "It still haunts me."

He threw 6 interceptions, and Gillman tightened the screws. Sid's confidence in the veteran quarterback wavered—because of the title-game flop, Van Brocklin felt. The coach split the quarterbacking between him and Wade. But after the Rams came up with a 4–8 record, first losing season of Van Brocklin's career, Gillman restored the veteran to first-string status for 1957.

However, Gillman insisted on sending in plays from the sidelines, à la Paul Brown. Van Brocklin wasn't buying. "You give the quarterback a 'ready' list and feed him information," he said, "but he's the only one who can get the actual feel of the play on the field. The quarterback has to be the leader." Besides which, the personalities of the intense Gillman and the wisecracking Van Brocklin didn't rub right.

After the 1957 season, Van Brocklin announced his retirement, a convenient way of saying he wanted out. Privately, he asked Pete Rozelle, then the general manager of the Rams, to trade him, preferably to a team like the Cleveland Browns and not the lowly Philadelphia Eagles. It had to be a team in the Eastern Conference because Rozelle wouldn't risk turning the Dutchman loose on his old teammates.

"Then I'll be a son of a gun," recalled Van Brocklin, "Buck Shaw, who was made coach of the Eagles, called me and said, 'I got you in a trade.' I told him I wasn't going to report." The price for the Eagles was cheap: defensive back Jimmy Harris, guard Buck Lansford and a draft choice.

Throwing footballs still beat working for a living, and Dutch did report. The Eagles burrowed through a miserable season that yielded just 2 victories. "We got a bunch of deadbeats," complained Van Brocklin, "but I'm not saying goodbye on that kind of record." Just for security, to keep the quarterback from running off and retiring again, the club paid him $1,000 a month to stick around and work during the off-season, instead of heading back to the warmth of the West Coast. He bought a home in Valley Forge, Pennsylvania, for his family, now expanded to three daughters, and immersed himself in Civil War history as a sideline, which seemed subjectively appropriate for someone like Van Brocklin.

The next season, as the Eagles improved to a second-place finish, Van Brocklin showed symptoms of being a teacher as well as a performer. He worked hard with misfits like Tommy McDonald and Pete Retzlaff. McDonald had been an All-American halfback at Oklahoma, but was too small to be a runner, and too flaky as a receiver, unable to remember his pass routes. He settled down to become a sensation under Van's urging. Retzlaff, a good-looking specimen, needed a position, and Dutch recommended end. He spent hours working with Pete, who tied for the NFL receiving crown in

237

Tommy McDonald (25) was a bust as a pro until the Dutchman worked with him on his pass routes. Pete Retzlaff (44) developed into a great receiver under Van Brocklin's tutelage.

1958. Dutch urged the Eagles to pick up safety Don Burroughs from the Rams when "The Blade" became available, a move that tightened the defensive secondary.

On a personal level, Van Brocklin entered the greatest phase of his career. The Eagles had no right to be a championship team. They lacked a good running game. Their offensive line was mediocre. The defense was porous. A fellow like Chuck Bednarik had to go both ways in key games against teams like the Browns and Giants. The Dutchman, however, was magnificent.

Buck Shaw was a low-keyed coach who let Van Brocklin do pretty much as he pleased. The confidence and responsibility brought a new balance to Van Brocklin's concept of offense. He mixed the short passes with the long and worked out a practical 50–50 ratio between running and throwing.

More than a decade of experience showed in his ability to avoid trouble. The blitz had become the big thing on defense, but in the first 7 games of 1960, he was thrown for a total loss of 6 yards. "It's impossible to put a rush on him," said his old Ram teammate, Andy Robustelli, then starring for the Giants.

"The toughest quarterback to get at in my time was Van Brocklin," said Gino Marchetti of the Colts, rated the finest defensive end in history. "No doubt about it. When I played against the Dutchman and was the offside end (Marchetti played left end, normally the strong side, but when the Eagles lined up in a left formation, he became the offside end), the Eagles wouldn't even bother to block me on a rollout pass. I used to be pretty fast, but I never got to him."

The Eagles came from behind in 8 games during the 1960 season as they rolled up a 10–2 record to win the Eastern Conference title. Van Brocklin, brash as ever, rode them harshly. "As well as I knew him off the field," said all-pro defensive back Tom Brookshier, "any time he thought I wasn't playing right, he'd bawl the hell out of me."

"With him," said Burroughs, "there is no substitute for winning."

Comparison of strength in the Western and Eastern divisions was already a favorite topic. Since Van Brocklin was exposed to both, the writer asked him for a comparison.

"Well," he said pointedly, "the West used to be stronger. But now we've got all the good quarterbacks over here."

The championship game against the Green Bay Packers on a gooey turf in Franklin Field was a masterpiece of play direction by the veteran quarterback. The sloppy going favored the Packers, who were oriented to a running attack and had young bucks like Jimmy Taylor and Paul Hornung to supply the power. The Packers outgained the Eagles on the ground, 223 yards to 99 with 22 first downs to 13. In the fourth quarter Green Bay took a 13–10 lead on a surprise 7-yard scoring pass from Bart Starr to Max McGee. Philadelphia got a lift when halfback Ted Dean cut loose with a 58-yard kickoff return to the Packer 39-yard line. If Van Brocklin followed his usual pattern, he would try to hit the Packers with the bomb. He played it cool and sent Dean off tackle, as the Green Bay defense dropped off. Then he called Billy Barnes into the middle on a trap. He alternated the two running backs, keeping the ball on the ground until the Eagles got inside the 20. He threw the ball just once. When the Packers closed in, he hit Barnes on a quick pop pass over the middle for 13 yards. With the ball on the 5-yard line, the Packers still expected the throw, but Van Brocklin swept Dean around end for the touchdown that won the game, 17–13.

Then he sat back and waited for the Eagles to name him their head coach. Buck Shaw, according to plan, announced his retirement. Van Brocklin said he had been promised the job as far back as '58, when he first came to the club. The Eagles, loath to lose the best quarterback in the league, wondered if he'd become a playing coach. He turned them down emphatically. According to Van Brocklin, the Eagle brass offered him a one-year contract as head coach but denied him the authority to hire or fire his assistants. Van Brocklin couldn't see that either. When they wondered if he'd settle for just playing quarterback, Dutch snapped, "I wouldn't play for you blankety-blanks if I was starving to death." That's one thing about Van Brocklin. He's not inconsistent. About that time, someone asked him if he'd consider a college coaching job.

"That's for idiots," he said, "—putting your career in the hands of eighteen-year-old kids."

Van Brocklin had a trump card left. The Minnesota Vikings, newly franchised, needed a coach. Bert Rose, their general manager, knew Van Brocklin from their association in Los Angeles, where Rose was the publicity man. Bert gambled that the Dutchman's natural leadership and undisputed knowledge of football would override his abrasiveness. Van Brocklin got the job.

The NFL conducted an expansion draft, and Van Brocklin came out of it saying, "we just paid half a million for a bunch of stiffs." From the original picks, only one man, tackle Grady Alderman, remained with the Vikings after the 1965 season. But the Vikings won the first league game they ever played, upsetting the Chicago Bears, 37–13. In their fourth season they tied the Green Bay Packers for second place in the Western Conference.

The early Viking training camps were exercises in physical survival. Van Brocklin, who had called himself a "spectator" quarterback, spared no one. From a Viking camp in 1962, quarterback aspirant Lee Grosscup wrote, "The Dutchman has his QB's do the wave drill, forward rolls, head-on tackling, sled popping, rope running, and even had us emulating corner linebackers for the benefit of our fullbacks in a pass-protection drill." Bemidji, Minnesota, is normally an idyllic summer retreat for virile young men since the teachers' college there is loaded with pert teachers on campus for refresher work. The football players were simply too exhausted to practice social coexistence.

The ultimate contradiction was that Van Brocklin the coach, the man who "ran only from sheer fright," wound up with a quarterback, Francis Tarkenton, who popularized the scramble in pro football. Against Baltimore, Tarkenton was nailed by Gino Marchetti and plopped on the ground in front of the Viking bench. Van Brocklin bent over his fallen, dazed quarterback and said, "Welcome to the National Football League."

Van Brocklin found coaching presented a different perspective. "I find it hard," he confessed, "to walk up to a player and tell him he did a helluva good job."

But in 1964, after the Vikings lost a tough game to the Baltimore Colts, the Western Conference champs that year, the Dutchman gushed with unexpected feeling, "I'm proud of these kids. I'm sure Baltimore respects us. If they say they don't, they're liars."

Mellowed? Not exactly. Mercurial? Still. After the same Colts dealt the Vikings a 41–21 whipping in the ninth game of the 1965 season, Van Brocklin spent a casual eve-

240

ning with Jim Finks, the general manager, discussing business as usual. At ten o'clock, he called Johnny McKay on the West Coast. McKay, the football coach at the University of Southern California, was Dutch's backfield teammate at Oregon and they kept touch. Van Brocklin was disappointed at the loss, which made the Viking record 5–4 and virtually eliminated them from a shot at winning the divisional title. But otherwise the conversation was normal chitchat. At midnight, however, Van Brocklin called the writers who covered the team for the Minneapolis and St. Paul newspapers and asked them to meet him in the morning.

The next day, he resigned. The loss soured him. He felt he couldn't help the Vikings win the "big" game. That he had taken the team as far as he could and it was time for a change. A hell of a time and a hell of a spot. The Vikings had the Green Bay Packers coming up in six days. The owners of the team, completely stunned, asked him to re-

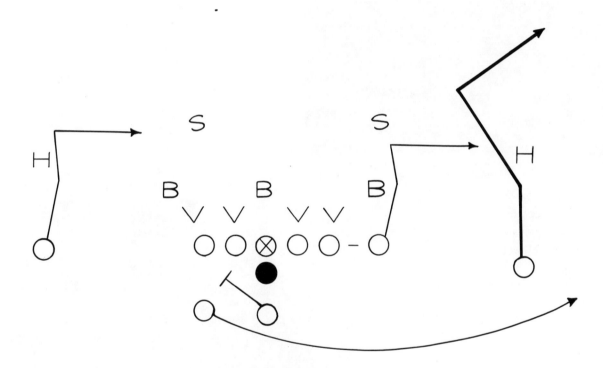

Norm Van Brocklin describes his favorite play:

"This play is called a 74 Away Switch.

"It's used when the left corner man is playing the flanker, who's the primary receiver, tough to the inside. When it works right, you can put six quick ones up on the scoreboard.

"The Eagles used it successfully in their championship game with the Green Bay Packers in 1960. Hank Gremminger, their corner back, was taking the inside move away from Tommy McDonald, our flanker. We had the ball on their 35-yard line.

"Tommy faked a cut to the middle of the field, drawing the corner man over. He was leaning that way anyhow. Then McDonald broke sharply to the flag in the right corner of the end zone and caught a touchdown pass to give us a 7–6 lead."

241

In his last active season, 1960, Norm Van Brocklin won the Jim Thorpe Trophy as the outstanding player in the National Football League.

Van Brocklin in his coaching cap with the Minnesota Vikings showed off his brilliant grasp of football in all phases.

consider. Van Brocklin went home and chewed on that awhile. Just as abruptly, he decided to stay on.

His resignation didn't surprise those who knew his volatility as much as did his turnabout decision to return to the Vikings. Van Brocklin is the kind of guy who sticks to his guns. But what he had done by quitting was basically unfair. It would hurt the kids, who still had a chance to retrieve the season. He wasn't the kind of man to run from a challenge, either.

Van Brocklin is a paradox in many ways. There's the calm, reflective side. He received his master's degree in education, just as Gloria, his wife, continued her studies for a master's in bacteriology. Coaching is detail work. Van Brocklin can pore over films for hours. His dedication affects the kids who play for him, who know he's a hard man and take his comments, which can sometimes be cruel, because they also know he doesn't drive them any harder than he does himself.

That's the way Dutch Van Brocklin played quarterback, too.

NORMAN VAN BROCKLIN

BORN: March 15, 1926   HEIGHT: 6'1"   WEIGHT: 200

Los Angeles Rams, 1949–57
Philadelphia Eagles, 1958–60
PASSING RECORD:

Year	Att.	Comp.	Yards Gained	T.D.	Pct.	Longest	Int.
1949	58	32	601	6	55.2	51	2
1950*	233	127	2061	18	54.5	58	14
1951	194	100	1725	13	51.5	81	11
1952*	205	113	1736	14	55.1	84	17
1953	286	156	2393	19	54.5	70	14
1954*	260	139	2637	13	53.5	80	21
1955	272	144	1890	8	52.9	74	15
1956	124	68	966	7	54.8	58	12
1957	265	132	2105	20	49.8	70	21
1958	374	198	2409	15	52.9	91	20
1959	340	191	2617	16	56.2	71	14
1960	284	153	2471	24	53.9	64	17
TOTALS	2895	1553	23,611	173	53.6	91	178

* Led NFL

RUSHING RECORD:

Year	Att.	Yards Gained	Longest	Ave.
1949	4	−1	2	−.3
1950	15	22	16	1.5
1951	7	2	4	.3
1952	7	−10	9	−1.4
1953	8	11	6	1.4
1954	6	−10	5	−1.7
1955	11	24	9	2.2
1956	4	1	1	0.3
1957	10	−4	3	−.4
1958	8	5	2	.6
1959	11	13	3	1.2
1960	11	−13	1	−1.2
TOTALS	102	40	16	.4

PUNTING RECORD:

Year	No.	Ave.	Longest
1949	2	45.5	46
1950	11	42.4	51
1951	48	41.5	62
1952	29	43.1	66
1953	60	42.2	57
1954	44	42.6	61
1955	60	44.6	61
1956	48	43.1	72
1957	54	44.3	71
1958	54	41.2	58
1959	53	42.7	59
1960	60	43.1	70
TOTALS	523	42.9	72

Charley Conerly

AT TWENTY-NINE, CHARLEY CONERLY
WAS EVERY BIT THE QUARTERBACK THAT
HE WAS AT THIRTY-NINE—BETTER, IN
FACT. ONLY NOBODY KNEW IT.

—Otto Graham, quarterback,
Cleveland Browns, 1946–56

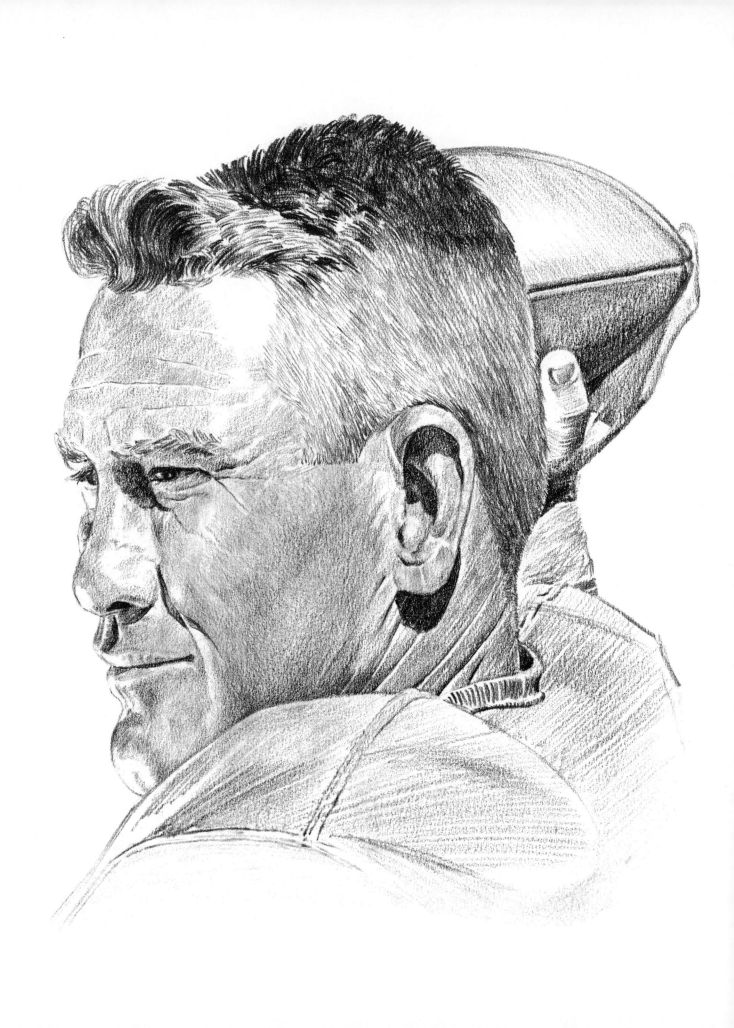

When Charley Conerly's hair showed gray at the temples and the lines in his forehead were permanent, an agency on Madison Avenue in New York thought he had just the right look for some outdoors-man cigarette ads. The dents in his nose told of rough days. And the tattoo on his forearm was the added touch. Charley didn't object. He got paid the scale for a male model. There was a tougher way to make a buck.

The burly linebacker of the Green Bay Packers sat in his lap, tugging on his ankle. Charley didn't like it. When they untangled and Charley had time to shake the mud from his pants and hitch his shoulderpads, he turned around and let the linebacker hear how he felt. The language was pure marine, the way they sometimes express themselves on a football field.

"You're too old," snapped young Tom Bettis of the Green Bay Packers, "to be talking to me like that."

At the time Conerly was thirty-eight years old. He played on until he was forty years old, through the 1961 season, the oldest quarterback in New York, or any other place in the history of pro football.

In his last years, as the skin got leathery and lined, Charley looked less like a vigorous football player than a Mississippi delta cotton farmer, which he also happened to be when he packed up his bags every December to go home to Clarksdale.

Except for a privy few, people around New York never really got to know Charley Conerly, who played there fourteen years. They knew him by the signs that festooned the old Polo Grounds, which used to say "Conerly, Go Home." They knew him from Conerly Day in the twilight of his career, 1959, when he stood in the more dignified setting of Yankee Stadium and made the longest speech of his life. He accepted $25,000 worth of gifts for himself and his wife Perian and said, "I've had my ups and downs here. I want to thank you all for sticking with me." They knew him from the 2,900 passes he threw in regular-season and championship games.

Charley wasn't an easy guy to know. "A man could never tell what Charley was thinking by looking at his face," said Y. A. Tittle, who shared his last season as quarterback of the New York Giants and saw Charley for the real pro he was.

He and Perian were people of the night who enjoyed the Broadway shows and selected bistros. With the right friends, he could be almost gregarious. But Charley always understood one thing. His social stature in New York depended entirely on his ability to throw a football. So when it was all over, after 1961, he went back to Clarksdale, Mississippi, where all his life he has been called "Roach," and went into the shoe business to start a new phase of life. Charley left New York with a sense of vindication and accomplishment. It could have been a lot different.

In June of 1954, Jim Lee Howell, the new head coach of the New York Giants, stood next to a railroad siding and pleaded with a farmer in coveralls. Jim Lee, as his first order of business, had tracked Charley Conerly down to this spot north of St.

Louis, in a place called Bowling Green, Missouri. Charley had a liquid-fertilizer business and was unloading equipment for a job in the lush Mississippi lowlands. He was thirty-three years old then and the creases from a half-dozen hard years of football with the Giants already showed. He had announced he was quitting the game, and Howell wanted him to change his mind.

"No sense," Charley shook his head, "a fella getting beat up all the time. I just don't get enough protection to do the job."

A new regime was starting for the Giants. Steve Owen, their coach for twenty-three seasons, was out. The record for 1953 was a poor 3 and 9, and Charley took most of the abuse for a faltering offense. He had 25 passes intercepted (the league record was 31). Howell, a big, white-haired man who played his last season with the Giants when Charley was a rookie and caught some of his passes, made a promise.

"We'll try to do something about protecting you," he told Conerly. "You can take my word for it." Howell is from Conerly's part of the country, the rice paddy region of Arkansas, across the river from Alligator, Mississippi, where Charley had cotton acreage.

"It's only fair then," answered Charley, "that if you try, I try."

When he came back to New York in the fall, Vince Lombardi was the new offensive coach of the Giants and fashioned a front line from young talent like Roosevelt Brown, Jack Stroud, Bill Austin and Ray Wietecha. Frank Gifford, who had fiddled around on defense, was consigned strictly to ball-carrying and receiving as a halfback. It took a couple of seasons to work the kinks out. In 1955, Alex Webster skipped Canadian football to team with Gifford in the backfield, and Kyle Rote was switched over to an end position to put less pressure on his bad knees. The old SMU star had more moves than a 29th Street bellydancer.

In 1956, the Giants won the Eastern Conference championship, their first in ten years. They followed up with 47–7 massacre of the Chicago Bears for the championship. It was their first season in the Yankee Stadium. The field was so hard for the title encounter, they had to wear sneakers. Charley didn't start the game. The Giants had worked out an alternating system in which Don Heinrich, a smart young field general who couldn't pass very well, opened the games and probed the defense for weak spots, mostly on the ground. On the bench, Charley made mental notes. At the right time, he would replace Heinrich and open up the offense. Charley was masterful against the Bears. He threw 10 passes and completed 7, 2 for touchdowns.

The Conerly-Heinrich entente lasted for five years and accounted, in part, for his longevity. In fact, the Giants made a fetish of age. Gifford, his best friend, his partner on road trips, called him "Pops." Conerly wasn't the only one growing old as the Giants won in 1958–59, skipped '60 when Norm Van Brocklin had a hot hand in Philadelphia, then came right back to start a new string in '61. The Giants capitalized on their experience. Here's how it worked:

In a game against the Pittsburgh Steelers, the Giants were hung up on their own 22-yard line with 1 minute to play, losing 17–12. It was fourth down. Conerly had failed to connect on 7 of his previous 8 passes. He was frankly stumped.

248

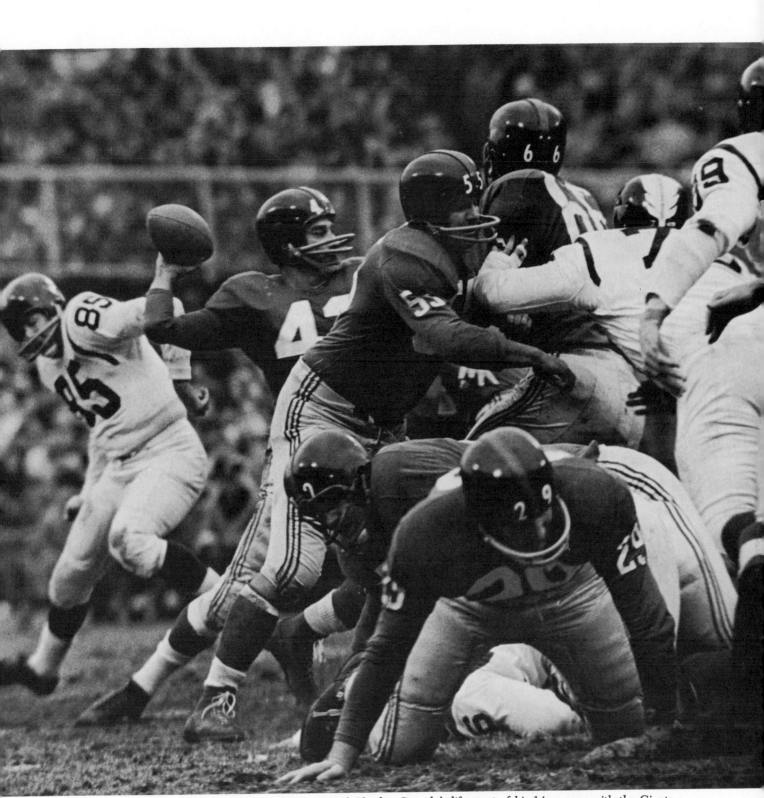

Passing in a crowd was a constant part of Charley Conerly's life most of his 14 seasons with the Giants.

He looked around, toward Gifford and Rote, and asked, "Got any ideas?"

"Yeah," said Rote. "Let's try that one we used against Cleveland three years ago."

"Okay," nodded Charley. "Rest of you guys, balanced left over inside formation, wing diagonal out, left acute in."

For the layman, it sounded complicated. Actually, it wasn't. Gifford, as the wing in the left formation, split wide and drew the Steelers' corner linebacker over with him. Rote, the left end, went straight down the field, then cut sharply inside, on a line with Conerly, deep enough to catch a pass for the first down.

As the play unwound, however, a hitch developed. The middle linebacker of the Steelers smelled out the pattern and backed up, standing directly in Conerly's passing lane. So Kyle simply improvised, moved over another notch to the right and was free for Conerly's pass. That was thinking.

Now the Giants needed execution. Kyle caught the ball in full stride (if he'd dropped it, the game would have been over). He was at the 40-yard line. As the Steelers converged on him, he improvised further and lateralled to Bob Schnelker, the other end, who snaked into Pittsburgh territory, to the 44.

On the next play, before the Steelers had time to recover their balance, Conerly faded back and located Gifford under the goalpost. Gifford gave the defender clinging to him a propitious nudge—the kind the field judge wasn't supposed to see—and caught the perfectly led pass for the winning touchdown. That was experience.

Like the fadeout in the old Hollywood western, Charley Conerly, in his fourteenth season as a Giant, saved his best almost for the last. Charley proved himself a lot of man in 1961. Allie Sherman was the new head coach, younger than his quarterback (Howell had resigned to lick the proverb that a coach's only future is to be fired). Physically, it was impossible for Charley to handle the job alone. Lee Grosscup, his heir apparent, had pooped out on a trial in training camp, like so many others before him. Conerly's rivals over the years included Travis Tidwell, Fred Benners, Bill Mackrides, Arnold Galiffa, Bobby Clatterbuck, Jack Kemp, Tom Dublinski, George Shaw, Heinrich and Grosscup. Even his buddy Gifford, a college quarterback at USC, took a shot at supplanting the old pro in 1960. But that last year they brought in Y. A. Tittle. Charley was forty; Yat was bald, but five years younger. Charley wasn't as spry as he should be. In the first game of the season, the St. Louis Cardinals surprised him with a safety blitz and upset the Giants, 21–10. Charley was painfully slow getting up every time the Card linebackers or safety man Larry Wilson mauled him. When the same thing happened in the second game against Pittsburgh, Sherman yanked him and put in Tittle, who rallied the Giants to a victory.

An athlete's pride outlasts his muscles. The Giant coach yanked Conerly early in the Redskin game, next on the schedule, after a pass had been intercepted for a touchdown. Charley flung his helmet angrily against the bench and sat down at the far end, stewing. Tittle played the rest of the game and was the regular quarterback the remainder of the season.

Sherman could have had a ticklish situation on his hands. Conerly helped him out of it. A feud over starting protocol would tear the club apart, and Sherman knew it. "Hell, Al," said Charley, "I've had my share of good years. I don't care who starts as long as we win this thing."

250

Tittle started, but Conerly made two big contributions. In the sixth game of the season, the Los Angeles Rams led, 14–10 in the second half, with Tittle obviously off his form. Charley relieved and threw touchdown passes to Rote and Del Shofner to win it, 24–14.

The Eagles, paced by the passing of young Sonny Jurgensen, were the Giants' big threat for the Eastern title, and the showdown arrived the next-to-last Sunday of the season, in a thick Philadelphia fog. The temperature hovered at freezing, while Conerly shrank deep in his hooded blanket on the bench as Tittle tried to warm the Giants up. A quick 7–0 lead, via a Tittle-to-Shofner bomb on the fourth play of the game, vanished as Jurgensen pushed the Eagles to a touchdown and a field goal. Tittle's passes skidded out of control. Charley watched the Eagles and made mental notes, as always. With 6 minutes left to go in the second quarter, Sherman turned around and said, "Okay, Charles. They're doubling Rote and Shofner. You see anything that'll work?"

Conerly said curtly, "Yep." And trotted stiffly on the field. He sent Shofner deep on the left side, and the Eagles halfback and free safety went with Del. Tight end Joe Walton crossed over into the cleared out medium-range zone and caught a pass for 35 yards and a touchdown.

In the second half, Charley was still in the game when the Giants recovered a fumble on the kickoff. He faked a play action to both set backs, pulling in the Eagle secondary, then hit Shofner with a 26-yard pass down the middle for a touchdown. When the Eagles crept close, he fired his third touchdown pass of the game, again to Shofner, gambling on a fourth-down play. That wrapped up the game, 28–24, and the Eastern Conference championship. For Charley it was an appropriate bow-out as a football player.

Charley Conerly wasn't supposed to be a Giant. Sure, Wellington Mara knew all about him. Wellington, son of the Giants' original owner, now the club president, was the team's purveyor of personnel when Charley enrolled at the University of Mississippi before World War II. He had a dossier starting with the season Charley played at Ole Miss before he enlisted in the Marines for two and a half years (remember that tattoo in those ads?). Charley was a corporal in the third invasion wave on Guam and saw his gunnery sergeant killed as they stepped into the shallow waters off shore. On a patrol, a Japanese sniper shot the carbine right out of his hands. It was the summer of 1944, and Charley endured three weeks of bloody jungle fighting. "It was kinda hot," he observed, typically.

When he came back to school, he was older than most college kids. In 1947, he made All-American at Mississippi. He was the nation's leading passer and played tailback in the single-wing, just what the Giants needed because Steve Owen, the coach, stubbornly bucked the T-trend and stayed with his favorite A-formation, a variation of the single-wing. The Giant quest for someone like Conerly was thwarted by George Preston Marshall, the owner of the Washington Redskins. In 1945 he'd been smart enough to draft Charley (since his original college class graduated). Though Marshall still had Sammy Baugh, he didn't want to give up Conerly because Sammy wasn't a young chicken. A lucky draw changed Charley's career. Marshall drew the bonus pick in the draft for 1948 and chose Harry Gilmer of Alabama, the hottest passer in the country. Every kid in the South imitated Gilmer jumping in the air and throwing the

Charley Conerly had the knack of studying an opponent and coming off the bench to pick up the New York Giant offense.

ball. Now Marshall traded Conerly to the Giants for halfback Howie Livingston and fullback Pete Stout, who both faded out in a couple of years. Brooklyn of the rival All-America Conference also bid for Conerly, in fact offered him more money, but he went with the Maras.

As a twenty-seven-year-old rookie with New York, Conerly stepped into a regular job running the offense. The Giants were in a down phase as a team, but Charley did all right. His first year, he completed 162 passes for 2,175 and 22 touchdowns. On December 5, 1948, against the Pittsburgh Steelers, he completed thirty-six passes, a league record. All those figures were to stand up over the next fourteen years as his career highs.

By 1950, with the absorption of the All-America Conference by the NFL, the Giants improved greatly, helped by a bonanza of defensive talent inherited from the extinct league. They were mixing the T-formation 50–50 with Owen's pet A. A young emigré from the Philadelphia Eagles, Allie Sherman, was brought in to be Charley's tutor. Conerly didn't say much. At the time he probably didn't like the idea because he was used to passing from his vantage point as a tailback, and he was still spry enough to handle his share of running. Charley was a wiry type, 6 feet and 185 pounds, who could handle himself. He was never very fast, but he was quick. Even a decade later, he could run sprints with the backs and stay with them for 20 yards. When he got into the T, Charley worked hard with Sherman to perfect the handoffs and other maneuvers essential to its trickery. He never was the smooth ball-handler like Frankie Albert or Eddie LeBaron because he didn't have their deftness, but he had a natural feel for the ball and seldom fumbled.

In the early 1950's, as the Cleveland Browns dominated the game, the Giants were the only team able to handle the young Turks from the AAC. New York won both games in 1950, achieving a 6–0 shutout in their first meeting, and tied the Browns for the Eastern Conference title. The playoff was a defensive battle. Conerly threw a fourth-quarter touchdown pass to lanky end Bob McChesney that would have won the game, but an offside penalty nullified the score. The Browns won, 8–3, without scoring a touchdown. And Charley, for the only time in his life, cried.

He's an emotional, introspective man who always managed to conceal his feelings. Charley claims there's 1/32nd Indian blood in him. It keeps a check on his Irish. He was stoic as the Giants crumbled around him. They lost to the Pittsburgh Steelers, 63–7, and to the Browns, 62–14. "The New York fans gave him as rough a going over as any player ever got," remembered Cleveland's Otto Graham.

"Some years it was so bad," Charley admitted, "that my wife and I just wouldn't go out evenings. I'd be recognized, and it doesn't matter to me so much what they say, but I didn't want my wife embarrassed."

Perian Conerly is a lovely woman who later wrote a syndicated column (when the years got kind to Charley and he was news). "Charley is a master at hiding his feelings," she said. "He never complains. He never offers an alibi. He accepts undeserved criticism and valid censure with equal calm."

Conerly once slapped a fan. A young tough accosted him with filthy language after a game. The abuse was ignored but the kid started to shove Conerly, who was leaving the field. Charley said, "Take your hands off." The hood persisted, and Conerly slapped him once in the face, hard.

He had firm opinions when he felt the situation warranted it. Lee Grosscup joined the Giants in 1960 in a swirl of controversy. The All-American quarterback from Utah had written letters to the writer which were published in *Sports Illustrated*. The Giants objected to some passages. In a burst of enthusiasm, Lee had described the Giants as a ". . . Great bunch! Fine gentlemen, very spirited, close-knit, good drinkers, great physical specimens . . ." The word "drinkers" got them. Their privacy had been invaded. In camp at Bear Mountain, New York, on the eve of the season, while Grosscup was ostracized, Conerly walked up to the writer and said, "That was a great article you wrote for that magazine."

"Oh, I didn't write any of it."

"Well, I want you to know it was the worst horse manure I ever read." That was all he said, impassive as always, and dropped the subject for good.

Charley had a quiet toughness as a player, too. Probably his greatest season, 1959, started with Conerly playing the full game on offense against the Los Angeles Rams in the opener on a hot September night in the Los Angeles Coliseum. The Giants had momentarily discarded their system of letting him alternate with Heinrich. In the middle of the third quarter, he was down on all fours behind the Giant bench, where no one could see him, retching from the tremendous exertion.

But in the fourth quarter, with the Giants trailing 21–20 and trying desperately to get in position for a field goal, Charley was still in the game. There were 4 minutes to go when the Giants lined up on their 45-yard line, fourth down and 11 yards to go. The percentage play was to punt and hope the defense held so the Giants could get better field position. However, Charley had waved off the kicking platoon. He was going for it. Again the percentage play was a hook or square-out, just enough for the first down. The Rams played it that way. But Bob Schnelker, the right end, faked a hook and took off down the field. Conerly, tired and whipped, staggered under a severe rush waiting for Schnelker to get loose. Defensive end Lou Michaels of the Rams was all over him. As Charley bent backwards, bracing himself for the shock, there was no way he could get rid of the ball. He was being ridden to the ground as he cocked the ball and let it fly with all his strength. Down on the 18-yard line Schnelker skidded to his knees and caught the football. Pat Summerall came into the game and kicked the winning field goal shortly after. Conerly held. "I don't know how," said Coach Jim Lee Howell. "He was so bushed I wasn't sure about letting him do it."

On the bus going to the airport after the game, Howell plopped down next to his quarterback. "How do you feel about it?" asked the Giant coach. "You like to start games?"

"Yes, sir," answered Charley. "I want to start. I want to play as much as I can."

He led the NFL in passing that year, with a percentage of 58.2 and an average gain of 8.79 yards per pass. Only 4 of his 194 passes were intercepted. Johnny Unitas of the world-champion Baltimore Colts was the all-pro quarterback, but Conerly, at the age of thirty-eight, got a rare honor. The players of the league voted him the Jim Thorpe Trophy—the prize of Charley's collection—signifying him as the most valuable. "For

254

having the Giants on top," said Colt linebacker Bill Pellington, "Conerly is the most deserving."

Charley wasn't the greatest. Sometimes he fell short. The Giants lost the sudden-death overtime to the Colts for the championship in 1958, and were defeated again for the title in 1959 after leading both times in the fourth quarter. He wasn't a spectacular passer, simply an efficient one.

Charley perfected the art of throwing the ball away when his receivers were covered without being called for intentional grounding. Lots of times when it looked like he was far off target, he was actually misfiring by design because his receivers were covered and he didn't want to risk an interception, or get caught for a loss.

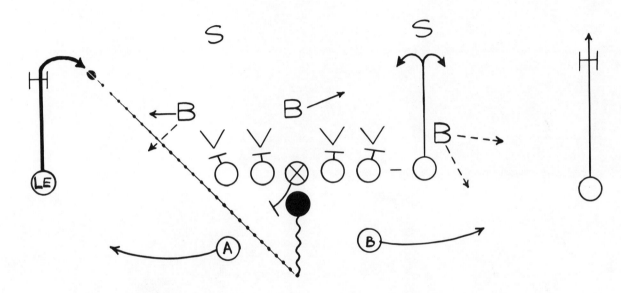

Charley Conerly describes his favorite play:

"This is one of your best hook passes when you aren't getting too much rush. You're sending out five potential receivers, so if they rush more than one linebacker, you could be in trouble.

"The Giants called it Balanced Right, L & R Hook, A Swing, B Flare. And we always considered it a very good first down play.

"Both ends hook at 8 to 12 yards. The left end is your most eligible receiver because the left halfback (or the A back) should pull the right linebacker into the flat as he swings out, giving the left end plenty of room to work on the right defensive halfback.

"The right end (also the tight end) hooks inside or outside, depending on the coverage they have on him.

"The blocking in the line is normal, with the center pulling and blocking where he's needed. The B back flares slowly to the right, so that if the corner backer on that side blitzes, he can pick him up. If the middle linebacker blitzes, the center will pick him up. If the right linebacker also comes, the quarterback should throw a swing pass to the A back.

"But basically, the idea is to get a one-on-one situation, which you should have with the left end."

Two battle-tested veterans got together when Frank Gifford (16) caught this long Conerly touchdown pass to beat the Philadelphia Eagles. Charley looked for Frank in a pinch.

With his gray hair and weatherbeaten face, Charley almost looked out of place. That's Jack Stroud, a great blocker for Charley, to his right.

Charley's biggest drawback was that he didn't fit the hero mold. A couple of kids ducked getting his autograph after a Giant victory because he was so tight-lipped and solemn-faced. They couldn't figure him with the winning team.

During one game, Frank Gifford's boy Jeff turned to his mom and asked, "How do you get to be a referee?"

"Mostly, they used to be football players," answered Maxine Gifford, "but they got too old."

"Then," asked Jeff, "are they going to make Charley be a referee?"

CHARLEY CONERLY

BORN: Sept. 19, 1922　　　　　　　　HEIGHT: 6'1"　　　　WEIGHT: 195
New York Giants, 1948–61
PASSING RECORD:

Year	Att.	Comp.	Yards Gained	T.D.	Pct.	Longest	Int.
1948	299	162	2175	22	54.2	65	13
1949	305	152	2138	17	49.8	85	20
1950	132	56	1000	8	42.4	61	7
1951	189	93	1277	10	49.2	69	22
1952	169	82	1090	13	48.5	70	10
1953	303	143	1711	13	47.8	60	25
1954	210	103	1439	17	49.0	68	11
1955	202	98	1310	13	48.5	71	13
1956	174	90	1143	10	51.7	48	7
1957	232	128	1712	11	55.2	70	11
1958	184	88	1199	10	47.8	44	9
1959*	194	113	1706	14	58.2	77	4
1960	134	66	954	8	49.3	70	7
1961	106	44	634	7	41.5	37	8
TOTALS	2833	1418	19,488	173	50.1	85	167

* Led NFL

RUSHING RECORD:

Year	Att.	Yards Gained	Longest	Ave.
1948	40	160	40	4.0
1949	23	42	7	1.8
1950	23	22	14	1.0
1951	17	65	18	3.8
1952	27	115	33	4.3
1953	24	91	24	3.8
1954	24	107	24	4.5

1955	12	10	12	.8
1956	11	11	8	1.0
1957	15	24	13	1.6
1958	12	−17	11	−1.4
1959	15	38	10	2.5
1960	14	1	17	.1
1961	13	16	9	1.2
TOTALS	270	685	40	2.5

PUNTING RECORD:

Year	No.	Ave.	Longest
1948	17	39.9	53
1949	2	35.0	36
1950	20	38.0	54
1951	72	39.7	55
1952	—	—	—
1953	—	—	—
1954	—	—	—
1955	—	—	—
1956	1	33.0	33
1957	—	—	—
1958	—	—	—
1959	—	—	—
1960	18	36.9	59
1961	—	—	—
TOTALS	130	38.9	59

Bobby Layne stands firm, in command of the action as he triggers his team into movement.

When the Dutchman cocked his arm, passing became a pure art form. Norm Van Brocklin throws for the Eagles.

Marvin Newman

The helmet hid a bald head. Y. A. Tittle has the look of an athlete—strong chin, strong resolve.

Eddie LeBaron was a midget mingling with the giants of the pro wars. He surveys the situation calmly.

The high cheekbones are a legacy of his Lithuanian ancestry. John Unitas is a study of unspoken confidence.

In the championship game against the Cleveland Browns on a snowy, muddy day,
Green Bay's Bart Starr never fumbled.

"Here, you take it." And Rudy Bukich of the Bears extends the ball with both hands in the classic handoff position.

Behind the goal line, Sonny Jurgensen makes his stand. He'll fire in the face of the
enemy, Jim Katcavage (75) of the Giants.

It takes iron discipline for John Brodie (12) to ignore the charge of Deacon Jones
(75) of the Rams and get off his pass.

Frank Ryan knew the percentages were with him every time the figure of Jim Brown (32) came into the picture.

Man on the move. With his Buffalo bench in the background, Jack Kemp of the Bills keeps a step ahead of the enemy as he passes on the run.

Malcolm Emmons

The line has held and Francis Tarkenton of the Minnesota Vikings has time to set and whip his arm over in classic style.

Face to face. With Willie Davis (87) coming at him head-on, Charley Johnson carries through his design for throwing.

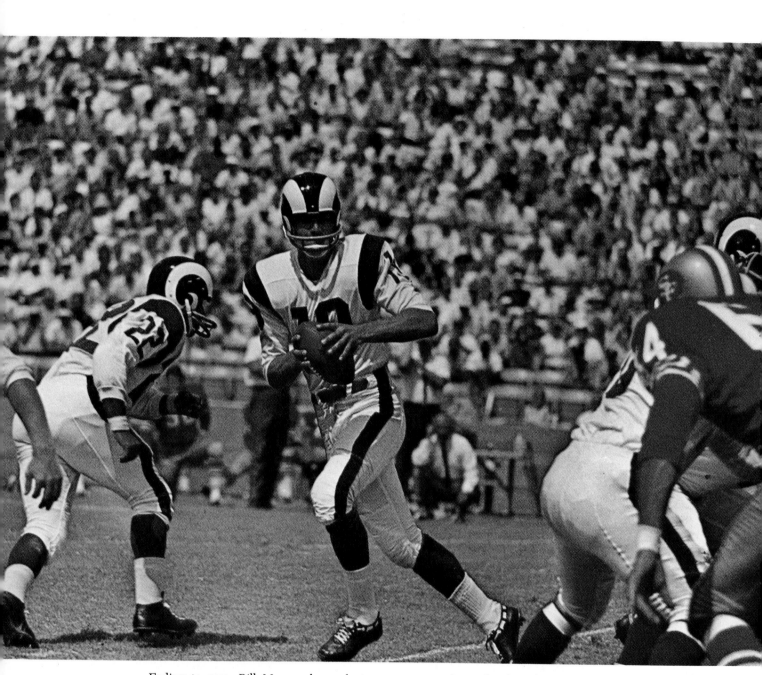

Fading to pass, Bill Munson has only two more seconds to decide on his receiver and get rid of the ball.

Joe Namath discovers the vocational hazards of a quarterback. He's about to be buried under 320 pounds of Ernie Ladd.

The panorama of professional football opens up for Gary Cuozzo (15) of the Colts—
and every other young quarterback of the future.

Eddie LeBaron

YOU CAN TEST ALL THE OTHER QUARTER-
BACKS IN THE LEAGUE, INCLUDING VAN
BROCKLIN, TITTLE AND THE REST, IN 10
FUNDAMENTALS OF FOOTBALL, AND
EDDIE LEBARON WILL BEAT THEM 8 OUT
OF 10.
—*Joe Kuharich, coach,*
Washington Redskins, 1956.

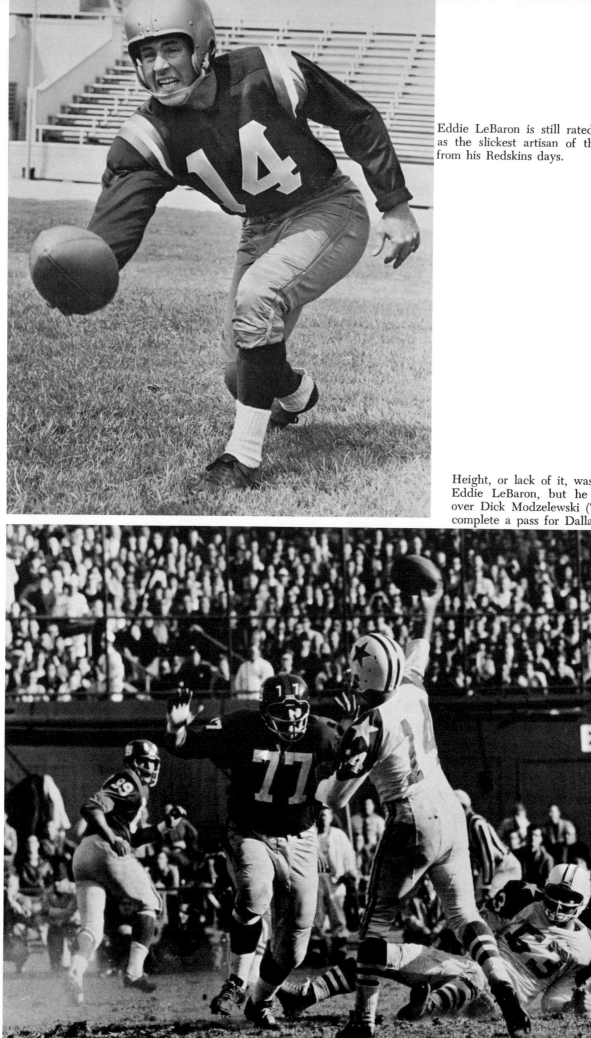

Eddie LeBaron is still rated by most football men as the slickest artisan of the T-formation. This is from his Redskins days.

Height, or lack of it, was a problem for 5'8" Eddie LeBaron, but he managed to throw over Dick Modzelewski (77) of the Giants to complete a pass for Dallas.

Eddie LeBaron spent his football career playing Little David and retired with a couple of shots left in his sling. It's a pity, too, since his aim was true and his heart was brave. Eddie never slew the Goliaths of the National Football League because even a doughty little general needed more soldiers than he was ever able to muster.

For the dozen years he was around as a pro, Eddie had his moments of triumph, though. For instance, there was his first year with the Washington Redskins in 1952, which was also incomparable Sammy Baugh's last year. Little Eddie, 5–7 and 175 pounds, played quarterback while the old pass master warmed the bench after the opening game. The Redskins weren't much. They were in the fourth-straight losing season. The week before the end they came up to New York to play the Giants, who were in a three-way battle with Cleveland and Philadelphia for Eastern honors.

On the third play after the kickoff, big Arnie Weinmeister, 250 pounds and the toughest tackle in pro football, lurched through the Redskin line and engulfed LeBaron. As they sprawled, Eddie's helmet went askew and his head ricocheted off the hard turf. He was carried off the field on a stretcher. The Giants moved to a fast 10–0 lead.

LeBaron sat on the sidelines holding his head in his hands, but as the teams changed sides at the end of the quarter, he asked Coach Curly Lambeau for a chance to get back in the game, then bounced on the field in his little-boy gait. The Redskins were stalled on their 35. Eddie faded far back to pass. Bones Taylor, the rangy end, got behind Giant safety Em Tunnell. On the dead run he caught the ball thrown diagonally 65 yards in the air for a Washington touchdown.

He later spotted Bones free across the field and angled another pass for 50 yards and a touchdown. In the third quarter the same combination clicked for another bomb that traveled more than half the length of the field. Eddie mopped up at the end by nailing fullback Johnny Papit with a pass in the end zone to round out a 27–17 upset and knock the Giants out of the race.

In quiet elation, Baugh, the veteran of sixteen seasons, drawled, "I guess he showed 'em if you give him enough time to throw, he'll hit them any place."

"What nobody knows," confessed Lambeau, "is that Eddie wasn't all there when he went back in the game. He was punchy from that knock on the head."

LeBaron repeated the process in the Philadelphia finale, flipping 2 touchdown passes and sneaking over from the 1-yard line with 18 seconds left to upset the Eagles and cost them a title tie.

It was kid's play for Eddie, a charade of battle. The year before he was in the middle of the real thing. Eddie hugged the ground on Heartbreak Ridge in Korea, leading a Marine infantry platoon. A mortar shell exploded 10 yards away and plastered the back of his legs with shrapnel.

"The truth is," said Eddie, "I was too scared to move, just then, because only a second or two before another mortar shell had landed 5 feet away." It was a dud. Otherwise, there would have been no LeBaron.

When Eddie first joined his platoon on the front line, he cautioned the men to take it easy. He wasn't in such good shape. Then weighed down with full pack, he took off into the hills. After the first peak, the battle-tough marines, sweating and panting, dispatched a message forward:

"Chicken —— lieutenant is requested to slow down; when you get in shape, you'll be up to your —— in gooks and alligators all by yourself."

LeBaron received a bronze star when he left cover under heavy fire to contact the forward observation post of a mortar platoon, in sight of the enemy. After an assaulting rifle platoon in his area lost its commander, he took charge and resumed the attack. He threw a grenade at 20 yards that blew a Chinese soldier to bits. "Had I time to think about it," he said, "it might have given me the creeps." He tried to rescue a wounded buddy while small arms and machine-gun fire sprayed the open area. A sniper's bullet killed the man draped over his shoulder, but didn't touch Eddie. Still, he returned home with two purple hearts, including a couple of pieces of shrapnel in his passing shoulder. He couldn't lift his elbow above his chest.

With his blond hair, clipped close on top, cherubic face and little-boy smile, Eddie never looked like a man of action, more like an Eagle Scout. When he left Korea, a hardened veteran of twenty-two, he had to prove something—that at 5 feet 7 inches, it was possible to be a quarterback in professional football. Eddie convinced the skeptics that one afternoon in New York.

But then he had to prove a team could win with him at quarterback, and this he never quite managed. "If only he were 6 inches taller," ran the refrain at the end of each season as the slick "Little Magician," the pet of every anxious mother who ever watched a football game, coexisted with the giants of the NFL and became the darling of the Washington tea set.

In 1953 he was the hero of a "This Is Your Life" saga on television and played golf with President Dwight Eisenhower at Burning Tree. In 1958 he received his law degree at George Washington University. In 1960 he retired to work in a rich Texas law firm but was conveniently reinstated with the organization of the Dallas Cowboys. The law firm belonged to Bedford Wynne, one of the Cowboy owners. The baby look faded. The cheeks became a little ruddy. He even shaved, a ritual that was unnecessary the first year he played college football. But on the field, he was still "The Pimple," his style crimped by a lack of height that forced coaches to use a rollout style of passing offense to give him looking room.

His throwing was still sharp, his ball-handling deft and his signal-calling brilliant when the Dallas Cowboys suddenly stopped using him in 1963. Eddie got the hint and retired to become president of a cement company in Nevada, where no one would say, "If he were only 6 inches taller. . . ."

Don't get the idea that Eddie LeBaron was a football failure. In 1955 he spurred the Redskins to an 8–4 second-place finish which has been their best showing in twenty years, or since Sammy Baugh led them to a division championship in the war season of 1945. The year before he retired, Eddie made the Dallas Cowboys, a collection of cast-offs and kids, the second-best offensive team in football, a powerhouse that averaged better than 28 points a game, same as the score-happy New York Giants.

262

During his term in Washington, owner George Preston Marshall was running an eccentric, segregated ship—shuttling coaches by whim, ignoring Negro talent—that made the building of a winning organization impossible. Eddie was his only selling point. And during the LeBaron residency in Dallas, the Cowboys, starting from scratch, didn't have time to come up strong enough.

Eddie had proved long ago what he could do under the right circumstances. College of the Pacific, in his backyard, became a football power on his inspired leadership. Eddie enrolled as a sixteen-year-old kid and played tailback for Amos Alonzo Stagg, who was eighty-six years old. Eddie, from California's San Joaquin Valley, really wanted to go to Stanford, but Coach Marchy Schwartz took one look and said, "Go home, little man, and grow up." The LeBarons were ranchers. His father once caught him breaking all the windowpanes in the chicken coops, throwing rocks. Eddie sawed off the handles on the garden tools to make them easier for a little fellow to use. At the age of ten, he could throw a football 50 yards. In high school he threw it 75.

The week before Eddie was to play his first college game for COP, at the age of sixteen (freshmen were eligible in 1946), he had his appendix removed. He played in the season's third game against the University of Arizona and completed 12 of 19 passes. Stagg made a dramatic return to Chicago that year, with Pacific visiting mighty Northwestern of the Big Ten. Little Eddie, who also played defense, intercepted a pass behind his goal line, ran it out and two laterals later, COP was in the other team's end zone to complete a 101-yard play. The man on the tag end was Wayne Hardin, who later became head football coach of the Naval Academy. Eddie also threw a touchdown pass as little COP lost respectably, 26–13.

In his sophomore year, LeBaron became a T-quarterback. Stagg was succeeded by Larry Siemering, a brilliant strategist who installed the new system by spending an entire winter studying films of the Chicago Bears. Three glorious years followed for Pacific. The little school in Stockton, California, lost one game in 1947, one game in 1948 and swept through 11 games undefeated in 1949, averaging 52 points a game. They beat Loyola 52–0, Utah 45–6 and nosed out the University of San Francisco team which eventually sent eleven men into professional football, among them all-pros Ollie Matson, Gino Marchetti and Dick Stanfel. Eddie made All-American and added a brilliant contribution to the development of the T-formation.

Eddie was a magician handling the ball. COP lost its only game during his junior year, to San Jose State, because the referees couldn't keep up with him. He faked a handoff to the fullback, who was tackled going into the line. The referee blew his whistle, automatically ending the play, while Eddie faded back and passed to his right end for a touchdown. It was nullified by the quick whistle.

In practice one afternoon, Eddie couldn't make an off-tackle slant by the fullback work because the defensive end on that side kept smelling it out. So Eddie put the ball in the fullback's stomach, watched the defender react, then quickly took the ball back and flipped it to a halfback who raced around the end. The maneuver was incorporated into the COP offense and became famous at Georgia Tech when Bobby Dodd labelled it the belly series—Dodd learned the maneuver while coaching Eddie in the Shrine East-West game.

LeBaron was a busy little man on campus, too. He worked in a clothing store, conducted a sports program on the college radio station, slung sacks of grain in a Stockton granary, had the campus agency for a flower shop and, for an additional fee, composed tender notes or poems for the bashful boyfriends who sent corsages.

Nobody believed this little man until he went to the East-West game in San Francisco on December 31, 1949, and he mixed in with the great All-Americans from all over the country (like 265-pound Leon Hart of Notre Dame). He came out the Most Valuable Player, although his team lost, 28–6! The next August he moved on to the College All-Star game in Chicago against the championship Philadelphia Eagles of the NFL and played quarterback in a backfield with Charley Justice, 170 pounds, and Doak Walker, 165. They called themselves "The Abnormal Midgets" and drank milkshakes. And in the game he teamed with Justice to spring a 17–7 upset of the pros.

The pros didn't believe him either. The Redskins had drafted him on the 10th round (Justice was their first choice). They brought him into Washington to meet the press. Eddie looked like a choirboy. When he sat down, he had to extend his toes to touch the floor. They asked him about his passing.

"I rifle-shot the short ones," he answered, "and loop the long ones—like Sammy Baugh." He grinned impishly. They measured his height and checked his weight on the scales. "We didn't draft him," said Redskin general manager Dick McCann. "We inducted him." Eddie went away to the Korean War before he reported to his first Redskin camp. He was a Marine lieutenant and served 8½ months in Korea. When he came out, he said he was interested in playing only a year or two of pro ball.

Eddie wasn't always happy with the Redskins. He ran into this phobia about little men early. Curly Lambeau was the coach his first two seasons and frowned at Eddie's inability to see over oncoming linemen, though he called the little man the best ballhandler he'd ever seen.

LeBaron was also a bold, imaginative signal-caller. He got better as he got older, especially adept at audibles to take advantage of switching defenses. But he got in trouble with Lambeau because of his daring in the last game of the 1953 season. The Redskins led the Pittsburgh Steelers, 13–7, with 5 minutes remaining. A victory would give them a second-place tie with the Eagles. Fired up, they repulsed a Steeler drive on the 5-yard line and recovered a fumble. Two plays into the line failed to budge the Pittsburgh defense.

"On third down," recounted Eddie, "I tried a pass that had been open before. It was a fairly long swing to Justice. But Jack Butler, the Steeler safety, guessed with me and took it right out of Charley's hands. He went 25 yards for a TD. They kicked the extra point and that was the game.

"I should have taken a safety and kicked from the 20. They would have had to score a touchdown to win. I hadn't wanted to kick from the end zone because there was canvas on it and about 3 inches of mud, tough to punt from. (Eddie was also the Redskin punter the early years of his career.)

"As it was, I called a bad play and cost us some money."

The Redskins drafted a couple of big prospects, Jack Scarbath of Maryland and Al Dorow of Michigan State, as his heirs apparent. So Eddie, rather than sit on the bench, skipped off to the Canadian league, to play with Calgary in 1954 under his old college coach, Siemering. He returned in 1955 under the more hospitable reign of Joe Kuharich, who had seen enough of Eddie in college (Joe was the USF coach) to know what he could do. "I've always maintained," said Joe, "that Eddie was as fine an all-around quarterback as I have ever seen in pro ball. He never had a real sound team around him in Washington."

Eddie was also a tough little cookie. He came back after a knee operation to repair cartilage damage in 1956. Two years later he was the No. 1 passer in the NFL, though the Skins won only 4 games. Against the Cardinals that season, he threw 5 touchdown passes one afternoon.

Moving to the Cowboys, he spearheaded a 17–16 upset of the Giants, outpassing the veteran combination of Tittle and Conerly. They never let him forget his size. "When

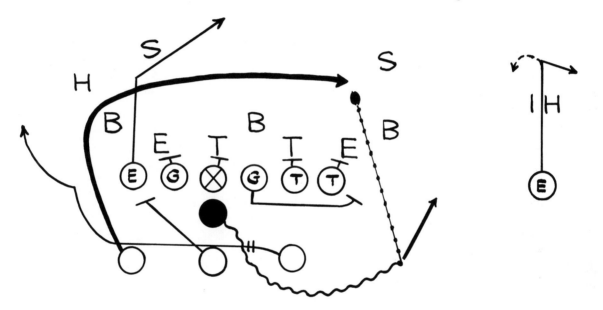

Eddie LeBaron describes his favorite play:
"My favorite play for years with the Washington Redskins was a bootleg off the unbalanced line. This was not a formation that lasted but we made a lot of yardage with this for two or three years.

"It was designed as a running formation, and when we faked the run and threw, it became quite effective.

"The play was called Slant 28 Keeper Pass.

"The left halfback would circle over the middle and was a primary receiver. The strong side or right end would run whatever pattern we called. I faked a handoff to the right halfback, who would keep running after the fake, bellying out around left end. He caught three touchdowns during the time we used it, as a secondary receiver.

"In fact, all our receivers caught touchdown passes off this play, and I've run for a touchdown, keeping the ball.

"The play was usable during any running situation, and we often used it on the goal line. I've always believed in throwing off the running fake as often as possible (play action), and this was a strong running play even when the quarterback didn't keep the ball."

Sam Huff picks up little Eddie and tackles him," said a Giant fan, "that's all right. But burping him—that's ridiculous."

Eddie made it part of his act, too. The Cowboys signed Sonny Gibbs, a quarterback from Texas Christian who stood 6 feet 7 inches—exactly a foot taller than Eddie. They were introduced together at a Dallas luncheon and Eddie asked the rookie, "What do you think, Sonny, would you be a better quarterback if you were 6 inches shorter?"

Funny? Gibbs never threw a pass in league competition for the Dallas Cowboys. With LeBaron, just check the record.

EDDIE LEBARON

BORN: Jan. 7, 1930   HEIGHT: 5'7"   WEIGHT: 165

Washington Redskins, 1952–53, 1956–59

Dallas Cowboys, 1960–63

PASSING RECORD:

Year	Att.	Comp.	Yards Gained	T.D.	Pct.	Longest	Int.
1952	194	96	1420	14	49.0	70	15
1953	149	62	874	3	41.6	66	17
1955	178	79	1270	9	44.4	70	15
1956	98	47	554	3	48.0	33	10
1957	167	99	1508	11	54.3	82	10
1958*	145	79	1365	11	54.5	71	10
1959	173	77	1077	8	44.5	49	11
1960	225	111	1736	12	49.3	76	25
1961	236	120	1741	14	50.8	80	16
1962	166	95	1436	16	57.2	85	9
1963	65	33	418	3	50.8	75	3
TOTALS	1796	898	13,399	104	50.0	85	141

* Led NFL

RUSHING RECORD:

Year	Att.	Yards Gained	Longest	Ave.
1952	43	164	32	3.8
1953	21	95	27	4.5
1955	37	190	25	5.1
1956	11	6	9	0.5
1957	20	—12	11	—.6
1958	12	30	13	2.5
1959	13	7	2	0.5
1960	17	94	23	5.5

Year	No.		Longest	
1961	20	72	21	3.6
1962	6	—1	3	—.2
1963	2	5	5	2.5
TOTALS	202	650	32	3.2

PUNTING RECORD:

Year	No.	Ave.	Longest
1952	51	42.2	63
1953	51	39.3	60
1955	62	41.6	57
1956	4	40.3	47
1957	—	—	—
1958	—	—	—
1959	—	—	—
1960	3	33.0	34
1961	—	—	—
1962	—	—	—
1963	—	—	—
TOTALS	171	40.9	63

Tobin Rote

TO KNOW THAT TOBIN ROTE IS ONE OF
THE GREAT QUARTERBACKS IS TO LOOK
AT HIS RECORD OVER THE YEARS.

—*Sid Gillman, coach,*
San Diego Chargers, 1960–

Tobin Rote started his third life as a quarterback when he took control of the San Diego Chargers in 1963.

Tobin Rote led three lives as a professional quarterback—not concurrently, however. He played ten years in the National Football League and made all-pro.

He skipped to Toronto of the Canadian league for three years and made All-Canada.

He returned to San Diego of the American Football League for two years and made all-league.

Tobin was a big, ruggedly built Texan designed for the long haul. He stood 6 feet 3 inches and weighed 215 to 220 pounds throughout most of his career. Just before he quit, Coach Sid Gillman of the San Diego Chargers said, "Rote can play another eight years if he takes proper care of the fine physique he has."

To look at Rote as he appeared in his last playing season of 1964 was to agree with Gillman. He still had a flat belly at the age of thirty-six. That weatherbeaten, perpetually tan face was a little more lined than usual, and the attempt at a crewcut showed only a few bristles that had mostly turned to gray. But Rote liked what he was doing. There was one major flaw. His arm was terribly old. Before each game the doctor had to stab it with needles of long-acting novocaine to ease the pain. Ligaments had been torn loose from his elbow, and although in the spring of 1964 he immobilized it for five weeks in a cast to let the tear heal and then lifted weights in a special program to rebuild strength in the arm, his service was limited.

Early in a game it was stiff and he couldn't get much distance on his throws. Sometimes as he warmed up, the limberness returned and he could fire long to young racehorses like Lance Alworth. His young understudy, John Hadl, played better than 50 percent of the time because the San Diego Chargers were a team that overwhelmed the opposition with its depth of talent and clinched the division title with a month remaining in the season. For the championship contest, however, Gillman went back to his old pro.

On the fourth play of the game, Rote fired a pass through the Buffalo defense 26 yards down the middle to tight end Dave Kocourek for a touchdown. The Bills, playing before their own crowd, rallied to take a 13–7 lead in the second quarter. Minutes before halftime, the Chargers were back on the move deep in Buffalo territory on the 15-yard line, threatening to go ahead. To stop the clock, Rote turned and flung the ball toward the sideline, obviously intending it to go out of bounds. But the throw had so little zip that linebacker Mike Stratton of the Bills intercepted and killed the Charger threat. That was the tipoff to Rote, who never played again after that game, which the Chargers lost, 20–7. When he couldn't get the ball out of bounds, he was done.

In a way it was sad to have the strength of his arm fail him at the end. Rote's contribution to the profession of quarterbacking was strength. He personified it with toughness, both spiritual and physical. No other quarterback in the history of the T-formation exposed himself more to the jolts of being tackled. He was the greatest running quarterback in the history of the T-formation. Over his fifteen years, Rote carried the ball from scrimmage 100 times more than his closest competitor, Bobby Layne. He gained 627 yards more on the ground during his ten seasons in the NFL than Layne did in fifteen, and Bobby was really the only other man who exposed himself consistently as a runner. Including his years in the Canadian and American leagues, Tobin gained 3,366 yards as a runner. Sammy Baugh, who played half his sixteen-year career as a single-wing tailback, had a career net of 324 yards.

Yet Tobin didn't neglect the main function, passing. The most prolific passer in the history of the T-formation was Y. A. Tittle. Tobin Rote was second and actually outgained old Yat over a comparable fifteen-year period and threw more touchdown passes. But, of course, Rote's efforts were spread over three leagues and suffer correspondingly in prestige. It took the NFL several years to acknowledge that professional football was even being played outside its precincts.

If Tobin had been compliant to the demands of The Establishment, he might have confined all his competition to the NFL, too. He cut out when he had a lot of playing left in both his arm and legs.

"I left the Detroit Lions of my own will after the 1959 season," he noted, "and for a principle. I had come to the Lions in 1957 from Green Bay with a two-year no-cut contract. We won a championship my first season. After '58, I wanted the same kind of contract. They refused me a no-cut. So I played out the option on my old contract the next season and quit."

A guy might ask why a man of Rote's experience and obvious achievement would need a no-cut contract (the club has to pay the player whether or not he is retained on the roster). He had been the key man on the '57 championship Lions. Faced with a choice, Detroit kept him and shipped off Layne, who was a year older, in 1958. There was slim chance of his being dropped.

"I had seen there's no sentiment in football," explained Tobin, who was a good buddy of Bobby, "and they don't honor service. I remembered the Lions had picked up Frank Gatski, a veteran center, from the Browns, and he had done a fine job for us. I know because I was the man closest to him on every play and would have suffered if he let down. Frank was thirty-five but in great shape and still wanted to play, yet the Lions released him outright. I didn't want that happening to me."

Tobin cloaks his devotion to principle in a soft personality. He's not gregarious. He still has the soft drawl of Texas in his voice, although he has been settled for the last decade in Birmingham, Michigan, a suburb of Detroit. He now devotes himself full time to his business as president of Tobin Rote and Associates, manufacturing lightweight concrete conduit.

The Rotes were a famous sports family back in San Antonio, Texas. Tobin went to Rice Institute and became the star quarterback of the 1949 team which lost only 1 game and whipped North Carolina in the Cotton Bowl. En route, they also beat Southern Methodist, which featured Doak Walker and cousin Kyle Rote. Kyle later starred for the New York Giants. Tobin was signed by the Baltimore Colts of the old All-America Conference, but when that league was absorbed in 1950, he was thrown back in the hopper and drafted by Green Bay.

272

Tobin spent seven rugged seasons leading the Green Bay offense. The Packers were right in the midst of a twelve-year decline and never had a winning record in all the time Rote played for Green Bay. He got them up to the .500 mark twice. Curly Lambeau, the founder of the Packers, was booted out of the coaching job just as Tobin arrived. He broke in as the quarterback for Gene Ronzani and later Lisle Blackbourn. Green Bay was the Siberia of pro football. Tobin was the big gun when Vince Lombardi was still an assistant coach at Army, and the Packers were doing well when they met the payroll.

Their offense was Rote dropping back to pass to Billy Howton, another product of Rice who arrived in 1952 to play end and eventually caught more passes in his career than the great Don Hutson. Or Rote tucking the ball under his arm and slashing into the line with long, ground-gobbling strides. In 1951, he gained an average of 6.9 yards per carry, high in the National League. Inevitably, they designed a spread formation where Tobin took a direct snap from center and ran or passed, like the old tailback. In 1956, he led the NFL in completions, yardage gained passing and touchdown passes. He also scored 11 touchdowns himself.

He was called the most underrated quarterback in the league, although the players on all the clubs held him in high enough esteem. In 1955, though Otto Graham bowed out grandly with a title team at Cleveland, the men of the NFL picked Rote as their quarterback on NEA's All-Player All-Pro team. But Rote wanted a chance to be a winner, and he got it when the Detroit Lions sent four players to the Packers for the big quarterback.

The Lions were a loose, roistering crew, but they absorbed Tobin readily as a man who could help them even if Bobby Layne still held sway as the quarterback. The two alternated time most of the season. When Layne's ankle was fractured the next-to-last game of the season, against Cleveland, Tobin took full charge. He produced two victories which tied the 49ers for the division title. He got a hot hand in the playoff to rally the Lions from a 27–7 deficit in the third quarter to a thrilling 31–27 victory.

Detroit had a score to settle in the championship game. Last time they had faced the Browns for the title, Cleveland had drubbed them, 56–10, in Graham's farewell. The key play came in the second quarter after Jimmy Brown, a rookie fullback with Cleveland, scored on a burst to make the score 17–7, Detroit leading. That's not a secure lead in pro football, especially in the second quarter. Rote's passing took the Lions into Cleveland territory, but they bogged down on the 26-yard line. It was fourth and 11 when Coach George Wilson sent in the field-goal-kicking unit. Rote knelt for the pass from center as Jim Martin, the kicker, carefully measured the distance. The Brown secondary moved up on the line, hoping to find a gap. Tobin grabbed the ball, but instead of placing it down he straightened up and rolled to his right. Lion end Steve Junker was alone near the goal line, and Rote's pass on the run hit him for the score. The rout was on.

The Lions crushed Cleveland, 59–14, as Rote threw for 4 touchdowns and scored once himself. Injuries hurt the Lions the next two years. Rote had a bursa removed from his shoulder in 1958 and was generally unhappy in '59. He also threw too many interceptions and had a poor passing year. The next fall he was gone, his contract expired.

He signed with Toronto for big money. His business in Birmingham was already established, and he wasn't too far from home, where he and his charming wife Betsy were raising their four children and a nephew who came to live with them. He led the Canadian loop in passing two of the three years he played. The Argos were an interesting team, with Cookie Gilchrist playing in the same backfield. Gilchrist, a 250-pound fullback, was colorful and controversial and itinerant. By this time the American Football League was established. Cookie, in a financial haggle with management, drew his release and signed with Buffalo in 1962.

After that season, Rote also became a free agent because he had signed a three-year contract with Toronto without an option for renewal. It was a convenient escape clause to get back to American football. He was convinced he was blackballed in the NFL. Buffalo held the AFL rights to Rote but the Bills figured they were well set at quarterback with Jack Kemp and young Daryle Lamonica. The Denver Broncos, regrouping under Jack Faulkner, thought they had made a deal for the rights to Rote. There was some crossfire, since San Diego, which had lost Kemp on a waiver slipup, also wanted Rote. Owner Ralph Wilson of Buffalo decided the only equitable settlement was to flip a coin. The Chargers won, and it came up California sunshine for the Rotes.

The Tobin Rote who returned to the American scene was like some long-lost uncle who went off to the other side of the world to seek his fortune. He looked vaguely familiar—a tall, imposing man who exerted authority when he gathered the men around him in the huddle. But a lot was changed from the vigorous, almost daredevil Rote they were used to in his Green Bay and Detroit youth. This one stepped gingerly, like he had discovered that bones can be brittle. He wasn't looking for ways to run with the ball. At the same time, he was more than a shadow standing in for some past great. The change from Canadian ball, with its three downs, wider field and twelfth man, didn't affect him. He adjusted easily to the new blitzing style of defense, drawing from his reservoir of experience. To the Chargers, a young team, Tobin Rote was a symbol of stability.

He moved right in as the All-AFL quarterback for the Chargers, who won the championship, trouncing the Boston Patriots, 51–10, with champagne served in the dressing room. There never was better proof how much a quarterback meant to a team. In 1962, the Chargers had a 4–10 record. With Rote, it became 11–3.

"In some ways," said Rote, "it was the most satisfying season of all. Our offensive unit was the most explosive I ever played on, better than the '57 Lions'. It had a definite edge in speed. There was no better back in football than Keith Lincoln, and I've never thrown to a receiver with the speed and jumping ability of Lance Alworth.

"But I didn't anticipate my elbow flaring up like it did. Or getting my ribcage torn loose on a hard tackle in the first exhibition game I played with San Diego."

His passing percentage of 59.4, his yardage total of 2,510 and his 20 touchdown tosses surpassed any mark he'd set in his seasons in the NFL. Rote had the enthusiasm of a kitten and the respect of a wise old owl. One of the charming tableaus of the league's all-star game, held in San Diego, was Rote winding up every practice session by running the length of the field half a dozen times. And running right with him was blonde Betsy, out to visit him from Michigan.

Tobin Rote, grizzled and balding, listens to Coach Sid Gillman outline the plan of attack.

But dedication to condition didn't help his passing arm. It never came back with the strength a quarterback needs in throwing the ball.

"Being a quarterback," said Rote, "is also a matter of discipline. You have to trust every guy will do his job, and that's asking a lot when a man runs the risk of being hit blind-side by a 260-pound giant with blood in his eye if a blocker muffs his job."

When Rote physically couldn't do his job any longer, he exercised that discipline and went out with the dignity of an old pro.

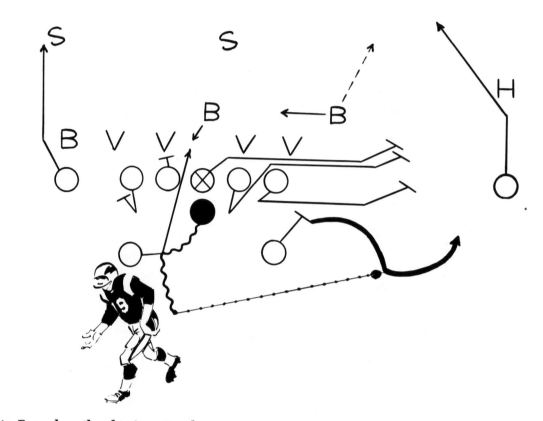

Tobin Rote describes his favorite play:

"The play we used quite successfully in San Diego is a fake draw to the strong side back and a screen pass to the weak side back. It's called 'Fake Draw to Len, Screen Right to Ray.'

"Len is the set back on the left side. Ray is the set back on the right side. In real life they were, respectively, Keith Lincoln and Paul Lowe.

"The draw play must have been working fairly well prior to the calling of this screen. With the San Diego Chargers, the draw was one of our most effective plays with Lincoln carrying. Therefore, this screen to Lowe gained a lot of yardage and resulted in frequent scores.

"I liked the play going to the right, as shown here because it was easier to make a good draw fake to the back on the left and conceal the ball on my belt buckle with my left hand, giving my empty right hand to the left back to fake over.

"Then, pivoting to my left, I changed the ball to my right hand in order to pass. All of this was done very deliberately, and a good fake into the left center of the line by the left back was very essential."

276

TOBIN ROTE

BORN: Jan. 18, 1928   HEIGHT: 6'3"   WEIGHT: 215

Green Bay Packers, 1950–56
Detroit Lions, 1957–59
Toronto Argonauts, 1960–62
San Diego Chargers, 1963–64

PASSING RECORD:

Year	Att.	Comp.	Yards Gained	T.D.	Pct.	Longest	Int.
1950	224	83	1231	7	37.1	96	24
1951	256	106	1540	15	41.4	85	20
1952	157	82	1268	13	52.2	81	8
1953	185	72	1005	5	38.9	80	15
1954	382	180	2311	14	47.1	82	18
1955	342	157	1977	17	45.9	60	19
1956	308	146	2203	18	47.7	66	15
1957	177	76	1070	11	42.2	48	10
1958	257	118	1678	14	45.9	65	10
1959	162	62	861	5	38.5	59	19
NFL TOTALS	2450	1082	15,144	119	44.2	96	158
1960	450	256	4257	38	55.6	103	25
1961	389	220	3093	16	56.6	108	16
1962	349	188	2538	13	53.9	75	17
CANADIAN TOTALS	1188	664	9888	77	55.9	108	58
1963	286	170	2510	20	59.4	85	17
1964	163	74	1156	9	45.4	82	15
AFL TOTALS	459	244	3666	29	54.0	85	32
COMBINED TOTALS	4097	1990	28,698	225	48.6	108	248

RUSHING RECORD:

Year	Att.	Yards Gained	Longest	Ave.
1950	27	158	29	5.9
1951	76	523	55	6.9
1952	58	313	30	5.4
1953	33	180	21	5.5
1954	67	301	30	4.5
1955	74	332	49	4.5

Tobin Rote, at 6'3", was an imposing figure when he dropped back to pass. He led the AFL in passing his first year with the Chargers.

1956	84	398	39	4.7
1957	70	366	23	5.2
1958	77	351	27	4.6
1959	35	156	31	4.5
NFL TOTALS	601	3078	55	5.1
1960	23	42	12	1.8
1961	31	95	12	3.1
1962	25	101	18	4.0
CANADIAN TOTALS	79	238	18	3.0
1963	24	62	8	2.6
1964	10	—12	9	—1.2
AFL TOTALS	34	50	9	1.5
COMBINED TOTALS	714	3366	55	4.7

13. The Big Guns

John Unitas

JOHN UNITAS IS MORE WILLING TO
SACRIFICE HIMSELF FOR THE SAKE OF
THE CONTEST THAN ANY QUARTERBACK
I KNOW. NONE COMBINE HIS SAVVY, HIS
REFLEXES AND HIS GREAT SPIRIT AS A
COMPETITOR.

—*Bill McPeak, coach,*
Washington Redskins, 1961–65

The tall crewcut man with the high Slavic cheekbones keeps it all inside. The fires burn within John Unitas of the Baltimore Colts—ambition, confidence, desire, guts—no one questions they're there. But they don't show on his phlegmatic face or in his calm bearing. He's ice-cold perfection, the classicist, the picture-book quarterback who throws the ball the way it's supposed to be spiralled, hands off with sureness and just the right fakes prescribed by the theoreticians, and directs the team with an awareness that makes coaches cite him as the beau-ideal of field generals in professional football.

A team that starts with Unitas is the team to be beaten, which is why the Baltimore Colts have been a strong factor in the Western Conference of the NFL for the decade in which Unitas has operated their offense.

He's in the $70,000 bracket as a wage-earner, with multiple business interests between seasons and a showcase home in the comfortable Maryland suburb of Towson with plenty of roaming room for his four kids. Unitas makes it all look so easy.

But it wasn't.

The career of John Unitas is an exercise in perseverance, ups and downs in which his important quality was not raw quarterbacking ability but a refusal to quit.

He could have gone to work in the steelmills like the other kids in his Pittsburgh neighborhood when the big football schools wouldn't give him a scholarship because he weighed only 145 pounds. But he shopped around and made a career for himself on a minor league level at the University of Louisville. He could have quit when he flunked his first pro trial with the Pittsburgh Steelers but he went to work as the "monkey," or high man, on a piledriver and played for the Bloomfield Rams on the side, so that when the Baltimore Colts tapped him on a chance phone call, he was ready. He could have quit the first time he took over at quarterback in a regular-season pro game and fumbled 3 handoffs, then threw an interception which led to a rout of the Baltimore Colts. But two years later he made the Colts the champions of the pro football world. He could have quit when the Colts collapsed after two championships in a row, and the fans in Baltimore booed him. But he eventually led them to another division title in 1964.

Not even a torn knee cartilage and damaged medial ligaments, suffered late in the 1965 season, will make John Unitas quit, though he's an aging veteran of thirty-three in a young man's sport.

"I've always had the greatest confidence in myself as far as ability as a player is concerned," says Unitas. "There's never been any doubt in my mind that I could do the job."

He's not cocky when he says it. The unemotional face—angular, the skin tautly drawn over the bones, the mouth almost cruel—is hard. The eyes, with a slight Mongolian cast, bore into the listener. When he's talking business, Unitas drops any pretense at petty chitchat. Football's his way of life, and in his own mind there's no nonsense about who deserves the credit for carrying Johnny Unitas as far as he has gone in his

283

business. Unitas suffered and worked and took all the chances that go into the making of a quarterback.

His character as a football player can be drawn from just one play in his career. It came moments before the end of "the greatest game ever played"—as the championship meeting between the Baltimore Colts and the New York Giants in 1958 has been called.

The setting was dynamic, in the dusk of Yankee Stadium, with the lights turned on to put an eerie glow on the late December chilling dampness. At the south end of the field, leading to the dugouts, Gino Marchetti, the defensive end of the Colts, lay on a stretcher and made the bearers wait. His left ankle was fractured. The injury occurred when Gino tackled Frank Gifford of the Giants inches short of a first down, forcing a fourth-down punt. Carl Taseff of the Colts raised his hands in a fair-catch signal. With less than 2 minutes to play, the Colts trailed, 17–14, the goal line a long 86 yards away. The first 2 passes by Unitas went incomplete, then he sent Lenny Moore on a trap off tackle for 11 yards. Three more passes missed fire and the Colts were faced with elimination. But on the crucial last down he hit Raymond Berry on the 35-yard line. The rangy end tacked on 15 more yards to midfield. The Colts stopped the clock, with 64 seconds left.

Twice more, he looked for Berry and was right on target. With no more timeouts left and the clock running, the Colts were on the Giant 13-yard line. The Colt field-goal team rushed on the field, sub quarterback George Shaw took the hasty snap from center, placed it down and Steve Myrha kicked the ball squarely. The clock showed 7 seconds as the ball went through the posts. Marchetti let them carry him inside. He'd catch the rest of it on radio.

With Gino gone, Unitas acted as captain and joined the officials and a couple of Giants for the toss at midfield to see who'd receive the kickoff in the historic first over-time period. Unitas called, "Tails," as referee Ron Gibbs flipped a half-dollar in the air. It came up "heads." But the Giants couldn't move the ball and had to punt again from their own territory. Taseff took the ball on his 20. Unitas went calmly to work. Twice he was confronted with third-down situations. He hit Alan Ameche on a swing pass, and the big fullback lumbered inches past the first-down pole. Unitas eluded a Giant rush and saw Berry loose, but the end wasn't far enough down the field. So John waggled twice with his left hand while he kept the ball cocked in his right and Giant tacklers took shots at him. Berry ran deeper and caught the ball on the Giant 44. Unitas faked a pass—play action—and gave the ball to Ameche as guard Art Spinney laid out Giant tackle Dick Modzelewski with a crackling trap block. Ameche sprang through the hole for 24 yards. This was field-goal territory, but the cool quarterback kept the Colts moving inexorably. He fired true to Berry on a slant-in pass that reached the 8-yard line.

As Unitas huddled his team, a spectator jumped the left-field railing and sprinted up the middle of the gridiron. The cops ran out and got him. Johnny called the play, a trap off tackle with Ameche. It was hardly the time to put the ball in the air. The fullback jammed into the hole, met stubborn resistance and gained only 2 yards. Should the Colts skip the suspense and go for the sure field goal? Ewbank, on the sideline, didn't make a move.

Now came the key play, the one that reveals Unitas. He faked the ball to Ameche again, drifted back 7 yards and threw the ball sharply across the field to his right. Jim Mutscheller, the tight end, grabbed it on the 1-yard line and fell across the sideline before he could veer over the goal. On the next play, "16 power," Ameche crashed through a gaping hole to win the game, 23–17.

But how about that pass call to Mutscheller? It was one of the most controversial in the history of football. The Colts didn't need a touchdown. A flat pass across the field looked risky. Three safe smashes into the line would have sufficed. One writer hinted the Colts went for a touchdown because a friend of owner Carroll Rosenbloom had a bundle riding on the game and they wanted to beat the point-spread. Otherwise, why risk the interception? Ridiculous.

"When you know what you're doing," shrugged Unitas, "you don't get intercepted. Mutscheller was there. All I had to do was hit him."

"But what if Mutscheller was covered?" one of the Colts later asked him.

"Then I'd have thrown the ball away. You don't risk anything in this game when you know where you're passing. Only I could have loused it up. And a guy's got to have confidence."

But with Unitas there's also a realization that he doesn't do it alone. "The quarterback's only as good as the men standing in front of him," he nodded. "You got to have ten other guys to go along with him. If they don't give him time to do his job, forget it."

When the Colts were going bad a couple of years back, he snapped peevishly, "I'm tired of patting 'em on the butt. Tired of begging them to do this and that. That's for the birds. I got to go out there and do whatever comes up that's necessary, like block. The man next to me should do the same thing. There's no priority for anybody."

However, there's also a softer, sensitive side to Unitas that relaxes, at first shyly, into a big wide smile when he feels comfortable in his own crowd; a side that made him stop just before he left the house to play in the 1959 championship game and change baby Chris' diaper. At such times he's the friendly, helpful next-door neighbor who wants to be accepted.

"He doesn't want to be any different than anybody else," said Jimmy Orr, the all-pro flanker of the Colts, a prime receiver for Unitas' passes. "But a quarterback is different. He can't be one of the boys."

Even among quarterbacks, Unitas is different. "The distinction between him and the others," said Bill McPeak, the former coach of the Washington Redskins, "is that Johnny's physically more a part of every game. He's not looking to eat the ball or throw a harmless incompletion if the pocket is invaded. He's more willing to take off and find a secondary open spot to throw from, to sacrifice himself." He also blocks, which is a violation of every canon of quarterbacking.

Unitas is a hybrid of greatness. He's not the greatest passer or faker or ball-handler. He has just enough quickness to keep out of trouble. But he's physical, as McPeak indicated, and has the elusive quality of being the boss when he's on the field. His supreme confidence is infectious. It reaches into the upper tier. The guy in the cheapest seat gets the feeling that somehow Unitas will find a way to win.

When Don Shula landed his first head coaching job in football, as leader of the Baltimore Colts, in January, 1963, he chortled happily, "Who else was ever able to start out with a Unitas? We were just scared to death of him in Detroit." Shula had been the defensive coach of the Lions, though his contact with the quarterback went back to the pre-championship days when they were teammates on the Colts.

His first official act as head coach was to call the quarterback, who was on the west coast practicing for the Pro Bowl game. Shula hadn't even considered who his assistants would be.

"I'd make you an assistant coach, too, John," he began, "only you got too much to do. How well I make out as coach depends on how well you do as quarterback."

Among all the great T-quarterbacks in pro history, John Unitas was the first bred to that system from the start of his playing days. The older ones, his predecessors, all came out of the single-wing. Unitas developed late. In high school he didn't throw a pass until his senior year.

Sports wasn't in the Unitas family scheme. Getting enough food on the table was the big struggle. His father died when John was five years old, leaving his mother with four children, the oldest only ten, and a shaky coal delivery business. By day Mrs. Unitas took the coal orders and by night, from nine to one, to make ends meet, she worked as a scrubwoman in downtown Pittsburgh office buildings. When the coal business failed, Mrs. Unitas went to work in a bakery, attended school at night, received the highest mark in a civil-service exam and became a bookkeeper for the city of Pittsburgh.

Meanwhile Johnny helped out when he got big enough by shoveling coal into bins around the neighborhood at 75 cents a ton. He tried to build himself up by working on construction gangs when he was old enough to get his working papers. At St. Justin's High School he turned out for football and played halfback for a couple of years, though his mother wasn't happy about it because she was afraid he'd get hurt. He was a skinny kid with long bony arms. St. Justin's was a small school. In his senior year, when the regular quarterback broke an ankle, the coach looked around for the kid with the strongest throwing arm to take his place. Unitas was elected. He went on to earn All-Catholic high school honors for the Pittsburgh area, but there was no rush to the front door on William Street by college scouts. Johnny barely scraped together 145 pounds.

A visit to Notre Dame in quest of a scholarship was followed by a curt note of refusal to the high school fathers. "The boy is too light," it read. He moved on to Indiana. They didn't even bother to explain there. He was finally steered to the University of Louisville in late April after nobody else showed any interest.

Since Louisville played freshmen, Unitas didn't waste any time earning his scholarship, although at first the scrawny quarterback played third-string and was almost cut from the squad. A big game against St. Bonaventure (11 completions in his first 12 attempts, 3 touchdowns, more than 300 yards) put him over the hump. Louisville football didn't mean much nationally, but the school played such powers as Cincinnati, North Carolina State and Tennessee. After Tennessee had Unitas on his back most of the game in a 59–6 drubbing, Vol Coach Bowden Wyatt called the tough Pittsburgher "the best quarterback I've seen this year." His senior year he suffered a hairline ankle fracture and

286

John Unitas of Baltimore keeps a sharp eye out for switchers in the defense as he calls signals.

Unitas prepares to hand off to Lenny Moore, left, while Colt linemen screen off Doug Atkins (81) of the Chicago Bears. The Colt quarterback is a sure ball handler.

missed only one game. He also grew into a sturdy 190-pounder, with some recognition as a prospect. The Pittsburgh Steelers picked him in the ninth round of the NFL draft, which should have been a natural parlay—the home-town kid and a club that needed help.

He reported to camp in 1955 with the cards stacked against him. Jim Finks (now the Minnesota general manager) was the Steeler quarterback—a sturdy veteran who had survived a broken neck, broken hand, torn ligaments, shattered cartilage and a smashed face (twice). Butch Kiesling, the coach, also had big hopes for Ted Marchibroda, a little passer coming out of the service, and Vic Eaton of Missouri. Unitas was fourth on the list. In a camp scrimmage he threw 2 touchdown passes and broke away for a 25-yard run. However, he never got into an exhibition game. When the Steelers cut him, he said to Kiesling, "I wouldn't mind, but I didn't get a chance to play." The Steelers even refused to put him on the taxi squad—that refuge of failures—at $125 a week. They gave him $10 to take a bus home to Pittsburgh.

At home, his wife Dorothy was pregnant. He was a 22-year-old guy out of work, living with her folks. Forget the college degree. He took the first job he could get, as the high man on a piledriving gang, climbing the rig for oil-and-grease jobs. On Saturday nights, instead of the movies, he made the Bloomfield Rams famous. They were a semi-pro team in a sandlot league. Unitas was paid $6 a game, but the money was inconsequential. There were no diathermy machines, or trainers to take the kinks out of tired muscles. You dressed in a shack, and took the caked mud home with you before you showered. Still, it kept him sharp because Unitas was determined to have another go at the pros, and Dorothy was sympathetic. He had to get it out of his system.

In February, while John was at work in the construction of a tin mill at Aliquippa, Dorothy answered the phone. General Manager Don Kellett of the Baltimore Colts wanted to talk to him. He said he'd call back later, and when he did, Unitas hesitated. With the baby coming, maybe he shouldn't try football again. It was too big a gamble. Kellett invited him down to a tryout in May. At Dorothy's insistence he went.

The phone call to Pittsburgh cost 80 cents. The myth has been propagated that Kellett called on a whim after scanning some old waiver lists. Actually, a fan had written Coach Weeb Ewbank, describing this kid quarterback for the Bloomfield Rams, and when Weeb checked out Unitas with his college coach, he passed the information on to the team's general manager.

The Colts liked his actions when they saw him in Baltimore and offered him a contract for $7,000 a year. ("When I went from the Bloomfield Rams to the Baltimore Colts," he once said, wryly, "I tripled my salary.") He still had to make the team, but was lucky because the Colts had an opening for a second-string quarterback behind incumbent George Shaw.

Shaw had been the rookie of the year in '55, a fine talent with a long future—until the fourth game of the season when the Chicago Bears damaged his knee. Ewbank had no choice but Unitas. The Colts had a slim 21–20 lead. Unitas fumbled the ball 3 times, all in his own end of the field, and the Bears converted those 3 fumbles into touchdowns. He threw a pass into the arms of J. C. Caroline of the Bears' secondary. Caroline ran it back 59 yards for a score, and from then on an interception became known in the Colt

288

terminology as a "Caroline Special." The Bears won the game 56–21. But, as noted, Ewbank was stuck.

In a dramatic switch, Unitas wound up saving Weeb's job. The Colts came down to the last game of the season needing a victory over the Washington Redskins to keep from dropping into last place in the Western Conference. A loss was supposed to mean that Ewbank was through. With 15 seconds to go, the Colts were mired on their own 47-yard line, behind 17–12. Unitas arched a desperation pass toward Jim Mutscheller, who was well covered at the goal line by two defenders. But Redskin halfback Norb Hecker misjudged the ball; it bounced off his shoulderpads and into Mutscheller's eager fingers. 'Skins were all over him, yet Mutscheller dragged them into the end zone for the job-saving triumph.

It was the first of many big plays in Johnny's career. Shaw, returning to action in 1957, was never able to reclaim his job. Unitas was firmly in charge—just how firm he proved in a game against the San Francisco 49ers. The Colts had the ball on their own 40, inches to go for a first down. They were going to gamble for it. Unitas went over to the sideline and asked, "What do you want, Coach?"

"Go for 16-Power," replied Ewbank, which meant fullback Ameche plowing into the line behind strong blocking. A logical play for such a spot.

When the Colts lined up, however, Unitas noted the middle backer of the 49ers had moved into the 6-hole where Ameche was heading. He also noticed that the left corner back of the 49ers was laying off Lenny Moore, who was flanked to the outside. Unitas quickly checked off.

He faked the ball to Ameche, wheeled and threw 15 yards across the field to Moore. The 49er defensive back reacted quickly and nailed Moore almost immediately, but Lenny wriggled ahead one step to save the gamble. Unitas shrugged. The play had worked.

The Colts missed a division title in '57 by blowing their last two games on the West Coast, but Unitas was voted the Jim Thorpe Trophy by the players of the NFL as the outstanding player of the season. And the next season he got the Colts their first world championship.

He was in the midst of the streak that would eventually reach 47 straight games in which he threw touchdown passes until the Los Angeles Rams stopped him in 1960. His style of pumping the ball two or three times before throwing was widely copied. "Every other quarterback," said safety Jimmy Patton of the Giants, "you look at his eyes and you know where he's going to throw. Not Unitas. He looks one way and throws another."

With Raymond Berry, he made the passer-to-receiver act a science. "It takes me 1.2 seconds to retreat 7 yards behind the line of scrimmage," he explained. "A quarterback should need protection up to 2.5 seconds, so now I've got 1.3 seconds to get rid of the ball. Then, if it's not too long a pass, the ball's in flight for 1 second. It should be in Raymond's hands at 3.5. If it isn't, we're not throwing the right distance for that particular play."

In 1959, leading the Colts to their second-straight NFL title, Unitas threw 32 touchdown passes, breaking Sid Luckman's sixteen-year-old record. Y. A. Tittle has since raised the mark to 36, but Unitas' total still stands as the best for a 12-game schedule.

Then, almost inexplicably, the Colts went haywire. They were leading the Western Conference in 1960. Playing in Chicago's Wrigley Field, against the rugged Bears, Unitas was subjected to a severe physical beating. His face was cut and bruised, and he was groggy from being mauled. There were 19 seconds left on the clock with the Colts trailing 20–17 and on the Bear 39-yard line. Unitas faded deeper than normal, almost to midfield, and threw one final desperation bomb. It dropped perfectly into Lenny Moore's arms in a corner of the end zone for the winning score.

That was their last victory of the year. From a 6–2 record, at which point Coach Vince Lombardi of Green Bay actually conceded them the Western championship, the Colts collapsed to a 6–6 season. It really started in Detroit, when Alan Ameche tore his Achilles tendon and was through for good as an effective fullback. The Colts also lost the game on the very last play when two defenders collided and let Lion end Jim Gibbons catch a 65-yard touchdown pass. Without Ameche, Unitas didn't have the running balance for his passing threat.

"You lose a guy like that," said Unitas, "you can't replace him. 'The Horse' was a tremendous blocker and a great runner. They couldn't key on me alone."

Reduced to the lone threat of Unitas, the Colts stumbled through two more disappointing seasons. In 1961, he dislocated the middle finger of his throwing hand, jamming it on the shoulderpads of Minnesota's Don Joyce as he followed through on a pass. It swelled so much he couldn't put pressure on the ball to get a firm grip, which affected his passing. In 1962, the Colts came within 49 seconds of playing 8 straight quarters without scoring a touchdown.

There was a rupture between Unitas and Ewbank on how a football game was supposed to be run. The success of the Green Bay Packers' running attack influenced the Colt coach. He wanted Unitas to stay on the ground more, throw short passes, forget about gambling on the bombs.

"In '58 and '59," said Unitas, "I'd throw from the end zone if I knew I could get a man open. I had a situation against Green Bay, fourth down and a yard to go. We were on their 35, the score tied. Weeb sent in a quarterback sneak. I couldn't get through with a bulldozer. I told Moore to slant in and take off, then bust out for the sideline. I gave the fullback a fake, held for half a count, then spun around and hit Lenny on the 12-yard line. We went for the score on the next play. I could have been a bum. As it worked out, we hit it. But as a quarterback, I also got to take orders."

When the Colts played Detroit, Weeb cautioned him to keep the ball away from Night Train Lane, their veteran cornerback, and Yale Lary, all-pro safety.

"If you don't throw at a man," argued Unitas "you give him an easy day. He hasn't got anything to worry about. But if you work on him a little, he's got to play it cautious."

The Colts faced the Lions after being humiliated by the Chicago Bears, 57–0. Owner Carroll Rosenbloom had already decided to make a coaching change after the season. He pulled Unitas aside and said, "You're the boss out there once the game starts. Call any plays you want."

Johnny pumped a covey of passes into Night Train's territory and beat him twice on long pitches for touchdowns. Given the green light, he never considered failure.

290

The quarterback's job is to concentrate on his passing target, and Unitas does, though Jim Marshall of the Minnesota Vikings lurks over his left shoulder.

George Preas, crouched at left, tries to ward off Cleveland end Paul Wiggin (84) as Unitas achieves a clear passing plane with his straight overhand motion.

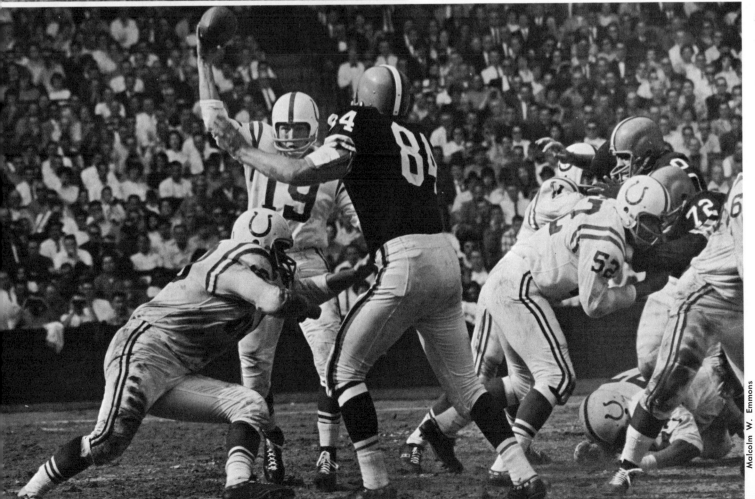

"If I was going to worry about that," he said, "I'd keep the ball on the ground all day and let someone else take the criticism. I'm not a conservative-type player. You've got to do something to break the routine, to let them know— 'Hell, I can't count on this guy for a down-and-in everytime there's a third and 5 situation. I've got to play it a little cautious, maybe watch for a down-and-out takeoff or down-and-in takeoff or boom, straight back.'"

They booed Unitas, and a friend of one of the Baltimore coaches explained to him, "I cheered him when he was winning. Why can't I boo him now that he's losing?" And the coach confessed, "You know, I couldn't argue with him."

Unitas heard the boos and said they didn't bother him. He was bothered, however, by the writer's revelations, in *Sport* magazine, of his differences with Weeb, who had already been dismissed and hired by the New York Jets. He called Weeb to apologize, but it's part of John's basic honesty that he never claimed he was misquoted. Unitas is essentially a noncontroversial guy and was embarrassed by the fuss created over his statements in the Baltimore newspapers. His color as an athlete is not in his personality, but in his performance.

With the Shula regime that started in 1963, he achieved a career high of 237 completions (also an NFL record until John Brodie broke it two years later). And when he led the Colts to the Western Conference title in 1964—also regaining all-pro status for the first time in five seasons—it was as if his skills had never been questioned. "All things considered," said Bob Waterfield, a quarterback great himself, "I would say Unitas is the greatest quarterback of all time."

There was one slight puzzle to mar the pattern—the mysterious collapse of the Colts in the 1964 championship game, 27–0. Unitas never got untracked.

"Beyond comprehension," said Giant coach Allie Sherman. "I never saw Unitas work a game like that. I kept saying, 'Now, John . . .' I kept waiting, but it never showed."

Still, he tore the NFL apart again in '65, until the Bears got to him in the twelfth game and put him in the hospital for knee surgery, severing the Colt title chances. It was the most severe injury of his career, though he also survived a punctured lung and three cracked ribs in 1958 and a bad back a couple of years later.

Unitas had good personal reasons to keep going. After ten seasons of play, he stood on the threshold of almost all the major passing marks. By 1967, under ordinary conditions, he should pass Y. A. Tittle in career pass attempts and completions, and he figured to dethrone him in 1966 for total yards gained and total touchdown passes (he was just two behind Tittle's 212 scoring throws, achieved in fifteen seasons of play).

In addition, the Colts needed the daring and imagination he invests in his job as a quarterback, plus a fervor for doing the unusual.

"You have to gamble in this league," he once said, analyzing his role, "—or die."

His eyes glowed with healthy animation.

292

Brilliant timing has marked the passing combination of John Unitas to Raymond Berry, who grabs a pass in mid-air with Jesse Whittenton of Green Bay in pursuit.

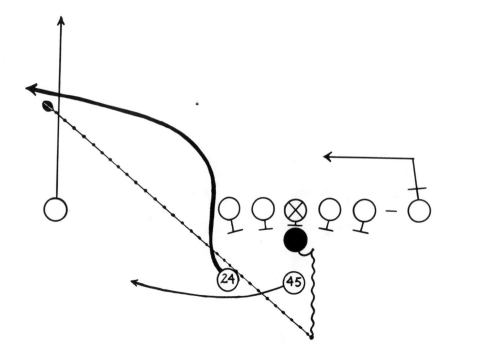

John Unitas describes his favorite play:

"A pass that has worked very well for the Colts is what we call an all-out pass to the weak side. When I say 'all out,' I mean just that. There are five possible receivers.

"The fullback is lined up directly behind me. That's Jerry Hill, No. 45, with the left halfback, Lennie Moore (24) on the weak side.

"Raymond Berry, the split left end, runs a pattern straight down the field. Moore cuts in behind him to the deep flat, and he's my primary receiver. If he's covered or there's a strong blitz on, I can hit the fullback swinging to his left.

"On the other side of the field, the right end checks and then cuts over the middle; the flanker dips to the inside and then straight downfield.

"I remember catching the Rams using a zone defense to the strong side. So I checked off and hit Moore to the weak side for a good gain."

294

JOHN UNITAS

Born: May 7, 1933   Height: 6'1"   Weight: 194
Baltimore Colts, 1956–65
PASSING RECORD:

Year	Att.	Comp.	Yards Gained	T.D.	Pct.	Longest	Int.
1956	198	110	1498	9	55.6	54	10
1957	301	172	2550	24	57.1	82	17
1958	263	136	2007	19	51.7	77	7
1959	367	193	2899	32	52.6	71	14
1960	378	190	3099	25	50.3	80	24
1961	420	229	2990	16	54.5	72	24
1962	389	222	2967	23	57.1	80	23
1963	410	237	3481	20	57.8	64	12
1964	305	158	2824	19	51.8	74	6
1965	282	164	2530	23	58.2	61	12
TOTALS	3313	1811	26,845	210	54.7	82	149

RUSHING RECORD:

Year	Att.	Yards Gained	Longest	Ave.
1956	28	155	34	5.5
1957	42	171	24	4.1
1958	33	139	38	4.2
1959	29	145	21	5.0
1960	36	195	27	5.4
1961	54	190	18	3.5
1962	50	137	35	2.7
1963	47	224	26	4.8
1964	37	162	20	4.4
1965	17	68	18	4.0
TOTALS	373	1586	38	4.3

Y. A. Tittle

IF IT WEREN'T TRADITIONAL TO PUNT
ON FOURTH DOWN, I'M CONVINCED
Y. A. TITTLE WOULD HAVE PASSED. AND
WITH HIS ABILITY, I WOULD HAVE GONE
ALONG WITH HIM 100 PERCENT.

—*Kyle Rote, back and end,*
New York Giants, 1951–61.

As the bald man behind the wheel paid the 25-cent toll on the San Mateo Bridge, his mind was made up. He was going to quit.

Behind him, in the Moraga Valley tucked in the San Leandro Hills, he left the San Francisco 49ers in their training quarters on the St. Mary's College campus. Coach Red Hickey had told him, succinctly, "Y.A., we've traded you. To the New York Giants, for Lou Cordileone. They're expecting you to join them up in Portland."

Y. A. Tittle had spent the biggest part of his athletic life, ten years, with the 49ers from 1951 to this August day in 1961. Who the hell was Lou Cordileone?

Ahead of him was home, across the San Francisco Bay, in Atherton, a prosperous suburban community on the Peninsula. Minnette was there. And the three children—Diane, Mike and Pat. They were all of school age. He had a good life there, with a thriving insurance business in Palo Alto, a couple of miles down the road.

If he were traded to Los Angeles, as it was once rumored, that wouldn't have been so bad. But New York? A good place to visit, like they say. "But I couldn't leave Minnette alone with the kids for four months," mused Tittle to himself as he drove along. "Better to make my break right now."

A kindly woman who lived in Tucson, Arizona, changed his mind and a little bit of the course of professional football history. If Mrs. Walter Risch hadn't been visiting her daughter Minnette that week, Y. A. Tittle probably would have retired as just another good quarterback who never quite made it, who would never be known from Coast to Coast.

Mrs. Risch is Tittle's mother-in-law. She made it all possible—the career after a career, his redemption as a great quarterback who could lead a team to a division championship.

"Tittle," said the scoffers, "never wins the big ones." He came close. A half game out in 1953, when he fractured his cheekbone. Down to a division playoff with the Detroit Lions in 1957, when the 49ers blew a 24–7 halftime lead. The failures bugged him.

Now as he came home, he told Minnette, "I said I would never go if they traded me to any team except the Rams. But—."

Mrs. Risch came in and sized up Y.A.'s self-debate. She offered to stay with the kids in the fall for a month so Minnette could join her husband in New York. That would make the move more bearable. And at Thanksgiving the children could come East for a visit, too, which would be exciting to them.

The next morning he flew off to Oregon.

Four months later, Tittle ran into the Giant dressing room, on the first-base side of Yankee Stadium—the same carpeted sanctum where the New York Yankees live in summertime—and went to a pay telephone in a private nook where the players can relax from prying eyes. He placed a call to California—Atherton—collect. It was 4:45

P.M. in New York, damp and chilly on December 17. In California, it was 1:45 P.M. and warm as Minnette picked up the phone and told the operator it was okay, she'd accept. "Well, honey," said Y.A., "we won."

Minnette started crying. So did the bald-headed man on the New York end of the phone, the tears filling his eyes. Four minutes later, the operator interrupted, "Your ti-yime is up." They were still crying.

"Most senseless call I ever made," said Tittle later. "All we did was cry. Never got a word in."

It was probably the single most emotional moment in the life of Y. A. Tittle, and he's had a lot of them, for old "Yat," as the players called him, was always transparent when it came to showing his feelings. On December 17, 1961, he became a winner for the first time in his life as a professional athlete.

A 7–7 tie with the Cleveland Browns, as Tittle went most of the way at quarterback, clinched the Eastern Conference title for the New York Giants. On their heels were the Philadelphia Eagles. Coach Allie Sherman told the Giants not to look at the scoreboard for the out-of-town game scores. "That's like not looking at a rattler at your feet," said Tittle. The Eagles won, so the Giants needed the tie. He threw his helmet high in the air, then looked around, embarrassed.

"After the final whistle," said Tittle, "I thought I was going to jump for joy. Instead, I broke down and bawled. Man, fourteen years is a long blankety time."

That's how long it took the aging quarterback, thirty-five years old when he joined the Giants, to prove himself. He had three more seasons with the Giants, filled with adulation and material goodies. Then the final frustration of not being able to do the job made him quit. Though he was disappointed, old Yat Tittle went out with all the respect an athlete can ask.

He had a much longer run than most pros bargain for. Altogether, Tittle played seventeen seasons, longer than any quarterback in history. His first two were with the Baltimore Colts of the old All-America Conference. The figures he piled up with the Colts don't count in the official pro records compiled by the National Football League, though the knocks were just as real as any he took later. Nevertheless, Yat stands out as the most decorated passer of all time.

He holds outright the record for most passes attempted in a lifetime (or the NFL version thereof), 3,817; most passes completed, 2,118; most yards gained in a lifetime, 28,339; most touchdown passes in a lifetime, 212; and most touchdown passes in a season, 36.

In 1965, his first year in a quarter of a century out of the uniform of an organized football team, Tittle became the backfield coach for the 49ers, his old team. He stood on the field before the game and told Billy Wilson, his old catching partner, "You know, Billy, I could go out right now and still throw the ball as good as these kids."

"That's right, Y.A.," said Billy, "but you're the only one who knows it."

For a man who is basically introspective and cautious, Y.A. had an adventurous flair as a football player. It was transmitted through his arm. "To me," said Tittle, "this game always has been putting the ball in the air." His bald head and jug ears and

300

prominent nose only made it easier for people to notice him. And the name was so unusual that they never forgot him.

He was born Yelberton Abraham Tittle, Jr., in Marshall, Texas, on October 24, 1926, a good year for long passers. Norm Van Brocklin was a progeny of that period. Marshall is a lumber town not far from the Louisiana border. All the kids had heard how Sammy Baugh, the great All-American at TCU, practiced passing by hanging an old tire in the backyard and throwing footballs through it. In the sixth grade young Y. A.—Yelberton Abraham was too much to saddle any kid with—discovered he could throw the ball better than any other kid his age in Marshall. He wore his first uniform in junior high school, and later at Marshall High he played tailback on a team that got as far as the state championship finals. In 1944, a boy who weighed 185 pounds and was 4-F because of asthma was choice recruiting material. The Louisiana schools just over the border came after him strong, and Y.A. accepted a scholarship offer from Louisiana State, though his older brother, Jack, had been a blocking back at Tulane.

The summer before enrollment, however, the University of Texas pirated the young passer and actually put him up in a boarding house on campus. Another kid in the house was a blond hotshot from Dallas, the All-State quarterback, Bobby Layne. To while away the time, they ran barefoot races in the street. To Y. A., from a small town, it seemed like every great football prospect in the Southwest had congregated in Austin, Texas, and he wasn't too confident about getting a chance to play. Especially with Layne to beat out. The competition never materialized because an LSU coach came to Texas and convinced Y.A. to go to LSU.

As a freshman in the war years, Tittle played with the varsity and was the starting tailback in half the games. Against Tulane he completed 15 out of 17 passes. Bernie Moore, now the commissioner of the Southeastern Conference, was the head coach. A year later he converted to the T-formation and imported Carl Brumbaugh, the original T-quarterback of the Chicago Bears, to teach Tittle the rudiments of taking the snap from center.

Playing seventeen-year-olds and 4-Fs, LSU had a 7–2 record in Tittle's first year as a quarterback, progressed to 9–1 in 1946 and played a scoreless tie with Arkansas in the Cotton Bowl. In 1947, they met Mississippi, which featured a tough ex-marine, Charley Conerly, at tailback. Late in the game, with the Bayou boys trying to overcome a 20–18 deficit, Tittle intercepted a pass by Conerly and lit out for the goal line. He had clear sailing when he crossed midfield, yanking himself free from the groping hands of an Ole Miss tackler. But the Rebel had a souvenir of their encounter on the 50, Tittle's belt, only Y.A. didn't know it. He felt a tightening around his knees. He looked down. His pants were falling. He grabbed hastily with his left hand, trying to hold the ball with his right. The pants kept falling, and the Mississippi posse was gaining. By the time he reached the 20-yard line, the baggy cotton knickers, the uniform of that prenylon period, were almost at his ankles. He couldn't run out of his pants, and he couldn't afford to stop. Tittle made a last hasty grab at them on the run and fell flat on his face. Nobody had touched him. What embarrassed him more than his drooping britches was the fact that LSU didn't score and lost the game.

"I recognize football is still a game," said Tittle years later, after a Giant defeat, "but to me it's the bitterest thing in the world when it's going on, and maybe for a short while afterward."

Although he was overshadowed by such great college stars as Layne, Conerly and Johnny Lujack of Notre Dame, Tittle was drafted and signed by the Cleveland Browns. He received a $2,000 bonus and a $10,000 contract, more money than he ever dreamed of, and promptly got married. He and Minnette had been going steady since their high school days together in Marshall.

Before Tittle ever played a game with the Browns, he was traded to the Baltimore Colts, the worst team in the All-America Conference. The Colts trained in the glamorous setting of Sun Valley, Idaho, with a plush Swiss chalet for their headquarters. The luxury didn't go to Tittle's head. He beat out veteran Charley O'Rourke, a former Boston College All-American, for the quarterback post and became the rookie of the year in the AAC. The Colts surprised everybody by tieing the rugged Buffalo Bills for the divisional title of the East. In the playoff, they led, 17–7, going into the final quarter. The Bills rallied to go ahead. In the final moments, a Tittle pass was intercepted by linebacker Buckets Hirsch of Buffalo and returned for a touchdown to finalize a 28–17 Baltimore defeat. It was the opening chapter of a pattern that would haunt Tittle for the next thirteen years. A team didn't win the "big one" with him.

The Colts were hopeless after that. In the last season of the AAC they fell apart, and when the leagues merged and Baltimore hung on as the thirteenth club, a swing team, they were even worse. The Colts went winless over a stretch of 19 straight games and were disbanded in 1951. All the players were thrown back into the draft. Tittle was picked third, behind a couple of college players—Kyle Rote of SMU and quarterback Bob Williams of Notre Dame. The San Francisco 49ers won the rights to him on the toss of a coin with Green Bay and Washington, two clubs they had tied in the 1950 standings in the won-and-lost records.

With the move to the West Coast, Tittle was like a rookie despite his three years of experience. Frankie Albert was the first-string quarterback, but Tittle was a half-dozen years younger, though you'd never know it when he took his helmet off.

The early pictures of Tittle as a college passer showed him with tufts of curly hair on a high forehead. They were thinning out when he got to Baltimore, and they were all gone by the time he arrived on the West Coast. Yat was a little sensitive about it. He always wore a cap in practice. An admirer, a retired air force colonel, gave his wings to Tittle, who pinned them on his cap. The 49ers called him "Colonel Slick," or sometimes the "Bald Eagle."

Coach Buck Shaw started working him into Albert's spot. Late in the season, Tittle pushed the 49ers into a 20–10 lead over Detroit. Shaw told him to play it safe, keep the ball on the ground in the fourth quarter. On the first play, Yat threw a long pass downfield, incomplete. Next play, he threw long again and the Lions almost intercepted the ball. The frantic coach signalled to Albert to get up off the bench, but Tittle had already taken himself out of the game.

"I'm sorry, Buck," he apologized as he came to the sidelines, "but all I want is touchdowns against those——."

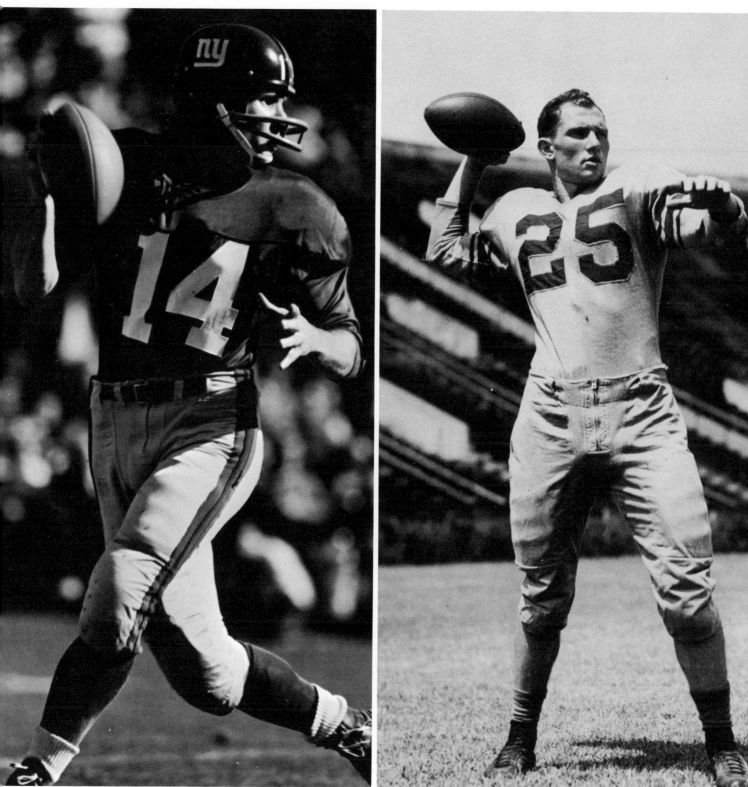

In the twilight of his career, Y. A. Tittle dominated the passing scene after he came to the New York Giants in 1961.

As a young quarterback at Louisiana State, Yelberton Abraham Tittle sported curly hair.

That's how fired up he got. It wasn't unusual, in San Francisco or later in New York, to see Tittle yank his helmet off after an incomplete pass and slam it to the ground while he kicked the turf a couple of times or pounded his thighs.

"I've been criticized for taking my helmet off during a game," he acknowledged, "and realize it might look ridiculous, but that's my own way of expressing myself. What do you do? You have emotion. I can throw two lackadaisical passes, and I'm quite concerned."

Tittle's spontaneous jigs of consternation and enthusiasm didn't communicate his personality to the fans of the Bay area. To them, he was a tight-lipped Texan, a rather colorless guy who went home every night. The Tittles were part of the postwar swarm of migrants to California. The newspapers carried the statistics . . . 15,200 a day . . . 20,000 a day. They were no different from their neighbors who came from Iowa or Oklahoma, Nebraska or Texas. Everybody in California builds a high fence around his backyard.

The only thing that distinguished Tittle was his way of making a living. He threw passes. And he was secretive about that, by design. In 1951, his first year with the 49ers, when he was used only spottily in the closing minutes, a San Francisco writer congratulated him on almost rallying the 49ers to a victory over the New York Yanks.

"Dammit," growled Tittle, "a guy can't win every week playing only the last 2 minutes."

This was picked up and mushroomed into a story that speculated about dissatisfaction on the 49ers, the quarterback criticizing the coach. After that, Tittle became dull copy, polite to all the media, but generally suspicious and uncooperative. "I got burned early," said Tittle when he came to New York. In the "big town," he was exposed to triple the amount of coverage he had received in San Francisco.

By contrast, however, his four years in New York were shared vicariously with the public. They were a happy interlude, almost a vacation in the reclusive life Tittle had made for himself and his family in the West. In New York he was a folk hero. He was the Walter Mitty brought to real life for the commuter to Darien, Great Neck or Scarsdale who had discovered violent pro football and needed to identify with the man on the field. This was no Nietszche superhero way out of his reach. Tittle even looked like this average fan when he put on streetclothes. He was bald, wore glasses to read the paper, dressed conservatively . . . and was a glorious gladiator every Sunday.

Tittle was camp—so far "out" he was "in." The Texas drawl, part of the melange of language in California, was quaint in the Big City. Y.A. also had a gift of phrase they found charming. He said he liked being with the Giants because of their history of success—"you can't criticize a trapper who's got the skins on the wall."

There's a tendency to forget Tittle was a great quarterback, particularly a great passer, before he ever came to New York. The bulk of his achievement, on a personal scale, was with the 49ers. At one time, in the mid-1950's, Y.A. was part of perhaps the greatest backfield ever put together. Joe Perry, who played with the 49ers for fourteen seasons and held all the ground-gaining records until Jimmy Brown came along, was the fullback. They called him "Joe the Jet." John Henry Johnson, a brutal runner and blocker who has played in the NFL for a dozen years and later was on a championship team in Detroit, played one halfback. Hugh McElhenny, the "King," a spectacular figure in the Bay area and all of pro football for a decade, was the other halfback. Tittle still considers McElhenny the greatest running back he has ever seen. Y.A. also had such receivers as Billy Wilson and Gordy Soltau. Wilson led the NFL in catches three different seasons.

From 1952, when Tittle displaced Albert at quarterback, through 1960, the 49ers finished second three times and were generally contenders. In 1953, Tittle ran a bootleg play against the Detroit Lions and crashed his face into Jim David's knee. The triple fracture of the cheekbone put him in the hospital for a week, with 16 bone chips removed. In the rematch with the Lions, he was in the game long enough to throw only one pass, intercepted, and the loss cost the 49ers the division title. In 1954, he played 10 games with a broken left hand. Tittle reached his peak with San Francisco in 1957. He made the all-pro lists for the first time as the 49ers won 8 games and lost 4 to tie the Lions for the Western Conference championship.

The 49ers had a rookie end, R. C. Owens, a great basketball rebounder in college. Tittle discovered in practice it was almost impossible to throw the ball over Owens' head. He beat the Rams and Bears with skyscraper tosses to Owens, who simply leaped higher than the defenders clustered around him to nab the ball. The 49ers trailed the Lions, 31–28, with a minute and 20 seconds to play and almost the length of the field to travel. Tittle moved them to the Detroit 41 with 19 seconds left. "Okay, R.C.," he said to Owens, "the Alley-Oop special." That was the name for their pet play.

Owens went step-for-step with Lion halfback Jim David, a great one, into the end zone. He was joined there by Jack Christiansen and Carl Karilivacz, of the Detroit secondary. Tittle arched the ball toward the cluster of uniforms. Owens went up for it, and so did the pride of Lions, all hacking at him. He came down with the ball, and they came down cussing. The 49ers won the game. Tittle considers that pass the greatest one he ever threw.

In the postseason playoff with the Lions, the 49ers were betrayed by their Achilles heel: defense. Throughout the Tittle years, the team never had a defensive unit to match its attack. In 1957, the 49ers actually gave up 4 points more than they scored. Against the Lions, they built up a 27–7 lead early in the third quarter but fell before a Detroit rally inspired by the passing of Tobin Rote.

Tittle discovered the difference in concept of defense the first week he joined the Giants in '61. They played an exhibition game in Los Angeles.

"We were beating them pretty good," recalled Tittle, "and the defensive team came off the field. I heard Sam Huff yelling, 'Come on, gang, we got to bear down. We got to get 'em.' This was in the fourth quarter and I looked up at the scoreboard. The Rams had three points."

He had another adjustment to make. A couple of nights before that exhibition game, he stood in the lobby of the Ambassador Hotel on Wilshire Boulevard, a bald, lonely man of thirty-five, hoping someone on the Giants would ask him to dinner.

No one did.

He wandered over to the Bull and Bush, a restaurant where players congregated, noticed an empty chair at one table and was finally asked to join a group of Giants.

The most exciting pass of Tittle's career was this grab by R. C. Owens, in white, to defeat the Detroit Lions in 1957 on the last play of the game. Jack Christiansen, left, and Jim David are helpless against the Alley Oop play.

Y. A. Tittle is presented the Jim Thorpe Trophy by the author, for being the outstanding player of the 1961 season in the NFL.

A study of purpose. Y. A. Tittle and Del Shofner, right, in practice togs, shared more than the same Giants' uniform. They were roommates, both from Texas, both intent, and they teamed to make a championship passing battery.

When Tittle was put into the preseason game just to get his feet wet, he bobbled the pass from center in his anxiety and hastily fell on the ball. A couple of Rams fell on top of him, knees first, and cracked two ribs. He was out five weeks before he ever threw a pass for New York.

The 49ers had let him go because he didn't fit into their plans. In the middle of the 1960 season, Coach Red Hickey, watching a college football game in the Southwest, got the inspiration for the shotgun formation. He moved the quarterback 5 yards behind the center, like the old single-wing tailback, and stationed the two running backs outside the tackles, where they could be receivers or carry the ball on reverses to the inside. It was a great passing formation because it immediately sent five men deep as receivers, but it needed some running balance. The quarterback was the logical man. That was all right for a young fellow like John Brodie, the other quarterback on the team. But a creaking old-timer like Tittle hardly fitted into Hickey's plans.

In January of 1961, the aging veteran was offered to the Giants, who refused. They had hopes for Lee Grosscup as incumbent Charley Conerly's stand-in. The Giants reached desperately for Tittle when Grosscup looked bad in the early workouts, and Tittle looked particularly sharp in an exhibition game against them in Portland. The price was cheap: Cordileone, a young untested lineman who never won a regular job. When told of the trade, Cordileone shook his head in disbelief and said, "Me for Tittle?" The "new" quarterback did the Giants an immediate turn. The Giants needed receivers as well as a passer. Del Shofner of the Los Angeles Rams was available. Tittle advised the Giants that they'd played together in the Pro Bowl and Shofner was "the best end I've ever thrown to." Old Yat and young Del arrived as an entry, two guys from Texas, roommates, and for the next few years an exciting combination.

Tittle, when he was healthy again, proved himself to the Giants the first time he went into action, in the second game of the season against the Steelers. He completed his first 8 passes, wound up with 10-for-12 and was responsible for a 17–14 victory. He had trouble absorbing the Giant system, but veterans like Kyle Rote helped him. When Tittle wanted to throw a square-out, his favorite pattern, he turned to Kyle, who translated it into Giant language. And Tittle put it into action.

"On a given day," said Rote, "Y. A. Tittle could throw the ball as well as anyone in the history of football. And he had the enthusiasm of a high school kid."

That's what impressed Grosscup, his young understudy. "He was a guy who'd been around for years," said Lee, "but if we made a mistake in practice, he'd be like a kid, slamming his hat to the ground, sounding off."

"I'm guilty, I know, of getting hot and bothered," said Tittle. "But I don't believe I'm just a Sunday player. I'm as much a football player when I'm out playing touch with the kids, or wherever I might be."

He handed off to a halfback in a dummy drill, swatted him on the tail as he went by and yelled, "Take off, baby." In a game he didn't spare himself. The Detroit Lions once gave him a brain concussion when he bootlegged the ball. But Yat also played it smart. His back was still taped from his exhibition injury as he went back to pass against the Dallas Cowboys, with two pursuers hot on his tail. Yat wheeled away from them to the left sideline and turned downfield. He knew, from experience, there'd be no other Cowboys coming up to hit him blind-side. He tightroped for 15 yards, into field-goal range, and gingerly stepped out of bounds before a group of Cowboys converged on him.

"Now wasn't that a pathetic run," he grimaced after the game. "I have this bum shoulder and didn't want to take any chances, but I don't want to look chicken either. I feel like a mummy, taped up. Sometimes I think the good Lord is telling me, 'This is a warning, boy. It's time to get out.'

"But man, you can't beat this winning."

The Giants won three-straight division titles with Tittle. The honors accumulated—All-Pro, the Jim Thorpe Trophy twice as the most valuable player in the league, a cabin cruiser for being the most popular Giant. He was a celebrity, and candid about it: "I'd be foolish to say I don't enjoy people asking for my autograph. It might not be fun during dinner, but I'd rather have it that way than the way I have in some other years. The big mistake is to think this is going on forever. The day I'm finished, I'm right back where I came from years ago in Marshall, Texas."

He was stuck on routine. He watched his weight carefully and kept it at 193 pounds. When others went to glamorous low-cut shoes, Tittle stuck with his old-fashioned hightops because he never had an ankle injury. So why change? He wore the same shoulderpads—rotten and ragged and put together with adhesive tape—for seventeen years. But he was lucky and never had a serious shoulder injury. When the team went down to the Roosevelt Hotel the night before a game, he always ate the same meal, a steak, at the same place and was in his room by nine-thirty. If any friends came to town, he didn't visit.

"I don't want to say the next day, if we lost the game, that I wasn't thinking football," he explained. "You got to pay the mental price. If it's universally accepted that you should be in bed by eleven, then to me that's paying the price."

Coach Allie Sherman disciplined Tittle's thinking and simplified his job by cutting out the frills and giving him a basic offense that Y.A. could master. "I was no great student in school," he admitted. "My senior year at LSU, our left halfback called most of the plays."

Tittle learned the value of an integrated attack. When the Giants played Detroit in 1962, Sherman gave him a game plan that stressed running. Tittle couldn't see it. The Lions had a great defensive unit, anchored by all-pro tackles Roger Brown and Alex Karras and backed up by Joe Schmidt. You weren't supposed to run against them. But the Giants took the ball right down the field on the ground and scored early to take control of the game. "You won me over, Coach," said Tittle.

Y.A. was a great passer. He threw 33 touchdown passes in 1962, for a new league record, including 7 in one afternoon against the Washington Redskins. Tittle refrained from trying for an eighth late in the fourth quarter. "It would have been in poor taste," he said simply. He increased the record to 36 in 1963, when there wasn't a single Giant ball carrier among the top ten, and Phil King led the Giants with 613 yards (Tittle's passing, best in the league, gained 3,145 yards).

Bill George, the capable linebacker of the Bears, was riled by his inability to blitz Tittle. He hit him with a forearm after a play, but not square, and promised, "I'll get you next time, Tittle."

308

"You do," blustered Y.A., "and you'll see what'll happen."

"What'll happen?" demanded George.

"You know," grinned Tittle later, "I didn't know what to tell him."

There was one flaw to his life. He could not win the big one, an NFL title. The Giants hadn't had much of a chance the first two years against the superior Green Bay Packers, but in 1963 they faced the Bears confidently in Chicago. "There is no doubt in my mind," said Tittle, before the game. "There is no way we can lose."

The Bears found a way. As Tittle threw a touchdown pass to Gifford in the first quarter, linebacker Larry Morris hit him across the leg on a blitz. Yat felt a twinge

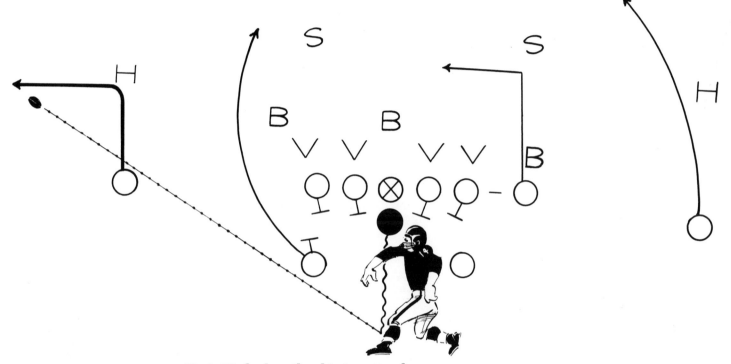

Y. A. Tittle describes his favorite play:

"There's only one pass that can't be stopped when it's done right. That's the weakside sideline pattern.

"I used it a lot when I teamed with Del Shofner, our left end on the New York Giants.

"It's a timing pass. You set up at seven yards. The receiver can go downfield 11 yards in the same period of time.

"I always believed in throwing to the outside, because in the middle there's always trouble. You can't predict how a linebacker or a safety is going to react. It looks like a man is open, and then a strange hand reaches up from nowhere.

"On this sideline pass, there's only one man can get at the receiver. The way this play works, the quarterback has only one choice. He hits the left end immediately or not at all. The beauty of it is, if the man isn't open, you can throw the ball out of bounds and not risk an interception.

"In running this pattern, incidentally, Shofner didn't break it off sharp like a lot of ends. He found out he could get to the spot of the ball faster, and also keep the defensive back off him by rounding the corner instead of cutting off his right foot, which had to slow him up a little."

behind the knee, which started to stiffen. In the same period Morris intercepted a screen pass and ran it back 61 yards to set up a touchdown. Before the half, Tittle went back to pass and Morris, shooting again, hit him just as he got rid of the ball. They were both clean shots, but they left Yat a cripple. At halftime he couldn't bend his knee, so the Giant doctor froze it with a spray and gave him a shot. The only other Giant quarterback was a nervous rookie, Glynn Griffing. Tittle came out and played the second half on guts but was generally helpless. In the third quarter, another screen pass was intercepted by end Ed O'Bradovich and returned deep into Giant territory to set up a Bear touchdown and a 14–10 lead. As the second hand on the clock in Wrigley Field tripped toward the zero mark, Tittle sat on the Giant bench with a blanket over his head like a shawl, crying.

It was the symbolic end to his football career. He played again in 1964 to finish out his contract. His daughter Diane was ready to go to high school, and Yat was worried about the constant shifting of schools. He also took a physical beating as the Giants slumped to their worst record in history, 2–10–2. John Baker of the Steelers caved his ribs in the second game of the season. Teams blitzed the hell out of him. "They were picking on a cripple," shrugged Tittle. He was supplanted at quarterback by a 5–10 rookie scrambler from the Ivy League, Gary Wood of Cornell.

"I knew it was time to quit," Tittle sighed and winked, "when Gary asked me if he could date my daughter."

He moved his family quietly back to Atherton, California, and concentrated on his lucrative insurance business. The 49ers took advantage of his presence and made him their quarterback coach in 1965. It's more than coincidence that John Brodie came up with the best season of his life, and the 49er offense led the league in scoring and yards gained. "I like to think," said Tittle modestly, "I helped John in getting prepared mentally to play football."

The regret at never winning a championship was tempered by the esteem he rated from his Giant achievements.

"In football," said Paul Brown, "the quarterback is the point of the spear. The Giants had that spear with Tittle."

YELBERTON ABRAHAM TITTLE

Born: Oct. 24, 1926   Height: 6'0"   Weight: 195
Baltimore Colts (AAC), 1948–50
San Francisco 49ers, 1951–60
New York Giants, 1961–64
PASSING RECORD:

Year	Att.	Comp.	Yards Gained	T.D.	Pct.	Longest	Int.
1948	289	161	2522	16	55.7	n.a.	9
1949	289	148	2209	14	51.2	n.a.	18

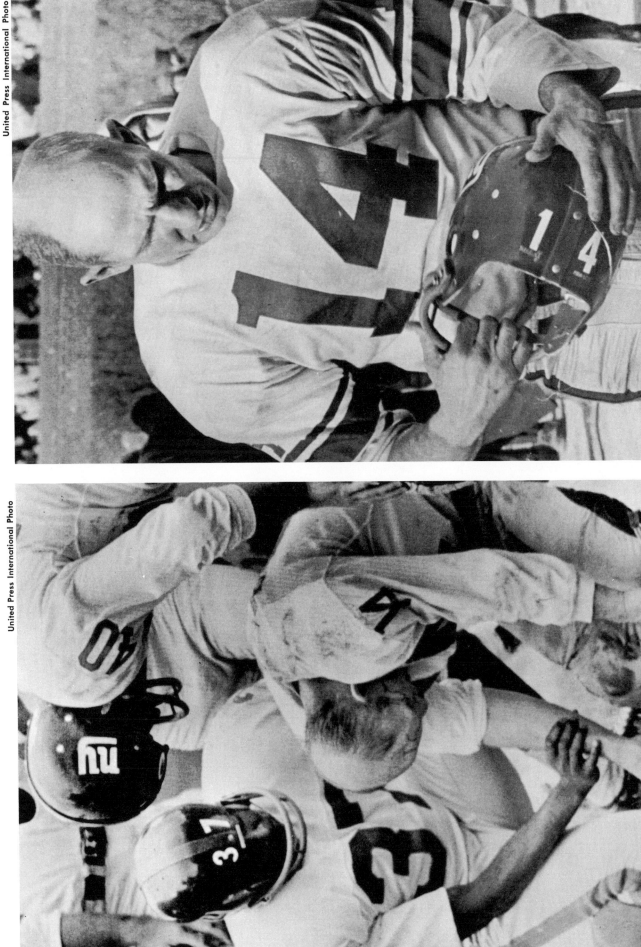

Despair covers Y. A. Tittle's face as he leaves the field after the Giants' 1963 championship game loss to Chicago. He never got another chance to win an NFL title.

Y. A. Tittle's days as an effective pro quarterback faded after his ribs were caved in by big John Baker of Pittsburgh. R. C. Owens (37) and Joe Morrison (40) offer help to bloodied, bowed Yat.

AAC TOTALS	578	309	4731	30	53.5		27
1950	315	161	1884	8	51.1	62	19
1951	114	63	808	8	55.3	48	9
1952	208	106	1407	11	51.0	77	12
1953	259	149	2121	20	57.5	71	16
1954	295	170	2205	9	57.6	68	9
1955	287	147	2185	17	51.2	78	28
1956	218	124	1641	7	56.9	77	12
1957	279	176	2157	13	63.1	46	15
1958	208	120	1467	9	57.7	64	15
1959	199	102	1331	10	51.3	75	15
1960	127	69	694	4	54.3	45	3
1961	285	163	2272	17	57.2	62	12
1962	375	200	3224	33	53.3	69	20
1963*	367	221	3145	36	60.2	70	14
1964	281	147	1798	10	52.3	54	22
NFL TOTALS	3817	2118	28,339	212	55.5	78	221
COMBINED TOTALS	4395	2427	33,070	242	55.2	78	248

* Led NFL

RUSHING RECORD:

Year	Att.	Yards Gained	Longest	Ave.
1948	n.a.	n.a.	n.a.	n.a.
1949	n.a.	n.a.	n.a.	n.a.
1950	20	77	23	3.9
1951	13	18	5	1.4
1952	11	—11	4	—1.0
1953	14	41	14	2.9
1954	28	68	10	2.4
1955	23	114	35	5.0
1956	24	67	13	2.8
1957	40	220	45	5.5
1958	22	35	12	1.6
1959	11	24	22	2.2
1960	10	61	28	6.1
1961	25	85	17	3.4
1962	17	108	23	6.4
1963	18	99	18	5.5
1964	15	—7	7	—.5
NFL TOTALS	289	999	45	3.5

Bart Starr

WHEN I FIRST CAME HERE, THE BOY WAS
NOT CONFIDENT. BUT NOW HE HAS A LOT
OF LEADERSHIP ABILITY, AND HE KNOWS
EXACTLY WHAT I WANT.
—*Vince Lombardi, coach,*
Green Bay Packers, 1959–

The mood was jubilation in the dressing room of the Green Bay Packers. Coach Vince Lombardi had his arms around a couple of big, mud-splattered tackles, the gap in his teeth showing as he smiled broadly. Jimmy Taylor wasn't feeling the bruised splotches on his body. He grinned crookedly.

Only Paul Hornung seemed disturbed as he tossed a stained T-shirt on the floor, which was cluttered with football gear and television wires. "Them not picking Bart Starr," he groused, "—it's ridiculous."

Taylor was the recipient of a gleaming new sports car as the most valuable player of the championship game between the Packers and the Cleveland Browns on January 2, 1966. The tough little fullback had hammered out 96 yards on the ground, and no one begrudged him the honor.

But next to Hornung's locker stood Starr, the upper right side of his body, from the ribs across the chest, encased in tape. He wasn't feeling pain, either. The Packers were the winners, 23–12, and again the champions of the NFL after a two-year hiatus in second place.

For the six days leading up to the game, Coach Lombardi wasn't sure Starr could play. A jarring block by Baltimore's Steve Stonebreaker bruised his ribs on the first play of the divisional playoff the week before and left him unable to raise his throwing arm. A quarterback who can't throw is like an opera singer with laryngitis. As Starr healed during the week, there was still a question: what would happen if the Browns got to him? Could he take another shot in the ribs?

Starr could, and did. He was in on every offensive play but one. Lombardi let 10-year vet Zeke Bratkowski run out the clock at the very end so he could always tell his grandchildren he'd played in a championship game. But Starr was the cool executioner who cut down the Browns. Handling a slush-heavy football, he never fumbled. He completed 10 out of 18 passes for 147 yards, the first one a long floater to Carroll Dale that went for 47 yards and the first score of the game. He carried out Lombardi's game plan with the precision of a diamond cutter, chipping away at the Cleveland defense to prepare them for the big plays—Dale's grab and Hornung's 13-yard touchdown run in the third quarter which cemented the victory.

And when it was over the cameras and the writers sought out Hornung and Taylor and some of the defensive heroes. They wanted Starr only as an afterthought to explain to them what had happened. Starr is the anomaly of all T-quarterbacks. In an era when the men who play that position are the most glorified of all football players, he gets skimpy attention. The kids in Baltimore, when they pick up a game on an empty lot, all want to wear No. 19—Unitas' numerals. The kids in Green Bay, they clamor for No. 5—worn by Hornung, a halfback. Starr wears No. 15.

Starting in 1960, the Packers have won four division championships in six years and converted three of them into NFL titles, all with efficient, quiet Bart Starr playing quarterback. Until the middle of Lombardi's first season, he wasn't sure he could win with Starr. At the end of it, he traded Lamar McHan to the Baltimore Colts and gave Bart the complete responsibility of leadership. It was significant. Lombardi's first move in Green Bay was the acquisition of McHan from the Cardinals because he felt he needed an experienced quarterback.

"This does a lot for a person," admitted Starr later in soft, measured tones, "to know that someone has the confidence to gamble on you. Believe me, I had nothing on my mind except justifying his decision to trade Lamar away.

"My first couple of years with the Packers if I'd throw an interception, it killed me. I worried about it all day, and this is bad. Now I'll throw an interception, I feel I can throw three more and it still doesn't bother me. If a drive used to bog down in '56–'57, I'd worry about it. Why heck, I forget about it now. When I first came to the Packers, criticism bothered me. I was sensitive about it. I'm not sensitive like that any more. I'm a sensitive person basically. At least, my wife tells me I am. But not playing football."

When the credits are passed out, Starr sometimes gets skipped because he's a mild, precise man by nature and it's reflected in the way he plays football. Winning has produced a libido of sorts. He stood up to Lombardi, who also is the general manager, for a salary raise one year. Lombardi shook his head, smiled sadly, "Like Frankenstein, I've created a monster." He gave Bart the raise he demanded.

Starr was selected for the January, 1963, Pro Bowl game, along with seven other Packers. Lombardi was sensitive about the number of his boys there, more than any other team, and named Johnny Unitas of the Colts as the starting quarterback.

"Bart is very unhappy about it," admitted Lombardi during the practice sessions leading up to the game. How did he know? Bart told him so.

"Sure, it bothered me," said the Packer quarterback. "I told him I thought I earned the right to start that game. I don't think it was the idea of starting. I couldn't care less. That's beside the point. But I had played on a championship team for two straight years. If there were eight of us there, we merited the right."

As Starr spoke, the thought occurred to the listener: could he have talked like that to Lombardi a half dozen years ago?

"No," he grinned bashfully, "I'd probably have hung my head and looked at my feet."

The mature Starr still isn't a dynamo who rallies his team around. He once told end Max McGee in a huddle to "Hush up!" The Packers broke up because the imploring Southern expression sounded funny in a tough football environment. Starr says only what has to be said.

"I'm back there trying to do the best I can," he explained, "and they're up front trying to do the best they can. No one feels worse about it when they miss a block than they do. When Fuzzy Thurston (veteran Green Bay guard) misses Roger Brown (Detroit defensive tackle), there's no guy in the stadium who feels worse than Fuzzy. So why eat him out? Hell, he knows it. I've had great pass protection and thrown an interception. So why blast him?"

Starr qualifies to play quarterback for a championship team on smartness and execution. He's the image that Lombardi tried to inculcate in the Packers—thoroughness and dedication. "Bart follows our ready sheet for a game perfectly," said Vince once. "We win because we make very, very few mistakes. We work on that."

There are important records in the NFL manual which stand high with Lombardi. One shows that Starr is the most effective passer in the history of football. In lifetime passing efficiency, including only those pros who've thrown more than 1,000 passes, he is listed No. 1 at 56.7 percent. Ahead of Sammy Baugh. Ahead of Otto Graham. His percentage of interceptions in the career category (4.26) is also the best in history. And Bart went one stretch of 277 passes, spanning the 1964–65 seasons, without throwing an interception, another all-time record. This kind of statistics breathe.

The Packers are a running team. Nobody denies it. But in 1965, they gained 625 more yards with Starr's arm than they did bruising the enemy's lines (2113 to 1488).

Figures like these should puncture the legend that Starr is a pedestrian passer, not to be mentioned with Unitas or such other practitioners as Tittle and Van Brocklin. When the Packers played the Eagles in the 1960 title game, Starr completed 21 out of 35 passes. Van Brocklin went 9 for 20. The Eagles won the game on a ground march. The next year, Bart threw 3 touchdown passes, while Tittle and Charley Conerly were blanked in a 37–0 championship rout of the Giants.

When the Packers beat the Giants again in 1962, the losers moaned that a wind which whipped Yankee Stadium with 50-mile-an-hour gusts took away their best weapon, Tittle's passing. "It didn't help me," shrugged Starr, who had led the league in passing that season and completed 62.5 percent of his pitches. "What nobody knew was that our game plan called for us to throw against the Giants. It discouraged me to read that they would have won if they'd had a dry field and a warm day. Why, if we had that, and the guys could have heard my automatics (the crowd noise and the wind were too much), we would have eaten them up." In the same gale and miserable cold that atrophied Tittle's passing, Starr didn't fumble once, didn't throw a single interception—in fact, completed 9 out of 21. But under the conditions, the Packers played conservative football, and Starr used mostly his head instead of his arm.

Protecting a slim 3–0 margin late in the second quarter, Green Bay recovered a fumble on the Giant 28. On the first play, Hornung threw to Boyd Dowler on the option play for a first down on the 7-yard line. On the second play, Taylor cut through the middle of the line for a touchdown and a commanding 10–0 lead. Starr explained how he set it up:

"After a team fumbles I like to come right back with something, hit 'em now. It's not like after a punt. They've got to collect themselves. The option run or pass by Hornung gave us a good threat. It came off play action, which was important. It wasn't the straight turn and hand to Paul, where he just runs a sweep from which he can throw. I thought they might be looking for that. But by faking a dive to Taylor up the middle and bringing Hornung across, it looked more like a run. I called on him to throw because the Giants might have been looking for me in that spot. The Taylor play was one of our best. It was designed to the right side with cross-blocking up front. We caught Sam Huff, the middle linebacker, guessing. Jimmy hit and slid left and had a clear alley.

"Some teams might prefer to go for the home run. We're not a big-bomb team. We throw enough fly patterns to keep 'em off of us. We try to control the ball."

Grimness and resolve are Bart Starr's trademark as the Green Bay field general.

Bart Starr is the most effective passer in football history, if completion percentages are the criterion.

Control is the clue to the Packers and why Starr is the antithesis of his own name. "Lombardi dominates that club," said Eddie LeBaron, the little lawyer who used to play for the Redskins and Cowboys. "They're building a strong corporate image with no great individual stars."

"That's cute," laughed Starr. "For me it's enough just to have the privilege and pleasure of playing on the Packers. We're basically a running team. Credit has to go to Hornung and Taylor and Tom Moore. They've been our bread and butter. If you're controlling the ball, moving downfield, I think you can see where an interception would wreck us. As long as we have the ball, they can't do anything with it.

"Who wouldn't like to rare back a few times and throw the bomb? It's tremendous. I don't do it because it's not our style of attack. If they gang up on us, sure, we throw the ball over their heads. That's an easy score then.

"A quarterback is only as good as his arm, basically. He can be the smartest guy in the world, the best runner, but you still have to throw. It's like hitting a baseball. Either you can or you can't. I can throw the ball far enough. I have to work on the accuracy of the long one. We don't throw it that much. I used to throw my long passes on a flatter trajectory that I do now. Then I went out to the Pro Bowl and noticed Unitas. I really study him because I think he's the greatest. A pass with a flat trajectory has to be dead on the money. There can be no leeway. But if you loft the ball, like Unitas, the receiver can adjust and run to it."

His scoring pass to Dale against the Browns last January was a prime example. It wasn't well thrown. Bart didn't get enough on the ball. Dale had his defender, halfback Walter Beach, beaten, backtracked to meet the ball, then did a smart bit of running to elude the safety who came across to double on him. Yet Bart has no desire to be a Unitas-type quarterback—gambling, unorthodox, daring.

"I'm not knocking it," he said diplomatically. "They made a living off it in Baltimore. But I'm like Coach Lombardi. I'd play it by the book if I had to. When you've got fourth and 1 yard, or half a yard, on the other guy's 20-yard line, there aren't too many times you'd throw the ball. I've seen John do it time and time again. I never have, not down there, though I have thought of gambling a lot more just to keep teams loose."

Starr's gambling is in the game of wits on the line of scrimmage, when the Packers are over the ball and the sharp-eyed quarterback squints over the heads of his linemen. The Packers "audible" 50 percent of the time in some games. Bart calls football a cat-and-mouse business. With automatics, he's pitting his skill of recognition against the opposition. That's where he gets his kicks.

"His greatest asset," asserted Bill Austin, a former Packer assistant who now heads the Pittsburgh Steelers, "is picking apart the defense. Any defense has a hole. The trick is to know where."

"We could never huddle if we wanted to," added Starr. "It's my ambition to play a whole game in which I call all the plays on the line of scrimmage. That'd really frustrate 'em."

He has the confidence of the players in his judgment. Jerry Kramer, an offensive guard, said, "If we're lined up ready to go, and I see the defense overloaded, I forget automatically the play that was called in the huddle. I'm that confident he's going to

319

change it. I'm already thinking of the next play. Sometimes we might 'check off' three or four times on one play."

Green Bay once got hooked on the myth that Bart was a Phi Beta Kappa at Alabama. He traced the rumors to one of his early roommates, end Gary Knafelc. "That's nothing," said Knafelc, "I'm going to make you a Rhodes scholar, too, before you're through here."

Actually, Starr was a straight-A student his last two years at Alabama. He had plenty of time to study. His last two years were spent mostly on the bench, though he had played as a sophomore and led 'Bama to the Cotton Bowl. His junior year was a fizzle because of a bad back, aggravated when he did some punting and damaged the tissue. Periodically, the old strain in the sacroiliac region kicks up on him and he receives chiropractic treatment. His senior year, he sat on the bench as Alabama achieved a perfect record, no wins, 10 defeats, the low point in Tide annals.

"Probably any confidence I had built up in twenty years of life was almost shattered," recalled Bart. "A guy sits there and he doesn't even play. Ears Whitworth was the new coach and he decided he'd rather lose with sophomores than gamble on winning with seniors. Just ridiculous."

He was lucky to be drafted by the Green Bay Packers for the 1956 season, on the seventeenth round, the 199th man chosen among college eligibles. Being chosen by Green Bay was hardly an honor. Bart scarcely knew where it was, or that in those days the airport terminal was a quonset hut. He knew he had a burning desire to try pro football from watching the Bears and Redskins on TV.

There wasn't much chance of displacing the reigning quarterback, big Tobin Rote. "There were four of us," remembered Bart, "and Tobin. It was a funny training camp. I never saw so many guys leave. Being a rookie, I said, 'Holy cow, maybe I should leave, too.' I wound up being behind Tobin and didn't play much."

Rote was traded to Detroit the following season. Babe Parilli, an ex-Packer, was returned by the Cleveland Browns, but Starr became the regular. He didn't know what was going on, but he was gaining experience. In 1958, he twisted his ankle badly and Parilli was the starter. Playing with the Babe was a privilege. As a high school player in Montgomery, Alabama, his home town, Bart had once been sent up to Kentucky for a three-week summer course in the T-formation. The Kentucky coach was Bear Bryant, and his All-American quarterback was Babe Parilli, Bart's tutor.

"Babe taught me more in three weeks about the fundamentals of ball-handling and technique," said Bart, "than I've learned the rest of my life." On his mirror at home he hung pictures of the Kentucky Babe, his first football idol.

In 1959, the start of the Lombardi regime, Starr's position was precarious. He threw an interception in the first scrimmage, and Lombardi barked, "One more like that and you're through."

The final squad cut produced the ultimate irony. It narrowed down to Starr or Parilli, and Starr stayed. It was no real vote of confidence. Lombardi needed bodies to fill out the roster. Newly-acquired Lamar McHan was the first-string quarterback. The Packers, who won just one game in 1958 while Starr sat around, opened up with three straight victories. And Starr continued sitting. McHan hurt his shoulder before the

320

Packers were due in New York to play the Giants. For Lombardi, the game was special. He had been the offensive coach of the Giants. He was a native New Yorker coming back before the home folks. He wanted the best going for him.

"I thought, boy, this was going to be my big chance," recalled Starr. "So I worked real hard all week and thought I had everything down cold. I had a good game plan. So what does he do when it's evident early in the game Mac can't throw. He sticks Joe Francis in there."

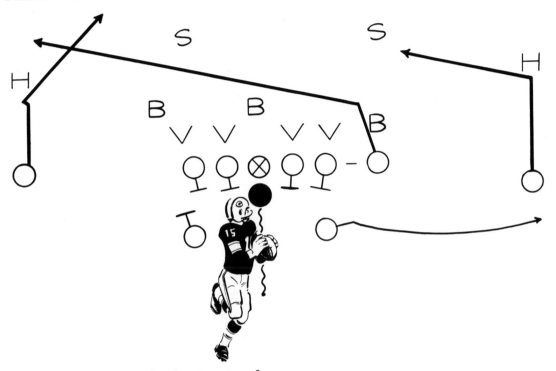

Bart Starr describes his favorite play:

"We have a pass in Green Bay we throw against everyone and all defenses and make it go. Against the Lions in Detroit, we used it several times very effectively in '65, once for a real long gain that got us started after we were down by some 20 points.

"It's a crossing action type of pass not easily covered by a defense and is known in our play book as Right Formation, Flare Wide L & R, Wing Trail. L & R merely denotes L (*left end*) and R (*tight end*) are crossing. Wing trail is just that. The wing, or flanker trails across.

"I like the pass specifically for three reasons: 1) it can be thrown against any defense very effectively; 2) there are four good choices of receivers, depending on how the defense covers; 3) there are easy take-off or companion routes the wing can run off this basic move to keep his defender completely off balance.

"The blocking is very sound and simple. Big linemen on big defensive linemen. The center is responsible for the middle linebacker. The remaining back, the left half-back, is responsible for the linebacker to his side. If the linebacker on the fullback's side comes, the ball is released quickly to the fullback flaring.

"Optional blocking is to delay flaring the fullback, in which case he takes the linebacker on his side if the red dog is on.

"This play was part of our championship game plan against the Browns and we completed it a couple of times for crucial gains."

Francis was a converted single-wing tailback with limited experience who played quarterback like he was still a halfback. The Giant defense ate him up, and the Packers lost, 20–3.

"I was so sick and so disgusted," continued Starr, "I couldn't see straight. I was so mad after the game I went out with Ron Kramer, another benchwarmer who later starred for the Packers at tight end, and we cried on each other's shoulder. Only time in my life I really felt sorry for myself." Well, New York's a big city and no one noticed.

The following week McHan's arm was okay, but he hurt his leg. Bart got the starting call against the Chicago Bears and played regularly the rest of the season. He passed beautifully in the last 4 games—52 completions in 79 attempts for 699 yards—and the Packers won them all to achieve their first winning record in twelve years.

Green Bay has been the most powerful team in the NFL ever since. Its most solid position has been quarterback. Starr has a high threshhold of pain, as football coaches say. In 1961, he played 6 games with a torn stomach muscle which he refused to reveal to Lombardi, and the Packers won 5. In 1965, he was badly shaken by a tackle against Chicago as the Packers lost their first game of the season in late October. But he kept on playing. Of course, his performance against the Browns in the championship game, with taped ribs, was heroic.

He's not the worst runner among the active quarterbacks nor the best, just as he's not the best or worst passer. He's good enough, with no real weakness, and built for the buffeting at 6–1 and 200 pounds. Starr has rounded out a decade of play in the pros. Perhaps his finest tribute came when the Packers slipped from the top in 1963 and 1964 and critics suspected many of the old champs were over the hill. Not a one of them mentioned Starr.

It's just possible they never thought of him.

BART STARR

BORN: Jan. 9, 1934   HEIGHT: 6'1"   WEIGHT: 200
Green Bay Packers, 1956–65
PASSING RECORD:

Year	Att.	Comp.	Yards Gained	T.D.	Pct.	Longest	Int.
1956	44	24	325	2	54.5	39	3
1957	215	117	1489	8	54.4	77	10
1958	157	78	845	3	49.7	55	12
1959	134	70	972	6	52.2	44	7
1960	172	98	1358	4	57.0	91	8
1961	295	172	2418	16	58.3	78	8
1962*	285	178	2438	12	62.5	83	9
1963	244	132	1855	15	54.1	53	10
1964*	272	163	2144	15	59.9	73	4
1965	251	140	2055	16	55.8	77	9
TOTALS	2069	1172	15,929	97	56.6	91	88

* LED NFL

322

That was no rocking chair injury. Jerry Kramer (64) helped Starr off the field after the Packer quarterback was injured on the first play from scrimmage in the 1965 Western Conference playoff against Baltimore.

Starr shovels the ball to Paul Hornung (5) to start the Packers rolling to a title win over Cleveland on Jan. 2, 1966.

RUSHING RECORD:

Year	Att.	Yards Gained	Longest	Ave.
1956	5	35	14	7.0
1957	31	98	16	3.2
1958	25	113	20	4.5
1959	16	83	39	5.2
1960	7	12	13	1.7
1961	12	56	21	4.7
1962	21	72	18	3.4
1963	13	116	20	8.9
1964	24	165	28	6.9
1965	18	169	38	9.4
TOTALS	172	919	39	5.3

14. The Moderns

Frank Ryan

FRANK RYAN HAS EXCELLENT POTEN-
TIAL, ALTHOUGH FOOTBALL OBVIOUSLY
HELD HIM UP.
—*Dr. B. Frank Jones, Jr.,*
mathematician, Institute for
Advanced Studies, Princeton Uni-
versity

When Frank Ryan was an undergraduate student at Rice Institute in Houston, Texas, the football coaches used to play a little game with him.

Frank, who majored in physics but had an affinity for mathematics, also played quarterback on the football team. The coaches couldn't tell him point-blank that he was the No. 2 quarterback because Frank obviously could count and his psyche might be wounded.

"They had different-color jerseys to denote the status on the squad," recollected Ryan, "so in practice sessions the first part of the week, I'd have a gold jersey, or first team. Then the last part, closer to game time, I'd pick up my basket and it'd be white again." Or second team.

In this way they played their little game with the man who wrote a thesis for his doctorate in advanced mathematics and entitled it: A Characterization of the Set of Asymptotic Values of a Function Holomorphic in the Unit Disc.

"I think," mused Frank, "the coaches in college used to try to make me feel good. I threw 22 passes as a senior at Rice."

The life of Frank Ryan is a dichotomy. On the one side there's the ascetic, completely disciplined mathematician who can pull together the most complex abstractions and derive from them a purity of meaning that brings excited pleasure to his sensitive face. On the other side there is the strident quarterback of the Cleveland Browns who produced a world championship, who absorbs himself in the swirl of violence where simplicity of purpose is the keynote to success and luck can be the overriding factor.

"It's absolutely false," he said, "to pursue any sort of notion that football and mathematics are related. The heart and soul of modern mathematics is very abstract symbolism. People think mathematicians are concerned with numbers, and they're not at all."

And the heart and soul of professional football?

"Pro football is a game of breaks and luck and opportunity. You can study the defense and call a play you think'll kill them, and they put on a line slant that squashes the play. What determines the course of a game is, as you threw the ball, did the guy you're throwing to slip down?"

These variables, plus such a mundane consideration as a $40,000 contract to help feed his wife and three kids, pose the lure of football to Frank Ryan, Ph.D. It took him seven years, concurrent with his study for the doctorate in geometric functions, to figure what the game was all about.

The moment of revelation came on December 27, 1964, the day Dr. Ryan became an athlete as well as a scholar. The Cleveland Browns beat the heavily favored Baltimore Colts, 27–0, for the NFL championship in one of the more mystifying contests in football history.

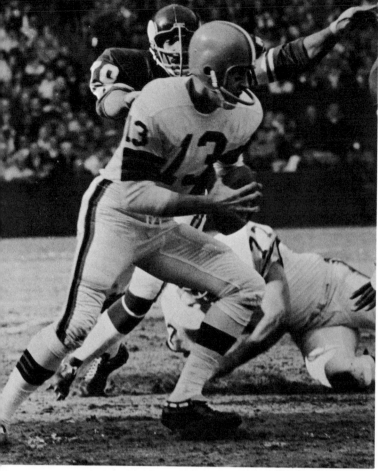

Mathematician Frank Ryan of Cleveland harbors no superstitions about wearing No. 13.

Frank Ryan is squared away to unleash a bomb against his old teammates, the Los Angeles Rams.

"I think we were very lucky against the Colts," said Ryan generously. "Take our second touchdown in the second quarter, which really broke the game open. We caught them in just the right defense for an 87 hook, the play I called. I remember that we had the Colts hook-conscious, so as Gary Collins came to the huddle, I whispered to him, 'Hook post.'

"That means he goes down around 10 yards, turns to the inside like a hook, the way the play is designed, and then breaks straight down the field again. The safety played him for the hook. They almost bumped, in fact. Then when Gary turned, the safety slipped and fell down and Gary was all alone by 20 yards for the touchdown pass."

Frank will admit that there is one contiguous benefit from his scholarly pursuits, as far as playing quarterback.

"If the math does anything," he said, "it helps me organize my football. Everything complicated is less complicated if you have a good organizational scheme. The playbook is like a memory bank. For every situation there's a play. The better you categorize them, the better play you come up with during a game.

"Football itself is a complex game, but the thing that made us play so well in Cleveland in 1964, when we won the championship, is that we decided we were becoming too fancy. We went through three-quarters of the season and we were fancier than we had to be."

The Browns got the message one afternoon in Dallas when the Cowboys ran them all over the field, and Cleveland only pulled the game out in the fourth quarter because defensive halfback Bernie Parrish picked off a pass and ran it back 54 yards for a 20–16 victory.

"We feared Dallas' defense," reviewed Ryan, "and we put in a lot of new formations to fool them, but what happened was we fooled ourselves. After that we went back to basic plays. We would run simple things and defy them to stop us.

"It's absolute trash to say a quarterback has to have 1,000 plays in his head. In our offense I could come up with 2,000 variations. But are they really different?

"We had 6 basic formations we ran against the Colts in the championship game, both right and left. With one play from each of these formations, we already have 12.

"The mental challenge is calling the right play at the right time. On third and 1, you're going for a dive or a power off-tackle. For short yardage, we have 5 or 6 running plays. We had 3 pass plays, or we could improvise. We had at most 10 different running plays in our game plan for the Colts."

Ryan has his own plan of logic for simplifying football. Like, say the running game:

"How many holes can a man hit. There's the 2–3 hole up the middle. Then the 4–5 between guard and tackle, the 6–7 between tackle and slot end, and the 8–9 wide. But actually, with right and left formations, you're only really thinking of four holes. How many ways can you hit these holes? Say, three ways. Then you have 12 plays you use. That's my way of organizing things.

"Why try to hit the 4-hole seven different ways? If you got something good going, why use another play? Only occasionally do you reach back. I remember a close game with Washington. We controlled the ball—I called no passes—for almost 10 minutes late in the game to clinch it. We used 11 plays. We hadn't even worked on three of the plays during the week."

This disciplined thinking was worked out for Ryan by Blanton Collier, the erudite coach of the Browns who is hipped on psychocybernetics, a study of the automatic control and communication processes of the mind, and found a willing guinea pig in the scholarly quarterback.

"When I was with the Los Angeles Rams," said Ryan, "I wasn't ready mentally to be a pro quarterback. Under Bob Waterfield (then the coach of the Rams), the quarterback had to call all the blocks and all the patterns on passes. It's too much. I think a young quarterback can play right away in pro ball if he's got good coaching. I could have done it under Blanton Collier after one year.

"I owe a lot to Coach Collier because he showed me what has to be done."

Collier was the only coach, since Ryan's senior year in high school, to entrust a first-string job completely to the tall mathematician, intrigued no doubt by Ryan's thought processes and adaptability to coaching. Frank was always an outstanding prospect, and obviously bright. He lacked steadiness.

"You'll find most of the quarterbacks are pretty bright," said Frank. "They have to be. The ones that make it this far, as pros, had to have something. King Hill was no scholar at Rice, but he had a good intuitive sense for football."

King Hill was the man who kept Ryan playing second-fiddle most of his college days. Rice had the best quarterback tandem in the country, but Hill was the one who attracted attention because he was the better all-around athlete. ("It was the most frustrating period of my life," admitted Ryan.) They frequently alternated. Rice met powerful Texas A & M in a game which would decide the Southwest Conference championship in 1957. The Aggies were undefeated and rated the No. 1 team in the country going into the game.

Ryan, in the third quarter, led the Owls on a 70-yard march which reached the Aggie 1-yard line just as the period ended. It was time for Hill's platoon to come in as the teams changed sides. On the first play of the fourth period, Hill went over on a quarterback sneak, and Rice won the game, 7–6. The game stories featured his score, naturally, and propelled him to All-American honors.

In the pro draft, Hill was the bonus choice of the Chicago Cardinals, picked above every man in the country. The Los Angeles Rams, with their proclivity for amassing quarterbacks, tapped Ryan on the fourth round and surprised everybody. He was, after all, a second-stringer and a double risk as a pro because he obviously intended to go into graduate study. His Rice professors persuaded him that he ought to switch from physics to pure mathematics.

The Ram move made sense in that Frank had already been accepted by UCLA in nearby Westwood for advanced work. And it made further sense when Frank took over for King Hill in the Cotton Bowl game against Navy and played the whole second half, while Hill was used as a flanker.

In his eight years as a pro, Hill has been unable to win a regular job, whether with the Cardinals or the Philadelphia Eagles, to whom he was traded in 1961. But that all-around-athlete bit has probably saved him, because King has made himself useful as a punter and spare signal caller.

The Rams regarded Ryan as a better passer and partially on his account, partially because they had Bill Wade, traded veteran Norm Van Brocklin away to the Eagles. It was a readymade setup for instant success. The Ram yearbook of 1958 featured a double-truck spread on a rookie reporting to training. The rookie: young Frank Ryan. He looked boyish and eager, and his dark hair hadn't yet turned to salt and pepper like it is now.

There's a curious thing about Frank Ryan. Put him in street clothes, and he looks exactly like a pedant who's been holed up for years in a library nook or some remote lab. His skin is pale and his eyes burn, and his face has the lean, hungry look of a man searching for the truth. His smile is tight and a shade skeptical. His voice is subdued. But put him in a football atmosphere, the disarray of a locker room, and he fits in, too. He is tall, 6–3, and weighs 200 pounds, though his long neck betrays him. His voice takes on a bit of a whine, especially when he's displeased. And Ryan has not been the happy warrior for most of his career.

"My rookie year," he reviewed, "the Rams switched their practices from afternoon to morning sessions to accommodate me because I had enrolled at UCLA and had an eleven-to-one class. Then after my rookie year, they drafted Buddy Humphrey from Baylor. And (Coach) Sid Gillman said, 'We've arranged to have practices in the afternoon. Fit your schedule to it.'

"That's when I quit school at UCLA and started returning to Rice during the off-season (to work on the masters and doctorate degrees). My wife and I were unhappy living in Los Angeles anyhow. We had an apartment in Hollywood and everything was too far away. It seemed like all our friends were always a couple of hours away."

He was unhappy with the Rams, too. It didn't show so much at first when he was breaking in under Wade and learning the job. In 1960, Bob Waterfield stepped in as the head coach and told Ryan he was the No. 1 man, then derricked him for sloppy play in the second game of the season. The Rams lost their first 4, extending their streak to 12 straight defeats over two seasons, when Frank started against the Chicago Bears and played all the way to salvage a 24–24 tie. Ryan started the next game against Detroit, too, and pushed the Rams to a 10-point lead at half time by throwing 3 touchdown passes. He felt like he was coming on. Early in the third quarter, he threw an interception and was removed from the game. He started the next game against Dallas and had the Rams out in front by 20 at half time. Dallas is only 30 miles from Fort Worth, Ryan's home town. He was on top of the world. He overthrew Jon Arnett on a pass to start the third quarter. Waterfield yanked him again.

"I got my chance to play with the Rams," noted Ryan, "but it was jerked out from under me." The bitterness lingers.

The Rams traded Wade to Chicago for Zeke Bratkowski in 1961, and Ryan wound up playing second-string again. He never got into the last 4 games. After the season finale, a 35–21 thumping by Green Bay in the Coliseum, Ryan strode angrily into the dressing room and confronted general manager Elroy Hirsch with a "trade-me-or-I-quit" ultimatum.

Ryan, the free-thinker, was traded to the Cleveland Browns, with halfback Tom Wilson, for an obscure defensive tackle and a couple of draft choices. He joined a team where the quarterback's mental processes were securely locked in by the head coach, Paul Brown, who believed in doing all the signal calling himself, and where the quarterback's job was allocated to Jim Ninowski, secured in a trade with Detroit for Milt Plum.

Two breaks solidified Ryan's position in Cleveland that first season of 1962. Collier had returned as an assistant coach in charge of the offense after eight years at Kentucky, and he started his simplicity program on Ryan immediately. The other break was to Ninowski's collarbone in the 8th game of the season against Pittsburgh, leaving Ryan in sole possession of the first-string job. He never relinquished it. When Collier was elevated to head coach in 1963, Frank was set.

"He was the first coach who ever really coached me," enthused Ryan. "He broke down passing into three basic steps: setting, aiming, throwing. He taught me to concentrate on one receiver. But he also gave me a concept. We don't have a primary receiver. We let the defense tell us.

"Take, for example, a play we call 87 all hook.

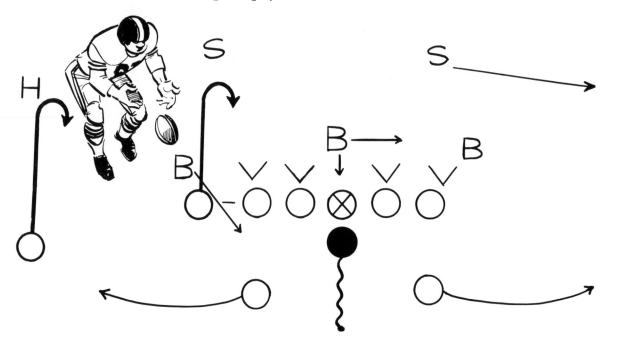

"What is the middle linebacker doing? I've got to watch him first. If he comes at me, I dunk it to the slot end. He's coached, if they blitz, to start looking in—that's to say, to cut in to the middle of the field or the territory the middle man has vacated. If the middle linebacker doesn't come, I know the center blocks to the weak side of the field. Then I checked the strong side linebacker. If he's blitzing, I quick-pitch to the tight end. There's no way the linebacker can reach me before I get the ball off. If neither is blitzing, then I'm throwing to the weak side end. If the middle linebacker goes to the weak side, I throw to the flanker." Ad infinitum, the thought processes go on and on.

Ryan threw 25 touchdown passes his first season as a regular quarterback, more than Otto Graham ever threw in a single year in the NFL. The Browns finished a respectable second with a 10–4 record. In 1964, Frank threw 25 touchdown passes again, and the Browns won the Eastern Conference title, their first in seven years, and then mopped up the Colts for the championship. The Browns repeated as division leaders in 1965, but lost to Green Bay and a bid for a second straight NFL title.

The Green Bay defeat was no discredit to Ryan. Upper Wisconsin, off Lake Michigan, is no place to be on January 2 of any year. And a slushy ball wasn't meant to be thrown. Yet Ryan completed 8 for 18. In the first period, when field conditions were fairly tolerable, he passed to Jimmy Brown for 30 yards and a first down, to Paul Warfield for 19 and a first down and to Gary Collins for 17 and a touchdown—on consecutive plays following the kickoff after Green Bay had opened up with a quick touchdown.

The Packers were simply better mudders, however, and won 23–12.

"Until he's won two titles in a row," said one of the coaches in the league skeptically, "he's just another guy. Ryan is not quick in either maneuver or release. His second selection of receiver doesn't come in as quickly as it should."

But a lot of coaches would settle for him. Besides his passing, Ryan is also a surprisingly good runner for a quarterback—better, in fact, than Unitas or Starr. The chief criticism of him has been a slow release, a split-second indecision in getting rid of the ball.

"I think you can get to him," claimed Bill Koman, the veteran linebacker of the St. Louis Cardinals. "He's not agile standing back there. He throws the ball into the ground when you give him a good rush. But he's a good quarterback and if he gets hot like he was in that title game against the Colts, he'll kill you."

Like every quarterback, Ryan is a devotee of football movies and tends to be self-deprecating: "It's sort of embarrassing to watch myself throw because I don't throw as pretty as I think I do. I've come down to a utilitarian delivery. In seven years I've also gotten a quicker delivery. I'm still not in the same league with Unitas, but I do compensate in other areas. I have less throwing ability than the best—it's all relative, of course, because I think I throw well. At the same time, I think my concentration is a little stronger.

"After I've read the defense, which tells me what receiver I'm going to throw to, I've got to concentrate on where I'm going to throw the ball—at his eyeballs or what have you. I probably take a little too long in this area. But if I try to throw faster, I throw bad passes. Technically and mechanically, Unitas is the best. There's no comparison. But I pride myself on being the quarterback who gets the most of what he's got."

Meanwhile he also continues his studies at Rice between seasons, with a schedule that starts at 7:40 A.M. and might carry him through till one o'clock in the morning. Even during the football season he works at his mathematics sporadically because that will be his life's work. He enjoys football, the intense competition, some of the acclaim and the sense of personal accomplishment.

If Ryan, finding playing maturity with experience, has any area of discontent, it's in the interpretation of his personality by writers. He shudders at the genius halo they've put over his head because he can speak French and German (to meet the language requisites for a Ph.D.) and knows all about geometric function theory and linear transformations. Commissioner Pete Rozelle, who signed Frank to his original pro contract while general manager of the Rams, said, "He's the only player I know with an IQ as high as Jill St. John's." Jill is a red-headed Hollywood cupcake whose convolutions of the frug and the watusi (those are dances, bub) match her 162 genius level. Ryan has gray-speckled hair, is the pipe-smoking father of three children and has an impish twist of mind that creates devilish situations. He posed for passing pictures one afternoon at a newspaper photographer's request. After they were developed back at the office the horrified sports department noted he'd held the ball in his left hand.

"They could have reversed them and made your number 31," someone suggested to Ryan. (He wears No. 13, not to defy superstition, but because it happened to be available when he joined the Browns.)

"That would have made it El," noted Ryan swiftly.

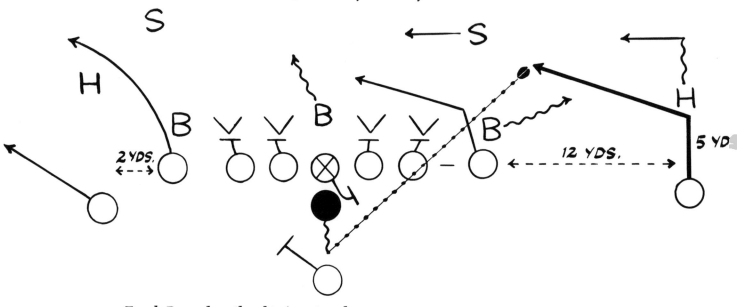

Frank Ryan describes his favorite play:

"We used a simple quick pass to great advantage against the New York Giants in 1964, when we won 52–20.

"I hit touchdowns to both Gary Collins, the right flanker, and Paul Warfield, the left end, in that game. This diagram shows it to the right, Collins' side, but it was just as effective to the left.

"In the huddle, I call it 2 Double Wing, Fire 70, Slot Cross, Rip Slant. Breaking that down, the double wing is the formation. Fire 70 is pattern No. 7, while 'fire' indicates aggressive pass blocking by the linemen. Slot cross means the tight end cleans out the throwing area by pulling the strong safety with him; also the middle linebacker. Rip slant is Collins on a slant pattern.

"The receiver just needs his body in front of the defensive halfback, and if I throw it properly it can't be broken up. However, Collins and Warfield are both great at getting fairly clear of the halfback, making the pass all the easier to complete.

"As it stands, a variety of defenses can stop this pattern—for instance, the standard zone defense. For this reason, it is most effective against a man-for-man type defense. In our game with New York, we happened to hit just the right defense."

When he played quarterback for the East team in the 1965 Pro Bowl, a story broke nationally that Frank Ryan felt he was worth $1 million if Joe Namath was worth the $400,000 just paid to him by the New York Jets. The prices have since gone up.

"They were taking pictures of the East squad," explained Ryan, "and I was kidding around and what I actually said was, 'If he's worth $400,000, I'm worth a million and John Unitas is worth $10 million—ha, ha, ha.'

"They didn't quote the Unitas part. Or the 'ha, ha, ha.'"

And that, in the orderly but abstract mind of Dr. Frank Ryan, who will some day devote himself fully to pure mathematics, was no laughing matter.

FRANK RYAN

BORN: July 12, 1936   HEIGHT: 6'3"   WEIGHT: 200

Los Angeles Rams, 1958–61

Cleveland Browns, 1962–65

PASSING RECORD:

Year	Att.	Comp.	Yards Gained	T.D.	Pct.	Longest	Int.
1958	14	5	34	1	35.7	14	3
1959	89	42	709	2	47.2	67	4
1960	128	62	816	7	48.4	61	9
1961	142	72	1115	5	50.7	96	7
1962	194	112	1541	10	57.7	65	7
1963	256	135	2026	25	52.7	83	13
1964	334	174	2404	25	52.1	62	19
1965	243	119	1751	18	49.0	80	13
TOTALS	1400	721	10,396	93	51.5	96	75

RUSHING RECORD:

Year	Att.	Yards Gained	Longest	Ave.
1958	5	45	12	9.0
1959	19	57	13	3.0
1960	19	85	24	4.5
1961	38	139	38	3.7
1962	42	242	39	5.8
1963	62	224	25	3.6
1964	37	217	19	5.9
1965	19	72	18	3.8
TOTALS	241	1081	39	4.5

John Brodie

JOHN BRODIE WAS COMING ON REAL
STRONG, AND I HAD A FEELING MY DAYS
IN SAN FRANCISCO WERE NUMBERED.

—*Y. A. Tittle, quarterback,*
San Francisco 49ers, 1951–60

John Brodie of the San Francisco 49ers flashed league-leading passing form in 1965.

The 49ers' John Brodie (12) can scramble away from tacklers when he's severely rushed.

The best golfer in professional football is John Brodie, the quarterback of the San Francisco 49ers. John is so good that he won't play in the National Football League Players Association annual tournament in Florida each January because that would mean he'd win a car.

John doesn't want to win a car because that would make him a pro, and he went that route once before.

When Y. A. Tittle was the quarterback of the 49ers, threatening to last as long as Little Orphan Annie, Brodie decided to double up on his careers and try the Professional Golfers Association tour. If he hustled and sneaked out to course late afternoons after football practice, he could be ready to tee off with the other pros at their traditional starting point in the Los Angeles Open early in January. He didn't worry about a conflict with the Pro Bowl, also played in Los Angeles. As a second-stringer, John wasn't going to make any all-star teams.

For two winters, he diligently chased par, and then he totalled up his earnings. They came to slightly under $1,000. From that point on, golf became a hobby and football his business.

"I could say I gave up golf because it interfered with my football," said John, "but the fact is there was only one big reason. The most I ever won in a tournament was something like $300. It took me years to regain my amateur status."

He's still a scratch golfer in local amateur tournaments in the northern California area, but his career as a quarterback really pushed ahead. And that, for Brodie, represents the real payoff.

In 1965, Brodie set a new National Football League record for pass completions in a single season with 242, breaking John Unitas' mark of 237 set in 1963. Brodie was the NFL leader in five different passing categories: attempts, completions, total yardage (3,112), percentage (61.9) and touchdown passes (30).

During the winter, Sid Luckman of the Bears' staff was discussing the great quarterbacks he's seen and noted thoughtfully, "Unitas is one of the great ones, the equal of anybody. But you can't sell this kid Brodie short."

Kid?

John Brodie had passed his thirtieth birthday. There's a lot of skin on top of his head where hair used to be. He totalled nine seasons of playing time in the NFL and more than 7 miles gained in the air. He spent his first four years as a pro in the shadow of Tittle. After old Yat departed, Brodie survived the rigors of the shotgun formation, a broken left arm in 1963 that caused him to miss 11 games of that season and a succession of challenges by passing neophytes, the latest of them George Mira.

Recognition has come late to a man who was picked out by Otto Graham in the College All-Star camp of 1957 as the finest passing prospect he had ever handled. "He was the best natural quarterback I coached," said Graham.

Brodie is a northern California product all the way. He went to Oakland Technical High School across the Bay—an all-city performer in football, baseball and basketball—but not highly regarded as a grid prospect. He enrolled at Stanford without a scholarship, turned out for the freshman football team and couldn't make the starting unit.

But by his senior year, 1956, Brodie led the nation in passing and total offense and was named to a majority of the All-American teams. The 49ers drafted him as their top pick for 1957. He was voted the most valuable player in both the Shrine East-West game and the College All-Star game, playing in a cast which included Jim Brown, Paul Hornung and Jon Arnett.

When John reported to the 49ers, Tittle was almost thirty-one years old. Coach Frank Albert, also a Stanford man, had so much faith in Brodie as Yat's eventual replacement that he didn't bother to carry another quarterback on the roster. The heir apparent got a chance to justify Albert's faith before the year was over. The 49ers were in a three-way battle with Detroit and Baltimore for Western Conference honors. On the next-to-last weekend, the Colts came into Kezar Stadium leading the other two clubs by a game. Tittle had played virtually every minute on offense all year, but in the second half he pulled leg muscles and was forced to the sideline with only a minute to play and the 49ers trailing, 13–10.

The rookie came into the game, cranked up and on the second play hit Hugh McElhenny with a touchdown pass to pull out a 17–13 victory. Brodie even started the finale against Green Bay, but Tittle came on in the last half to finish out the campaign with a win that tied Detroit for the division lead. In the playoff, it was Tittle all the way as the 49ers tried to play safe with a 24–7 half time margin and were routed by a remarkable Lion rally. It was the closest the 49ers, or Brodie, have ever come to a division crown.

When Tittle looked bad during the 1958 exhibition season, Albert abruptly switched to Brodie as his starting quarterback. Brodie was the man at the controls as the 49ers began their championship schedule. This caused quite a fuss in the Bay area, since Tittle had long been entrenched as the favorite son. It's a situation that faces every club stocked with more than one outstanding quarterback. Detroit was finding it out with Layne and Rote. The Rams had been through it with Van Brocklin and Waterfield. And earlier, San Francisco had experienced it when Tittle came to the club in Albert's fading days as a quarterback.

The 49ers eventually went back to Tittle as the No. 1 man, but Brodie played almost half the time in '58 and had an impressive 60 percent completion mark, which showed his arm, at least, was major league. Albert quit after the season and was succeeded as head coach by Red Hickey, who put Tittle back in full charge. The 49ers opened the '59 campaign by winning 6 of their first 7 games with Y. A. in magnificent form. But in the eighth game, Tittle missed a couple of passes and Hickey yanked him for Brodie. The 49ers lost that game, and altogether 6 of their last 7. Brodie played the last 3 alone after Tittle was carried out on a stretcher against Baltimore with severely damaged ligaments.

"He had good leadership," recalled a man who was with the 49ers during that period. "He was intelligent. But intelligence demands work. And John Brodie at that time was just not a dedicated football player. He wouldn't work or study like he should have. Sometimes he wouldn't even have the game plan memorized.

"But John's got a great arm. I always felt that if he applied himself he'd be a helluva quarterback, because he always thought he was the best and the guys on the club rallied to him."

Maybe it was always the presence of Tittle blocking him. Or the obsession with golf. Or even a conflicting interest in bridge, which absorbed a lot of his free time. But Brodie coasted along for years as a cocky kid on the verge of doing big things but never quite achieving them. The 49ers went through a couple of rousing periods that didn't help him either.

In 1960, Hickey reached the conclusion that Tittle wasn't ever going to lead the 49ers any place. In November he brought them into Baltimore for a game against the Colts, who had won two straight world championships and were again leading the league. The 49ers were staggering along at a .500 pace. Early in the week, Hickey unveiled a new shotgun offense to throw at the champs.

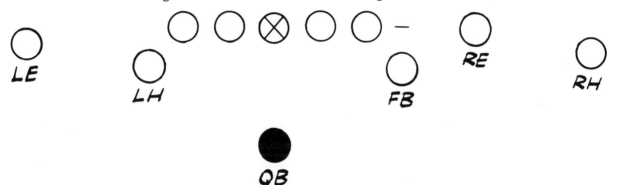

The quarterback was positioned 5 yards behind the center. The running backs moved into the slots between tackle and end. The tight end was split 3 to 5 yards out from the tackle. Five receivers could be flooded downfield instantly. It was obvious that most of the running had to be handled by the quarterback, and that was no job for Tittle. Brodie was more suited to the new offense. He could run, although he didn't particularly like to and never bothered to hide his disaffection. The only other candidate was a third-string quarterback from Presbyterian named Bobby Waters, who had never thrown a pass in competition.

With Brodie riding shotgun, the underdog 49ers took the Colts by surprise and engaged them in a rousing battle. Late in the fourth quarter, Brodie was kayoed by a hard tackle. Waters came in and threw a pass to R. C. Owens. Owens lateralled to rookie end Dee Mackey, who raced for the decisive touchdown as the 49ers upset the champs, 30–22.

The 49ers won 3 of their last 4 games while relying heavily on the shotgun, and Brodie, playing 90 percent of the time, racked up a gaudy 9.5-yard rushing average for the year with 171 yards gained in 18 carries. Hickey took his team to camp firmly committed to exploit his new offense. There was no place in it for Tittle, who was quickly traded to New York.

Red added another gimmick to the shotgun in the third game of the season, against Detroit. The 49ers had drafted Bill Kilmer, an All-American single-wing tailback at UCLA. He was a strong runner; Brodie was a strong passer. Young Waters could do a

341

fair job running and passing. Red gathered all three around him on the sidelines and shuttled them on every play—Brodie when the situation called for a pass, Kilmer for the short-yardage thrusts, Waters for special spots. He turned the troika loose on the Detroit Lions in the third game of the season. The Lions, as usual, were one of the best defensive teams in the NFL. They were also undefeated and in first place. The 49ers clobbered them, 49–0.

"It looked like the Drake Relays," sighed Lion linebacker Wayne Walker after watching the three alternating backs race on and off the field.

Red's little picnic lasted five weeks, during which the 49ers averaged 33.4 points a game and led the league in rushing, passing and total offense. The panic was on. Teams that built defenses only against the T didn't know how to key against the shotgun. The normal 4–3 defense wasn't adequate.

The Chicago Bears suddenly brought them up short, 31–0. Bill George, the middle linebacker of the Bears, took up a position in the line right over the center, and charged mercilessly on every play. Whenever the tailback tried to hand off to one of the wings on an inside reverse, George was right on top of the transaction. If he tried to pass, George was on him like a shot, too. The 49ers fumbled the ball 7 times to disrupt their offense. The Bears cued the league on how to muffle the shotgun.

The Steelers beat the 49ers the next week, the Lions tied them in a rematch and the Rams upset them. Poof, the high velocity of the shotgun had vanished. The attrition rate on the tailbacks was high. And the predictability of the offense was too closely related to the talents of whichever tailback happened to be in the game. Just as suddenly as he had unveiled his new weapon, Hickey wrapped it up and put it in limbo, never to be used again. The mystery to football students has always been why he didn't attempt to integrate the surprise effect of the shotgun with the natural deception of the T, keep it as part of his offense and therefore force other teams to prepare defenses for it every week, using the shotgun just enough to keep them wary. But Red was stubborn that way.

And Brodie didn't exactly cry over the abandoned experiment. He went back to his job as the regular T-quarterback—in fact, the only experienced one on the squad. Career-wise, it was probably to his advantage, because Brodie, though nimble on his feet and one of the best scramblers in the league, didn't have the innate physical toughness to play at being a running threat. Kilmer, who did, was injured in a car wreck after the '62 season and never was the same again.

Brodie missed most of the '63 campaign himself with a broken left arm in a car accident but reclaimed his job with a flair the next year. He threw bombs of 80 and 83 yards to Dave Parks, an exciting rookie receiver from Texas Tech. In 1965 they became the most potent battery in football as Parks led the NFL in receiving and Brodie blossomed out as the most prolific passer in the game. In addition to Parks, Brodie also had strong backs in rookie Ken Willard and veteran retread John David Crow. Willard and Crow, besides providing a running threat, were strong blockers and facile receivers on screens and flares. With a well-rounded attack the 49ers scored more points than any team in pro football.

They also gave up more.

342

Backed up to his goal line in a game against the Colts, Brodie threw a hitch pass that was intercepted by Bobby Boyd and returned for a touchdown. The Colts had rotated their defense on the play, and Brodie failed to spot the rotation, or if he did, failed to throw the ball safely out of bounds. Even at 30, a quarterback's learning processes aren't complete.

John Brodie describes his favorite play:

"A successful pass play for the 49ers actually splits off into three different plays, using the talents of David Parks, our split left end.

"We go strong side left and I always use the tight end to keep the safety on that side occupied, leaving the wing (or corner back) alone on David.

"All three plays look the same until the ball is released:

"1. The Pole—Parks runs this so well that if a wingback has to watch him alone, he must play David to the inside or he hasn't got a chance against a well-thrown ball.

"2. The Post corner—if the wingback plays him too strong inside, David breaks to the left corner of the field. This is commonly called a zig-out and is actually my favorite pass play. The success depends on the release of the ball just as he turns out at the pole.

"3. The Hook. I can best illustrate by using the Green Bay game, to end the '65 season. The Packers doubled up on him and had two men outside waiting for either a pole or a post corner. David and I recognized the problem simultaneously. He hooked up and caught a touchdown pass to tie the score and force the Packer playoff with the Colts."

343

In the same game he also threw two bombs to Parks. After the season he received two honors that were firsts in his nine-year career: selection to the all-pro team, and nomination to the Pro Bowl as the starting quarterback for the West team.

The Pro Bowl experience turned into something of a fiasco when 6 of Brodie's passes were intercepted. Afterwards, he shook his head and smiled, "I'm scared that if I don't laugh, I'm going to cry." Another year it might have worried him more.

Now, entrenched at last as a recognized quarterback and leader, he knew he'd be back to pass another day.

JOHN BRODIE

BORN: August 14, 1935   HEIGHT: 6'1"   WEIGHT: 210

San Francisco 49ers, 1957–65

PASSING RECORD:

Year	Att.	Comp.	Yards Gained	T.D.	Pct.	Longest	Int.
1957	21	11	160	2	52.4	28	3
1958	172	103	1224	6	59.9	61	13
1959	64	30	354	2	46.9	34	7
1960	207	103	1111	6	49.8	65	9
1961	283	155	2588	14	54.8	70	12
1962	304	175	2272	18	57.6	80	16
1963	61	30	367	3	49.2	41	2
1964	392	193	2498	14	49.2	83	16
1965	391	242	3112	30	61.9	59	16
TOTALS	1895	1042	13,686	95	55.0	83	94

RUSHING RECORD:

Year	Att.	Yards Gained	Longest	Ave.
1957	2	0	0	0.0
1958	11	—12	6	—1.1
1959	5	6	6	1.2
1960	18	171	30	9.5
1961	28	90	29	3.2
1962	37	258	21	7.0
1963	7	63	24	9.0
1964	27	135	38	5.0
1965	15	60	13	4.0
TOTALS	150	771	38	5.1

344

Sonny Jurgensen

I MADE A GREAT PASSER OUT OF NORM
VAN BROCKLIN, AND I'LL MAKE A GREAT
ONE OUT OF SONNY JURGENSEN.

—Tommy McDonald, flanker,
Philadelphia Eagles, 1957–63.

Sonny Jurgensen took charge of the Eagle offense in 1962 and had his greatest season in his first year as a regular.

Malcolm W. Emmons

The Jurgensen passing style is marked by ultra-quick release as Cleveland's Bill Glass rushes up on the right.

Malcolm W. Emmons

The undeniable factor in any assessment of Christian Adolph Jurgensen is talent. He's the best dancer on the team, the best pool player, Ping-Pong player and golfer. He's also the best tennis player, handball player and comedian. He once was offered a major league baseball contract.

And for pure passing arm, Sonny Jurgensen can match any man who throws a football. "Sonny's a great pocket passer," said Coach Don Shula of the Baltimore Colts. "He gets the ball off quickly and can beat a rush. He's a real good play caller; he's working at it now."

But there is a flaw somewhere in the chemistry of Christian Adolph Jurgensen. At times, he is not always the best quarterback on his own team, the Washington Redskins. His leadership, while unquestioned, has not inspired success.

In his nine years in professional football, Sonny has only been the regular for one winning season, a statistic that must surely be annoying at the age of thirty-two, when most quarterbacks less talented than he have been sated with success.

Sonny looks at the world through baleful blue eyes under a carrot-colored wisp of short hair surrounded by a pinkish complexion and slightly bucked white teeth. The effect is one of a grown-up Huckleberry Finn with a little potbelly, and that in truth has been the image Sonny has carried almost since he came to the pros in 1957. An impish grin has sustained him through a spotty career.

He's originally from Wilmington, North Carolina, where he starred orthodoxly in baseball, football and basketball. He went to Duke on a football scholarship and emerged after four years with a gift for handing off right and handing off left. Those were his main exercises as a split-T-quarterback.

"I didn't even know how to set up to pass," he confessed. "We had no straight dropback passes. Only rollouts. When it was third and 15 we ran the ball."

He also played defense. "Safety," he explained. "I hung way back. Even had trouble following the coaches."

But Ace Parker, the old Brooklyn Dodger great who was on the Duke coaching staff, recommended Sonny to the pros as "the finest quarterback prospect I've seen in years," and the Philadelphia Eagles drafted him on the fourth round for 1957. Jurgensen broke in behind Bobby Thomason, a veteran sidearm flipper playing his last year. When the Eagles lost their first 3 games, Jurgensen was allowed to start against the Cleveland Browns and staged an upset 17–7 triumph. He was instrumental in 3 of the 4 Eagle victories that season. They regarded him as a strong-armed prospect.

Then came the Norm Van Brocklin era. The Dutchman arrived from the Rams in 1958, along with Buck Shaw as head coach. Jurgensen, who threw 70 passes as a rookie, totalled exactly one more than that the next three years. Van Brocklin played, and Jurgensen cracked jokes.

"Show me anybody who hasn't responsibility," said Sonny, "and I'll show you a happy-go-lucky guy. No matter how hard I worked and studied films, I knew I wasn't going to play on Sunday."

Van Brocklin said Jurgensen might be a good team quarterback some day—if he stopped being the team clown.

Timmy Brown, the zippy halfback who came to the Eagles during that period, remembered Sonny as a glib, bantering comedian who refused to get depressed in his secondary role.

"I'm no psychiatrist," said Pete Retzlaff, the Eagles' fine end, "but if Sonny didn't have the personality makeup he did, I don't think he could have lasted all that time on the bench. You have to realize what an exceptionally talented person Sonny is."

Jurgenson started to get serious about halfway through the 1960 season when it dawned on him the Eagles were making a rush for the NFL championship, and if anything happened to Van Brocklin en route, the responsibility would all fall into his generous lap (the years of inactivity had produced a little bulge in his belly that has never disappeared). Dutch didn't get hurt, but he retired right after the season, and Sonny's four years as a stand-in expired.

In the spring of 1961, Steve Van Buren, the old Eagle piledriver, was doing public relations for the club and telling anyone who would listen that Sonny Jurgensen was a better quarterback than Van Brocklin, which was like trying to convince critics that the Beatles were musically superior to the Budapest String Quartet.

The best anyone remembered of Jurgensen was that he was a loose-lipped kid who used to be a rollout college quarterback and had a rusty arm. The Eagles, though a championship team, lacked solid defense and good running. Their plus was the same set of receivers which had served Van Brocklin—Tommy McDonald, Retzlaff and Walston. When McDonald said he'd make Sonny as great as Dutch, facetiously, Jurgensen retorted, "You'll be nothing until I get the ball to you, McDonald."

The Eagles themselves wondered about Sonny's ability to step into Van Brocklin's shoes—particularly as a leader.

He answered their questions in the first game in which he took command, against the College All-Stars in August, 1961. "He had a sharper tone when he barked signals," said McDonald. "You could see the change in him immediately." When the Stars put a strong rush on him and apparently had all his passing alleys sealed off, Jurgensen astounded both them and his own teammates by flipping the ball behind his back for a completion to Retzlaff.

Sonny was a revelation that entire year. In his first regular season as a pro quarterback, he broke the NFL record for pass completions (235), set a passing-yardage record of 3,723 yards which still stands and tied the then-existing mark of 32 touchdown passes in a single season. No one could have broken in more sensationally.

Against the Washington Redskins one afternoon, the Eagles netted —12 yards on the ground, but Sonny passed for 436. They had him trapped behind the line for a long loss, but Sonny spun off the mass of Redskin burgundy jerseys hemming him in, gripping the ball in his left hand. As he wheeled to get away, he drew his left arm back and passed the ball southpaw on a flat line complete to halfback Billy Ray Barnes, who

348

galloped for a 27-yard gain. In the final 40 seconds of the game, Sonny took the Eagles 80 yards in the air, passing to Tommy McDonald from midfield for the winning, touchdown.

The wire services picked him as their all-pro quarterback. Sonny took the Eagles to 7 victories in their first 8 games of the campaign. The only achievement that eluded him was the championship. Two defeats to New York knocked the Eagles out of first place, but they carried the Giants down to the last weekend of the season and missed by only half a game.

The merry world of Sonny Jurgensen turned sadder after the first of the year, though. In the Playoff Bowl at Miami, the "nothing" battle of second-place teams, offensive tackle J. D. Smith severely damaged a knee and Jurgensen went out of action with a severely dislocated shoulder. The injuries set a pattern for the following fall, in which the Eagles tumbled to last place, while Sonny had 26 passes intercepted.

And then veteran center Chuck Bednarik, getting ready to retire after fourteen seasons in the league, got up at a luncheon in New York and said you could blame the Eagles' lousy season directly on their quarterback.

"They look for faults when you lose," shrugged Jurgensen. "Four ends broke their arms that year, and one broke his leg. Who'd they expect me to throw the ball to, the guards and tackles?"

The last-place decline of the Eagles persisted through 1963, and then Jurgensen was gone. His marriage had broken up. He was booed lustily every time he trotted into Franklin Field. His laughing-boy reputation now extended to all the boites around the Philadelphia area. "Go back to the tap rooms!" bellowed his acquaintances of the night by the light of day. Philly fans are notoriously irreverent.

Jurgensen cupped his hands and yelled back, "It's Sunday—they're closed. That's the only reason you're here."

A new regime swept into Eagle football. The personalities of new Coach Joe Kuharich and easygoing Sonny weren't mated. Kuharich hardly got settled in town before he traded Jurgensen to Washington in a big swap which amounted to Sonny for Redskin quarterback Norman Snead, even up.

"When I left Philadelphia," laughed Sonny, "all the bartenders wore black armbands."

A training-camp injury kept him out of most of the exhibition games in 1964. The Redskins started off miserably, losing their first 4 league games. Then he met his old mates, the Eagles, and everything was right for a day. Sonny flung the Skins to a 35–20 icebreaker, and he had another big day beating them a second time in Philadelphia.

His old buddies in Franklin Field roared, "Take that bum back to Washington. We still don't want him!"

Sonny developed a hot hand down the stretch part of the season. He threw 24 touchdown passes as the Redskins rallied to a third-place finish (tied with the Eagles) and was voted to play in the Pro Bowl game with the Eastern All-Stars.

The Redskins were regarded as the possible surprise team in the Eastern Conference because of Jurgensen's resurgence, the addition of Sam Huff to their defense and the brilliant rookie performance of Charley Taylor, a versatile halfback with an all-pro future. But Taylor cracked an ankle during a camp scrimmage in the summer of '65. Sonny was bothered by calcium deposits in his throwing shoulder. The Redskins couldn't get untracked again in the opening month. They extended themselves and lost their first 5 games in a row. Jurgensen was benched momentarily for young Dick Shiner, then came back and threw 3 touchdown passes in a 24–20 upset of the St. Louis Cardinals. He led them to 5 wins in their next 6 games. The Skins even had a

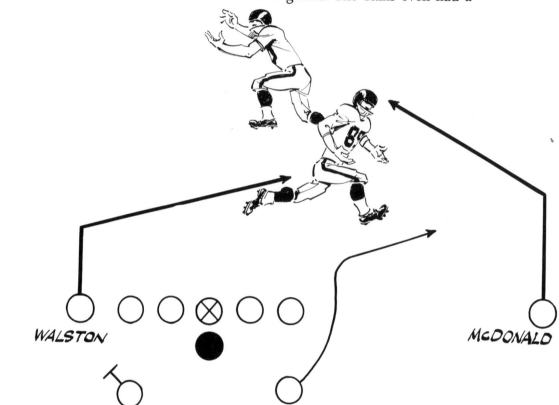

RETZLAFF   WALSTON   McDONALD

Sonny Jurgensen describes his favorite play:

"We used one play when I was with the Philadelphia Eagles that had memorable success.

"At that time I had Pete Retzlaff, Tommy McDonald and Bobby Walston as the primary receivers.

"The pass terminology was Open Left 55 Y-Slot Cross.

"Retzlaff would isolate his defender by running a sideline pattern. Walston would run approximately seven yards and break across the middle, gradually gaining ground after McDonald crossed his path.

"Our weak side halfback would run a fan pattern to isolate the weak side linebacker. Then McDonald would run a pattern similar to that of Walston, also breaking across the middle, except that he went deeper.

"My most memorable recollection of this particular pass was against the Washington Redskins in 1961. They had scored with less than a minute to play to take the lead. After the kickoff we completed 3 short passes to move the ball to their 40-yard line. With time running out, we threw the forementioned pass.

"McDonald was open, caught the ball and raced over for the game-winning touchdown with less than 15 seconds left on the clock."

350

shot at second place and took a 10–0 lead against the Giants in the key game, then collapsed miserably for a 27–10 rout which committed them to another losing season.

And so Sonny Jurgensen stood in the debris of frustration wondering where the season went wrong, and whether it would ever go right for him again like it had during that one brief spree of 1961 when he was a fresh young quarterback. He's the kind of guy you have to stick with because there's that innate talent for throwing a football. Sonny can fire short and long. He can zip it or float it softly, tricks he picked up in his stewardship under Van Brocklin. The little pot and a flat-footed stride make him look awkward, but he's as quick as anybody in the game getting rid of the ball. Sonny also has those accumulated years of experience in recognizing and picking apart pro defenses.

He's not the kind of guy a team gives up on easily, especially with the precedent set by Y. A. Tittle, who was three years older than Jurgensen when he got a reprieve on his career and was transformed from a perennial also-ran into a winner.

The Redskins entered a new era in 1966 with the appointment of Otto Graham as the head coach. For Jurgensen, particularly, it was significant since Graham more than anybody should appreciate Sonny's gifts as a quarterback. At the same time, Graham's personality as a quarterback was the antithesis of Jurgensen's. He was never the bon vivant. But underneath Sonny's debonair crust there's supposed to be a severity of purpose which the public doesn't see.

Graham'll have to see it. He's already stated that his quarterback, whoever it may be, will have to be a man respected both on and off the field by his teammates.

CHRISTIAN A. (SONNY) JURGENSEN

BORN: August 23, 1934   HEIGHT: 6'0"   WEIGHT: 208
Philadelphia Eagles, 1957–63
Washington Redskins, 1964–65
PASSING RECORD:

Year	Att.	Comp.	Yards Gained	T.D.	Pct.	Longest	Int.
1957	70	33	470	5	47.1	61	8
1958	22	12	259	0	54.5	61	1
1959	5	3	37	1	60.0	19	0
1960	44	24	486	5	54.5	71	1
1961	416	235	3723	32	56.5	69	24
1962	366	196	3261	22	53.6	84	26
1963	184	99	1413	11	53.8	75	13
1964	385	207	2934	24	53.8	80	13
1965	356	190	2367	15	53.4	55	16
TOTALS	1848	999	14,950	115	54.1	84	102

RUSHING RECORD:

Year	Att.	Yards Gained	Longest	Ave.
1957	10	—3	8	—.3
1958	1	1	1	1.0
1959	—	—	—	—
1960	4	5	9	1.3
1961	20	27	14	1.4
1962	17	44	30	2.6
1963	13	38	13	2.9
1964	27	57	24	2.1
1965	17	23	27	1.4
TOTALS	109	192	30	1.8

Jack Kemp

I ENJOY THE POLEMICS OF THE CLEAR-
CUT DEBATE BETWEEN LIBERAL PRINCI-
PLES AND CONSERVATIVE ONES.
   —*Jack Kemp, quarterback,*
   Buffalo Bills

JACK KEMP

Credit the election defeat of presidential aspirant Barry Goldwater for making a better pro quarterback of Jack Kemp. Jack is freckled, snub-nosed and disputatious. In the fall of 1964, while Goldwater ran against Lyndon B. Johnson, Master Kemp stumped the hustings of western New York state, quoting Ludwig von Mises, blasting the Keynesian philosophy of economics, pleading for the rugged individualism of good old Barry.

On Sunday afternoon, it was sometimes touch-and-go whether Jack would pull a play out of William Buckley's *National Review* or Lou Saban's recipe for the Buffalo Bills. Saban barely won out as the Bills and Kemp moved on to their first championship in the American Football League.

Jack's espousal of conservative causes posed some problems because in the course of duty he was supposed to hand the ball off to Chester Carlton ("Cookie") Gilchrist, the 250-pound fullback who was diametrically opposed to his political point of view. The successful melding of their football talents is a tribute to the democratic way of life.

But in the course of events, Barry Goldwater lost the election, Cookie Gilchrist was shipped off to the Rocky Mountains (Denver) and Jack decided to become a football player. Instead of running back to his four-bedroom ranch home in the Point Loma section of San Diego, he took up winter residence in the Buffalo suburb of Hamburg, New York, to pursue an advanced course in football study under Saban. "I am," he said, "serious about becoming a twelve-month-a-year quarterback."

It was a time of reappraisal, that winter of 1965, because Jack, the perennial baby-face, was approaching thirty. His career, dating back to 1958, had been somewhat spotty. A young quarterback, Daryle Lamonica, was hot on his neck and had, in fact, retrieved many of the Bill victories in '64 with his clutch relief work. Kemp would start a game and when the attack bogged down, Lamonica would come in and rally the Bills from behind. Daryle performed that rescue trick six times as Buffalo reeled off 9 straight victories.

"My ultimate goal," said Lamonica, "is to be the No. 1 quarterback."

As training camp dawned for the '65 campaign, Don Klosterman, the superscout who had helped Jack get his start in the AFL, said, "I have a hunch you're going to see a new Kemp this year. He's finally matured. He'll be the best in our league."

Klosterman, who went on to become the general manager of the Houston Oilers, was right on the button. Kemp was the All-AFL quarterback in an unbelievable season. The Bills showed their class by winning their second straight championship. Kemp was the inspirational leader, with almost no help from Lamonica. He started brilliantly by completing 71 passes in the first 4 games. But in the third game, his best receiver, Elbert Dubenion, went out for the season with a knee injury. Glenn Bass, the other deep threat, was lost for the year in the next game. Veteran tight end Ernie Warlick was hurt and replaced by a rookie from the taxi squad, Paul Costa. The leading receivers for the Bills were Bo Roberson, a midseason pickup from the Oakland Raiders, and Billy Joe, the fullback who was supposed to make them forget Cookie Gilchrist. Joe was a fizzle and faded to Miami in the expansion draft. Roberson went that route, too, after the season.

Kemp suffered knee, ankle and shoulder injuries. There wasn't a wide-running threat on the club. Wray Carlton, his chief ball carrier, had played only 5 games the previous two seasons because of a damaged groin muscle.

Jack scratched and scrambled and found ways to keep the Bills alive. On Thanksgiving Day they played the San Diego Chargers on the West Coast. The talent-laden Chargers had walloped them, 34–3, earlier in the year. Buffalo was losing 20–17 with a minute and 25 seconds to go, stuck on their own 25-yard line, and no timeouts remaining. The Chargers were in a "prevent" defense, dropping eight men back, as Kemp faded to pass on third down. He looped the ball high over the reach of 6–9 Ernie Ladd. At midfield, Paul Costa reached over his shoulder with a Charger hanging on to him and went down clutching the ball. Jack hastily threw incomplete to stop the clock with 24 seconds left. On the next play he connected with Roberson, who stepped out of bounds. The Bills had one, at the most two, more shots. Kemp couldn't find a receiver, scrambled desperately for the sideline and stepped out of bounds after a 9-yard scamper. On the final play of the game, Pete Gogolak kicked a field goal to give the Bills a 20–20 tie and clinch at least a tie for the Eastern title.

Now flick to the championship game a month later in San Diego. Warlick, the old pro, made his first start since October as Coach Saban played two tight ends to control the ball and keep it from the explosive Chargers. On the opening kickoff the Bills lost Billy Shaw, their best offensive lineman, but Kemp stuck to the game plan. He smashed Joe and Carlton inside the tackles to hold the Chargers in a conventional defense. Late in the first half neither team had scored, and Buffalo controlled the football. At the right moment, Kemp spotted Costa for a big 22-yard gain to the San Diego 18. Then he sent Warlick, who had caught only 8 passes all year, on a post pattern into the end zone and hit him with a bullet toss. The Bills were on their way to a smashing 23–0 championship triumph, and Kemp was the unanimous choice as the game's most valuable player.

If he looked over at the other side of the field and snickered to himself . . . well, a guy could understand it. Jack once played for the Chargers, and for Sid Gillman, their coach. That's how come he owned that house in San Diego. In fact, Jack was the first player ever signed by the Chargers, to a $20,000 no-cut contract, three weeks before Gillman was hired as a coach. If the timing had been the other way around, Gilman later admitted, he wouldn't have given the young quarterback a no-cut contract. This was in 1960, and Kemp immediately led the Chargers to two straight Western Division titles. The first year they were in Los Angeles, Kemp's home town; the second year they moved to San Diego. Both years they blew the championship game to Houston.

When the critics started looking around for a guy to blame after the second debacle, they settled on Kemp. Even Coach Gillman.

"Jack was the victim of a double press," said Sid. "He pressed, and the Oilers pressed him, too."

The San Diego press book for 1962 stated curtly. "Kemp had an off-year." In that "off-year" the Chargers won 12 games and lost 2 and were unbeaten in 5 exhibition games.

"Jack wasn't as serious about football as he should have been," continued Gillman. "His enthusiasm was superficial. I doubt if he cracked the play book all season. He got the idea that Jack Kemp was doing it all."

In 1960 his right shoulder was injured in the third game and Jack spurned X-rays. A post-season examination revealed he had played with a hairline fracture. In 1961 his left shoulder was in a harness. It was dislocated at the acromial clavicular joint. The pain was so severe that Kemp took novocaine injections before each game to deaden the agony involved in the simplest quarterback maneuvers. His handoffs and fakes were limited.

In November, Jack, a member of an army reserve unit, was declared 4-F after a physical examination. Around the league he was baited as a draft-dodger and developed a deep injury psyche. When the state of his health was brought up by the writer, he drew back sensitively and said, "You're not going to write about that, are you?"

Early in 1962 he ruptured the middle finger of his throwing hand and was put on the injured-reserve list. Gillman neglected to pull him off the list after the required interval. The Buffalo Bills claimed him for the bargain price of $100. "His confidence," said Joel Collier, now the Bills' head coach, "was shaken."

The years he had spent trying to prove himself as an athlete were a threatened waste. Jack is a bona fide product of Hollywood.

"Like a lot of other kids," he reminisced, "I dreamed of playing for a school like USC or California or UCLA. I went to Fairfax High School in Hollywood, and no college approached me. I was real small—5–9 and weighed 170. I pitched on the baseball team."

He was the third-string pitcher behind Larry Sherry and Barry Latman, who both went to the major leagues in baseball.

"My older brother Tom was a better ballplayer than I was," added Jack. "My little brother Dick won the national soapbox derby when he was fifteen. My dad was an all-city baseball player. I didn't make anything. The only thing that saved me was an alumnus of Occidental. He took me out to the school and I said to myself, 'Here at least, I'll get to play.'"

Occidental is a fine little college tucked in the Eagle Rock Hills near Burbank and Glendale. The Washington Redskins used to train there. It was in a college conference with Whittier, Redlands, Claremont and Pomona. Cal Tech dropped out of the football competition. Too stiff.

The best thing that happened to Kemp at Occidental was Payton Jordan. Jordan, a prominent track coach who moved to Stanford, made Jack grow up. Kemp threw the javelin on Jordan's track team. He was put on a weightlifting program and in one year went from 180 to 215 pounds and stretched out to 6 feet.

What kind of football did he play at Occidental?

"The lowest. I even called pass patterns in the huddle. We didn't have any."

But the Detroit Lions heard of him and drafted him on the seventeenth round for the 1957 season. He signed a contract for $6,500 "because all they had was Bobby Layne and Jerry Reichow for quarterback, and Layne was already getting old." The week after he reported, the Lions made a trade with Green Bay for Tobin Rote.

Kemp got into one exhibition game and threw 8 passes, none complete. "Heck," he said, "I never played before more than 4,000 people until I got into pro ball. The night the Lions played the Browns, I couldn't warm up I was so nervous just being on the field, and I wasn't even going to play."

Buddy Parker resigned as the Detroit coach on the eve of the season and was hired by Pittsburgh. He immediately traded for the kid quarterback, giving the Lions seventh and ninth draft choices. The Steelers also acquired Earl Morrall from San Francisco and had Lenny Dawson, Jack Scarbath and Ted Marchibroda on hand. The Steelers had to learn about Kemp quickly. They had one exhibition game remaining. Jack started and went all the way in a 13–13 tie against Green Bay. He made the club ahead of Scarbath, an All-American from Maryland, and Marchibroda, once the Steeler first-stringer, but played very little that year behind Morrall. He threw 18 passes and completed 8. That's the extent of his activity in the NFL record books.

The next year, 1958, the Steelers decided to go with two quarterbacks. Morrall played as the regular, and Dawson represented too great an investment to cut loose— the Steelers had picked Lenny No. 1 over Jimmy Brown in the draft. Jack was cut loose after the first league game. He had a chance to catch on with the Giants or the Colts. "The Colts said they'd put me on the roster right away," said Jack, "but I couldn't see going to a team that had Unitas. So I went to New York as a taxi-squader. When Charley Conerly was hurt in midseason, I was activated for the rest of the year but never got into a game. Conerly was getting on. Don Heinrich wasn't a great passer, and I saw a real future there . . . until they drafted Lee Grosscup after the season and gave him a no-cut contract. That really burned me up. I asked to be traded."

The Giants arranged for him to go to Calgary of the Canadian league on an informal lendlease basis, and he ran into typical Kemp luck. The Stampeders had signed Joe Kapp of California at a fancy figure. Kemp was released at midseason. He went back to Los Angeles, where he enrolled at Occidental again to get the few credits he needed for his degree in administrative education. "I thought I was through with football," he said, shaking his head.

But the urge kept nagging him, and he made contact with Coach Red Hickey of the San Francisco 49ers. "Come on up and learn our system," Red urged. Then Y. A. Tittle got hurt, leaving only John Brodie to run the club. Kemp was activated to face Cleveland in late November, but a league ruling knocked him off the roster—he wasn't eligible because he'd played in Canada that same year.

"Some good came out of it," said Jack. "I got some publicity around the country. I would have signed with the 49ers again, but the American Football League started up in 1960 and put a club in Los Angeles. One of their scouts was Fido Murphy, who once worked for the Steelers."

Suddenly everything Kemp had waited for was thrown in his lap—a team in a new league, with a fresh outlook, and in his home town. The Chargers went for a bundle, $20,000, to sign a kid who'd never held a regular job.

358

"Sid Gillman stood behind me beautifully," said Jack. "He talked himself and me into feeling I could do the job. Mentally, I had to get over the idea of being a second-string quarterback."

Kemp was the first bona fide quarterback star produced by the AFL. The others—George Blanda, Babe Parilli, Frank Tripucka, Lenny Dawson, Al Dorow—were all veterans cast off by the NFL after plenty of chances to prove themselves. Despite his wanderings, Kemp was really a rookie in experience when he came to the Chargers.

His assets were a naturally strong arm—he could heave the ball 80 yards—a robust physique that he didn't hesitate to expose to danger, and a quick release. While Fran Tarkenton ran rings around NFL rushers with his mad scrambles, Kemp was running all over the lot in the other league. His first year he hung on to the ball 90 times and wound up with a net total of minus 103 yards.

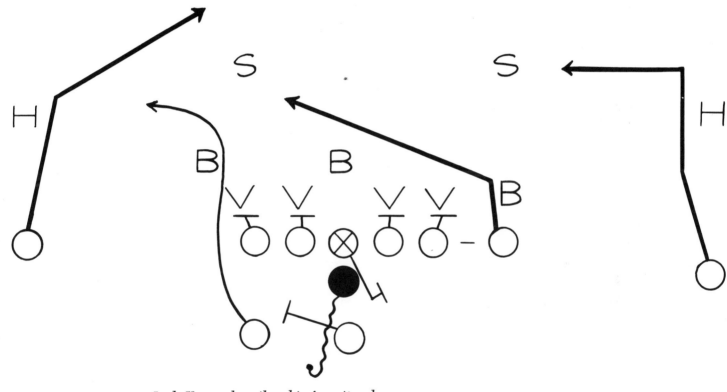

Jack Kemp describes his favorite play:

"Favorite plays are difficult to define because plays are pragmatically chosen according to the defense, score, field position, etc.

"But I like this one—Opposite Right, 65 Flanker Square In—because you have several alternatives.

"The key is the weakside safety and how he reacts. If he plays the tight end as he slants across, then I throw deep to Glenn Bass, the split left end. If the weakside safety covers deep, then I throw to either Paul Costa, the tight end, or Elbert Dubenion, the flanker on the right side.

"We like it because the play goes equally well against zone or man-to-man defenses. We used it extensively in our drive to two AFL championships.

"With it, we scored several touchdowns, but equally important, it was a big third down play for us to control the ball."

359

"His biggest problem," said Al Davis, who was a Charger assistant and later coached Oakland, "is that he's got to stay in the pocket longer. Jack has a very quick delivery, but he doesn't throw real quick."

He also didn't live and breathe football. At the first sign of snow, Kemp would rush off to Mammoth Mountain skiing. He's a natural on the slats, too, and keeps up his interest between football seasons, taking along his growing family of three children, the oldest six. Because Jack personified the All-American boy, the Copley Newspapers in San Diego hired him as a goodwill man. He still served them as a sometime correspondent after his Buffalo move and also worked for a bank. Then there was his absorption with the political arena.

A visit to Kemp in training camp found him surrounded by economic treatises as well as game films and his play book. "I feel these other pursuits," he said, "are legitimate and do not interfere with football." Before the 1964 elections he made speeches supporting the conservative Republican cause.

"I was disappointed in the campaign," said Jack, "because it never got down to political philosophy." Or maybe because his man Goldwater lost.

It's probably true that Kemp used to lack the maturity of purpose and dedication that goes with being a first-class quarterback. "He has all the equipment," his former coach, Sid Gillman, once said. "I think he needs a little adversity." Sid provided that element by bouncing Jack Kemp to Buffalo in the waiver slipup. No one's certain if it was an oversight or Gillman's convenient excuse to get rid of Kemp. Sid isn't talking.

He can't afford to, after San Diego lost champion games to Buffalo in 1964 and '65, with Kemp profiting from the adversity.

JACK KEMP

BORN: July 13, 1935   HEIGHT: 6'0"   WEIGHT: 201

Pittsburgh Steelers, 1957

New York Giants, 1958

San Diego Chargers, 1960–62

(Los Angeles until 1962)

Buffalo Bills, 1962–65

PASSING RECORD:

Year	Att.	Comp.	Yards Gained	T.D.	Pct.	Longest	Int.
1957	18	8	88	0	44.4	21	2
1958	—	—	—	—	—	—	—
1959			(Canada)				
1960	406	211	3018	20	52.0	69	25
1961	364	165	2686	15	45.3	91	22
1962	139	64	928	5	46.0	74	6
1963	384	194	2914	13	50.5	89	20
1964	269	119	2285	13	44.2	94	26

It took Jack Kemp of Buffalo nine seasons to settle down as a championship quarterback.

Jack Kemp's passing style features one of the strongest arms in football and a lot of mobility.

The author, left, presents Jack Kemp with the Third Down Trophy at the AFL All-Star game in January, 1966. He was voted the most valuable Buffalo player in a poll of his teammates.

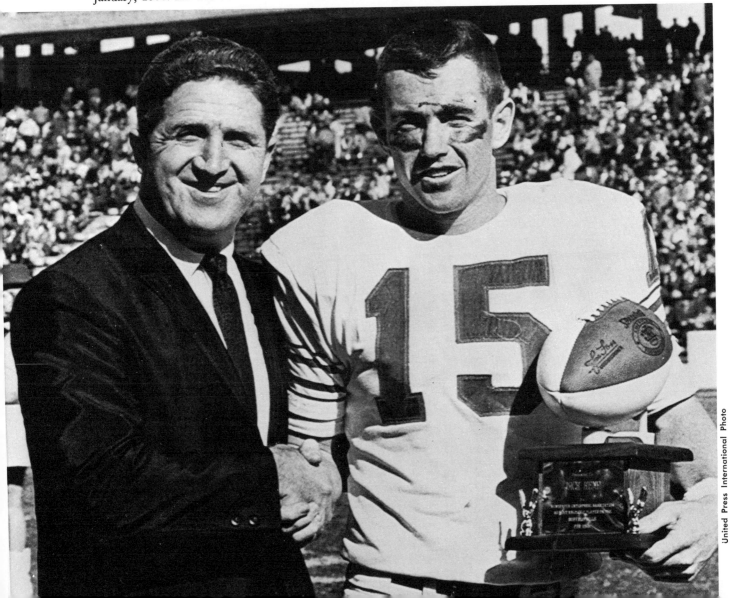

1965	391	179	2368	10	45.8	78	18
AFL TOTALS	1953	932	14,199	76	45.2	94	119

RUSHING RECORD:

Year	Att.	Yards Gained	Longest	Ave.
1957	3	−1	2	−.3
1958	—	—	—	—
1959	—	—	—	—
1960	90	−103	31	−1.1
1961	43	105	23	2.4
1962	12	56	28	4.7
1963	52	226	26	4.3
1964	37	124	14	3.4
1965	36	49	12	1.4
AFL TOTALS	270	456	31	1.7

15. The Young Turks

Francis Tarkenton

FRANCIS TARKENTON MAKES THE MIN-
NESOTA TEAM—BECAUSE HE MAKES
THE GREAT PLAYS WHEN HE SHOULDN'T.

—*Tom Landry, coach,*
Dallas Cowboys, 1960–

Francis Tarkenton—now isn't that a name for a quarterback—looked up at the open end of Lambeau Stadium in Green Bay, where the second hand stopped at 54 and the minute indicator showed zero, and he knew he was in trouble. The Minnesota Vikings clustered around him, waiting to see what would happen next.

("A quarterback has got to have leadership qualities," says Francis Tarkenton. "He has to be able to lead a group of men who are professionals who come from different parts of the country, with different personalities. He's got to be able to have the leadership to get the very best from them while he's on the field. He has to take charge.")

The ball was on the Minnesota 36-yard line, fourth down. Tarkenton had been trapped for an 8-yard loss on the first play. He'd crossed the line of scrimmage to throw a pass and that cost them 5 more, plus another down. A running play by rookie back Tom Michel gained only 1 yard. By quick calculation, and checking the chains, Francis knew he had to pick up at least 22 yards to keep the Vikings alive. The score was Green Bay 23, Minnesota 21.

("Another requisite," says Francis Tarkenton, "is ability to learn the professional offense and defense. In other words, having a football mind. Not a classroom mind. He's got to have an intense desire to learn football. He's got to love the game of football. More so than at any other position, because he has to spend more time than anyone else to perfect his abilities.")

Tarkenton called a play in which the split receivers, Tom Hall and Paul Flatley, went deep to the outside. He circled the backs, Michel and Bill Brown, deep down the middle, with Gordie Smith, the tight end, running a zig-out shallow on Hall's side. The idea was to flood all the passing zones. The Packers were in a "prevent" defense, rushing only their front four. The quarterback, who'd been having good luck finding Hall all day, told him to get as far down as he could and keep his eyes open, because he'd get the ball to him.

("I don't think a quarterback is drafted to play professional football," says Tarkenton, "unless he's got the ability to throw the ball. This is the first thing that gets him into pro ball. Being able to throw is just the start, though, because there are many people who have strong arms. When I came up to the pros I needed to strengthen my arm somewhat. Actually, the short ball is the hardest to throw. The long ball is the easiest.")

With the snap of the ball, Tarkenton beat a hasty retreat as his five possible receivers fanned downfield. Francis knew that if he took his normal "drop" he wouldn't have time to get off a deep pass because he had weakened his backfield blocking on the play. The only way to get time was to skip around as long as possible behind the line. He looped and reversed and twisted to throw the Packer rushers off. Willie Davis, the fastest man in the Green Bay line, was on his tail as Francis got back almost to the 10-yard line. Willie reached out and got a hand on the quarterback's heel. Tarkenton turned and started to move up, with Willie still clawing at him. More than 30 yards down the field, Tom Hall was all alone at the right sideline. Tarkenton wound up and threw. Another white Viking jersey, belonging to tight end Gordie Smith, flew into the quarterback's line of vision. "No, Gordie, no," gasped Tarkenton to himself. Smith reached up, grasped the ball and cut around the astonished Hall down to the Green Bay 21-yard line.

("The quarterback's got to win the confidence of his team by performing well, where they know on third and 7 he can do it for them. Or where they go into a big game, they know this guy can win for them if they block well, catch the ball, play decent defense and stay alert.")

Tarkenton used up a few more seconds by sending Michel into the line for a couple of yards to position the ball in the middle of the field. Specialist Fred Cox came in with the field-goal unit. Tarkenton held, and Cox kicked the ball between the uprights as time ran out. Minnesota won, 24–23, their first victory ever over the mighty Packers.

("The only criterion a quarterback is judged by," says Francis Tarkenton, "is how many he wins and how many he loses.")

In their five-year history, the Minnesota Vikings have had virtually no other quarterback but Tarkenton. He was picked on the third round in December, 1960, when the Vikings participated in their initial draft of college talent.

"It bothered my pride I wasn't a first-round choice," he admitted. "I had indications from various people that I would be. I understood the Washington Redskins liked me. I was surprised they didn't take me, and very disappointed. I got a better offer from Boston to play in the AFL. But I just had to prove to everybody I could play in the National league, and play well. If I had been a first-round pick, I might have leaned more to the money."

Tarkenton wanted to be another Sammy Baugh. He was born in Washington, D.C., and Sammy Baugh was his first idol. His father, a Methodist minister, moved to Athens, Georgia, for Fran's school years. It was logical for him to enroll at the University of Georgia, located in Athens. He started his sophomore year as the third-stringer behind Charley Britt and Tommy Lewis. Tarkenton felt they were going to hold him out of action the whole season, as a redshirt, to save his eligibility. He took direct steps to avoid that in the opening game against Texas.

Georgia was losing 7–0 in the third quarter, and young Francis was right at Coach Wally Butts' elbow, cajoling him for a chance to get in the game. Texas punted to the Georgia 5-yard line.

"I ran five steps on the field," recalled Francis, "before I turned around and almost begged him to let me go the rest of the way. He finally gave in. We took the ball 95 yards, and I threw a touchdown pass to an end named Aaron Box. Then we went for the 2-point conversion to go ahead, 8–7. Texas scored again. We got the ball back for a last chance with 2 minutes left. I looked around again at Coach Butts. He made me sit on the bench. Charley Britt went in."

Georgia lost, but by the end of his sophomore season, Tarkenton was playing half the time on offense. In his junior year he went 80 percent, with Britt playing 20 per-

366

A chase all over the field at Yankee Stadium ended with Hal Bedsole nabbing a 20-yard pass from Francis Tarkenton (10), left background. Jimmy Patton of the Giants hauled down the Viking end.

A typical Tarkenton passing pose finds him ready to take off on a moment's notice.

Francis Tarkenton doesn't always throw on the run. The Minnesota quarterback plants himself against the Cleveland Browns.

cent and full-time on defense. Charley later made it in the NFL as a defensive back for the Rams but achieved his greatest fame for sharing a pad in Hollywood with Ricky Nelson. Tarkenton was all-conference as a junior and piloted the Bulldogs to a 14–0 Orange Bowl victory over Missouri. He was picked for All-American honors before his senior season, but Georgia slipped to a 6–4 season and in the last two games Tarkenton couldn't throw at all because of a hip pointer. Mississippi won the national title behind quarterback Jake Gibbs, who signed with the New York Yankees for a big baseball bonus. Jake was the All-American in 1960.

"I had to prove I could be a regular quarterback in the NFL," said Tarkenton, "and let some of the people eat crow who had passed me up. You just don't know about a quarterback. It's an intangible. Usually you're drafted by teams not doing well, which creates an immediate handicap."

At Minnesota, he stepped into a situation which had not even been charted. Van Brocklin, looking around the league for possible leaders, had his choice of George Shaw, Y. A. Tittle and Bill Wade, all in disfavor with their teams. The Vikings probably settled on Shaw because of his age and the price was right (a No. 1 draft pick).

"We're going to bring you along slowly as the No. 2 quarterback," the Dutchman told Tarkenton. In the last preseason game Tarkenton had a good second half against the Los Angeles Rams.

"On Tuesday," reviewed Tarkenton, "Norm told me I was going to start the opener against the Bears. On Friday, he said, 'Shaw should get an opportunity.' George did start and played the first two series of downs and then I came in."

The Vikings, in their NFL debut, pulled a sensational 37–13 upset of the Bears. Tarkenton was phenomenal, running in and out of the Bears' clutches and finding receivers in the most unlikely places. That game probably set the stage for his reputation as the super scrambler deluxe of all time. When the Vikings almost upset the mighty Baltimore Colts in the third game, losing only on a last-second field goal, 34–33, defensive end Gino Marchetti warned, "The kid's going to get killed!"

The prescribed method for breaking in a quarterback is to let him spend three years patiently absorbing the intricacies of the modern T before exposing him to fire. But this conflicts with the old theorem that says there's no substitute for experience. The Vikings chose the latter course for Tarkenton because they had nothing to lose except games which nobody expected them to win.

Looking back, Tarkenton said, "I just didn't know enough football. There were times I'd send both backs out with second down and 9 yards to go, which I know now is a blitz situation. I'd get trapped and I had nobody to blame but myself."

So he learned to run for his life.

Fortunately, Francis has some built-in warning clock which buzzes in times of danger. He also has a deceptively strong constitution—190 pounds, 6 feet tall and good legs. And he's a leader. Electricity crackles from him. The Vikings respect his toughness, both spiritual and physical. Hal Bedsole, a cocky rookie end from Southern California, once dropped 3 passes in a game. Tarkenton, furious, walked up to him after the game. Bedsole is 6–4 and 235. "Next time you drop 3 passes," spat Tarkenton, "you're going to have to answer to me."

368

The quarterback's language is impeccable, and so are his personal habits. He's active in the Fellowship of Christian Athletes. Yet he doesn't flaunt his piety. After a Pro Bowl game, when a group of the Viking stars and their wives stopped off at Las Vegas en route home, Fran and his wife Elaine made the scene, too. And he got trapped at the green velvet tables with the rest of them.

Between seasons, he goes back to Georgia and makes his home in Atlanta, where he's a budding advertising executive.

In the January, 1965 Pro Bowl, Tarkenton relieved John Unitas and completed 8 out of 13 passes for 172 yards, directing the West to a 34–14 win and walking off with the Most Valuable Player award. But the main thing he got out of the experience was a week shared with Unitas on the practice field.

"The important thing in passing," he said, "is to get the ball away when the guy is open. This is the thing Unitas does better than anyone in football. The whole week, I talked to John about his timing, and I learned something. The Colts have a definite pattern. He'll tell Raymond Berry to hook at 12 yards and to come back at 15, and he knows exactly the area Berry'll be coming to. John sets up at 7 yards behind the center. He has had success with it and continually repeats.

"A young quarterback like myself experiments with things. He might drop back 8 yards on one type of pass, 6 yards on another. But I think I've grasped the game pretty well by now. I came a good way because Van Brocklin is a former quarterback and has been able to teach me more than the average coach could.

"Essentially, Dutch knows this—a quarterback knows his own style. He doesn't try to make me like Norm Van Brocklin or like Bart Starr. He lets me develop my own personality."

Van Brocklin didn't always agree with Tarkenton's football personality. He shook his head when Francis deserted the pocket and started roaming all over the field. He worked on getting Tarkenton to set his feet when he passed, to throw while on balance.

While Francis became a more disciplined quarterback as he matured, and as the Vikings matured as a team, he couldn't help reverting periodically. He was in the Pro Bowl game again in 1966, scrambling typically. Jim Parker, the beefy offensive guard of the Baltimore Colts, playing for the West with Tarkenton, came back to the huddle wheezing and out of breath. He turned to Grady Alderman, the offensive tackle from the Vikings, who's used to Tarkenton's tactics.

"How the heck do you keep up with that Tarkenton?" puffed Parker. "He runs all over and you have to kill yourself getting there to block for him."

"No, you don't," advised Alderman. "Just stand still and wait for ol' Fran to come past you again, and then throw another block."

Tarkenton blamed some of his indiscretions as a scrambler on the youth of the Vikings, the five years it has taken them to become stabilized in personnel.

"The main trouble I've had," insisted the young quarterback, "is with different receivers. We had six different end combinations one year with the Vikings. I've never worked consistently with the same receivers, except in the last year, and that's how a quarterback builds confidence—by knowing the angles, the habits, the capabilities of the men he's working with.

"Football is a team game. Every player wants more than anything else success for his team. The thing I want most of all is a world's championship, not a division title, for my team. And we're going to get it. I feel this; I know this; I believe in it. And my teammates believe in it."

Will Tarkenton be the leader to get them that championship?

"How can you evaluate your own self effectively? You don't know. You think and you hope and you feel you're respected by your teammates, that they believe in you and you can win for them. I hope this is true in my case."

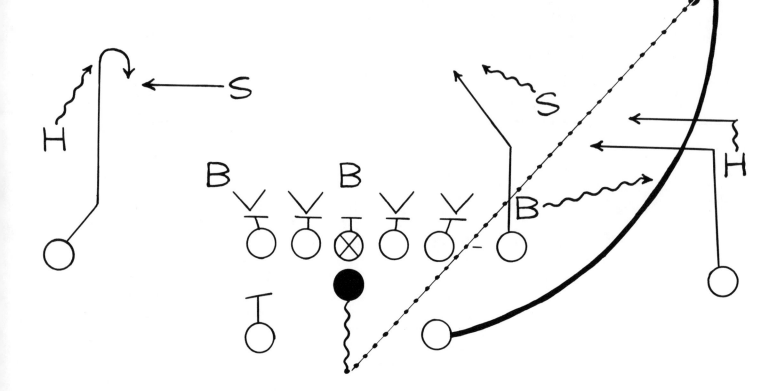

Francis Tarkenton describes his favorite play:

"This is a swing and up pass play to either halfback Tommy Mason or fullback Bill Brown. The object of the play is to set up a situation where a 230-pound linebacker has to cover a halfback man-to-man on a deep pass route.

"We have scored about 25 touchdowns on this play in five years.

"In 1964 we played the Giants in New York. In the fourth quarter, with the score close we caught New York blitzing our weak side to our left. We sent Brown on a swing and up pattern down the right side of the field. Their left linebacker had to cover him, and Bill simply outran him. He caught the ball for a touchdown of 40 yards.

"It works essentially the same way when we're lined up strong left, and Mason runs the swing. I've been fortunate in that both our backs are good receivers."

370

FRANCIS TARKENTON

BORN: Feb. 3, 1940   HEIGHT: 6'0"   WEIGHT: 193

Minnesota Vikings, 1961–65

PASSING RECORD:

Year	Att.	Comp.	Yards Gained	T.D.	Pct.	Longest	Int.
1961	280	157	1997	18	56.1	71	17
1962	329	163	2595	22	49.5	89	25
1963	297	170	2311	15	57.2	67	15
1964	306	171	2506	22	55.9	64	11
1965	329	171	2609	19	52.0	72	11
TOTALS	1541	832	12,018	96	53.9	89	79

RUSHING RECORD:

Year	Att.	Yards Gained	Longest	Ave.
1961	56	308	52	5.5
1962	41	361	31	8.8
1963	28	162	24	5.8
1964	50	330	31	6.6
1965	56	356	36	6.4
TOTALS	231	1537	52	6.7

Charley Johnson

I WISH I WAS CHARLEY JOHNSON'S AGE.
AND HAD HIS FUTURE. WHOOEE!

—*Y. A. Tittle, quarterback,*
New York Giants, 1963

With fullback Joe Childress (35) as his bodyguard, quarterback Charley Johnson of the St. Louis Cardinals fades to pass.

Malcolm W. Emmons

Center Bob DeMarco (61) of the Cards shields Charley Johnson as the young quarterback flings a sideline pass.

Malcolm W. Emmons

The regular quarterback of the St. Louis Cardinals when Charley Johnson came upon the scene in 1961 was Sam Etcheverry. Sam was a legendary passer from Canadian ball. He showed St. Louis a mythical arm. It couldn't propel a football more than 25 yards in the air.

The second choice, on the basis of experience, was Ralph Guglielmi, whose mother made good spaghetti. Ralph was good-looking but didn't look good passing.

And then there was Charley. He had guts and was smart enough to keep his mouth shut. That's how he made the team.

"We knocked hell out of him in training camp that first year," remembered Bill Koman, the exuberant linebacker of the Cardinals, "and he didn't say a word."

The next year, by a process of attrition, Johnson was the No. 2 quarterback. Guglielmi was traded to New York. And Etcheverry still couldn't throw. So when the Cards fared poorly in an early-season game against the New York Giants, behind 31–7, Coach Wally Lemm said, "What the hell, it can't get any worse." And put Charley in the game. He threw 7 straight completions.

The next week Lemm started the young crewcut sophomore against Washington. The Redskins jumped into an early lead. Charley got a little panicky, forgot about the game plan, and started throwing the ball all over the lot. As the Cardinals trotted to the dressing room at half time down 14–3, Lemm made a mental note to himself about reassuring Charley everything would be all right. The young quarterback walked over to him and placed a hand on Wally's shoulder.

"Coach," he said, "I think we'd be better off if we got back on the field and worked this thing out like we planned."

Charley rallied the Cardinals to a 17–17 tie. After the game, Etcheverry stood on a locker and threw the game ball to Johnson. It was virtually the last completion of Sam's career because Charley became the starting quarterback of the St. Louis Cardinals, and never gave it up.

Charley needed only three seasons to break every career and season passing record in the history of a team which can trace its lineage back to 1898, on a field on the south side of Chicago.

They were the Chicago Cardinals when Charley was drafted as a "future" at New Mexico State University. They were already transplanted to St. Louis by the time he joined them in the late summer of 1961 at their training camp in Lake Forest, Illinois. Charley's chances of making a living in professional football seemed remote. He was the fifth in a list of quarterbacks the coaches had checked as their possibilities. Charley said all along he only wanted to try the pros so he could see fellows like Unitas and Tittle, whom he'd read about back in Las Cruces, New Mexico, up close.

However, Johnny Roach, the starter in 1960, and King Hill, his alternate, were traded to other teams before training camp opened. George Izo, a youngster from

Notre Dame, went to the Redskins for Guglielmi. Charley was in business after impressing the Card coaches with his intellect, his sturdiness and his skill in passing.

A few years later, he had all those team records: most passes, most completions, most yards, most touchdowns . . . oh yes, most interceptions, too. Lemm, his coach through the 1965 season, left the Cardinals and was free to criticize. "Charley's biggest problem," said Wally, "is in feeling when to get rid of the ball. He tries to force the pass through. That's why he gets so many interceptions."

Charley had a valid reason for this when he was just starting out and lacked experience. He was as much aware of his weakness as Lemm. "When receivers were covered," he recalled, "I'd run around back there, waiting and hoping somebody would get clear. I just hated to see a play go down the drain. But I would have had fewer interceptions and lost less yards if I'd just thrown the ball away."

Now, as a five-year veteran at the ripe age of 27, what's his excuse?

Charley's passing has fluctuated like the weather in west Texas, where he was born and raised. When he's hot, he can melt the insides of a freezer in Alaska. When he's cold, forget it and wait till next week.

The Cardinals have been that kind of team, too. They went into the 1965 season fully expecting Charley to lead them to their first championship in seventeen years. They were young, cocky (parenthetically, Charley is also young, but not cocky) and boasted they had the best personnel in their division. In 1964 they finished only half a game behind Cleveland. The Cardinals were generally picked to win and showed why in the second game of the season when they thoroughly plucked the Browns, 49–13, as Johnson threw 6 touchdown passes. After 5 games they were tied with Cleveland at 4 won, 1 lost.

But Charley's left shoulder was severely bruised in the fourth game against Washington and reinjured the next week against Pittsburgh. He sat out the sixth game completely. With Buddy Humphrey filling in at quarterback, the Cardinals were upset by the Redskins, winless to that point. No calamity. Charley would be back in another week, and the Cardinals faced the New York Giants, who shaped up as easy pickings. Nothing went right. A 10–0 lead evaporated. Charley's chin leaked blood where a Giant elbow had got in under the protective bar, and later it would take four stitches to close the gash. The Cardinals trailed, 14–10, when they got a last chance with 2 minutes to play. The ball was on their own 5-yard line.

A flare pass to fullback Willis Crenshaw gave them a little breathing room and a third-down completion brought them out to the 24. Within a minute, tossing precisely, Charley got the Cardinals down to the Giant 14-yard line. Three plays misfired. Charley tried a fourth-down pass and the intended receiver fell down as the Cards blew the ball game. As it turned out, they blew the season, too, and wound up losing their last 6 games in a row. Charley missed two of them completely, and was not 100 percent when he did play. The shoulder bruise turned out to be a bone separation and required an operation in December. His timetable for becoming a championship quarterback was shattered.

Whom do you blame? The Cardinals as a team? They were unhappy because of big money paid to some rookies who didn't pull their weight. Charley Johnson? You can't give up on a kid with his credentials, and his latent class.

On December 9, 1962, in his ninth game as a regular for the Cardinals, Charley threw 5 touchdowns against the bewildered Dallas Cowboys at distances varying from 5 to 74 yards. The logical place to find Charley late that night would have been at Stan and Biggie's or Gaslight Square or wherever a pro football player goes to drain the tension that builds up on a Sunday afternoon.

But on that particular night a guy would have found Charley at the kitchen table with a bunch of books sprawled around him and one big looseleaf getting special attention. Neatly lettered on a corner of the cover was the title: "Expansion of Laminar Jets of Organic Liquids Issuing from Capillary Tubes." Charley was studying for a test, and this was his master's thesis.

(A graduate student in chemical engineering at Washington University in St. Louis, Charley has since progressed to his doctor's degree, and from a garden apartment to a house in the suburbs.)

A woman doctor was his neighbor and the next morning she saw Charley carrying his textbooks, en route to the chemistry laboratory at Washington University. Whenever the neighbors asked him what he did, Charley drawled politely in his flat Texas accent, "I'm a graduate student, ma'am."

"Now," said the woman doctor, "I know who you are. I saw your picture in the morning papers." (For having thrown the 5 touchdown passes.)

Coach Wally Lemm knew Charley from the other end of the tangent. He was introduced to him first as a football player. "He appeared to have the ability to throw," noted Wally. "I didn't realize at the time how intelligent he was."

Pro football has become the thinking man's game. The coaches who move the O's and X's around on dressing-room blackboards look for the bright young field generals to carry out their design. Charley Johnson is the prototype, just like Frank Ryan, the Cleveland mathematician, or Bart Starr, the Green Bay A-student.

For five years, until he completed work for his doctorate, Charley's daily routine was to attend classes until noon, then transfer his thoughts to football for the afternoon. At night he was back concentrating on the flow of liquid plastics and their peculiar properties. It required rigid mental discipline for Johnson to keep the two, football and chemistry, separated. Occasionally rheology mixed with red dogs and polymers fused with play-action passes. And Charley wound up on his rear end looking at the malevolent eyes of a blitzing linebacker.

As his prominence around St. Louis increased, he took on a third career—sportscaster—and conducted a daily radio sports show, taped at six o'clock in the morning. But Charley has managed to juggle his different careers without becoming a victim of hypertension.

He maintains a subdued family life with his wife Barbara, whom he started courting in high school, and their two young children. Charley doesn't look like a young man who will get too excited. His eyes are a cool gray-green, curious but unemotional. His face is broad and plain. The lips, which curve up at the ends, are pressed firmly together. His high cheekbones are his only prominent feature. Charley wears his straight blond hair clipped close to his head.

He's built like an athlete, with a strong neck and sloping shoulders, and he carries himself like one. He has the disciplined touch to be a fine golfer. When the U.S. Open was held in St. Louis in June, 1965, there was a strong rumor passed around that Charley was considering a stab at the pro golf tour. He once shot a double eagle on a par 558-yard hole, putting his tee shot 300 yards straight down the middle of the fairway, then walloping a No. 2 wood that bounced a couple of times and plopped into the cup.

But Charley has a future assured in chemical engineering if he wants it, and so far it has fitted in neatly with his football. He has a facility for breaking the complex down into simple elements. In football he has reduced the whole problem of quarterbacking down to two words—"recognizing defenses."

"The most important aspect of Charley's progress as a quarterback was his ability to catch on to situations," said Lemm.

"Coming into a game," said Charley, "I try to have the same outlook that I once read Johnny Unitas has. Complete preparation, so that there's instant recall of things you should know to meet any situation."

Once he has the right play in mind, nothing stops Charley. "I've always had the confidence that if a receiver is loose down the field, I can get the ball to him." He was trained for it.

Before Charley could walk, his father propped him up against a wall and slipped a football in his belly to get used to the feel of it. His dad was the city tax assessor of Big Spring in west Texas, where the dry winds blow ruts in a man's face and football ranks with cotton and oil as a commodity.

When he was three, the local high school tried to get baby Charley on the field at half time for a passing exhibition. But he was no quick-budding genius. He didn't make starting quarterback in high school until his senior year. "There were eight schools in our district," Charley reminisced. "Seven quarterbacks got some kind of all-star mention after the season. I was the eighth."

He wanted to go to Southern Methodist but would have settled for any school in the Southwest Conference, or Hardin-Simmons over in Abilene, where Sammy Baugh was the coach. No one wanted him, and the Johnsons weren't rich, so Charley settled for a scholarship at a little junior college in Kerrville, Texas, called Schreiner Institute. Schreiner dropped football after one year and still nobody was interested in recruiting Johnson. He returned for another term—to play basketball.

New Mexico State was trying to build up its basketball team and sent its trainer to scout a tournament in Big Spring. Charley has an uncle named Jack Johnson who is big (6–3 and 250 pounds), and persuasive because he is big. Uncle Jack adopted the trainer for the run of the tournament. Late one night, Uncle Jack persuaded him that even if Charley didn't make it in basketball, he was worth a look in football.

The timing was right. After Charley got to New Mexico State, Warren Woodson was hired as football coach. As a rollout quarterback, Charley, with average speed, wasn't much. Woodson, partial to the pass, put in a pro-type attack in which the quarterback sets up by dropping straight back. He providently supplied an offense that had Pervis Atkins and Bobby Gaiters at the halfbacks, Bob Jackson at fullback, Bob Kelly and E. A. Sims at the ends.

Atkins became an All-American halfback and played for the Los Angeles Rams and

Washington Redskins. Gaiters led the nation in rushing and was the first pick of the New York Giants in 1960. Jackson, drafted No. 2 by the Cardinals a year later, chose to play with San Diego in the American Football League. Kelly, also a Card choice, went with Houston as a tackle. Sims migrated to Canada.

While they were together, New Mexico State went to the Sun Bowl in consecutive years, and each time Charley was named the game's most valuable player.

The pros were intrigued by all those high-powered backs, and the Cardinals requested some game films. "Gaiters was the guy who interested us," recalled Ray Pro-

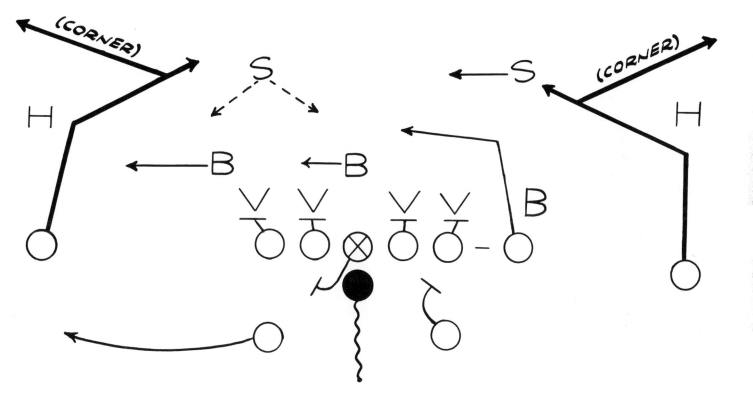

Charley Johnson describes his favorite play:

"The Cardinals have used a simple pattern called a Double Quick Post effectively in recent years. The audible for it was 94. Most of the defensive backs in the league know it, so there's no secret involved.

"It's especially effective against the blitz or any rush, and we're helped by having two fine outside receivers in Sonny Randle and Bobby Joe Conrad. They have scored on it numerous times—I would guess, against every team in the East and perhaps almost every team in the West.

"The play really is two in one: the break to the middle, and the complementary fake to the middle and back to the outside, or corner.

"As sort of an unwritten rule to avoid congestion in the middle, Randle always ran the deeper pattern. He's the left end in this diagram.

"The free safety was the key. We threw to the side opposite his move in the coverage."

379

chaska, an assistant coach. "Chuck Drulis and I were running the projector and pretty soon we nudged each other, 'Wait a minute. Let's look at that quarterback. The heck with the others.'

"You could tell then that Charley was class."

St. Louis drafted him in the tenth round of the 1960 draft as a "future" with a year of college eligibility remaining. The AFL, just beginning operations, skipped him, though the San Diego Chargers picked him No. 8 a year later. "Their coach called me one night," remembered Charley. "His offer was $3,000 under what I could get from the Cardinals."

It's easy now to see why pro teams wouldn't knock themselves out to get Johnson. He's compact enough, at 190 pounds, to take the beating a quarterback must endure. But the pros like their passers to look a 270-pound tackle in the eye instead of the armpits, and Charley barely qualifies as a 6-footer. In fact, he looks shorter.

Charley doesn't throw a pretty pass. His delivery isn't pure overhand past the ears —more the three-quarters type like Tittle used to throw. And the ball travels on a flat trajectory. Even in practice it wobbles.

"A ball that wobbles is easier to catch," claimed Bobby Joe Conrad, who caught enough Johnson passes (73) in 1963 to lead the NFL in receiving. "Those pretty spirals rifle right through your hands."

"Charley throws a soft ball, and he knows when to zing it and when not to zing it," said Sonny Randle, his other favorite receiver. "His first season as a regular he was three years ahead of any quarterback that's ever come along."

That was four years ago. Charley Johnson will have to come up a winner to maintain his lead.

CHARLEY JOHNSON

BORN: Nov. 22, 1938   HEIGHT: 6'½"   WEIGHT: 190
St. Louis Cardinals, 1961–65
PASSING RECORD:

Year	Att.	Comp.	Yards Gained	T.D.	Pct.	Longest	Int.
1961	13	5	51	0	38.4	16	2
1962	308	150	2440	16	48.7	86	20
1963	423	222	3280	28	52.5	78	21
1964	420	223	3045	21	53.1	78	24
1965	322	155	2439	18	48.1	78	15
TOTALS	1486	755	11,255	83	50.8	86	82

RUSHING RECORD:

Year	Att.	Yards Gained	Longest	Ave.
1961	1	−3	−3	−3.0
1962	25	138	19	5.5
1963	41	143	16	3.5
1964	31	93	19	3.0
1965	25	60	15	2.4
TOTALS	123	431	19	3.5

16. The New Breed

JOE NAMATH'S NOT ONLY THE BEST
ATHLETE I'VE EVER COACHED, BUT THE
BEST ATHLETE I'VE EVER SEEN.

—*Paul (Bear) Bryant,*
head football coach,
University of Alabama.

Beaver Falls is a dingy steel-mill town up the Ohio River from Pittsburgh, in the midst of a major industrial and mining complex. Men look for release from the grimness and soot that puts a grayness in their lives.

The center of activity in town is a pool hall. Joe Willie Namath, like most of the other kids in Beaver Falls, knew it well.

But Joe Willie was cut out for other things besides chalking a cue stick. Recreation in a mill town also takes violent form, which is why high school football flourishes in the clusters of smokestacks in western Pennsylvania. It relieves the drabness of the lunchbox and the timeclock for those sturdy second-generation workers and provides an escape for their kids.

The skinned turf of Beaver Falls High School's stadium has been the springboard for Joe Walton and Jim Mutscheller, who became All-American ends—Walton at the University of Pittsburgh and Mutscheller at Notre Dame. Both had distinguished careers in professional football as tight ends. Just across the river, Vito (Babe) Parilli went from Rochester, Pennsylvania, to stardom at the University of Kentucky and a thirteen-year tenure as a pro quarterback.

However, Joe Willie Namath has become the *ne plus ultra* in the ambitions of every little kid who grows up in Beaver Falls or the football-rich communities that pockmark the Ohio River basin above and below Pittsburgh. First, Joe led Beaver Falls High to the Double-A championship of western Pennsylvania—the highest a team can go. Joe Willie was a swinger who climbed the school flagpole, which doesn't sound like much until you stop to realize that it jutted out three stories above the ground.

Whatever he tried, he was a smashing success. Star guard on the basketball team and slugging centerfielder on the Junior Legion baseball team, with slouch-hatted big-league scouts in the stands every time he played. The Chicago Cubs offered him $50,000.

Then Joe Namath went away and became a big wheel at the University of Alabama.. He wore dark glasses and let his black hair grow long, and sometimes smoked a big cigar after the Crimson Tide won a big game. He also graduated to a $400,000 contract, drove a big green Lincoln convertible, escorted blond movie queens like Mamie Van Doren and flashed his sharp green eyes in the fruggy smoke of New York's most "in" discothèques.

Joe Willie Namath had it made. Instant quarterback. Monogrammed shirts. And Bob Hope cracked jokes about him.

Those are the superficial aspects of the making of a pro. Joe Namath was a national figure from the moment he became the target of a bidding contest between the St. Louis Cardinals of the NFL and the New York Jets of the AFL. Because of him a whole new set of values was created about the worth of rookie talent. The $400,000 quarterback became part of the lexicon of professional football. The Jets signed him and never denied the figure.

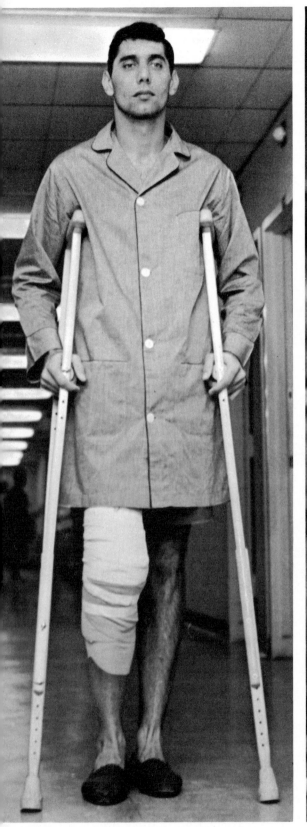

The knee on which the New York Jets staked a $400,000 investment gets its first outing. Joe Namath recovered from the operation to become the AFL Rookie of the Year.

White shoes became Namath's trademark in the uniform of the Jets.

Nobody ever came into professional football like young Namath did in the summer of 1965. Before he drew on his first uniform in the Jet camp at the Peekskill Military Academy up the Hudson River from New York City, Joe and his noble Hungarian nose were on the cover of *Sports Illustrated* in four vivid colors. W. C. Heinz hovered at his elbow preparing a lengthy text piece for *Life*. Dave Anderson had already written one for *True;* and *Sport* was out with a penetrating portrait of this new personality. *Look* had a picture treatment in the meld. The roving cameras of NBC were everywhere for a one-hour documentary telecast; and tape recorders were all over the place stocking up his pronouncements for present and future programs.

This was the New Breed of pro quarterback. Instant celebrity. White football shoes with taped spats to protect the ankles. And Howard Cosell clucking over him like a mother hen.

The most notable thing about Joe Namath is that with all the adulation and attention that has invariably followed him since he impressed people with his ability to complete a forward pass, he never lost sight of his primary objective—to be a dedicated, proficient athlete. Joe has never wanted to be anything else.

The sharp clothes, the glib personality, the affected Southern accent that he has carried out of Alabama are incidental trappings to his true self, a quarterback who embodies the physical equipment, mental attitude and competitive temperament to become one of the great performers of professional football history. He's graded A-plus by every competent scout, coach and observer in either major pro football league. Except for the physical risk of a badly damaged knee, Joe has done nothing to diminish this assessment. He is 6–2, weighs 195 sinewy pounds and throws a football with the overhand purity of John Unitas and a remarkable quickness in flicking it long or short with his wrist action.

He withstood more pressure than any rookie in history to complete his first pro season as the most exciting new talent ever seen in the six-year annals of the American Football League. Joe Namath has lived his young life with a cocksureness that everything would turn out right, from the time he indulged in gang rock fights on Jungle Hill and Bunny Hill and Tin Hill in Beaver Falls.

He had a choice of 52 colleges and wanted to go to Notre Dame but couldn't get in because of grades. Joe was a perfunctory student. He did just enough to get by with innate brightness. He wasn't the first college man in the family. His older brother Frank went to Kentucky for a couple of years on a football scholarship. When Joe flunked his college boards to get into the University of Maryland, an assistant coach at that school steered him to Bear Bryant at the University of Alabama. That way Maryland wouldn't have to play against him.

Joe arrived with a blue straw hat, a pearl in the band around it, and a toothpick in his mouth. He was invited by Bear Bryant to come up on the viewing tower overlooking the practice football field, a rare privilege. By his sophomore year, Joe was the regular quarterback of a team that won 10 out of 11 games, including an Orange Bowl victory over Oklahoma, 17–0. In his junior year, Joe received the one serious setback of his young career. He broke training during the season and was suspended from the squad.

This meant missing a trip to the Sugar Bowl in New Orleans. It also meant exile from the athletes' dormitory, which is the Taj Hilton of living in Tuscaloosa, Alabama. "Roughest thing I've had to face," admitted Joe. "It helped me to grow up." As a chastened senior, Namath was on the way to a great campaign, cinch All-American honors, maybe a shot at the Heisman Trophy, when he rolled out around right end in the fourth game of the season against North Carolina State.

"Nobody hit me," said Joe. "I think the cleats on my right shoe were bent. I stumbled and fell when my right knee went out on me."

The knee was destined to become one of the celebrated hinges of sport. During that senior season, Joe knew he was going to need a cartilage operation but postponed it to help Alabama's quest for a national championship. He played only a few minutes of each game. The Crimson Tide was locked in a scoreless duel with Georgia Tech with a minute and 20 seconds to go in the first half when Bryant put Joe, heavily taped, in the game.

He threw 8 passes in 9 plays, and 2 of them went for touchdowns to break open the game. Alabama finished the regular season the top-ranked team in the country and met Texas in the Orange Bowl. The Tide fell behind, 14–0, until Namath limped onto the field with his gimpy knee in the second quarter. He had reinjured it just four days before the game. He rallied 'Bama by completing 18 passes, a new Orange Bowl record, for 255 yards and 2 touchdowns. With his team trailing 21–17 late in the game, Namath led a drive which took Alabama to a first down on the 6-yard line. Three shots into the line, called from the bench by Bryant, took the ball to the 1-yard line. On fourth down, Namath tried to sneak across and was stopped inches short of the goal as Alabama was toppled from a national championship.

"I didn't plan to play Namath at all," said Bryant, "but he said that he wanted to go in. I thought he was the most courageous player I've ever seen. His knee was badly hurt, but he still wanted to play."

In the meantime the Cardinals and the Jets had both drafted Namath as their No. 1 choice. Joe himself was playing it cool. A dark-haired young lawyer named Mike Bite of the law firm of Bite, Bite & Bite in Birmingham, Alabama, represented the quarterback in his negotiations. The bidding escalated until Sonny Werblin, the president of the Jets, personally signed Namath to a long-term contract the day after the Orange Bowl and handed him the keys to a green (Jets' color) convertible. Joe, of course, wanted to know if the insurance was paid up, too.

The exact figures of Namath's deal with the Jets have never been revealed. The Cardinals, losers in the bidding, said that their offer was almost $400,000. Ergo, the Jets had to top them. Werblin, a shrewd publicity man, never bothered to deny the $400,000 figure, which has been generally accepted as Namath's deal.

One of the New York club's first steps was to put Joe on the operating table. The incision on the knee revealed some ligament as well as cartilage damage. Recuperation was slow. Back in school at Alabama, Namath had to take special exercises, lifting 40-pound weights strapped to his foot. When Coach Weeb Ewbank of the Jets visited Namath on campus and watched him throw, he was satisfied he had his quarterback for '65.

388

A quarterback's lot can be lonely as Joe Namath looks for a receiver in the swirl of battle.

A friendly figure, fullback Matt Snell, flits across his field of vision as Joe Namath winds up to throw the football against Kansas City.

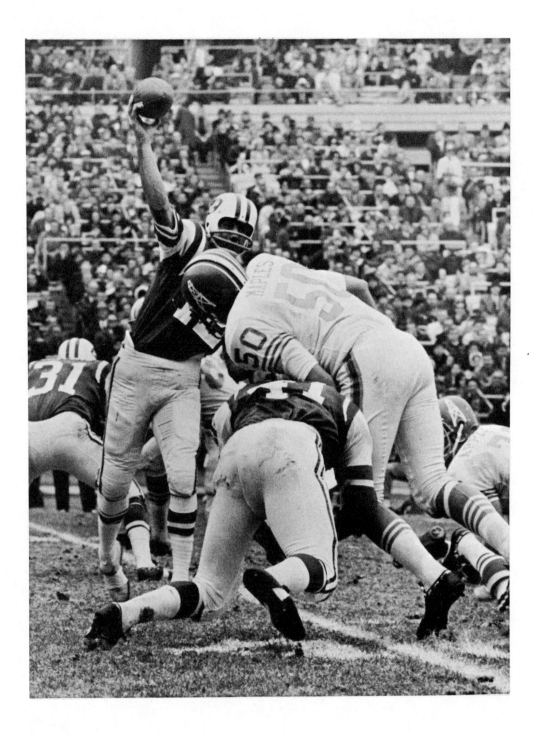

On Joe Namath's greatest day as a pro, he threw four touchdown passes against the Houston Oilers. Bill Mathis (31) and Matt Snell (41) block for him.

The Jets were in a curious position. They'd also signed John Huarte of Notre Dame, the Heisman Trophy winner, for $200,000. The only other quarterback on the roster was Mike Taliaferro, a second-year man who had seen limited service as a rookie. Because of his knee, Namath was excused from the College All-Star game. Huarte went, starred, but was so far behind when he rejoined the Jets that he never caught up to the other two, was never activated and finally was traded to the Boston Patriots after the season.

Ewbank, meanwhile, went slow with Namath. The knee limited Joe's mobility. The quarterback, with a fine instinctive grasp of football, adjusted quickly to the pro system but still had to learn to read defenses and establish rapport with his receivers. His targets—Don Maynard, Bake Turner and Dee Mackey—developed a dismaying habit of dropping passes. Namath alternated with Taliaferro during the exhibition season, but when the Jets opened the regular campaign in Houston, the $400,000 quarterback sat on the bench, answering the phone. He stayed that way the whole day, too, as the Jets lost.

Joe didn't start until the third game of the year, against Buffalo. Two weeks later he lost his starting role back to Taliaferro as the New York attack sputtered miserably. Namath, who had played in only 4 losing games in five years of college and high school football, was on a team that lost its first 4 games, tied 1, then lost another. He wasn't throwing the ball well in practice. He wasn't setting up as quickly as he should. A pro passer throws off his front foot. Joe was wobbling the ball off his rear foot. Maybe he was favoring his knee. His communication with the receivers broke down.

The Jets have a system where the receiver is allowed some freedom in his routes under certain conditions. If the quarterback calls a pass play predicated on man-to-man coverage and the receiver sees the defense shift to a zone, he automatically changes his route. The quarterback is supposed to notice the change in coverage, too, and look for the receiver's new pattern. In theory, it sounds easy. In practice, it puts a lot of pressure on a young quarterback.

The Jets had a chance to beat Oakland in their fifth game. But Maynard, who was supposed to run a sideline pattern on a key fourth-down play, broke his route and took off straight down the field. He fooled Namath, too. Joe threw the ball out of bounds.

He never lost his poise, however. Joe played his first full game as a pro against the blitzing Boston Patriots and rifled two touchdown passes to Maynard to pace a 30–20 victory. He reached his peak as a rookie by bombing the Houston Oilers with 4 touchdown passes in a 41–14 rout. It was the Jets' fourth-straight triumph, and a Buffalo observer, watching Namath's passes fill the TV screen, mused, "You know, he just might be the best quarterback in our league right now."

"I can't figure out whether he's the best I've ever seen," said Cookie Gilchrist, the loquacious veteran fullback of the Denver Broncos, "or is going to be. Tell you this—he's the best quarterback in the AFL right now."

Namath, who walks around with shoulders stooped and a hangdog expression that's the antithesis of the cockiness in his personality, shrugged, "It's just a matter of knowledge. You keep accumulating it every game, every day in practice. Everybody believed the publicity and expected me to come right in and be a hero. You don't do that in the pros."

For his rookie season, he showed respectable figures: 164 completions in 340 attempts, for 2,220 yards and 18 touchdowns. He was the third-ranked passer in the league and was picked for the All-Star squad.

The Buffalo Bills led the Stars, 13–6, at half time with Namath riding the bench while John Hadl of San Diego led the attack. Namath started the third quarter and touched off a scoring spree that led to a 30–19 victory for the All-Stars. He threw two touchdown passes to Lance Alworth, was brilliant in his direction of the attack and walked off with the game's Most Valuable Player Award.

It was the final fillip of his rookie season and established him as the most brilliant young player in football. He also became something of a character. For most of the week in Houston, Joe had sported a little goatee and a mustache to go with the long black hair that he likes to tease. He was also seen in the company of Mamie Van Doren, a Hollywood chanteuse who has adorned the arm of baseball's Bo Belinsky from time to time. At game time, however, Joe showed up clean-shaven.

"My mother," he explained, "might be looking at the game and see me. I tried coming home that way one time when I was at Alabama. She took one look and said, 'Shave it off. You don't even look Hungarian.'"

Joe gave the AFL its first authentic young quarterback star. The league in its formative years had lagged behind the NFL in signing the good passers coming out of football. Only one other AFL-bred quarterback, John Hadl, could be considered a regular.

Hadl was an All-American triple-threat back at Kansas who signed with the San Diego Chargers in 1962 because they promised him a full shot at quarterback, whereas the Detroit Lions of the NFL, who also drafted him, hinted they'd prefer him as a halfback.

Although he has led the Chargers to one division championship on his own and helped in producing two others as the back-up man for Tobin Rote, Hadl operates under a distinct handicap as a quarterback. He doesn't throw a football in the classic style.

"He threw the greatest end-over-end pass I'd ever seen," winced Coach Sid Gillman of the Chargers as he recollected his first exposure to Hadl's passing. "The receivers almost died till it got there."

Hadl admitted he couldn't spiral a ball the first two or three weeks in camp. He throws the ball from the shoulder like a snub-nose howitzer. After four seasons, the kidding hasn't eased.

End Don Norton of the Chargers ran a route during a passing drill, stuck one hand up nonchalantly for the ball and dropped it. When he came back to the huddle, Hadl chided him, "Ever hear of two hands, Don?"

"Yeah," answered Norton. "You ever hear of a spiral?"

Yet this unpretty passer led the AFL in 1965 with 174 completions in 348 attempts, an even .500, and had 20 touchdown passes to his credit. Hadl is an athlete. He's a strong runner, has a quick release with his shoulder-holster delivery and is an assertive leader. When the Chargers had a bad game against Boston, he mounted a bench in the

392

Bill Munson was one of those rare rookies who stepped into a regular role for the Los Angeles Rams in 1964.

Munson has exhibited amazing poise against such veteran defensive terrors as Doug Atkins (81) of the Chicago Bears.

Malcolm W. Emmons

Bill Nelsen solidified his position as the regular quarterback of the Pittsburgh Steelers in 1965, though he played on a bad knee.

dressing room and yelled, "Only reason we lose is because we beat ourselves. You guys goofed off in practice. Me, too. From now on we all work."

He's inured to criticism of his throwing style. "When I first came into the league," he shrugged, "people said I wouldn't make it. I made it. Now they say I won't be great. They don't bother me. The only guy I worry about is Sid Gillman."

The AFL in the last couple of years has produced a bevy of young quarterbacks who are on the verge of a breakthrough. The one with the most native talent is Pete Beathard of Kansas City. If his arm ever went dead, Pete could become a regular defensive back. He has the size (6–2, 205), the intelligence and the strong arm to be an outstanding pro. He needs only experience.

At the University of Southern California, he was the regular quarterback on a Rose Bowl team, as a junior, with senior Bill Nelsen playing second-string. Nelsen went on to become the starting quarterback for the Pittsburgh Steelers in 1965. Beatherd, in his first two years with the KC Chiefs, was stymied by the presence of veteran Len Dawson. He also showed a tendency to stray from his passing pocket. But he'll be outstanding some day.

Daryle Lamonica of Buffalo is another strong-running quarterback. The big Notre Dame graduate was a twenty-fourth-round draft choice for the 1964 season. As a high school kid in Fresno, California, he was better known for his shortstop prowess in baseball and spurned a $50,000 contract offer from the Chicago Cubs. With the Bills, he became a football relief pitcher instead. As a rookie on the '64 Bills, Lamonica showed a facility for coming off the bench and picking up the offense from Jack Kemp. The Bills, on a steamroller to the championship, won their first 9 games of the year, and husky (6–3) Daryle was the man who led them from behind in 6 of those victories. He was the third-best rusher on the Buffalo team, with 289 yards gained in 55 carries, and in passing had a phenomenal total of 1137 yards on 55 completions.

Daryle recognized the futility of being pegged as a scrambler. "The only friend a quarterback has when he runs with the ball," said Daryle, "is the sideline." Like Beatherd, he has been stuck behind an established pro, Kemp. Lamonica's service was limited in '65 because of Kemp's great season.

In Houston, Don Trull has to wait for George Blanda to wear out. Trull led the nation's colleges in passing two years in a row, 1962–63, at Baylor. He has to fight a tendency to scramble, too. Trull still must prove himself as a long passer. Otherwise, his credentials are sound.

The turnover to the kids has been, surprisingly, faster in the older National Football League.

The foremost example of a young quarterback who wasted no time in making a place for himself is Bill Munson of the Los Angeles Rams. Bill was an outstanding quarterback on a fine Utah State team but attracted little national attention at a time when Roger Staubach of Navy, George Mira of Miami and Don Trull of Baylor were the big names in college passing. The Rams drafted him first in 1964, which surprised some people. But Coach Harland Svare said he had a quicker release than Norm Van Brocklin. They called him the fastest in the West since Wyatt Earp.

The quarterback spot in Los Angeles was supposed to be reserved for Roman Gabriel, heralded as a potential great almost every year since he first showed up in 1962. Gabriel has not been a decisive leader, however. When he bruised a knee during the '64 exhibition season, Munson jumped into a starting job as a rookie, yielded the job briefly to Gabriel at mid-season and then reclaimed it in the final month. Munson is 6–2, 197, with a smooth throwing motion.

He was the Ram regular again in '65 until he hurt his knee and missed the last month after submitting to a cartilage operation. Los Angeles is firmly committed to Munson as the man who'll make the Rams a winner again.

As a rookie with the Washington Redskins in 1964, Dick Shiner threw exactly 1 pass. But as a sophomore pro, he briefly supplanted Sonny Jurgensen as the regular quarterback. The blond 6-footer was the greatest passer in Maryland history as a collegian.

Bill Nelsen has never been a first-choice passer. He was a second-stringer at Southern California, though recognized as an outstanding long thrower. The Pittsburgh Steelers kept him around for a couple of years to fill out the roster while veteran Ed Brown did almost all the work. When they soured on Brown, they tried to give the job to rookie Tommy Wade of Texas. But Nelsen did such a brilliant job in an exhibition game in Atlanta against the Baltimore Colts that the Steelers were forced to promote him to No. 1. Bill played most of the 1965 season with a floating cartilage but refused treatment until it was over.

George Mira has had limited opportunities to play behind John Brodie at San Francisco. Mira is in the Francis Tarkenton modern mold of quarterback—an elusive scrambler, tough to nail behind the line. Mira sometimes has to run because he lacks the ideal height for a quarterback. He's under 6 feet, but he was an All-American at Miami and passed for more than 5,000 yards in his varsity career. The little dynamo from Key West, Florida, remains an exciting prospect.

Craig Morton of the Dallas Cowboys is at the other end of the pole. He looks the field over from a commanding height of 6 feet 4 inches but doesn't have the quickness of a Mira behind the line. He's slower than the others in setting up, too. Craig's greatest asset is a powerful, accurate arm. The Cowboys put the former California star in some tough spots last year. He played all the way, for instance, against the Green Bay Packers.

Nevertheless, for playing under pressure, the blue ribbon goes to Gary Cuozzo of the Baltimore Colts. Here's an example of why no young quarterback should ever despair. Gary has had the thankless role of playing second-string to John Unitas since the Colts picked him up as a free agent in 1963.

Gary could have had a shot at a Rhodes scholarship when he was a straight-A student at Virginia. He was actually accepted by Yale Medical School, studied law at Johns Hopkins and in recent terms has been attending the Tennessee Dental School. None of this has much to do with playing quarterback for the Baltimore Colts but should show how bright Master Cuozzo is.

He wasn't drafted by the pros at Virginia because the impression had been fostered that Gary wanted only to become a doctor. But he responded to the challenge when the

John Hadl (21) of San Diego has convinced skeptics leadership can compensate for mechanical defects in his passing.

The Kansas City Chiefs have brought Pete Beathard (10) along slowly as their quarterback of the future.

Colts contacted him, even though it meant sitting by a phone every Sunday while John Unitas played interminably.

The Colts tested him in preseason trials, however, and liked what they saw. He's built along the same lines as Unitas. He throws the same sharp kind of pass. There's no question about his brightness. The toughest thing, he said, was to come into the dressing room after a game the Colts had won and know that he wasn't really part of it, that he hadn't contributed.

"The biggest problem," he said, "is how to keep myself ready. On game day, I'm as ready to play as John Unitas."

In November of 1965, Unitas was bruised by the Chicago Bears and relieved by Cuozzo, who threw an important touchdown pass in a 26–21 triumph. The next week Unitas could have played, but Coach Don Shula demonstrated faith in his young apprentice by letting him start and play all the way against the Minnesota Vikings. After a sputtering first half, Cuozzo wound up the afternoon throwing 5 touchdown passes. He knew that day that he had contributed, though Unitas was restored to the starting lineup the next week.

Late in the year, the Bears again damaged Unitas, this time permanently. Cuozzo couldn't retrieve a losing cause in that game, but he was the man entrusted with quarterback command the following week against the Green Bay Packers. A victory would have clinched the title for Baltimore. Gary couldn't produce it. In the third quarter he suffered a shoulder separation. But the gutty stand-in came back from hasty repairs in the dressing room to take the field again and fire 2 touchdown passes which kept the Packers on the hook until late in the final period.

Gary played no more once the X rays confirmed the separation. However, the Baltimore Colts felt no tremors as they contemplated the future. Unitas, with a knee operation, might be a risk. But the percentages are with a team that also has a talent like Gary Cuozzo on the roster.

The New Breed is the quarterback insurance of tomorrow.

17. The Wrapup

THE OLD SOLDIER NEVER DIES . . . HE
SIMPLY FADES AWAY.

> —*General of the Army
> Douglas MacArthur,
> addressing the Congress.*

Rudy Bukich of Chicago hit the jackpot as a pro passer in his 11th season.

Malcolm W. Emmons

The quarterback is bred for longevity. As long as he can raise his trusty right arm there is a place for him in professional football. The skills fade so subtly that a team is loath to let the veteran field general fade into obscurity, because his specific blending of experience and tactical execution is so integral to good performance.

The quarterback may be slightly flawed. Not everyone combines the diverse qualities of John Unitas. But once a man reaches the professional level, the shades of difference are so pale that few can discern them technically. One man throws a little sharper than the other; one man thinks a little better in the clutch. But the variations are not enough to matter. If the man is a pro he's worth retaining indefinitely. He may not always win for you, but he'll be competent.

And so quarterbacks have made careers for themselves without reaching the heights of an Otto Graham or a Sid Luckman or a John Unitas. These are some of them.

RUDY BUKICH, Chicago Bears:

For ten years in the National Football League, Rudy Bukich made more money for doing less than almost any man in professional football history. He was the perennial benchwarmer. He kept his nose clean, showed up punctually for practice and almost never played. He came into pro ball with the Los Angeles Rams as the possessor of a great passing arm, which he had displayed in firing the University of Southern California to the Pacific coast's first Rose Bowl victory over a Big Ten team. He stayed on the Ram's roster for five years (including a couple in military service) behind such established performers as Norm Van Brocklin and Billy Wade. If Rudy was unhappy, nobody ever knew about it. In practice he threw his usual pretty pass. On Sundays he kept his uniform spotless. Word got around slowly. Great arm, but he wasn't smart enough to be a quarterback in pro ball. The Rams traded him to the Washington Redskins, who didn't keep him past training camp. He was picked up by the Bears, who were collecting quarterbacks by the "B"—Ed Brown, Zeke Bratkowski, George Blanda. In 1960 the Bears sent him to the Pittsburgh Steelers in one of those peculiar lendlease deals that only a patriarch like George Halas could effect, and Rudy sat some more— behind Bobby Layne. But in 1961, Layne got hurt and Rudy played in 7 straight games, more than he had in seven years. The next fall he was back in Chicago, rejoined with his old Ram pal, Billy Wade. He threw 13 passes the whole year. But imperceptibly, ambition had grabbed Rudy. He went to school in the off-season and got his master's degree in educational administration and started working on his doctorate. Say, this guy was smart after all. When Wade slumped in '64, Rudy threw 12 touchdown passes in one stretch of 4 games, then suffered a shoulder separation. When the Bears lost their first 3 games in '65, Bukich replaced veteran Billy as the Bear regular. In his eleventh year as a pro he had finally won a starting job on his own merit. Handsome Rudy made capital of the opportunity. The Bears, also sparked by rookie Gale Sayers at halfback, became the hottest team in football. Rudy dealt a torrid hand at quarterback. He led the league in passing. At the age of thirty-three he had arrived as a pro.

403

EARL MORRALL, New York Giants:

On first impression, Earl Morrall is a mousy type of character. He doesn't offer that firm handshake. His smile is bashfully aloof. He doesn't come on strong. He never did. Earl's football career is full of peaks and valleys. He was an All-American quarterback on a very good Michigan State team a decade ago. This caused the San Francisco 49ers to make him their No. 1 draft choice for 1956, athough they already had Y. A. Tittle on hand. The 49ers let him absorb one season of relief work, then shipped him to the Pittsburgh Steelers because they had drafted John Brodie of Stanford. Earl stepped into a regular job with the Steelers and absorbed a valuable year of playing experience. But when the Steelers had a chance to acquire Bobby Layne early in '58 they sent Morrall in exchange to the Lions, and Earl was back home in his native Michigan. He stayed for seven years, carefully nurturing a reputation as a relief man. The Lions didn't hesitate to use him in a game, but they stopped just shy of entrusting their offense to him. In succession, he played behind Tobin Rote, Jim Ninowski and Milt Plum. The breakthrough came in 1963 when he ousted Plum as the regular quarterback and threw 24 touchdown passes. But the next season he was back in his old relief role at the start. Then after he had ousted Plum again, a fractured collarbone in the sixth game put him out of commission for the year. The Plum-Morrall entente looked like a perpetual see-saw until Harry Gilmer was named head coach of the Lions for 1965. Gilmer believed in the one-quarterback system. Morrall and Plum were too good to be sitting around half the time. During the preseason games he made his choice: Plum. Morrall was traded to the New York Giants, who were desperate for quarterback help. Coach Allie Sherman discovered he had a pro who mastered his system overnight and led the Giants to an amazing second-place finish in the Eastern Conference. For the first time since his brief tenure in Pittsburgh, Earl was in complete charge. The Giants were a young team. The ten-year vet offered them stability. His passing was sharper than ever. At Detroit he had a reputation for being erratic in his throwing. With the Giants he was uniformly accurate up until the last day of the season. New York already was making comparisons with the amazing revival Y. A. Tittle had experienced when he came to the Giants late in his career.

NORMAN SNEAD, Philadelphia Eagles:

In his five seasons in the National Football League, Norman Snead has never played on a team whose victory total matched its losses. This has, of course, labelled him a loser. In Philadelphia, there is one dissenter. Pete Retzlaff, the veteran all-pro end, had been harboring thoughts about retirement. "But Norm was so tremendous the last half of the season," said Pete, "I'm confident he could quarterback us to an Eastern title in '66." Whereupon he decided to come back for another year. Snead has always attracted this kind of tribute. When Otto Graham saw the lanky Virginian in the College All-Star camp of 1961, he glowed, "Best-equipped kid I've had to step right into pro ball. He's a natural." Snead stands 6–4 and has a limber arm. The Washington Redskins had chosen him as their first draft choice ahead of such other possibilities as Francis Tarkenton of Georgia. Snead played at Wake Forest and broke 15 Atlantic

404

Norman Snead of the Eagles has never been anything but a regular since he broke in with Washington in 1961. His old Redskin mates put a rush on Snead (16).

Earl Morrall found the Giants just as comforting to a veteran quarterback as did Y. A. Tittle, his predecessor.

The maturing of Don Meredith had a lot to do with the second place finish of the Dallas Cowboys in 1965.

The latent talents of Milt Plum keep the Detroit Lions hopeful he'll put a big season together.

Coast Conference records in passing, though his team managed just one winning season in his three varsity years. Big Norman always seems to have fought the battle of inadequate support. With his arrival, the Redskins gave up on Ralph Guglielmi as the regular quarterback and installed Snead in his rookie season. It was a tough baptism. The Redskins won just 1 game that year. But in 1962, they broke the color line by trading with Cleveland for Bobby Mitchell, who was converted from halfback to flanker. Snead-to-Mitchell became the biggest act in football for 7 games as the Redskins roared through the first half of the season undefeated (they tied 2). Defenses became bomb-conscious against the Redskins. They double- and triple-teamed Mitchell the second time around. The Skins collapsed and lost 7 straight. The slide continued through another year. Though Snead continued as the regular, the opposition felt they could read him clearly. He didn't mix up his attack. It was Mitchell, or else. With the coaching regime on the spot, Snead was traded to the Eagles in 1964 for Sonny Jurgensen in one of those moves by losers that figure a change of scenery will help both sides. After two years with the Eagles, Snead could count up five seasons of experience in pro ball, and Coach Joe Kuharich was confident they added up to a mature, poised signal caller who had acquired the knack of recognizing defenses and was ready to be a leader. Norm had once entertained thoughts of joining the Peace Corps. But there was still a personal battle to be won at home.

DON MEREDITH, Dallas Cowboys:

"The quarterback is the difference in pro ball," said Tom Landry, the coach of the Dallas Cowboys. "He has to make the big play to win, and Don now can make it." Tom's confidence in Don Meredith has not always been that positive. He could be accused of fickleness. Landry was an original Meredith fan when Tom was still the defensive coach of the New York Giants and Don was throwing passes for Southern Methodist University. He said at that time young Meredith was the best passing prospect he had ever seen for pro ball because of his mobility and snappy arm delivery. So when Landry became the coach of the newly-formed Cowboys in 1960 and Meredith was the first man drafted, it looked like a natural weld of talents. But Tom is a grimly devoted football tactician, with controlled emotions, and he found in Meredith an opposite personality. Don is glib, outwardly cocky, fun-loving. He didn't apply himself to the job of mastering the nuances of quarterbacking. The slow development could be tolerated for a couple of years because the Cowboys had little Eddie LeBaron to shoulder the heavy work while Don learned his lessons. In 1962 Landry accelerated Meredith's program. He played more than LeBaron, but his work was spotty. He scrambled more than he had to; his passing was erratic. "He's okay when things are going normal," said veteran end Bill Howton, "but he can't reach back in a tight spot and give you that big play." Meredith's reckless running also made him injury prone. He played the '64 season with injuries ranging from torn knee cartilage to shoulder sprains, ankle sprains, bone bruises and stomach-muscle rupture. Hampered by a bad shoulder in training for the '65 season, feuding with the coaches, Meredith passed poorly at the start of the campaign. Landry even tried running his quarterbacks in by shifts, alternating Meredith and rookies Craig Morton and Jerry Rhome. For an important

407

game against Green Bay, he sidetracked Don altogether for young Morton. But at mid-season the Cowboys suddenly gave the reins completely to the lanky (6–3) native Texan. He drove them to 5 victories in 7 games and a second-place finish, highest in Cowboy history. He also threw for 22 touchdowns, a career high, and showed, at the age of 27, a maturity and definite purpose in his play that indicated he still may bear out Landry's original evaluation. The Cowboys are a young, coming team. Meredith fits that groove, too.

MILT PLUM, Detroit Lions:

Milt Plum is everything a quarterback should be, except a leader. He could evade that responsibility as long as he played for the Cleveland Browns during the time Paul Brown treated his quarterbacks as robots. Paul sent in the plays, and Milt carried them out. He never dreamed of countermanding the boss's orders. But Milt faced a moment of decision in one game when Brown forgot to send in the usual messenger. The clock was running out at the end of the half. There was time for only one play, and the Browns were in scoring position. A pass was the obvious call, but Milt kept looking to the sideline. On the previous play, Brown had ordered a fullback sweep to the short side. "So Milt played it real cool," said Jimmy Brown. "He simply called me again on the same play, although we were hemmed in on that side of the field." The Browns, of course, did not score. After five years with Cleveland, Milt boasted the best passing completion average in pro history, but the Browns had never won a championship. So he was traded to the Detroit Lions for Jim Ninowski. "We were depending on a running back to be the No. 1 man," explained Paul Brown, "instead of the quarterback. To win in pro ball, you must have the big gun." Plum retorted that Brown never gave him the option of changing the plays in his stereotyped offense. "You've got to recognize defenses," shrugged Brown, "before you can do anything about them." And it was pointed out that in a game against New York, the Cleveland quarterback was given an audible to call at the line of scrimmage against a certain Giant defense. The game films showed that the Giants used that defense eleven times, and Plum never called the audible. Given new freedom when he went to Detroit in 1962, Milt sparked the Lions to an 11–3 record and a strong second-place finish behind Green Bay. The season turned on a third-down pass play late in a game with the Packers. The Lions held a slim 7–6 margin. Plum's receiver slipped and fell as the ball was thrown, and the Packers' Herb Adderley picked off the pass to set up the winning field goal. Coach George Wilson of the Lions shouldered the blame for the call. Plum lost his job to Earl Morrall in 1963, regained it in 64 and then was the man the Lions kept when they had to make a choice between him and Morrall as the regular in '65. He tends to be phlegmatic. Defeats don't touch him like they do some other players. But Milt is also a picture-book passer and physically strong. He once beat the Colts on a 45-yard keeper up the middle. Coaches are loath to give up on him.

BILLY WADE, Chicago:

Billy Wade is a picture of dignity. A spot of gray hair at the temples imparts just the right touch of authority. He speaks with the zeal of an evangelist. Billy's been ex-

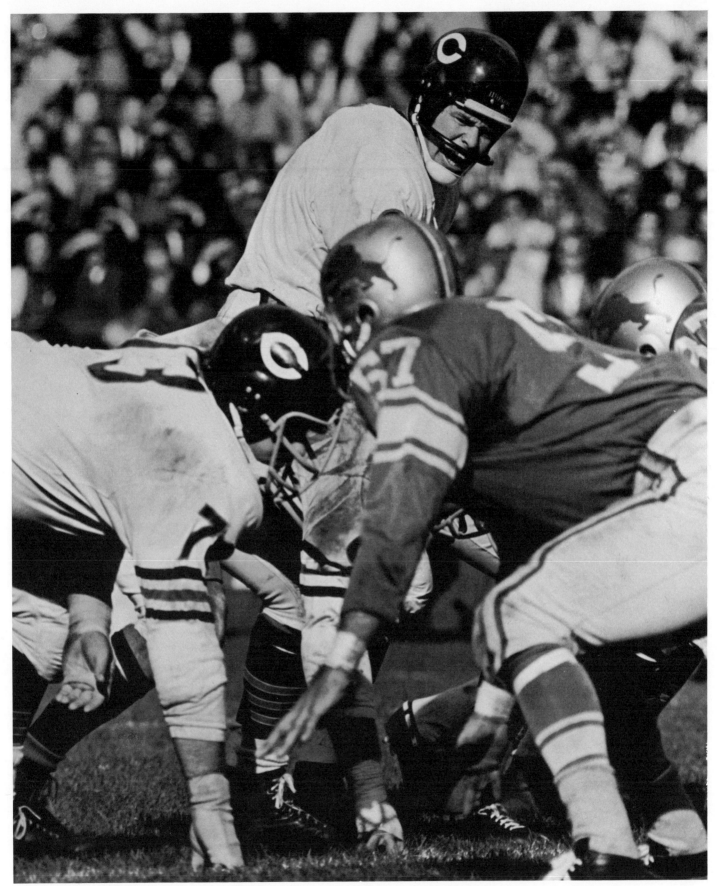

For at least one year, 1963, Billy Wade proved he could lead a team (the Chicago Bears) to a championship.

When Bart Starr was hurt in '65, the Green Bay Packers had a competent replacement in veteran Zeke Bratkowski.

tremely active in the Fellowship of Christian Athletes movement. His own life is exemplary. But his football career, except for one brief year, has been a series of frustrations. Billy's father was the captain of an undefeated football team at Vanderbilt University in 1921, and Billy followed in his footsteps as a star quarterback for the Commodores. The Los Angeles Rams drew the bonus choice in the college draft of 1952 and picked Billy above every man in the country. That was one of the great rookie crops of all time, including such stars as Ollie Matson, Frank Gifford, Hugh McElhenny and Gino Marchetti. When Wade reported to the Rams after two years in service, they made room for him alongside Norm Van Brocklin. Eventually, Billy chased the Dutchman to the Philadelphia Eagles. A good runner, a strong thrower and a fine ball-handler, Billy settled down for a long tenure as the Ram quarterback. But Los Angeles is a pressure spot when the team isn't winning. Billy got them a respectable 8–4 record and second-place money in 1958; the Rams became steady losers after that. The flaw in Wade was a certain indecision. He was frequently dropped for long losses while debating whether to run or throw. In 1961 the Rams gave up and traded him to the Chicago Bears. Billy passed the ball to his heart's content—412 attempts in 1962—yet the skeptics insisted that he wasn't the type to carry a team to a championship. So the Bears won the championship of the Western Conference in 1963, then toppled the New York Giants in the title playoff as Wade scored 2 touchdowns. Still the cynics derided his part in the victory and credited an amazing defensive effort for the championship surge of the Bears. Billy, as a result, tends to be a little bitter in his relations with the press and their slow acceptance of him as a top-flight quarterback. After a decade of pro football, he also found himself struggling to hold a job after producing a title. Rudy Bukich displaced him during the '64 season and again the following fall, while Wade went to the bench. At the age of thirty-six, Billy's future could no longer be called bright. The gray at the temples only accentuated his plight.

ZEKE BRATKOWSKI, Green Bay:

Probably the greatest tribute that has come to Edmund (Zeke) Bratkowski as a pro was his omission from the expansion list of players made available to the new Atlanta franchise in 1966. In the strict sense of the word, Zeke should have been an expendable. He would be thirty-five years old the next football season. After a full decade of experience Zeke could not be considered anything more than a spot performer to be used only in case of emergency. Fortunately for Zeke and his immediate future with the champion Green Bay Packers, such emergencies arose frequently enough in his last couple of years with them to make Coach Vince Lombardi consider him an indispensable member of the cast. A notable example was the playoff game for the Western Conference title between the Packers and the Baltimore Colts on December 26, 1965. On the first play from scrimmage, Bart Starr was helped off the field with severely bruised ribs which prevented him from raising his arm in a normal throwing motion. Zeke responded to the call and gave the Packers a workmanlike performance at quarterback which carried them into a sudden-death overtime and a thrilling victory. Zeke completed 22 of 39 passes for 248 yards, exceeding his total of completions for the

411

Although George Blanda began his pro career in 1949, the Houston Oilers keep him exercising his passing arm.

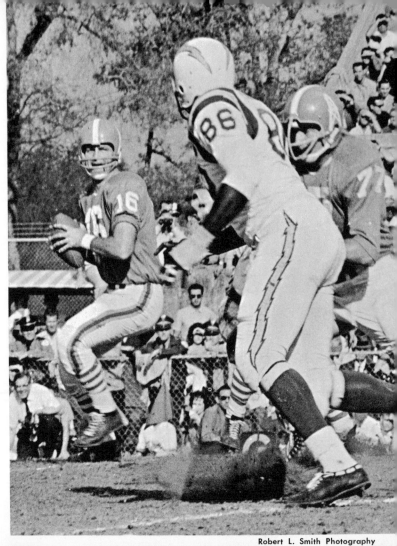

It takes an old hand like Babe Parilli (15) of the Boston Patriots to keep cool in this kind of jam against Buffalo.

regular season by one. A man who can respond like that "cold" is worth retaining. And if you think there's no sentiment left in football, consider this: Starr was back for the championship game against Cleveland and delivered his usual superb effort. With the clock running out, the Packers had a safe 23–12 lead and possession of the ball. From the sidelines, Zeke Bratkowski ran on the field, at Lombardi's behest, to handle the last snap from center. He would always be able to say he had played in a championship game. Zeke might have made it in 1956 with the championship Chicago Bears, but he was in the army. When the Bears first displayed him as a rookie in 1954, they felt the Georgia graduate would be the next great quarterback in football, even exceeding their own Sid Luckman. But two years in service rusted his skills. In five seasons with the Bears he was never able to pin down a regular job and was traded to the Rams for Billy Wade. Zeke lacked that little bit of extra quickness to be a top-notch quarterback. In his second year in Los Angeles, he was supplanted by rookie Roman Gabriel, and in 1963 the Packers picked him up as an insurance quarterback in case anything happened to incumbent Bart Starr. It was a provident move, both for them and Zeke.

GEORGE BLANDA, Houston Oilers:

Young Joe Namath was just entering the first grade in Beaver Falls, Pennsylvania, when George Blanda, who also comes from western Pennsylvania, played his first game of professional football. The year was 1949, and George was fresh out of the University of Kentucky, where he played for Bear Bryant, who was to coach Namath as a collegian, too. The Chicago Bears were choosy about their quarterbacks in those days. They had men like Sid Luckman, Johnny Lujack and Bobby Layne. Blanda lasted ten years with the Bears, a quarterback tenure exceeded only by Luckman in that team's illustrious history. He is still the top scorer in Bear history, because George early in his career demonstrated a proficiency at place-kicking. Only three quarterbacks in Bear history completed more passes. George's quarterbacking was eclipsed by his kicking, so it's not generally remembered that from 1952 through 1954, when he suffered a severe shoulder injury, he reigned as the field general of the Bears, too. All this, however, served as a prelude to George Blanda's real career in professional football. He had retired in 1959 to become a Chicago businessman for a trucking firm. A year later the American Football League was organized, and George wangled his release from the Bears to become a charter member of the Houston Oilers. In a league where inexperience was rampant, Blanda was a dominant figure. The tough old pro led the Oilers to three straight Eastern Conference titles and two championships. He holds virtually every passing record in the AFL, and in six years gained 10 miles through the air. George also holds the record for being controversial. As Blanda grew older—he was thirty-three years old when he started in the AFL—Oiler coaches like Pop Ivy tried to induce him to cut down his activity. George demurred. Youngsters Jackie Lee and Don Trull tried to break his stranglehold on the job. The Oilers always went back to Blanda because you can't beat that experience. With the 1966 season he will tie Y. A. Tittle for longevity in professional football (seventeen seasons). Blanda's arm is apparently tireless. He set a pro record of 505 attempts and 262 completions in 1964. He keeps in good shape. His kicking is still important to the Oilers. "I'll know it's time to quit," he said, "by whether or not I can get rid of the ball, whether I can still elude some people and when I can't get the ball to the ball carrier on a handoff." Since he pulls down $38,000 a year, it'll take a lot to convince him.

VITO (BABE) PARILLI, Boston Patriots:

Mike Holovak, the coach of the Boston Patriots, has skimped on filling out his staff because of Babe Parilli. He anticipates that Babe might quit playing quarterback some day, and he's saving a spot as an assistant coach for him. The problem, from Mike's standpoint, is that he needs Parilli more as a player, although the Kentucky Babe's hair is flecked with gray and he undoubtedly has lost a shade of his spryness. Parilli has been around professional football since 1952; only Blanda has lasted longer. The Babe, a high school fullback in Rochester, Pennsylvania, followed Blanda at Kentucky and was converted to quarterback. He was a unanimous All-American for Bear Bryant, a brilliant stylist both in his maneuvers behind center and in his passing. When the Green Bay Packers, in the doldrums, drafted the Sweet Kentucky Babe in 1952, they envisioned him as the man who would save the franchise because he seemed to have every qualification necessary for pro success. The Packers already had an established quarterback, Tobin Rote, but let the Babe divide time with him for two years. Parilli's progress was aborted by an army call which kept him away from football for two years. While he was gone the Packers traded him to the Cleveland Browns, who desperately sought a successor for the retired Otto Graham. When Babe reported in 1956, he was rusty and unsure of himself. Coach Paul Brown was impatient. The Babe is a sensitive man. He couldn't take Brown's prodding and broke out with a case of nervous hives. The experience was demoralizing. When he was returned to Green Bay a year later, his confidence was shattered. Eventually he was released and played a year in Canada. The formation of the AFL gave him a shot with the Oakland Raiders. After the first year he was traded to the Boston Patriots and under the gentle touch of Mike Holovak reestablished himself as a first-class quarterback. The Patriots, without many name players, were never expected to do much. With the Babe directing their attack, they were always in contention and even won a division title in 1963. In 1964 he tossed 31 touchdown passes and was a unanimous choice for All-League quarterback.

LEN DAWSON, Kansas City:

Len Dawson's special niche in pro football comes from the toss of the coin. He was the pawn as the Pittsburgh Steelers and the Cleveland Browns, tied in the standings, flipped to see who would get the chance to pick first in the college draft for the 1957 season. Both wanted Dawson, who had concluded a sensational career at Purdue by leading the Big Ten in total offense and passing for three straight years. The Steelers won and got Dawson. The Browns, of course, had to settle for a young fullback from Syracuse named Jimmy Brown, who was their second choice. Before Dawson had a chance to develop with the Steelers, they acquired veteran Bobby Layne and Lenny was stuck in the shadow of the big man. "Lenny Dawson can outrun me any day in the

414

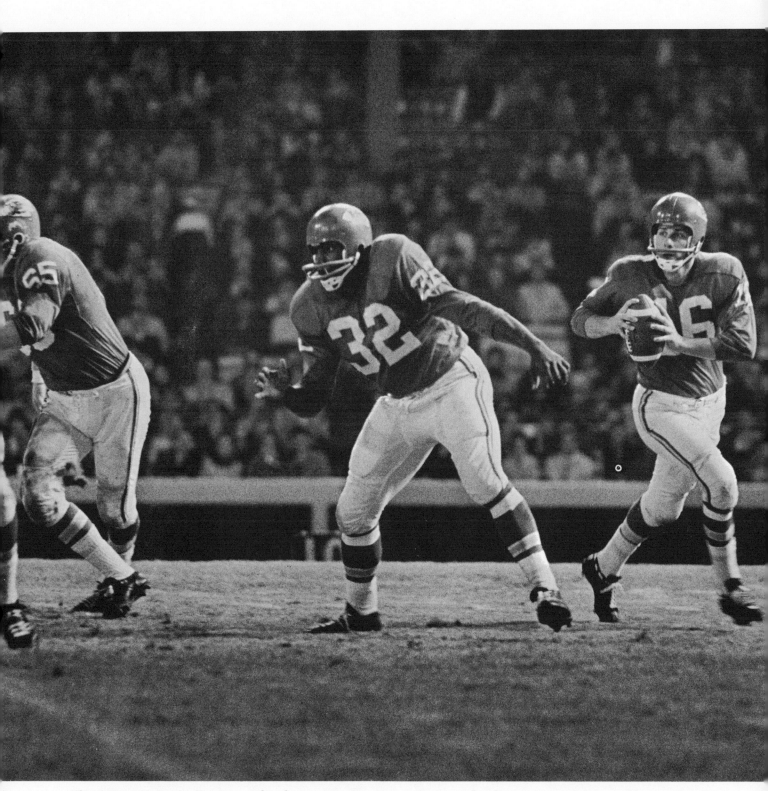

The AFL gave Lenny Dawson, right, the opportunity to prove he was a big league passer, for the Dallas Texans and Kansas City Chiefs.

week," said Layne, "and has just as strong and accurate an arm as me. He should be great some day. All he needs is a chance to get into an important game and click." In three years, Dawson threw a total of 17 passes. The Steelers traded him to the Browns, the team that wanted him in the first place. It was just as futile for Lenny playing behind Milt Plum. He rarely got in a game. Maybe it was his personality. Lenny's on the quiet side. He's not impressive to look at—barely 6 feet, on the slim side, almost ascetic-looking. When he saw he was getting no place again during the 1962 training camp, he requested and received his release from the Browns. He joined the Dallas Texans of the AFL in time to start the season. Why the Texans? Their coach was Hank Stram, who was well acquainted with the young quarterback since he had been Lenny's back-field tutor at Purdue. Lenny shook the dust off his five years on the bench and flipped the Texans to an AFL championship. He had a great year, completing 61 percent of his passes, throwing for 29 touchdowns, stabilizing a young team on which he was the only one who had ever played in the NFL. The Texans were moved to Kansas City in 1963 and became the Chiefs. The move didn't bother Lenny—who was that much closer to his old home in Alliance, Ohio—or affect his passing. He has stayed consistently near the top of the league in passing, and led the AFL for a second time in 1964. However, the young Chiefs were visibly disturbed by the switch and floundered below their potential as a team. At various times, Lenny has been hurt but missed very little action. He's a sound, conservative quarterback who doesn't excite the people but has definitely proved in the younger league that he's better than a perennial bench-warmer.

416

18. The Composite

The ideal quarterback in professional football doesn't have to be a combination of Frank Merriwell, Clark Kent, Tom Swift and Batman. He can relate to actual flesh and blood, and by drawing out the best qualities of the men who have been featured in this position over the last quarter of a century, it's possible to draw a composite portrait.

The qualities embrace both the tangible—the ability to complete passes—and the intangible—leadership, intuition. The shades of definition aren't always too distinguishable in analyzing the individual talents of the great T-formation quarterbacks, so it can be a provocative composition. For instance, how do you know Norm Van Brocklin threw a better long pass than Y. A. Tittle, or Eddie LeBaron was a better ball handler than Frankie Albert?

I know it'll raise some argument but based on personal observation and consultation with coaches, this is how the ideal quarterback can be assembled:

• Give him the confidence of Otto Graham, who never wavered.

• He must have the passing arm of Sammy Baugh, who threw a football better than any man who ever lived.

• Let him handle the ball like Eddie LeBaron, who didn't have big hands but revealed a dexterity you find only in Las Vegas dealers.

• He should run like Francis Tarkenton, the super-scrambler of the Minnesota Vikings, to avoid the posse of tacklers.

• Imbue him with the leadership of Bobby Layne, a benevolent despot in getting the most out of his team.

• I want him to have the mental alertness of Sid Luckman, the original model for the pro T quarterback.

• He needs the analytical finesse of Bart Starr, who has more discipline than any signal caller in history.

• He can use the dedication of Y. A. Tittle, for whom the game of football became a ritual of living.

• And all the qualities are best combined in John Unitas, who borrowed from all and made himself into the best quarterback of his time.

The most successful quarterback in history has been Graham, who once listed the six basic skills that go into the making of a winning quarterback:

1. *Ability to throw the football.* "A successful pro quarterback must be able to hit his target 99⁴⁴⁄₁₀₀ percent of the time," said Otto. But percentages aren't the criterion. The great passer knows when to throw the ball—the intuitive moment his receiver is open. He also sacrifices his completion average occasionally to avoid an interception or a long loss. Bobby Layne threw long bombs that had minimal chance of clicking because they spread the defense for his short yardage game, on the ground and in the air.

2. *Natural instincts.* These are directly allied with the ability to pass, as noted, in the instinctive timing that tells a passer when to release the ball. The delicate mechanism of timing is a gift of nature. So is the coordination of hand and eye which enables him to carry out what the quick reflexes of the brain tell him must be done. The natural instincts also invade the field of signal calling and recognition of defenses, when a split second reaction lets the quarterback know, without any lengthy reasoning process, what has to be done to meet the particular situation. In other words, some got it and some ain't.

3. *Leadership.* Another intangible quality which can be manifested in diverse ways. Bobby Layne espoused the tough, marine drill sergeant line, driving his men through the absolute dynamism of his personality. Bart Starr, quiet and resolved, is very much the leader, too, though his coercion is gentle. His approach is more professional. Each has merits.

4. *Ability to run.* There are two types. Tarkenton is the super-scrambler, always a dodge ahead of trouble, improvising as he scampers, depending on his quickness to avoid tacklers. Tobin Rote, when he was with Green Bay and Detroit, ran planned patterns with the strength of a fullback. But he was unusual. Except for one brief period in the mid-1950s, most coaches have hesitated to risk their quarterbacks on running plays from scrimmage and don't carry more than one or two in their repertoire. Essentially, a quarterback's running ability boils down to quickness, and even a notorious slow-foot like Van Brocklin had the quickness to set up in a hurry, though he was handicapped when he was forced to leave his passing pocket.

5. *Play calling.* Again there are two schools of thought. There is the conservative, percentage brand espoused by Bart Starr, predicated on confidence in execution. And there is the daring, unorthodox gamble practiced with just as much confidence by such strategists as Bobby Layne and particularly John Unitas. The important thing is for a quarterback not to get into a pattern. Even Unitas, who boldly passed on third and fourth down, in short yardage situations, had to change because the opposition began expecting the pass in such spots. Behind all good play calling, no matter which school the quarterback favors, is a great amount of homework and film study. A lazy quarterback is a losing quarterback.

6. *Faking.* The element of surprise is the essence of the T formation and a man who can manipulate the football so that the defense thinks it's going in one direction while he sends the ball carrier or the pass in another is just that much ahead of the game. Good ball handling also keeps the defense in place and gives him the extra split second he needs to set up and spot his receiver. However, Graham calls ball handling the least important of the quarterback's requisites, possibly because Otto was self-admittedly poor in that department. For the record, a man can be a great field general without being a ball handling magician. The old converts from the single wing—Baugh, Graham, Charley Conerly—didn't concern themselves too much with the intricacies of footwork and slick handoffs. They mastered just enough of those maneuvers to get by. On the other hand, George Ratterman, who once understudied Graham at Cleveland, was a great faker but didn't measure up on the other counts and so never had much success in the NFL.

420

There are, of course, nuances of the qualities mentioned above which give quarterbacks distinctive personalities. Take the area of passing, the single most important asset of a quarterback. Sammy Baugh had a slingshot delivery and great range. Men who faced him, like Jim Lee Howell of the New York Giants, still speak of him with awe, especially, they point out, since Sammy never had a cordon of great receivers to complement his throwing—as for instance, Graham had in Cleveland with Mac Speedie, Dante Lavelli, Dub Jones and Ray Renfro. Partly because the league wasn't too bomb-conscious in his day and partly because he didn't have the swifties to go deep, Sammy concentrated on the short pass.

The long throw was the domain of Norm Van Brocklin. The Dutchman had a feathery touch and fellows on the Rams like Elroy Hirsch, Tom Fears, Bobby Boyd, Vitamin Smith and Tommy Kalmanir to race downfield under his passes. When Dutch moved to the Eagles, and only Tommy McDonald had the zip to go deep, he adjusted his sights and polished the other facets of his passing skills.

For a varied passing repertoire, Tittle came closest to the ideal. He had equal facility, long or short and personally favored sideline square-out patterns. Because Yat didn't panic under a strong rush, he was a master of the screen. Tittle could wait until the last possible moment, until the defense had been sucked out of the screen area, then turn and throw a little floater with precisely the right amount of lead to the screened target. It takes a certain knack of timing to pull off the deception.

Although Conerly was a proficient passer, he had trouble making connections with the screen. Charley's forte was passing in adverse weather. It didn't matter whether the ball was wet or dry, the weather hot or cold. Charley had perfect cradle and got the ball to his man.

The softest pass was thrown by Graham. The receivers never had to worry about the ball ricocheting off their hands like a bullet. Luckman threw soft, too, but his passes had a tendency to hang, like a rainbow, which makes them vulnerable to interception.

Concomitant with good passing is quick release. The ability to hit the bull's-eye doesn't mean a thing if the projectile is never launched. Frank Ryan of Cleveland used to be criticized for holding the ball too long. Milt Plum is in the same boat. Van Brocklin and his successor on the Eagles, Sonny Jurgensen, had the quickest release—although, ironically, there were almost no slower quarterbacks afoot in the NFL. They compensated with fast hands. An offshoot of quick release is the science of throwing the ball away rather than being stabbed for a loss. Conerly was the best. He developed this skill under duress, in the early days when the Giants didn't give him much protection and it was either ground the ball or be grounded himself, with the physical danger much more acute under the latter option.

Like passing, leadership has its distinctions, too. Layne was the prototype of absolute command. "If a decoy receiver loafed during passing drills," he said, "I straightened him out by hitting him in the back of the head with a pass. There's nothing more embarrassing to a receiver."

On the other hand, Graham theorized, "I always felt a pat on the back would go much further with most players."

Both worked, because both won. Much depends on the personality of the man. Layne's leadership is an extension of his own brash, bold self. Graham was just as much a competitor, but less of an extrovert. Layne led the rookies on an annual beer bust. Graham went the other way. But both were take-charge guys once the game was under way. They dominated the field.

"A quarterback may be good and he may be bad and he may be mediocre," Tittle once said, "but he has to be himself. The worst thing a quarterback can do is call a game for somebody else. If you have a feeling you should throw a sideline-and-down, then by God you should throw it. You should not have to answer to anybody for it. If you can't win, they should find somebody else."

Tittle felt that Johnny Unitas of Baltimore was the most dangerous quarterback he saw in his 17 years of pro ball because "he has the supreme courage to do the things that he really wants to do." So Unitas made a career of throwing passes on third and one.

Command decision on the field is born of confidence. A timid quarterback sacrifices alertness. Once, against the Green Bay Packers, a rookie signal caller took his team up to the line of scrimmage to start a play. In the middle of the Packer line was a 300-pound middle guard named Ed Neal, who used to break beer bottles over his forearms and worked as a blacksmith.

As the quarterback prepared to call signals, he heard a whisper in the line. "What's the number?" the voice asked softly.

This indicated to the quarterback that one of his linemen had forgotten on what count the ball was supposed to be snapped from center. "Three," he whispered back, and started his countdown.

On "three" the ball hit the quarterback's hands, and Neal hit the quarterback, who fell like a collapsed accordion. As he lay stunned, Neal squashing him, he heard Ed say through the fog, "Thanks." The Packer middle linebacker was the man who had asked the question.

The art of quarterbacking isn't quickly assimilated. Earl (Jug) Girard had been a quarterback in college, at Wisconsin, but spent most of his career in the National Football League as a fine halfback and flanker with the Green Bay Packers and Detroit Lions. Occasionally, Jug shifted to quarterback in an emergency. He led the Packers out of the huddle in one such jam, strode snappily up to the line of scrimmage, and began barking, "Hut one, hut two! . . ."

His hands reached eagerly for the ball on "two" but came up with the air. Jug looked around bewildered as bodies crashed in front of him. The football had gone straight up in the air. Jug had lined up behind his right guard instead of the center, leaving no one to take the direct snap.

The ultimate judgment of a quarterback is in the final score. It helps to settle the debates on relative ability. Comparisons may be odious, but they're stimulating and they lead to the question asked most often when a man pretends to be an expert. This is especially true when he can say that he has seen in action, and known, all the outstanding quarterbacks in the quarter of a century since the T-formation made them the most important men in football. Who was the best?

This is my personal rating of the pro quarterbacks of modern football:

1. Otto Graham

Over a decade of action with Cleveland, Otto never lost. Critics derided his role with the Browns because plays were sent in from the bench. But on the field, Otto was always the master of the situation. He could adjust quickly. If one receiver was not open, he spotted another immediately. He was fast in delivery and in picking out the next man, and even if he didn't make the play selection, he inspired confidence with his ability to execute.

2. John Unitas

He could get the job done in more ways than his contemporaries. The Baltimore star exemplified versatility. He had no visible weakness. He even developed into a fine runner under pressure. The greatest tributes always came from the opposition. As a passer, he had classic form and never tipped off his target before throwing. He introduced the pumping fake motion. He also had supreme faith in himself under all conditions.

3. Bobby Layne

Bobby thrived in clutch situations. He was the man best able to meet the challenge of a single game, to rally a team. He spurned passing records in his quest for victories. He had a great football mind. George Wilson, one of his coaches at Detroit, called him the greatest competitor he's ever seen in football. Sunday at 2 o'clock, he gave 100 percent. He was also a great handler of players on the field.

4. Sammy Baugh

If the modern T-formation had been born a decade earlier, Slinging Sammy probably would have surpassed them all, for he was ideally suited to play quarterback. No one ever matched his arm. Sammy was also a great all-around athlete who could kick, run and play defense. He never had the great receivers some of the other great quarterbacks had and still compiled an amazing completion record.

5. Sid Luckman

The Bears claimed he had no peer in handling players. Sid was most considerate of all leaders in his dealings with teammates. He didn't throw a pretty pass or have a fast delivery, but he was effective. He was great because he wanted to be great. Sid was the pioneer of the T-formation in pro ball and set a pattern for living by one's brains. He also set a standard for field generalship that few have matched.

6. Norm Van Brocklin

The Dutchman had superb control of himself. He was caustic, even cruel, but his energies were always directed to winning. Van Brocklin had a professor's grasp of football and a technician's ability to execute. In his early years, he was a little mule-headed in his concepts and sometimes erratic as a passer. As he progressed, he learned to adapt, and on a hot day no one ever threw the ball better. The only man ever to produce a title (for Philadelphia) with mediocre running and defense to balance his passing.

7. Y. A. Tittle

Old Yat performed at the peak of his abilities longer than any quarterback, including Baugh. He was second only to Baugh as a natural thrower, first in wanting to play. He became better in his later years. Old Yat was also a deceptive runner and a fine ball handler. He learned to boil the complexities of a pro attack down to a few simple patterns. The big regret of his career was the failure to win an NFL title.

8. Bob Waterfield

Buckets didn't play as long as most of the others, by choice. He was like Unitas in his versatility. "He was the greatest athlete I've ever seen," said George Wilson. "A great passer, runner, field goal kicker, punter and defensive back." Waterfield, a silent type, also had natural dignity as a leader. First and only rookie quarterback ever to produce a championship.

9. Bart Starr

Probably the most underrated of quarterbacks because he subordinated himself to his team's style of play. Everybody should be as conscientious. Bart has been rapped for inability to throw the long bomb, but the records show he has completed his share of 50-yarders. A passer doesn't have to put the ball in the air any farther than that. He's a serious student who'll be coaching material some day. A lot tougher spiritually and physically than he looks.

424

10. Charley Conerly

Charley did a good job of masking his emotions, but he won for the Giants because he cared. And along with his pride he was a fine passer. Charley didn't have finesse as a quarterback. He lacked color, too. But the guys who played with him respected him because he never whimpered and always accepted his share of the blame when things didn't go right. He took more punishment than most quarterbacks and was the oldest of all when he bowed out.

Those are the ten best. Some day a Joe Namath might develop to supplant one of them. The species always improves. But one factor is constant—attitude. All the great ones have a positive approach which enables them to survive in this intense arena of sport.

"If you're an average person who can't raise his emotions over 100 percent," said Norm Van Brocklin, "you can't play professional football."

Appendix

STARTING QUARTERBACKS

BALTIMORE (NFL)

1950—Adrian Burk, Y. A. Tittle
1953—Fred Enke
1954—Gary Kerkorian
1955—George Shaw
1956—George Shaw, John Unitas
1957—John Unitas
1958—John Unitas
1959—John Unitas
1960—John Unitas
1961—John Unitas
1962—John Unitas
1963—John Unitas
1964—John Unitas
1965—John Unitas

CHICAGO (NFL)

1940—Sid Luckman
1941—Sid Luckman
1942—Sid Luckman
1943—Sid Luckman
1944—Sid Luckman
1945—Sid Luckman
1946—Sid Luckman
1947—Sid Luckman
1948—Sid Luckman
1949—Johnny Lujack
1950—Johnny Lujack
1951—Johnny Lujack
1952—George Blanda, Steve Romanik
1953—George Blanda
1954—George Blanda, Zeke Bratkowski
1955—Ed Brown
1956—Ed Brown
1957—Ed Brown
1958—Ed Brown
1959—Ed Brown
1960—Ed Brown
1961—Billy Wade
1962—Billy Wade
1963—Billy Wade
1964—Billy Wade, Rudy Bukich
1965—Rudy Bukich

CLEVELAND (NFL)

1950—Otto Graham
1951—Otto Graham
1952—Otto Graham
1953—Otto Graham
1954—Otto Graham
1955—Otto Graham

1956—Babe Parilli, George Ratterman, Tom O'Connell
1957—Tom O'Connell
1958—Milt Plum
1959—Milt Plum
1960—Milt Plum
1961—Milt Plum
1962—Jim Ninowski, Frank Ryan
1963—Frank Ryan
1964—Frank Ryan
1965—Frank Ryan

DALLAS (NFL)

1960—Eddie LeBaron
1961—Eddie LaBaron, Don Meredith
1962—Eddie LeBaron, Don Meredith
1963—Don Meredith
1964—Don Meredith
1965—Don Meredith

DETROIT (NFL)

1947—Clyde LeForce
1948—Fred Enke, Clyde LeForce
1949—Fred Enke, Clyde LeForce
1950—Bobby Layne, Fred Enke
1951—Bobby Layne
1952—Bobby Layne, Jim Hardy
1953—Bobby Layne
1954—Bobby Layne
1955—Bobby Layne, Harry Gilmer
1956—Bobby Layne, Harry Gilmer
1957—Bobby Layne, Tobin Rote
1958—Tobin Rote
1959—Tobin Rote, Earl Morrall
1960—Jim Ninowski
1961—Jim Ninowski, Earl Morrall
1962—Milt Plum
1963—Earl Morrall
1964—Milt Plum, Earl Morrall
1965—Milt Plum

GREEN BAY (NFL)

1950—Tobin Rote
1951—Tobin Rote
1952—Tobin Rote
1953—Tobin Rote

1954—Tobin Rote
1955—Tobin Rote
1956—Tobin Rote
1957—Bart Starr
1958—Bart Starr, Babe Parilli
1959—Lamar McHan, Bart Starr
1960—Bart Starr
1961—Bart Starr
1962—Bart Starr
1963—Bart Starr
1964—Bart Starr
1965—Bart Starr

LOS ANGELES (NFL) (Cleveland until 194?)

1944—Albie Reisz
1945—Bob Waterfield
1946—Bob Waterfield
1947—Bob Waterfield
1948—Bob Waterfield, Jim Hardy
1949—Bob Waterfield
1950—Norm Van Brocklin, Bob Waterfield
1951—Norm Van Brocklin, Bob Waterfield
1952—Norm Van Brocklin, Bob Waterfield
1953—Norm Van Brocklin
1954—Norm Van Brocklin
1955—Norm Van Brocklin
1956—Norm Van Brocklin, Billy Wade
1957—Norm Van Brocklin
1958—Billy Wade
1959—Billy Wade
1960—Billy Wade
1961—Zeke Bratkowski
1962—Zeke Bratkowski, Roman Gabriel
1963—Zeke Bratkowski, Roman Gabriel
1964—Bill Munson, Roman Gabriel
1965—Bill Munson, Roman Gabriel

MINNESOTA (NFL)

1961—George Shaw, Francis Tarkenton
1962—Francis Tarkenton
1963—Francis Tarkenton
1964—Francis Tarkenton
1965—Francis Tarkenton

NEW YORK (NFL)

1948—Charley Conerly

428

1949—Charley Conerly
1950—Charley Conerly
1951—Charley Conerly
1952—Charley Conerly
1953—Charley Conerly
1954—Charley Conerly
1955—Charley Conerly
1956—Charley Conerly, Don Heinrich
1957—Charley Conerly, Don Heinrich
1958—Charley Conerly, Don Heinrich
1959—Charley Conerly, Don Heinrich
1960—Charley Conerly
1961—Charley Conerly, Y. A. Tittle
1962—Y. A. Tittle
1963—Y. A. Tittle
1964—Y. A. Tittle, Gary Wood
1965—Earl Morrall

PHILADELPHIA (NFL)

1941—Tommy Thompson
1942—Tommy Thompson
1943—Roy Zimmerman
1944—Roy Zimmerman
1945—Roy Zimmerman
1946—Tommy Thompson
1947—Tommy Thompson
1948—Tommy Thompson
1949—Tommy Thompson
1950—Tommy Thompson
1951—Adrian Burk
1952—Adrian Burk, Bobby Thomason
1953—Adrian Burk, Bobby Thomason
1954—Adrian Burk, Bobby Thomason
1955—Adrian Burk, Bobby Thomason
1956—Adrian Burk, Bobby Thomason
1957—Bobby Thomason, Sonny Jurgensen, Al
   Dorow
1958—Norm Van Brocklin
1959—Norm Van Brocklin
1960—Norm Van Brocklin
1961—Sonny Jurgensen
1962—Sonny Jurgensen
1963—Sonny Jurgensen
1964—Norman Snead, King Hill, Jack Con-
   cannon
1965—Norman Snead, King Hill

PITTSBURGH (NFL)

1952—Jim Finks
1953—Jim Finks
1954—Jim Finks
1955—Jim Finks
1956—Ted Marchibroda
1957—Ted Marchibroda
1958—Earl Morrall
1959—Bobby Layne
1960—Bobby Layne
1961—Bobby Layne
1962—Bobby Layne, Ed Brown
1963—Ed Brown
1964—Ed Brown
1965—Bill Nelsen

ST. LOUIS (NFL) (Chicago until 1960)

1945—Paul Christman
1946—Paul Christman
1947—Paul Christman
1948—Paul Christman, Ray Mallouf
1949—Paul Christman, Jim Hardy
1950—Jim Hardy
1951—Jim Hardy, Charley Trippi
1952—Charley Trippi
1953—Jim Root
1954—Lamar McHan
1955—Lamar McHan
1956—Lamar McHan
1957—Lamar McHan
1958—Lamar McHan, M. C. Reynolds
1959—King Hill
1960—John Roach
1961—Sam Etcheverry
1962—Sam Etcheverry, Charley Johnson
1963—Charley Johnson
1964—Charley Johnson
1965—Charley Johnson

SAN FRANCISCO (NFL)

1946—Frank Albert
1947—Frank Albert
1948—Frank Albert
1949—Frank Albert
1950—Frank Albert
1951—Frank Albert

1952—Y. A. Tittle
1953—Y. A. Tittle
1954—Y. A. Tittle
1955—Y. A. Tittle
1956—Y. A. Tittle
1957—Y. A. Tittle
1958—Y. A. Tittle
1959—Y. A. Tittle
1960—Y. A. Tittle, John Brodie
1961—John Brodie (rotated with Billy Kilmer and
     Bobby Waters in shotgun, ran T himself)
1962—John Brodie
1963—John Brodie
1964—John Brodie
1965—John Brodie

WASHINGTON (NFL)

1944—Sammy Baugh
1945—Sammy Baugh
1946—Sammy Baugh
1947—Sammy Baugh
1948—Sammy Baugh
1949—Sammy Baugh
1950—Sammy Baugh
1951—Sammy Baugh
1952—Eddie LeBaron
1953—Eddie LeBaron
1954—Jack Scarbath
1955—Eddie LeBaron
1956—Al Dorow
1957—Eddie LeBaron
1958—Eddie LeBaron
1959—Eddie LeBaron
1960—Ralph Guglielmi
1961—Norman Snead
1962—Norman Snead
1963—Norman Snead
1964—Sonny Jurgensen
1965—Sonny Jurgensen

BOSTON (AFL)

1960—Ed Songin
1961—Ed Songin, Babe Parilli
1962—Babe Parilli
1963—Babe Parilli
1964—Babe Parilli
1965—Babe Parilli

BUFFALO (AFL)

1960—Tommy O'Connell, Johnny Green
1961—Johnny Green, M. C. Reynolds
1962—Al Dorow, Warren Rabb, Jack Kemp
1963—Jack Kemp
1964—Jack Kemp, Daryle Lamonica
1965—Jack Kemp

DENVER (AFL)

1960—Frank Tripucka
1961—Frank Tripucka
1962—Frank Tripucka
1963—Mickey Slaughter, Don Breaux
1964—Jackie Lee, Mickey Slaughter
1965—John McCormick, Mickey Slaughter

HOUSTON (AFL)

1960—George Blanda
1961—George Blanda
1962—George Blanda
1963—George Blanda
1964—George Blanda
1965—George Blanda

KANSAS CITY (AFL) (Dallas until 1963)

1960—Cotton Davidson
1961—Cotton Davidson
1962—Len Dawson
1963—Len Dawson
1964—Len Dawson
1965—Len Dawson

NEW YORK (AFL)

1960—Al Dorow
1961—Al Dorow
1962—Ed Songin, Lee Grosscup, Johnny Green
1963—Dick Wood
1964—Dick Wood
1965—Mike Taliaferro, Joe Namath

OAKLAND (AFL)

1960—Tom Flores, Babe Parilli
1961—Tom Flores
1962—Cotton Davidson
1963—Tom Flores, Cotton Davidson

1964—Cotton Davidson, Tom Flores
1965—Tom Flores, Dick Wood

SAN DIEGO (AFL) (*Los Angeles until 1961*)

1960—Jack Kemp

1961—Jack Kemp
1962—Jack Kemp, John Hadl
1963—Tobin Rote
1964—Tobin Rote, John Hadl
1965—John Hadl

CHAMPIONSHIP QUARTERBACKS

NATIONAL FOOTBALL LEAGUE

1940—Sid Luckman, Chicago Bears
1941—Sid Luckman, Chicago Bears
1942—Sammy Baugh, Washington Redskins
1943—Sid Luckman, Chicago Bears
1944—Irv Comp, Green Bay Packers
1945—Bob Waterfield, Cleveland Rams
1946—Sid Luckman, Chicago Bears
1947—Paul Christman, Chicago Cards
1948—Tommy Thompson, Philadelphia Eagles
1949—Tommy Thompson, Philadelphia Eagles
1950—Otto Graham, Cleveland Browns
1951—Bob Waterfield, Norm Van Brocklin, Los
    Angeles Rams
1952—Bobby Layne, Detroit Lions
1953—Bobby Layne, Detroit Lions
1954—Otto Graham, Cleveland Browns
1955—Otto Graham, Cleveland Browns
1956—Charley Conerly, New York Giants
1957—Tobin Rote, Detroit Lions
1958—John Unitas, Baltimore Colts

1959—John Unitas, Baltimore Colts
1960—Norm Van Brocklin, Philadelphia Eagles
1961—Bart Starr, Green Bay Packers
1962—Bart Starr, Green Bay Packers
1963—Billy Wade, Chicago Bears
1964—Frank Ryan, Cleveland Browns
1965—Bart Starr, Green Bay Packers

AMERICAN FOOTBALL LEAGUE

1960—George Blanda, Houston Oilers
1961—George Blanda, Houston Oilers
1962—Len Dawson, Dallas Texans
1963—Tobin Rote, San Diego Chargers
1964—Jack Kemp, Buffalo Bills
1965—Jack Kemp, Buffalo Bills

ALL-AMERICA CONFERENCE

1946—Otto Graham, Cleveland Browns
1947—Otto Graham, Cleveland Browns
1948—Otto Graham, Cleveland Browns
1949—Otto Graham, Cleveland Browns

PASSING LEADERS

National Football League

Year		Att.	Comp.	Yards	T.D.	Pct.	Int.
1965	Rudy Bukich, Chicago	312	176	2641	20	56.4	9
1964	Bart Starr, Green Bay	272	163	2144	15	59.9	4
1963	Y. A. Tittle, New York	367	221	3145	36	60.2	14
1962	Bart Starr, Green Bay	285	178	2438	12	62.5	9
1961	Milt Plum, Cleveland	302	177	2416	18	58.4	10
1960	Milt Plum, Cleveland	250	151	2297	21	60.4	5
1959	Charley Conerly, New York	194	113	1706	14	58.2	4

1958	Eddie LeBaron, Washington	145	79	1365	11	54.5	10
1957	Tommy O'Connell, Cleveland	110	63	1229	9	57.3	8
1956	Eddie Brown, Chicago	168	96	1667	11	57.1	12
1955	Otto Graham, Cleveland	185	98	1721	15	53.0	8
1954	Norm Van Brocklin, Los Angeles	260	139	2637	13	53.5	21
1953	Otto Graham, Cleveland	258	167	1722	11	64.7	9
1952	Norm Van Brocklin, Los Angeles	205	113	1736	14	55.1	17
1951	Bob Waterfield, Los Angeles	176	88	1566	13	50.0	10
1950	Norm Van Brocklin, Los Angeles	233	127	2061	18	54.5	14
1949	Sammy Baugh, Washington	255	145	1903	18	56.9	14
1948	Tommy Thompson, Philadelphia	246	141	1965	25	57.3	11
1947	Sammy Baugh, Washington	354	210	2938	25	59.3	15
1946	Bob Waterfield, Los Angeles	251	127	1747	18	50.5	17
1945	Sammy Baugh, Washington	182	128	1669	11	70.3	4
1944	Frank Filchock, Washington	147	84	1139	13	57.1	9
1943	Sammy Baugh, Washington	239	133	1754	23	55.7	19
1942	Cecil Isbell, Green Bay	268	146	2021	24	54.5	14
1941	Cecil Isbell, Green Bay	206	117	1479	15	56.8	11
1940	Sammy Baugh, Washington	177	111	1367	12	62.7	10
1939	Parker Hall, Cleveland	208	106	1227	9	51.0	13
1938	Ed Danowski, New York	129	70	848	8	54.3	8
1937	Sammy Baugh, Washington	171	81	1127	7	47.3	14
1936	Arnie Herber, Green Bay	173	77	1238	9	44.5	13
1935	Ed Danowski, New York	113	57	795	9	50.4	9
1934	Arnie Herber, Green Bay	115	42	799	8	36.5	12
1933	Harry Newman, New York	132	53	963	8	40.5	17
1932	Arnie Herber, Green Bay	101	37	639	9	36.6	9

PASSING LEADERS

American Football League

Year		Att.	Comp.	Yards	T.D.	Pct.	Int.
1965	John Hadl, San Diego	348	174	2798	20	50.0	21
1964	Len Dawson, Kansas City	354	199	2879	30	56.2	18
1963	Tobin Rote, San Diego	286	170	2510	20	59.4	17
1962	Len Dawson, Dallas	310	189	2759	29	60.9	17
1961	George Blanda, Houston	362	187	3330	36	51.7	22
1960	Jack Kemp, Los Angeles	406	211	3018	20	52.0	25

432

Index

Adderley, Herb, 61, 74, 77, 408
Agase, Alex, 132
Aiken, Jim, 234
Albert, Frank, 18, 115, 169–175 (chapter), 181–2 (statistics), 225, 253, 302, 305, 340, 419
Albert, Jane, 175
Alderman, Grady, 240, 369
Aldrich, Ki, 159
Aldridge, Lionel, 74, 131
Alworth, Lance, 271, 274, 392
Ameche, Alan, 88, 284–5, 289–90
Anderson, Bill, 4, 5, 136
Anderson, Dave, 387
Andrews, LeRoy, 14
Angsman, Elmer, 163, 177–8
Arnett, Jon, 331, 340
Artoe, Lee, 161
Atkins, Pervis, 378
Austin, Bill, 248, 319

Bach, Joe, 21
Baker, John, 104, 310
Baker, Terry, 84
Barabas, Al, 145
Barnes, Billy Ray, 239, 348
Bass, Glenn, 355, 359
Battles, Cliff, 157, 159
Baugh, Sammy, 15, 20, 25, 26, 148, 150, 153, 155–65 (chapter), 165–67 (statistics), 171, 180, 205, 208, 226, 251, 261, 264, 271, 301, 317, 366, 378, 419, 421, 423–4
Beach, Walter, 319
Beals, Allyn, 172
Beatherd, Pete, 395
Bednarik, Chuck, 239, 349
Bedsole, Hal, 119, 368
Belinsky, Bo, 392
Bell, Bert, 180
Benners, Fred, 250
Benton, Jim, 148, 205, 208
Bergman, Dutch, 20
Berry, Connie, 148
Berry, Raymond, 89, 284, 289, 292, 369

Berwanger, Jay, 14
Bettis, Tom, 247
Bible, Dana X., 222
Bierman, Bernie, 193
Bingaman, Les, 98, 224, 226
Bite, Mike, 388
Blackbourn, Lisle, 273
Blanda, George, 43, 151, 174, 359, 395, 403, 413–14, 425
Blitz, 97–112 (chapter)
Bowman, Ken, 5, 65
Box, Aaron, 366
Box, Cloyce, 224, 228–9
Boyd, Bobby (Colts), 54, 56, 130, 135, 343
Boyd, Bobby (Rams), 30, 203, 209, 236, 421
Bratkowski, Zeke, 59, 61, 62, 64–6, 136, 315, 331, 403, 411, 413, 425
Bray, Ray, 193
Brewer, John, 56
Britt, Charley, 366, 368
Brodie, John, 35, 97, 123, 135, 174–5, 307, 310, 337–44 (chapter), 344 (statistics), 358, 396, 404
Brookshier, Tom, 239
Brown, Bill, 36, 124, 365, 370
Brown, Ed, 134–5, 396, 403, 425
Brown, Jimmy, 54, 87, 192, 273, 304, 333, 340, 358, 408, 414
Brown, Paul, 46, 132, 172, 187, 189–99, 226, 237, 310, 332, 408, 414
Brown, Roger, 308, 316
Brown, Roosevelt, 90, 248
Brown, Timmy, 348
Brown, Tom, 74, 132
Brumbaugh, Carl, 17, 145, 147, 301
Bryant, Bear, 193, 320, 383, 387–8, 413–4
Bukich, Rudy, 403, 411
Bumgardner, Rex, 199
Burk, Adrian, 36, 150, 425
Burke, Vern, 135
Burroughs, Don, 104, 239

Butler, Jack, 264
Butts, Wally, 366

Caffey, Lee Roy, 74, 136
Cagle, Chris, 14
Cannon, Billy, 79
Caroline, J. C., 288–9
Carlton, Wray, 356
Carr, Joe (trophy), 208
Chandler, Don (Babe), 65, 131, 136
Cherry, Blair, 222
Childress, Joe, 71
Christiansen, Jack, 224, 305
Christman, Mark, 176–7
Christman, Paul, 25, 26, 163, 171, 176–9 (chapter), 185 (statistics), 222
Claridge, Dennis, 64–5
Clark, Harry, 35, 148
Clatterbuck, Bobby, 250
Cochran, Red, 62–4, 151
Collier, Blanton, 87, 196, 198, 199, 330, 332
Collier, Joel, 357
Collins, Gary, 54, 56, 87, 329, 333–4
Collins, Ted, 222
Conerly, Charley, 7, 21, 29, 43, 44, 97, 120, 181, 220, 245–58 (chapter), 257–8 (statistics), 265, 301–2, 307, 317, 358, 420–1, 424
Conerly, Perian, 247, 253
Conrad, Bobby Joe, 379–80
Conzelman, Jimmy, 176–7
Cordileone, Lou, 299, 307
Cosell, Howard, 387
Costa, Paul, 356, 359
Costello, Vince, 4, 86–7
Cox, Fred, 366
Craft, Russ, 190
Creekmur, Lou, 219, 224
Crenshaw, Willis, 376
Cristigna, Steve, 59, 63
Cross, Bobby, 236
Crow, John David, 342
Cruice, Wally, 61–2

Cuozzo, Gary, 126, 129–32, 138, 396, 399

Dahms, Tom, 236
Dale, Carroll, 4, 5, 59, 64–5, 315, 319
Daniels, Clem, 84
Danowski, Ed, 14
David, Jim, 305
Davidson, Cotton, 79, 80, 124
Davidson, Gen. Gar, 144
Davies, Bob, 193
Davis, Al, 77, 124, 360
Davis, Fred, 150
Davis, Glenn, 198, 211, 236
Davis, Willie, 25, 74, 77, 130, 136, 365
Dawson, Len, 358–9, 395, 414, 416
Dean, Ted, 239
DeCorrevont, Bill, 193
DeGroot, Dud, 169
Dewell, Billy, 178
Dibble, Dorne, 219, 224
Dimancheff, Babe, 179
Dodd, Bobby, 263
Dorais, Gus, 14
Doran, Jim, 219
Dorow, Al, 264, 359
Dowler, Boyd, 66, 112, 131, 317
Dressen, Charley, 15
Drulis, Chuck, 71, 300
Dubenion, Elbert, 355, 359
Dublinski, Tom, 250
Duncan, Mark, 103

Eaton, Vic, 288
Edwards, Turk, 159
Eller, Carl, 62
Enke, Fred, 425
Etcheverry, Sam, 375
Ewbank, Weeb, 44, 89–90 (game plan), 104, 284, 288–90, 294, 388, 391

Falk, Bib, 226
Faulkner, Jack, 274
Faurot, Don, 176–7
Fears, Tom, 30, 211, 236, 421
Feathers, Beattie, 14
Feller, Bob, 208
Ferrante, Jack, 180–1
Filchock, Frank, 147, 150, 162
Finks, Jim, 241, 288
Fiss, Galen, 4, 87
Flaherty, Ray, 25, 162
Flatley, Paul, 36, 365
Flores, Tom, 124
Fortmann, Danny, 18
Fortunato, Joe, 97
Francis, Joe, 321–2
Frank, Clint, 14, 145
Freeman, Bobby, 199
Friedman, Benny, 14, 144

Gabriel, Roman, 135, 396, 413
Gaiters, Bobby, 378–9
Galiffa, Arnold, 250
Gallarneau, Hugh, 18
Garrett, Bobby, 8
Gatski, Frank, 272
Gedman, Gene, 134
George, Bill, 8–9, 308–9, 342
Gibbs, Jake, 368
Gibbs, Ron, 284
Gibbs, Sonny, 267
Gifford, Frank, 248, 250, 257, 284, 309, 411
Gilchrist, Chester (Cookie), 274, 355–6, 391
Gillette, Jim, 208
Gillman, Sid, 43, 237, 269, 271, 331, 356–7, 359–60, 392, 395
Gilmer, Harry, 162, 165, 221, 251, 404
Girard, Jug, 422
Glass, Bill, 4
Gogolak, Pete, 356
Goldberg, Marshall, 14, 163, 176
Graham, Otto, 7, 8, 29, 35–6, 52, 116, 120, 132–3, 172, 174, 187–201 (chapter), 201–2 (statistics), 205, 220, 245, 253, 273, 317, 333, 339, 350, 403–4, 414, 419–23
Grange, Red, 14, 17, 124, 144
Green, Ernie, 54, 87
Gregg, Forrest, 5
Gremminger, Hank, 241
Grier, Roosevelt, 89, 98, 115
Griffing, Glynn, 310
Grosscup, Lee, 44, 240, 250, 253, 307, 358
Groza, Lou, 199, 211
Guglielmi, Ralph, 375–6, 407

Hadl, John, 124, 271, 392
Halas, George, 13, 17, 20, 71, 141, 143–51, 219, 234, 403
Hall, Parker, 15
Hall, Tom, 365–6
Hapes, Merle, 150
Harder, Pat, 163, 177
Hardin, Wayne, 263
Hardy, Jim, 43, 209, 234
Harmon, Tom, 14
Harris, Jimmy, 237
Hart, Doug, 74
Hart, Leon, 219, 224, 228–9, 264
Hawkins, Alex, 134
Hawkins, Rip, 59
Hayes, Woody, 131
Haymond, Alvin, 135
Hecker, Norb, 289
Hein, Mel, 165
Heinrich, Don, 29, 248, 250, 254, 358
Heinz, W. C., 387

Herber, Arnie, 15
Hewitt, Bill, 17
Hickerson, Gene, 54
Hickey, Red, 44, 211, 299, 307, 340–2, 358
Hickey, Dan, 145
Hill, Jerry, 87, 130–1, 138, 292
Hill, King, 330, 375
Hirsch, Ed (Buckets), 302
Hirsch, Elroy, 30, 211, 236, 331, 421
Hoerner, Dick, 211
Hoernschemeyer, Bobby, 115
Holland, Brud, 145, 150
Holovak, Mike, 414
Holzman, Red, 193
Hope, Bob, 385
Hornung, Paul, 3–5, 64–6, 112, 131–2, 239, 315, 317, 319, 340
Horvath, Les, 206
Houston, Jim, 4
Howell, Jim Lee, 247–8, 250, 253, 421
Howton, Billy, 273, 407
Huarte, John, 391
Huff, Sam, 89, 98, 266, 305, 317, 349
Humphrey, Buddy, 331, 376
Hutson, Don, 15, 273

Isbell, Cecil, 15
Ivy, Frank (Pop), 98, 413
Izo, George, 375

Jackson, Bob, 378
Joe, Bill, 356
Johnson, Charley, 71, 97, 103, 124, 373–81 (chapter), 380–1 (statistics)
Johnson, Jack, 378
Johnson, John Henry, 304
Johnson, Walter, 157
Johnsos, Luke, 18
Johnston, Jim, 18
Jones, Deacon, 25
Jones, Dub, 190, 195, 198–9, 421
Jones, Edgar (Special Delivery), 198
Jones, Ralph, 17
Jones, Stan, 97, 129
Jordan, Henry, 74, 103, 136
Jordan, Payton, 357
Joyce, Don, 163, 290
Junker, Steve, 273
Jurgensen, Sonny, 43, 251, 345–52 (chapter), 351–2 (statistics), 396, 407, 421
Justice, Charley, 264
Justice, Ed, 18, 157

Kalmanir, Tommy, 30, 211, 421
Kanicki, Jim, 87
Kapp, Joe, 358

434

Karilivacz, Carl, 305
Karr, Bill, 17
Karras, Alex, 124, 308
Kavanaugh, Ken, 35, 148
Kellett, Don, 288
Kelly, Bob, 378–9
Kelly, Bob (announcer), 101
Kemp, Jack, 124, 225, 250, 274, 353–62 (chapter), 360–62 (statistics), 395
Kerkorian, Gary, 425
Kessing, O. O., 189
Kiesling, Butch, 288
Kilmer, Bill, 123, 341–2
King, Phil, 101, 103, 308
Klosterman, Don, 355
Kmetovic, Pete, 18, 171
Knafelc, Gary, 320
Kocourek, Dave, 271
Koman, Bill, 333, 375
Kostelnik, Ron, 74
Kramer, Jerry, 5, 8, 9, 319
Kramer, Ron, 322
Krause, Max, 148
Kuharich, Joe, 259, 265, 349, 407
Kutner, Mal, 177

Lahr, Warren, 199, 219
Lambeau, Curly, 15, 261, 264, 273
Lamonica, Daryle, 124, 274, 355, 395
Landry, Tom, 46, 123, 363, 407–8
Lane, Dick (Night Train), 290
Lansford, Buck, 237
Larson, Greg, 103
Lary, Yale, 290
Lavelli, Dante, 190, 195, 196, 421
Layne, Bobby, 4, 5, 98, 115–6, 120, 134, 151, 153, 176, 205, 217–30 (chapter), 229–30 (statistics), 272–3, 301–2, 340, 358, 403–4, 413–4, 416, 419–23
Leahy, Frank, 20
LeBaron, Eddie, 123, 134, 163, 253, 259–67 (chapter), 266–7 (statistics), 319, 407, 419
Lee, Jacky, 413
Leggett, Earl, 97, 129, 130
Lemm, Wally, 103, 375–8
Levane, Fuzzy, 193
Levy, Fred, 213
Lewis, Cliff, 132, 196, 199
Lewis, Tommy, 366
Lincoln, Keith, 274, 276
Little, Lou, 18, 144
Livingston, Cliff, 89, 98
Livingston, Howie, 253
Lombardi, Vince, 3, 8, 44, 46, 61–5, 86, 112, 116, 129, 248, 273, 290, 313, 315–7, 319–21, 411, 413
Lowe, Paul, 276

Luckman, Sid, 18, 25, 35, 36, 101, 115, 141–53 (chapter), 154 (statistics), 161, 171, 180, 222, 289, 339, 403, 413, 419, 423–4
Lujack, John, 151, 222, 302, 413, 425
Lyles, Lenny, 36, 112, 136
Lynch, Dick, 9

MacArthur, Gen. Douglas, 401
Mackey, Dee, 341, 391
Mackey, John, 129, 132, 134–5, 138
Macklem, Friday, 225
Mackrides, Bill, 250
Malone, Charley, 148, 159
Maniaci, Joe, 148
Manske, Ed, 145
Mara, Tim, 14
Mara, Wellington, 14, 251
Marchetti, Gino, 116, 126, 239, 240, 263, 284, 368, 411
Marchibroda, Ted, 288, 358
Marciano, Rocky, 189
Marion, Marty, 159
Marshall, George Preston, 13, 15, 147, 158–9, 162, 189–90, 257, 262
Marshall, Jim, 59, 62
Martin, Jim, 273
Martin, Slater, 226
Mason, Tommy, 370
Masterson, Bernie, 17, 147, 161, 171
Matson, Ollie, 263, 411
Matte, Tom, 126, 131–8
Maynard, Don, 391
McAfee, George, 18, 147–8, 151
McChesney, Bob, 253
McCord, Darris, 124
McDonald, Tommy, 233, 237, 241, 345, 348–50, 421
McElhenny, Hugh, 305, 340, 411
McGee, Max, 239, 316
McGraw, Thurman, 224
McHan, Lamar, 316, 320–2
McIlhenny, Don, 226
McKay, Johnny, 241
McKee, Paul, 162
McPeak, Bill, 281, 285
Meador, Ed, 135
Meadows, Ed, 134, 225
Meredith, Don, 43, 98, 124, 407–8
Meyer, L. R. (Dutch), 158
Michaels, Lou, 135, 136, 254
Michel, Tom, 365–6
Michelosen, John, 21
Miller, Clark, 97
Millner, Wayne, 157, 159, 162
Mira, George, 36, 106, 115, 123–4, 339, 395–6
Mitchell, Bobby, 407

Modzelewski, Dick, 4, 87, 89, 98, 284
Molesworth, Keith, 17
Moore, Lenny, 86–7, 89, 130–1, 284, 289–90, 292
Moore, Sammy, 14
Moore, Tom, 319
Moore, Wilbur, 161
Morabito, Tony, 172
Morrall, Earl, 106, 358, 404, 408
Morris, Larry, 97, 309–10
Morrow, John, 56
Morton, Craig, 30, 396, 407–8
Motley, Marion, 190, 196, 198
Munson, Bill, 97, 124, 135, 395–6
Murphy, Fido, 358
Musial, Stan, 29
Mutcheller, Jim, 89, 285, 289, 385
Myrha, Steve, 89, 284

Nagurski, Bronko, 17
Namath, Frank, 387
Namath, Joe, 104, 192, 335, 383–92 (chapter), 413, 425
Neal, Ed, 422
Neale, Earle (Greasy), 20, 26, 35, 178–81
Nelsen, Bill, 97, 395–6
Newman, Harry, 14
Ninowski, Jim, 332, 404, 408
Nitschke, Ray, 74, 131
Nolting, Ray, 18, 35, 148
Norton, Don, 392

O'Bradovich, Ed, 310
O'Brien, Davey, 15, 43, 145
O'Connell, Tommy, 25
Oosterbaan, Benny, 14, 144
Orff, Bud and Babe (twins), 177
O'Rourke, Charley, 301
Orr, Jimmy, 7, 39, 129, 130, 138, 285
Osmanski, Bill, 18, 147–8
Owen, Steve, 20, 148, 198, 248, 251, 253
Owens, R. C., 305, 341

Papit, Johnny, 261
Parilli, Vito (Babe), 320, 359, 385, 414
Parker, Ace, 148, 347
Parker, Buddy, 123, 219, 221–2, 224–6, 358
Parker, Jim, 86–7, 131, 369
Parks, David, 110, 342–4
Parrish, Bernie, 329
Passing, 25–39
Passing Leaders, 429–30
Patton, Cliff, 181, 190
Patton, Jimmy, 98, 289
Paul, Don, 209
Pauley, Ed, 213

435

Pellington, Bill, 56, 219, 254
Perry, Joe, 304
Pihos, Pete, 181
Pinckert, Ernie, 159
Plum, Milt, 106, 332, 404, 408, 416, 421
Poillon, Dick, 162
Polsfoot, Fran, 71
Pool, Hamp, 148, 231
Powell, Art, 78, 81
Preas, George, 130
Prohaska, Ray, 379
Purvis, Chuck, 25

Quarterbacks, championship, 429
Quarterbacks, starting, 425–9

Randle, Sonny, 71, 233, 379–80
Ratterman, George, 132, 134, 199, 420
Reeves, Dan, 209, 212, 234
Reichow, Gerry, 358
Renfro, Ray, 421
Retzlaff, Pete, 233, 237, 348, 350, 404
Rhome, Jerry, 407
Richter, Pat, 201
Risch, Mrs. Walter, 299
Roach, Johnny, 375
Roberson, Bo, 81, 356
Robinson, Dave, 74, 130–1
Robustelli, Andy, 98, 103, 131, 239
Rockne, Knute, 14
Romanik, Steve, 151, 425
Ronzani, Gene, 273
Rooney, Art, 221, 222, 225
Rose, Bert, 240
Rose, George, 39
Rosenbloom, Carroll, 87, 285, 290
Rote, Kyle, 248, 250–1, 272, 297, 302, 307
Rote, Tobin, 65, 116, 120, 124, 171, 225, 269–79 (chapter), 277–79 (statistics), 305, 320, 340, 358, 392, 404, 414, 420
Rozelle, Pete, 101, 237, 334
Rush, Cleve, 104
Russell, Jane, 162, 205–9
Ryan, Frank, 52, 54, 56, 86–7, 97, 106, 124, 134, 325–35 (chapter), 335 (statistics), 377, 421

Saban, Lou, 355
Sacrinty, Nick, 151
Sayers, Gale, 192, 403
Scarbath, Jack, 264, 358
Schafrath, Dick, 54
Schmidt, Francis, 158
Schmidt, Joe, 308
Schnelker, Bob, 250, 253
Schwartz, Marchy, 263
Scramble, 115–26

Sewell, Harley, 219
Shaughnessy, Clark, 17, 18, 98, 171–2, 234–6
Shaw, Buck, 172, 174, 237, 239–40, 302, 347
Shaw, George, 7, 250, 284, 288–9, 368, 425
Sherman, Allie, 9, 20, 26, 29–30, 35 (pass technique), 44, 46, 78, 98, 101, 103, 143, 178, 250, 253, 294, 300, 308, 404
Shiner, Dick, 350, 396
Shinnick, Don, 52, 54, 112, 136
Shofner, Del, 43, 72, 251, 307, 309
Shula, Don, 86–7, 124, 126, 129, 131, 134–6, 138, 286, 294, 347, 399
Siemering, Larry, 263, 265
Sims, E. A., 378–9
Skoronski, Bob, 4, 5
Smith, Billy Ray, 103
Smith, Gordie, 365–6
Smith, J. D., 349
Smith, Kate, 222
Smith, Riley, 159
Smith, V. T. (Vitamin), 30, 211, 421
Smyth, Bill, 211
Snead, Norman, 97, 349, 404, 407
Snyder, Bob, 147–8, 205
Soltau, Gordy, 305
Speedie, Mac, 190, 195–9, 421
Spencer, Ollie, 219
Spinney, Art, 284
Sprinkle, Ed, 174
Stagg, Amos Alonzo, 13, 263
Standlee, Norm, 18, 172
Stanfel, Dick, 219, 224, 263
Starr, Bart, 4–5, 8–9, 46–51 (breaking down a play), 57–67 (week in the life of), 86, 97, 112, 131, 136, 239, 313–24 (chapter), 322–34 (statistics), 333, 369, 377, 411, 413, 419–20, 424
Starr, Cherry, 59–67
Staubach, Roger, 116, 395
Stautner, Ernie, 8
Steele, Ernie, 181
Stonebreaker, Steve, 136, 315
Stout, Pete, 258
Stram, Hank, 416
Stratton, Mike, 271
Stroud, Jack, 248
Strzykalski, John, 172
Stydahar, Joe, 211, 236
Summerall, Pat, 253
Sutherland, Dr. Jock, 21, 222
Svare, Harland, 98, 395
Swisher, Bob, 35
Szymanski, Dick, 86–7, 130

Taliaferro, Mike, 391
Tarkenton, Francis, 7, 36, 39, 51–2, 109, 115, 116–26 (scramble), 240, 359, 363–71 (chapter), 371 (statistics), 396, 404, 419–20
Taseff, Carl, 284
Taylor, Charley, 192, 349–50
Taylor, Hugh (Bones), 155, 162–3
Taylor, Jim, 3–4, 61, 112, 130, 239, 261, 315, 317, 319
Thomason, Bobby, 33, 347
Thompson, Tommy, 36, 132, 171, 178–81 (chapter), 185 (statistics)
Thorpe, Jim, 13, trophy: 233, 254, 289, 308
Thurston, Fuzzy, 61, 316
Tinsley, Gaynell, 159
Tipton, Eric, 145
Tidwell, Travis, 250
Tittle, Jack, 301
Tittle, Y. A., 7, 29, 35–6, 43–4, 72, 104, 106, 109–10, 112, 115, 131, 134, 150, 153, 174–5, 220, 225, 247, 250–1, 265, 271, 289, 294, 297–312 (chapter), 310–12 (statistics), 317, 337, 339–41, 358, 368, 373, 404, 413, 419, 421, 423–4
Towler, Dan, 211
Trippi, Charley, 163, 177–9
Tripucka, Frank, 359
Trull, Don, 395, 413
Tunnell, Emlen, 26, 89, 163, 261
Turley, Doug, 162
Turner, Bake, 391
Turner, Bulldog, 101, 222

Unitas, John, 5, 7–8, 26–7, 35–6, 39, 44, 52, 56, 89, 97, 109, 120, 123, 126, 129–30, 132, 136, 138, 153, 254, 281–95 (chapter), 295 (statistics), 315–6, 319, 333, 335, 339, 358, 369, 378, 387, 396, 399, 403, 419–20, 423–4

Van Brocklin, Norm, 3, 7, 30, 115, 120, 129, 171, 199, 205, 209, 211–3, 220, 225, 231–44 (chapter), 242–4 (statistics), 248, 301, 317, 331, 340, 345, 347–8, 350, 368–9, 395, 403, 411, 419–21, 424–5
Van Buren, Steve, 178, 180, 181, 199, 209, 211, 348
Van Doren, Mamie, 392
Van Tassell, Irvin, 14
Vander Kelen, Ron, 201

Wade, Bill, 43, 237, 331, 368, 403, 408, 411, 425

436

Wade, Tommy, 396
Waldorf, Lynn (Pappy), 8, 193
Walker, Doak, 219, 221–2, 224, 226, 228, 234, 264
Walker, Wayne, 342
Walsh, Adam, 205, 208
Walston, Bobby, 348, 350
Walton, Joe, 250, 385
Warfield, Paul, 54, 87, 333–4
Warlick, Ernie, 355–6
Warner, Glenn (Pop), 13
Waterfield, Bob, 7, 33, 162, 171, 181, 198, 199, 203–13 (chapter), 213–5 (statistics), 225, 234–7, 294, 330–1, 340, 424
Waters, Bobby, 123, 341–2

Webster, Alex, 248
Weinmeister, Arnie, 261
Welch, Jim, 54, 56
Werblin, Sonny, 388
White, Byron (Whizzer), 14, 145
Whitsell, Dave, 126
Whitworth, Ears, 320
Wietecha, Ray, 248
Wiggin, Paul, 86–7
Wilkins, Willie, 165
Willey, Norm (Wild Man), 190
Williams, Bob, 302
Williams, Ted, 233
Willard, Ken, 342
Wilson, Billy, 300, 305
Wilson, Butch, 131, 134

Wilson, Camp, 224
Wilson, George, 18, 20, 148, 273, 408, 423–4
Wilson, Larry, 98, 250
Wilson, Ralph, 274
Wilson, Tom, 332
Wood, Dick, 124
Wood, Gary, 310
Wood, Willie, 74, 77
Wyatt, Bowden, 286
Wynne, Bedford, 262

Younger, Tank, 211

Zilly, Jack, 211
Zimmerman, Roy, 180